Deuteronomy

Deuteronomy

A Direct Translation

by

Daniel A. Elias

Tzeruf Co

Author: *Daniel A. Elias, J.D.*

Publisher: Tzeruf Co
             235 S. Lyon Ave. # 39
             Hemet, CA 92543   USA
             admin@tzeruf.com

SAN Number   853-0203

© 2013 by Tzeruf Co.
Printed in USA

All rights reserved. No part of this publication may be reproduced or transmitted in any form or by any means, electronic or mechanical, including photocopying, recording, or by any information storage an d retrieval system, without permission in writing from Tzeruf Co.

First Edition Published 2013

Publisher's Cataloging-in-Publication data

Author: Elias, Daniel A..

Title: Deuteronomy

English Paperback   ISBN 978-0-9792826-8-3

Dedication:

    I dedicate this book to

        Moses......

the most spiritual man to every have lived

Table of Contents

Preface	ix
Devarim...	11
Chapter 1	11
Chapter 2	20
Chapter 3	27
Vetchanan...	33
Chapter 3 cont	33
Chapter 4	34
Chapter 5	45
Chapter 6	52
Chapter 7	57
Ekev..	60
Chapter 7 cont	60
Chapter 8	63
Chapter 9	68
Chapter 9	75
Chapter 11	80
Rehei..	86
Chapter 11 cont	86
Chapter 12	87
Chapter 13	95
Chapter 14	100
Chapter 15	105
Chapter 16	111
Shofatim...	116

CHAPTER 16 CONT	116
CHAPTER 17	117
CHAPTER 18	122
CHAPTER 19	126
CHAPTER 20	131
CHAPTER 21	135
Ki Tetzeh	138
CHAPTER 21 CONT	138
CHAPTER 22	141
CHAPTER 23	148
CHAPTER 24	153
CHAPTER 24	158
Ki Tavo	163
CHAPTER 26	163
CHAPTER 27	168
CHAPTER 28	173
CHAPTER 29	187
Nitzavim	190
CHAPTER 29 CONT	190
CHAPTER 30	194
Vayeilech	200
CHAPTER 31	200
Ha'azinu	208
CHAPTER 32	208
Ha Barakah	217
CHAPTER 33	217
CHAPTER 34	222

Preface

TRANSLATIONS

The objectives of the translated Hebrew in this book are;
1) to help becoming more fluent in the reading of Hebrew,
2) to learn Hebrew vocabulary by seeing the translation directly below the Hebrew word that one is reading.
3) to memorize parts of the verses of the sacred scriptures
4) to easily increase kavanah or thought in the Psalms and Prayers
5) to feed the soul the subliminal and spiritual effects of bible code while reading the biblical verses

One translated Hebrew word of a verse contains so much subtle information. There is the root, the prefix, the affix, dropped weak letters, gutturals, dagesh lene, dagesh forte, it's sentence grammatical name, etc. There is only space for a one word translation. Much of the english grammar has been left out by necessity; ic. the translation "the" was put in only when there was a specific prefix letter Heh.

Every expression in the [ongoing] present tense can variably be expressed in the future tense as well as in the past tense. This is because anything that is ongoing is in the present and has already happened and will continue to happen.

I would have preferred to translate the tenses of the verbs as they actually appear instead of looking to the sentence meaning to infer the past, present or future. This best reflects the Hebrew language spiritual thought. However in order to make the text as simple to understand for the majority of people who do not understand this concept I have kept the verb tenses simple to optimize understanding.

The vast majority of the Hebrew words in the Bible are very easy to translate. Generally everyone agrees on their meanings and these words are used in everyday life in Israel. But there are hebrew words that have questionable roots or could be derived from one of several roots from words that have different meanings. Then the question is which meaning was intended. Many times they all seem to fit just that each has a different thought.

I have listed hard to translate words and made notes on what other translators have used for their translations, and what possible roots the word could be derived from.

The Eskimos have 20 words for snow. The same detail is found in the Hebrew words found in the Bible. Many times there is no english word to match the Hebrew word and especially when using only one or two words. Hopefully the english words I have chosen will help in understanding the hard to translate words. Hebrew words themselves have an intuitive meaning that one feels when one knows a large Hebrew vocabulary.

Devarim

Chapter 1

ספר דברים פרק א

[פרשת דברים]

אֵ֣לֶּה הַדְּבָרִ֗ים אֲשֶׁ֨ר דִּבֶּ֤ר מֹשֶׁה֙ אֶל־כָּל־יִשְׂרָאֵ֔ל

these   the speakings   which   Moses   spoke   unto - all - Israel

בְּעֵ֖בֶר הַיַּרְדֵּ֑ן בַּמִּדְבָּ֞ר בָּעֲרָבָ֗ה מ֥וֹל ס֛וּף

in side   the Jordan   in wilderness   in plain   against   end

בֵּֽין־פָּארָ֧ן וּבֵֽין־תֹּ֛פֶל וְלָבָ֥ן וַחֲצֵרֹ֖ת וְדִ֥י זָהָֽב׃

between - Paran   and between - Tophel   and Laban   and Hazeroth   and Di   zhab

1 These be the words which Moses spake unto all Israel on this side Jordan in the wilderness, in the plain over against the Red sea, between Paran, and Tophel, and Laban, and Hazeroth, and Dizahab.

אַחַ֨ד עָשָׂ֥ר יוֹם֙ מֵֽחֹרֵ֔ב דֶּ֖רֶךְ הַר־שֵׂעִ֑יר עַ֖ד קָדֵ֥שׁ בַּרְנֵֽעַ׃

---eleven--   day   from Horeb   way   Mountain - Seir   till   Kadesh   Barnea

2 (There are eleven days' journey from Horeb by the way of mount Seir unto Kadesh-barnea.)

וַיְהִי֙ בְּאַרְבָּעִ֣ים שָׁנָ֔ה בְּעַשְׁתֵּֽי־עָשָׂ֥ר חֹ֖דֶשׁ בְּאֶחָ֣ד לַחֹ֑דֶשׁ

and it was   in fortieth   year   --in eleventh--   month   in first   to month

דִּבֶּ֤ר מֹשֶׁה֙ אֶל־בְּנֵ֣י יִשְׂרָאֵ֔ל

spoke   Moses   unto - sons   Israel

כְּ֠כֹל אֲשֶׁ֨ר צִוָּ֧ה יְהֹוָ֛ה אֹת֖וֹ אֲלֵהֶֽם׃

like all   which   commanded   ihvh   to him   unto them

3 And it came to pass in the fortieth year, in the eleventh month, on the first day of the month, that Moses spake unto the children of Israel, according unto all that the LORD had given him in commandment unto them;

אַחֲרֵ֣י הַכֹּת֗וֹ אֵ֚ת סִיחֹן֙ מֶ֣לֶךְ הָֽאֱמֹרִ֔י

after   the his kill   that   Sihon   king   the Amorite

אֲשֶׁ֥ר יוֹשֵׁ֖ב בְּחֶשְׁבּ֑וֹן

which   reigning   in Heshbon

וְאֵ֗ת ע֚וֹג מֶ֣לֶךְ הַבָּשָׁ֔ן

and that   Og   king   the Bashan

אֲשֶׁר־יוֹשֵׁ֥ב בְּעַשְׁתָּרֹ֖ת בְּאֶדְרֶֽעִי׃

which - he dwelt   in Ashtaroth   in Edrei

4 After he had slain Sihon the king of the Amorites, which dwelt in Heshbon, and Og

the king of Bashan, which dwelt at Astaroth in Edrei:

בְּעֵ֥בֶר הַיַּרְדֵּ֖ן בְּאֶ֣רֶץ מוֹאָ֑ב

    Moab   in land   the Jordan   in side

הוֹאִ֣יל מֹשֶׁ֔ה בֵּאֵ֛ר אֶת־הַתּוֹרָ֥ה הַזֹּ֖את לֵאמֹֽר׃

  to say the this the torah - that in declaring Moses he began

5 On this side Jordan, in the land of Moab, began Moses to declare this law, saying,

יְהֹוָ֧ה אֱלֹהֵ֛ינוּ דִּבֶּ֥ר אֵלֵ֖ינוּ בְּחֹרֵ֣ב לֵאמֹ֑ר

  to say in Horeb unto us he spoke our Elohim and ihvh

רַב־לָכֶ֥ם שֶׁ֖בֶת בָּהָ֥ר הַזֶּֽה׃

  the this in mountain have dwelt to you - much

6 The LORD our God spake unto us in Horeb, saying, Ye have dwelt long enough in this mount:

פְּנ֣וּ ׀ וּסְע֣וּ לָכֶ֗ם וּבֹ֛אוּ הַ֥ר הָאֱמֹרִ֖י

  the Amorites mountain and you come to you and you journey you turn

וְאֶל־כׇּל־שְׁכֵנָיו֒ בָּעֲרָבָ֣ה בָהָ֗ר

  in mountain in plain his neighbors - all - and unto

וּבַשְּׁפֵלָ֥ה וּבַנֶּ֖גֶב וּבְח֣וֹף הַיָּ֑ם אֶ֥רֶץ הַֽכְּנַעֲנִ֖י

  the Canaanites land the sea and in coast and in Negev and in foothill

וְהַלְּבָנ֔וֹן עַד־הַנָּהָ֥ר הַגָּדֹ֖ל נְהַר־פְּרָֽת׃

  Euphrates - river the great the river - till and the Lebanon

7 Turn you, and take your journey, and go to the mount of the Amorites, and unto all the places nigh thereunto, in the plain, in the hills, and in the vale, and in the south, and by the sea side, to the land of the Canaanites, and unto Lebanon, unto the great river, the river Euphrates.

רְאֵ֛ה נָתַ֥תִּי לִפְנֵיכֶ֖ם אֶת־הָאָ֑רֶץ

  the land - that before you I gave see

בֹּ֚אוּ וּרְשׁ֣וּ אֶת־הָאָ֔רֶץ אֲשֶׁ֣ר נִשְׁבַּ֣ע יְהֹוָ֣ה לַאֲבֹתֵיכֶ֗ם

  to your fathers ihvh swore which the land - that and you possess you come

לְאַבְרָהָ֨ם לְיִצְחָ֤ק וּֽלְיַעֲקֹב֙ לָתֵ֣ת לָהֶ֔ם וּלְזַרְעָ֖ם אַחֲרֵיהֶֽם׃

  after them and to their seed to them to give and to Jacob to Isaac to Abraham

8 Behold, I have set the land before you: go in and possess the land which the LORD sware unto your fathers, Abraham, Isaac, and Jacob, to give unto them and to their seed after them.

וָאֹמַ֣ר אֲלֵכֶ֔ם בָּעֵ֥ת הַהִ֖וא לֵאמֹ֑ר

  to say the that in time unto you and I said

לֹא־אוּכַל לְבַדִּי שְׂאֵת אֶתְכֶם:
to you   carry   myself   I can - not

9 And I spake unto you at that time, saying, I am not able to bear you myself alone:

יְהוָה אֱלֹהֵיכֶם הִרְבָּה אֶתְכֶם
that you   caused to multiply   your Elohim   ihvh

וְהִנְּכֶם הַיּוֹם כְּכוֹכְבֵי הַשָּׁמַיִם לָרֹב:
to many   the skies   like stars   the day   and here you

10 The LORD your God hath multiplied you, and, behold, ye are this day as the stars of heaven for multitude.

[שני]

יְהוָה אֱלֹהֵי אֲבוֹתֵכֶם יֹסֵף עֲלֵיכֶם כָּכֶם אֶלֶף פְּעָמִים
times   thousand   like you   upon you   added   your fathers   Elohim   ihvh

וִיבָרֵךְ אֶתְכֶם כַּאֲשֶׁר דִּבֶּר לָכֶם:
to you   he spoke   when   that you   and he bless

11 (The LORD God of your fathers make you a thousand times so many more as ye are, and bless you, as he hath promised you!)

אֵיכָה אֶשָּׂא לְבַדִּי טָרְחֲכֶם וּמַשַּׂאֲכֶם וְרִיבְכֶם:
and your strife   and your burden   your cumbrance   me alone   I bear   how

12 How can I myself alone bear your cumbrance, and your burden, and your strife?

הָבוּ לָכֶם אֲנָשִׁים חֲכָמִים וּנְבֹנִים וִידֻעִים
and knowing ones   and understanding ones   wise ones   men   to you   the come

לְשִׁבְטֵיכֶם וַאֲשִׂימֵם בְּרָאשֵׁיכֶם:
in your leaders   and I will set them   to your tribes

13 Take you wise men, and understanding, and known among your tribes, and I will make them rulers over you.

וַתַּעֲנוּ אֹתִי וַתֹּאמְרוּ טוֹב־הַדָּבָר אֲשֶׁר־דִּבַּרְתָּ לַעֲשׂוֹת:
to do   you spoke - which   the matter - good   and you said   to me   and you answered

14 And ye answered me, and said, The thing which thou hast spoken is good for us to do.

וָאֶקַּח אֶת־רָאשֵׁי שִׁבְטֵיכֶם אֲנָשִׁים חֲכָמִים וִידֻעִים
and knowing ones   wise ones   men   your tribes   leaders - that   and I took

וָאֶתֵּן אוֹתָם רָאשִׁים עֲלֵיכֶם שָׂרֵי אֲלָפִים
thousands   officers   upon you   leaders   to them   and I gave

וְשָׂרֵי מֵאוֹת וְשָׂרֵי חֲמִשִּׁים וְשָׂרֵי עֲשָׂרֹת
tens   and officers   fifties   and officers   hundreds   and officers

וְשֹׁטְרִ֖ים לְשִׁבְטֵיכֶֽם׃
    to your tribes   and judge ones

15 So I took the chief of your tribes, wise men, and known, and made them heads over you, captains over thousands, and captains over hundreds, and captains over fifties, and captains over tens, and officers among your tribes.

וָאֲצַוֶּה֙ אֶת־שֹׁפְטֵיכֶ֔ם בָּעֵ֥ת הַהִ֖וא לֵאמֹ֑ר
to say the it in time your judging ones - that and I commanded

שָׁמֹ֤עַ בֵּין־אֲחֵיכֶם֙ וּשְׁפַטְתֶּ֣ם צֶ֔דֶק
fairly and you judge your brothers - between hear

בֵּֽין־אִ֥ישׁ וּבֵין־אָחִ֖יו וּבֵ֥ין גֵּרֽוֹ׃
his stranger and between his brothers - and between man - between

16 And I charged your judges at that time, saying, Hear the causes between your brethren, and judge righteously between every man and his brother, and the stranger that is with him.

לֹֽא־תַכִּ֨ירוּ פָנִ֜ים בַּמִּשְׁפָּ֗ט כַּקָּטֹ֤ן כַּגָּדֹל֙ תִּשְׁמָע֔וּן
you hear it like great like small in judgment faces you be partial - not

לֹ֤א תָג֙וּרוּ֙ מִפְּנֵי־אִ֔ישׁ כִּ֥י הַמִּשְׁפָּ֖ט לֵאלֹהִ֣ים ה֑וּא
he to Elohim the judgment like man - from faces you fear not

וְהַדָּבָר֙ אֲשֶׁ֣ר יִקְשֶׁ֣ה מִכֶּ֔ם תַּקְרִב֥וּן אֵלַ֖י וּשְׁמַעְתִּֽיו׃
and I will hear it to me you bring it from you it hard which and the matter

17 Ye shall not respect persons in judgment; but ye shall hear the small as well as the great; ye shall not be afraid of the face of man; for the judgment is God's: and the cause that is too hard for you, bring it unto me, and I will hear it.

וָאֲצַוֶּ֥ה אֶתְכֶ֖ם בָּעֵ֣ת הַהִ֑וא אֵ֥ת כָּל־הַדְּבָרִ֖ים אֲשֶׁ֥ר תַּעֲשֽׂוּן׃
you do which the matters - all that the it in time that you and I commanded

18 And I commanded you at that time all the things which ye should do.

וַנִּסַּ֣ע מֵחֹרֵ֗ב וַנֵּ֡לֶךְ אֵ֣ת כָּל־הַמִּדְבָּ֣ר הַגָּד֣וֹל
the great the wilderness - all that and we went from Horeb and we journeyed

וְהַנּוֹרָ֣א הַה֗וּא אֲשֶׁ֤ר רְאִיתֶם֙ דֶּ֚רֶךְ הַ֣ר הָאֱמֹרִ֔י
the Amorites mountain way you saw which the it and the awesome

כַּאֲשֶׁ֥ר צִוָּ֛ה יְהוָ֥ה אֱלֹהֵ֖ינוּ אֹתָ֑נוּ וַנָּבֹ֕א עַ֖ד קָדֵ֥שׁ בַּרְנֵֽעַ׃
Barnea Kadesh till and we came to us our Elohim ihvh commanded when

19 And when we departed from Horeb, we went through all that great and terrible wilderness, which ye saw by the way of the mountain of the Amorites, as the LORD our God commanded us; and we came to Kadesh-barnea.

Devarim - Chapter 1

וָאֹמַ֖ר אֲלֵכֶ֑ם בָּאתֶם֙ עַד־הַ֣ר הָאֱמֹרִ֔י
the Amorites   mountain - till   you came   unto you   and I said

אֲשֶׁר־יְהוָ֥ה אֱלֹהֵ֖ינוּ נֹתֵ֥ן לָֽנוּ׃
to us   gives   our Elohim   ihvh - which

20 And I said unto you, Ye are come unto the mountain of the Amorites, which the LORD our God doth give unto us.

רְאֵ֠ה נָתַ֨ן יְהוָ֧ה אֱלֹהֶ֛יךָ לְפָנֶ֖יךָ אֶת־הָאָ֑רֶץ
the land - that   before you   your Elohim   ihvh   gave   see

עֲלֵ֣ה רֵ֗שׁ כַּאֲשֶׁר֩ דִּבֶּ֨ר יְהוָ֜ה אֱלֹהֵ֤י אֲבֹתֶ֙יךָ֙ לָ֔ךְ
to you   your fathers   Elohim   ihvh   spoke   when   possess   rise up

אַל־תִּירָ֖א וְאַל־תֵּחָֽת׃
discourage - and don't   you fear - don't

21 Behold, the LORD thy God hath set the land before thee: go up and possess it, as the LORD God of thy fathers hath said unto thee; fear not, neither be discouraged.

[שלישי]

וַתִּקְרְב֣וּן אֵלַי֮ כֻּלְּכֶם֒
all you   unto me   and you came near

וַתֹּאמְר֗וּ נִשְׁלְחָ֤ה אֲנָשִׁים֙ לְפָנֵ֔ינוּ וְיַחְפְּרוּ־לָ֖נוּ אֶת־הָאָ֑רֶץ
the land - that   to us - and they search out   before us   men   we send   and you said it

וְיָשִׁ֤בוּ אֹתָ֙נוּ֙ דָּבָ֔ר אֶת־הַדֶּ֙רֶךְ֙ אֲשֶׁ֣ר נַעֲלֶה־בָּ֔הּ
in it - we ascend   which   the way - that   speak   to us   and they return

וְאֵת֙ הֶֽעָרִ֔ים אֲשֶׁ֥ר נָבֹ֖א אֲלֵיהֶֽן׃
unto them   we will come   which   the cities   and that

22 And ye came near unto me every one of you, and said, We will send men before us, and they shall search us out the land, and bring us word again by what way we must go up, and into what cities we shall come.

וַיִּיטַ֥ב בְּעֵינַ֖י הַדָּבָ֑ר וָאֶקַּ֤ח מִכֶּם֙
from you   and I took   the matter   in my eyes   and it was good

שְׁנֵ֣ים עָשָׂ֣ר אֲנָשִׁ֔ים אִ֥ישׁ אֶחָ֖ד לַשָּֽׁבֶט׃
to tribe   one   man   men   -- twelve --

23 And the saying pleased me well: and I took twelve men of you, one of a tribe:

וַיִּפְנוּ֙ וַיַּעֲל֣וּ הָהָ֔רָה
the mountain   and they ascended   and they turned

וַיָּבֹ֖אוּ עַד־נַ֣חַל אֶשְׁכֹּ֑ל וַֽיְרַגְּל֖וּ אֹתָֽהּ׃
to it   and they explored   Eshcol   valley - till   and they came

24 And they turned and went up into the mountain, and came unto the valley of Eshcol, and searched it out.

וַיִּקְחוּ בְיָדָם מִפְּרִי הָאָרֶץ וַיּוֹרִדוּ אֵלֵינוּ
and they took   in their hands   from fruit   the land   and they descended   unto us

וַיָּשִׁבוּ אֹתָנוּ דָבָר וַיֹּאמְרוּ
and they returned   to us   speech   and they said

טוֹבָה הָאָרֶץ אֲשֶׁר־יְהוָה אֱלֹהֵינוּ נֹתֵן לָנוּ׃
good   the land   ihvh - which   our Elohim   gives   to us

25 And they took of the fruit of the land in their hands, and brought it down unto us, and brought us word again, and said, It is a good land which the LORD our God doth give us.

וְלֹא אֲבִיתֶם לַעֲלֹת וַתַּמְרוּ אֶת־פִּי יְהוָה אֱלֹהֵיכֶם׃
and not   you come   to ascend   and you rebelled   mouth - that   ihvh   your Elohim

26 Notwithstanding ye would not go up, but rebelled against the commandment of the LORD your God:

וַתֵּרָגְנוּ בְאָהֳלֵיכֶם
and you murmured it   in your tents

וַתֹּאמְרוּ בְּשִׂנְאַת יְהוָה אֹתָנוּ הוֹצִיאָנוּ מֵאֶרֶץ מִצְרָיִם
and you said it   in hate   ihvh   to us   he brought us out   from land   Egypt

לָתֵת אֹתָנוּ בְּיַד הָאֱמֹרִי לְהַשְׁמִידֵנוּ׃
to give   to us   in hand   the Amorites   to destroy us

27 And ye murmured in your tents, and said, Because the LORD hated us, he hath brought us forth out of the land of Egypt, to deliver us into the hand of the Amorites, to destroy us.

אָנָה אֲנַחְנוּ עֹלִים אַחֵינוּ הֵמַסּוּ אֶת־לְבָבֵנוּ לֵאמֹר
where   we   rising ones   our brothers   they discouraged   our heart - that   to say

עָרִים גְּדֹלֹת וּבְצוּרֹת בַּשָּׁמָיִם
cities   great   and stone walls   in the heavens

וְגַם־בְּנֵי עֲנָקִים רָאִינוּ שָׁם׃
sons - and also   Anakims   we saw   there

28 Whither shall we go up? our brethren have discouraged our heart, saying, The people is greater and taller than we; the cities are great and walled up to heaven; and moreover we have seen the sons of the Anakims there.

וָאֹמַר אֲלֵכֶם לֹא־תַעַרְצוּן וְלֹא־תִירְאוּן מֵהֶם׃
and I said   to you   you be terrified - not   you fear - and not   from them

29 Then I said unto you, Dread not, neither be afraid of them.

לִֽיהוָ֨ה	אֱלֹהֵיכֶ֜ם	הַהֹלֵ֣ךְ	לִפְנֵיכֶ֗ם
to ihvh	your Elohim	the going one	before you

ה֖וּא	יִלָּחֵ֣ם	לָכֶ֑ם
he	he will fight	to you

כְּ֠כֹל	אֲשֶׁ֨ר	עָשָׂ֧ה	אִתְּכֶ֛ם	בְּמִצְרַ֖יִם	לְעֵינֵיכֶֽם׃
like all	which	he did	to you	in Egypt	to your eyes

30 The LORD your God which goeth before you, he shall fight for you, according to all that he did for you in Egypt before your eyes;

וּבַמִּדְבָּר֙	אֲשֶׁ֣ר	רָאִ֔יתָ	אֲשֶׁ֤ר	נְשָׂאֲךָ֙	יְהוָ֣ה	אֱלֹהֶ֔יךָ
and in wilderness	which	you saw	which	he carried you	ihvh	your Elohim

כַּאֲשֶׁ֥ר	יִשָּׂא־אִ֖ישׁ	אֶת־בְּנ֑וֹ
when	man - he carried	his son - that

בְּכָל־הַדֶּ֙רֶךְ֙	אֲשֶׁ֣ר	הֲלַכְתֶּ֔ם	עַד־בֹּאֲכֶ֖ם	עַד־הַמָּק֥וֹם	הַזֶּֽה׃
the way - in all	which	you went	you came - until	the place - till	the this

31 And in the wilderness, where thou hast seen how that the LORD thy God bare thee, as a man doth bear his son, in all the way that ye went, until ye came into this place.

וּבַדָּבָ֖ר	הַזֶּ֑ה	אֵֽינְכֶם֙	מַאֲמִינִ֔ם	בַּיהוָ֖ה	אֱלֹהֵיכֶֽם׃
and in way	the this	you weren't	believing ones	in ihvh	your Elohim

32 Yet in this thing ye did not believe the LORD your God,

הַהֹלֵ֨ךְ	לִפְנֵיכֶ֜ם	בַּדֶּ֗רֶךְ	לָת֥וּר	לָכֶ֛ם	מָק֖וֹם	לַחֲנֹתְכֶ֑ם
the going one	before you	in journey	to search	to you	place	to you camping

בָּאֵ֣שׁ ׀	לַ֗יְלָה	לַרְאֹֽתְכֶם֙	בַּדֶּ֙רֶךְ֙	אֲשֶׁ֣ר	תֵּֽלְכוּ־בָ֔הּ
in fire	night	to show you	in way	which	in it - you go

וּבֶעָנָ֖ן	יוֹמָֽם׃
and in cloud	by day

33 Who went in the way before you, to search you out a place to pitch your tents in, in fire by night, to shew you by what way ye should go, and in a cloud by day.

וַיִּשְׁמַ֥ע	יְהוָ֖ה	אֶת־ק֣וֹל	דִּבְרֵיכֶ֑ם
and he heard	ihvh	sound - that	your speakings

וַיִּקְצֹ֖ף	וַיִּשָּׁבַ֥ע	לֵאמֹֽר׃
and he wroth	and he swore	to say

34 And the LORD heard the voice of your words, and was wroth, and sware, saying,

אִם־יִרְאֶ֥ה	אִישׁ֙	בָּאֲנָשִׁ֣ים	הָאֵ֔לֶּה	הַדּ֥וֹר	הָרָ֖ע	הַזֶּ֑ה
if - he will see	each	in men	the these	the generation	the evil	the this

אֶת הָאָרֶץ הַטּוֹבָה אֲשֶׁר נִשְׁבַּעְתִּי לָתֵת לַאֲבֹתֵיכֶם:
    to your fathers   to give   I swore   which   the good   the land   that

35 Surely there shall not one of these men of this evil generation see that good land, which I sware to give unto your fathers,

זוּלָתִי כָּלֵב בֶּן־יְפֻנֶּה הוּא יִרְאֶנָּה
  he will see it   he   Jephunneh - son   Caleb   excepting

וְלוֹ־אֶתֵּן אֶת־הָאָרֶץ אֲשֶׁר דָּרַךְ־בָּהּ
  in it - way   which   the land - that   I will give - and to him

וּלְבָנָיו יַעַן אֲשֶׁר מִלֵּא אַחֲרֵי יְהוָה:
  ihvh   after   he was filled   which   because   and to his sons

36 Save Caleb the son of Jephunneh; he shall see it, and to him will I give the land that he hath trodden upon, and to his children, because he hath wholly followed the LORD.

גַּם־בִּי הִתְאַנַּף יְהוָה בִּגְלַלְכֶם לֵאמֹר
  to say   in your account   ihvh   became angry   in me - also

גַּם־אַתָּה לֹא־תָבֹא שָׁם:
  there   you will come - not   you - also

37 Also the LORD was angry with me for your sakes, saying, Thou also shalt not go in thither.

יְהוֹשֻׁעַ בִּן־נוּן הָעֹמֵד לְפָנֶיךָ הוּא יָבֹא שָׁמָּה
  to there   he will come   he   to before you   the standing one   nun - son   Joshua

אֹתוֹ חַזֵּק כִּי־הוּא יַנְחִלֶנָּה אֶת־יִשְׂרָאֵל:
  Israel - that   he will inherit it   he - like   encourage   to him

38 But Joshua the son of Nun, which standeth before thee, he shall go in thither: encourage him: for he shall cause Israel to inherit it.

[רביעי]

וְטַפְּכֶם אֲשֶׁר אֲמַרְתֶּם לָבַז יִהְיֶה
  it will be   as captive   you said   which   and your little ones

וּבְנֵיכֶם אֲשֶׁר לֹא־יָדְעוּ הַיּוֹם טוֹב וָרָע
  and bad   good   the day   they knew - not   which   and your children

הֵמָּה יָבֹאוּ שָׁמָּה וְלָהֶם אֶתְּנֶנָּה וְהֵם יִירָשׁוּהָ:
  possess it   and they   I will give it   and to them   to there   they will come   they are

39 Moreover your little ones, which ye said should be a prey, and your children, which in that day had no knowledge between good and evil, they shall go in thither, and unto them will I give it, and they shall possess it.

וְאַתֶּם פְּנוּ לָכֶם וּסְעוּ הַמִּדְבָּרָה דֶּרֶךְ יַם־סוּף:
  end - sea   route   to wilderness   and you journey   to you   turn   and they

40 But as for you, turn you, and take your journey into the wilderness by the way of the Red sea.

וַתַּעֲנוּ   וַתֹּאמְרוּ אֵלַי חָטָאנוּ לַיהוָה אֲנַחְנוּ נַעֲלֶה
we will ascend   we   to ihvh   we sinned   unto me   and you said   and you answered

וְנִלְחַמְנוּ כְּכֹל אֲשֶׁר־צִוָּנוּ יְהוָה אֱלֹהֵינוּ
our Elohim   ihvh   commanded us - which   like all   and we will fight

וַתַּחְגְּרוּ אִישׁ אֶת־כְּלֵי מִלְחַמְתּוֹ
his war   weapons - that   each   and they girded

וַתָּהִינוּ לַעֲלֹת הָהָרָה׃
the towards mountain   to ascend   and you were ready

41 Then ye answered and said unto me, We have sinned against the LORD, we will go up and fight, according to all that the LORD our God commanded us. And when ye had girded on every man his weapons of war, ye were ready to go up into the hill.

וַיֹּאמֶר יְהוָה אֵלַי אֱמֹר לָהֶם לֹא תַעֲלוּ וְלֹא תִלָּחֲמוּ
you fight   and not   you ascend   not   to them   say   to me   ihvh   and he said

כִּי אֵינֶנִּי בְּקִרְבְּכֶם וְלֹא תִּנָּגְפוּ לִפְנֵי אֹיְבֵיכֶם׃
being your enemies   before   you be defeated   and not   in your midst   I isn't   like

42 And the LORD said unto me, Say unto them, Go not up, neither fight; for I am not among you; lest ye be smitten before your enemies.

וָאֲדַבֵּר אֲלֵיכֶם וְלֹא שְׁמַעְתֶּם
you listened   and not   unto you   and I spoke

וַתַּמְרוּ אֶת־פִּי יְהוָה וַתָּזִדוּ וַתַּעֲלוּ הָהָרָה׃
towards the hill   and you went up   and you were arrogant   ihvh   mouth - that   and you rebelled

43 So I spake unto you; and ye would not hear, but rebelled against the commandment of the LORD, and went presumptuously up into the hill.

וַיֵּצֵא הָאֱמֹרִי הַיֹּשֵׁב בָּהָר הַהוּא
the it   in mountain   the one dwelling   the Amorite   and he came out

לִקְרַאתְכֶם וַיִּרְדְּפוּ אֶתְכֶם כַּאֲשֶׁר תַּעֲשֶׂינָה הַדְּבֹרִים
the bees   they do   when   to you   and they chased   to meet you

וַיַּכְּתוּ אֶתְכֶם בְּשֵׂעִיר עַד־חָרְמָה׃
Hormah - till   from Seir   to you   and they beat

44 And the Amorites, which dwelt in that mountain, came out against you, and chased you, as bees do, and destroyed you in Seir, even unto Hormah.

וַתָּשֻׁבוּ וַתִּבְכּוּ לִפְנֵי יְהוָה וְלֹא־שָׁמַע יְהוָה בְּקֹלְכֶם
in your voice   ihvh   listened - and not   ihvh   before   and you wept   and you returned

וְלֹא הֶאֱזִין אֲלֵיכֶם:

unto you · he gave ear · and not

45 And ye returned and wept before the LORD; but the LORD would not hearken to your voice, nor give ear unto you.

וַתֵּשְׁבוּ בְקָדֵשׁ יָמִים רַבִּים כַּיָּמִים אֲשֶׁר יְשַׁבְתֶּם:

you stayed · which · as days · many · days · in Kadesh · and you dwelled

46 So ye abode in Kadesh many days, according unto the days that ye abode there.

Chapter 2

ספר דברים פרק ב

וַנֵּפֶן וַנִּסַּע הַמִּדְבָּרָה דֶּרֶךְ יַם־סוּף

end - sea · route · the wilderness · and we journeyed · and we turned

כַּאֲשֶׁר דִּבֶּר יְהוָה אֵלָי

unto me · ihvh · spoke · when

וַנָּסָב אֶת־הַר־שֵׂעִיר יָמִים רַבִּים:

many · days · Seir - mountain - that · and we went around

1 Then we turned, and took our journey into the wilderness by the way of the Red sea, as the LORD spake unto me: and we compassed mount Seir many days.

ס

[חמישי]

וַיֹּאמֶר יְהוָה אֵלַי לֵאמֹר:

to say · unto me · ihvh · and he said

2 And the LORD spake unto me, saying,

רַב־לָכֶם סֹב אֶת־הָהָר הַזֶּה פְּנוּ לָכֶם צָפֹנָה:

towards north · to you · you face · the this · the mountain - that · going around · to you - much

3 Ye have compassed this mountain long enough: turn you northward.

וְאֶת־הָעָם צַו לֵאמֹר

to say · command · the people - and that

אַתֶּם עֹבְרִים בִּגְבוּל אֲחֵיכֶם בְּנֵי־עֵשָׂו הַיֹּשְׁבִים בְּשֵׂעִיר

in Seir · the dwelling ones · Esau - sons · your brothers · in border · ones passing · to you

וְיִירְאוּ מִכֶּם וְנִשְׁמַרְתֶּם מְאֹד:

very · and you heed · from you · and they will fear

4 And command thou the people, saying, Ye are to pass through the coast of your brethren the children of Esau, which dwell in Seir; and they shall be afraid of you: take ye good heed unto yourselves therefore:

Devarim - Chapter 2

אַל־תִּתְגָּרוּ בָם
in them   you meddle it - don't

כִּי לֹא־אֶתֵּן לָכֶם מֵאַרְצָם עַד מִדְרַךְ כַּף־רָגֶל
leg - palm   breath wide   till   from their land   to you   I will give - not   like

כִּי־יְרֻשָּׁה לְעֵשָׂו נָתַתִּי אֶת־הַר שֵׂעִיר:
Seir   mountain - that   I gave   to Esau   possession - like

5 Meddle not with them; for I will not give you of their land, no, not so much as a foot breadth; because I have given mount Seir unto Esau for a possession.

אֹכֶל תִּשְׁבְּרוּ מֵאִתָּם בַּכֶּסֶף
in silver   from them   you buy   and food

וַאֲכַלְתֶּם וְגַם־מַיִם תִּכְרוּ מֵאִתָּם בַּכֶּסֶף וּשְׁתִיתֶם:
and you drink   in silver   from that them   you buy   waters - and also   and you eat

6 Ye shall buy meat of them for money, that ye may eat; and ye shall also buy water of them for money, that ye may drink.

כִּי יְהֹוָה אֱלֹהֶיךָ בֵּרַכְךָ בְּכֹל מַעֲשֵׂה יָדֶךָ
your hand   your work   in all   blessed you   your Elohim   ihvh   like

יָדַע לֶכְתְּךָ אֶת־הַמִּדְבָּר הַגָּדֹל הַזֶּה
the this   the big   the wilderness - that   your going   he knows

זֶה אַרְבָּעִים שָׁנָה יְהֹוָה אֱלֹהֶיךָ עִמָּךְ
with you   your Elohim   ihvh   year   forty   these

לֹא חָסַרְתָּ דָּבָר:
matter   you lacked   not

7 For the LORD thy God hath blessed thee in all the works of thy hand: he knoweth thy walking through this great wilderness: these forty years the LORD thy God hath been with thee; thou hast lacked nothing.

וַנַּעֲבֹר מֵאֵת אַחֵינוּ בְנֵי־עֵשָׂו
Esau - sons   our brothers   from that   and we passed

הַיֹּשְׁבִים בְּשֵׂעִיר מִדֶּרֶךְ הָעֲרָבָה מֵאֵילַת
from Elath   the plain   from way   in Seir   the dwelling ones

וּמֵעֶצְיֹן גֶּבֶר [פסק באמצע פסוק]
Geber   and from Ezion

וַנֵּפֶן וַנַּעֲבֹר דֶּרֶךְ מִדְבַּר מוֹאָב:
Moab   wilderness   way   and we passed   and we turned

8 And when we passed by from our brethren the children of Esau, which dwelt in Seir, through the way of the plain from Elath, and from Ezion-gaber, we turned and passed by the way of the wilderness of Moab.

וַיֹּאמֶר יְהוָה אֵלַי
and he said   ihvh   to me

אַל־תָּצַר אֶת־מוֹאָב וְאַל־תִּתְגָּר בָּם מִלְחָמָה
don't - you distress - that Moab   and don't - you provoke   in them   war

כִּי לֹא־אֶתֵּן לְךָ מֵאַרְצוֹ יְרֻשָּׁה
like   not - I will give   to you   from his land   possession

כִּי לִבְנֵי־לוֹט נָתַתִּי אֶת־עָר יְרֻשָּׁה׃
like   to sons - Lot   I gave   that - Ar   possession

9 And the LORD said unto me, Distress not the Moabites, neither contend with them in battle: for I will not give thee of their land for a possession; because I have given Ar unto the children of Lot for a possession.

הָאֵמִים לְפָנִים יָשְׁבוּ בָהּ עַם גָּדוֹל וְרַב וָרָם כָּעֲנָקִים׃
the Emims   before   they dwelt   in it   people   strong   and many   and tall   like Anakims

10 The Emims dwelt therein in times past, a people great, and many, and tall, as the Anakims;

רְפָאִים יֵחָשְׁבוּ אַף־הֵם כָּעֲנָקִים
giants   they were considered   thus - them   the Anakims

וְהַמֹּאָבִים יִקְרְאוּ לָהֶם אֵמִים׃
and the Moabites   they called   to them   Emims

11 Which also were accounted giants, as the Anakims; but the Moabites call them Emims.

וּבְשֵׂעִיר יָשְׁבוּ הַחֹרִים לְפָנִים
and in Seir   they lived   the Horims   before ones

וּבְנֵי עֵשָׂו יִירָשׁוּם וַיַּשְׁמִידוּם מִפְּנֵיהֶם וַיֵּשְׁבוּ תַחְתָּם
and sons   Esau   they drove out them   and they destroyed them   from before them   and they settled   in their place

כַּאֲשֶׁר עָשָׂה יִשְׂרָאֵל לְאֶרֶץ יְרֻשָּׁתוֹ אֲשֶׁר־נָתַן יְהוָה לָהֶם׃
when   he did   Israel   in land   his possession   which - he gave   ihvh   to them

12 The Horims also dwelt in Seir before time; but the children of Esau succeeded them, when they had destroyed them from before them, and dwelt in their stead; as Israel did unto the land of his possession, which the LORD gave unto them.

עַתָּה קֻמוּ וְעִבְרוּ לָכֶם אֶת־נַחַל זָרֶד וַנַּעֲבֹר אֶת־נַחַל זָרֶד׃
now   you get up   and you cross   to you   that - brook   Zered   and we crossed   that - brook   Zered

13 Now rise up, said I, and get you over the brook Zered. And we went over the brook Zered.

וְהַיָּמִים אֲשֶׁר־הָלַכְנוּ מִקָּדֵשׁ בַּרְנֵעַ
and the days   which - we left   from Kadesh   Barnea

DEVARIM - CHAPTER 2

עַד אֲשֶׁר־עָבַרְנוּ אֶת־נַחַל זֶרֶד שְׁלֹשִׁים וּשְׁמֹנֶה שָׁנָה
year and eight thirty Zered brook - that we passed - which till

עַד־תֹּם כָּל־הַדּוֹר אַנְשֵׁי הַמִּלְחָמָה מִקֶּרֶב הַמַּחֲנֶה
the camp from among the war men the generation - all perish - till

כַּאֲשֶׁר נִשְׁבַּע יְהוָה לָהֶם׃
to them ihvh he swore when

14 And the space in which we came from Kadesh-barnea, until we were come over the brook Zered, was thirty and eight years; until all the generation of the men of war were wasted out from among the host, as the LORD sware unto them.

וְגַם יַד־יְהוָה הָיְתָה בָּם לְהֻמָּם
to eliminate them inthem it was ihvh - hand and also

מִקֶּרֶב הַמַּחֲנֶה עַד תֻּמָּם׃
finish them till the camp from among

15 For indeed the hand of the LORD was against them, to destroy them from among the host, until they were consumed.

וַיְהִי כַאֲשֶׁר־תַּמּוּ כָּל־אַנְשֵׁי הַמִּלְחָמָה לָמוּת מִקֶּרֶב הָעָם׃
the people from among to die the war men - all they finished - when and it was

16 So it came to pass, when all the men of war were consumed and dead from among the people,

ס

וַיְדַבֵּר יְהוָה אֵלַי לֵאמֹר׃
to say unto me ihvh and he said

17 That the LORD spake unto me, saying,

אַתָּה עֹבֵר הַיּוֹם אֶת־גְּבוּל מוֹאָב אֶת־עָר׃
Ar - that Moab border - that the day pass you

18 Thou art to pass over through Ar, the coast of Moab, this day:

וְקָרַבְתָּ מוּל בְּנֵי עַמּוֹן אַל־תְּצֻרֵם וְאַל־תִּתְגָּר בָּם
in them you meddle - and don't you distress them - don't Ammon sons against and you near

כִּי לֹא־אֶתֵּן מֵאֶרֶץ בְּנֵי־עַמּוֹן לְךָ יְרֻשָּׁה
possession to you Ammon - sons from land I will give - not like

כִּי לִבְנֵי־לוֹט נְתַתִּיהָ יְרֻשָּׁה׃
possession I gave it Lot - to sons like

19 And when thou comest nigh over against the children of Ammon, distress them not, nor meddle with them: for I will not give thee of the land of the children of Ammon any possession; because I have given it unto the children of Lot for a possession.

אֶרֶץ־רְפָאִים תֵּחָשֵׁב אַף־הִוא רְפָאִים יָשְׁבוּ־בָהּ לְפָנִים
giants - land   it considered   it - so   giants   in it - they dwelled   before ones

וְהָעַמֹּנִים יִקְרְאוּ לָהֶם זַמְזֻמִּים׃
and the Ammonites   they call   to them   Zamzummims

20 (That also was accounted a land of giants: giants dwelt therein in old time; and the Ammonites call them Zamzummims;

עַם גָּדוֹל וְרַב וָרָם כָּעֲנָקִים
people   great   and many   and tall   and Anakims

וַיַּשְׁמִידֵם יְהוָה מִפְּנֵיהֶם
and he destroyed them   ihvh   from before them

וַיִּירָשֻׁם וַיֵּשְׁבוּ תַחְתָּם׃
and they drove out them   and they settled   in their place

21 A people great, and many, and tall, as the Anakims; but the LORD destroyed them before them; and they succeeded them, and dwelt in their stead:

כַּאֲשֶׁר עָשָׂה לִבְנֵי עֵשָׂו הַיֹּשְׁבִים בְּשֵׂעִיר
when   he did   to sons   Esau   the dwelling ones   in Seir

אֲשֶׁר הִשְׁמִיד אֶת־הַחֹרִי מִפְּנֵיהֶם
which   and they drove out them   and they settled   in place of them

וַיִּירָשֻׁם וַיֵּשְׁבוּ תַחְתָּם עַד הַיּוֹם הַזֶּה׃
till   the day   the this

22 As he did to the children of Esau, which dwelt in Seir, when he destroyed the Horims from before them; and they succeeded them, and dwelt in their stead even unto this day:

וְהָעַוִּים הַיֹּשְׁבִים בַּחֲצֵרִים עַד־עַזָּה
and the Avims   the dwellers   in Hazerim   Azzah - till

כַּפְתֹּרִים הַיֹּצְאִים מִכַּפְתֹּר הִשְׁמִידֻם
Caphtorims   the ones coming out   from Caphtor   they destroyed them

וַיֵּשְׁבוּ תַחְתָּם׃
and they settled   in their place

23 And the Avims which dwelt in Hazerim, even unto Azzah, the Caphtorims, which came forth out of Caphtor, destroyed them, and dwelt in their stead.)

קוּמוּ סְּעוּ וְעִבְרוּ אֶת־נַחַל אַרְנֹן
you get up   you set out   and pass   brook - that   Arnon

רְאֵה נָתַתִּי בְיָדְךָ אֶת־סִיחֹן מֶלֶךְ־חֶשְׁבּוֹן הָאֱמֹרִי
see   I gave   in your hand   Sihon - that   Hesbon - king   the Amorite

Devarim - Chapter 2

וְאֶת־אַרְצ֑וֹ הָחֵ֣ל רָ֔שׁ וְהִתְגָּ֥ר בּ֖וֹ מִלְחָמָֽה׃
war   in it   and fight   possess   begin   his land - and that

24 Rise ye up, take your journey, and pass over the river Arnon: behold, I have given into thine hand Sihon the Amorite, king of Heshbon, and his land: begin to possess it, and contend with him in battle.

הַיּ֣וֹם הַזֶּ֗ה תֵּת֙ אָחֵ֣ל תֵּ֖ת פַּחְדְּךָ֣
your terror   to give   I will begin   the this   the day

וְיִרְאָ֣תְךָ֔ עַל־פְּנֵי֙ הָֽעַמִּ֔ים תַּ֖חַת כָּל־הַשָּׁמָ֑יִם
the heavens - all   under   the nations   faces - upon   and your fear

אֲשֶׁ֤ר יִשְׁמְעוּן֙ שִׁמְעֲךָ֔ וְרָגְז֥וּ וְחָל֖וּ מִפָּנֶֽיךָ׃
from your face   and they will be in anguish   and they will tremble   report of you   they will hear   which

25 This day will I begin to put the dread of thee and the fear of thee upon the nations that are under the whole heaven, who shall hear report of thee, and shall tremble, and be in anguish because of thee.

וָאֶשְׁלַ֤ח מַלְאָכִים֙ מִמִּדְבַּ֣ר קְדֵמ֔וֹת
Kedemoth   from wilderness   messengers   and I sent

אֶל־סִיח֖וֹן מֶ֣לֶךְ חֶשְׁבּ֑וֹן דִּבְרֵ֥י שָׁל֖וֹם לֵאמֹֽר׃
to say   peace   speakings   Heshbon   king   Sihon unto

26 And I sent messengers out of the wilderness of Kedemoth unto Sihon king of Heshbon with words of peace, saying,

אֶעְבְּרָ֣ה בְאַרְצֶ֔ךָ בַּדֶּ֥רֶךְ
in way   your land   I pass through

בַּדֶּ֣רֶךְ אֵלֵ֔ךְ לֹ֥א אָס֖וּר יָמִ֥ין וּשְׂמֹֽאול׃
or left   right   I will turn   not   high   in way

27 Let me pass through thy land: I will go along by the high way, I will neither turn unto the right hand nor to the left.

אֹ֣כֶל בַּכֶּ֤סֶף תַּשְׁבִּרֵ֙נִי֙ וְאָכַ֔לְתִּי
and I eat   you sell me   in silver   food

וּמַ֛יִם בַּכֶּ֥סֶף תִּתֶּן־לִ֖י וְשָׁתִ֑יתִי רַ֖ק אֶעְבְּרָ֥ה בְרַגְלָֽי׃
in my feet   I pass   only   and I drink   to me - you give   in silver   and water

28 Thou shalt sell me meat for money, that I may eat; and give me water for money, that I may drink: only I will pass through on my feet;

כַּאֲשֶׁ֨ר עָֽשׂוּ־לִ֜י בְּנֵ֣י עֵשָׂ֗ו הַיֹּֽשְׁבִים֙ בְּשֵׂעִ֔יר
in Seir   the dwellers   Esau   sons   to me - they did   when

וְהַמּ֣וֹאָבִ֔ים הַיֹּשְׁבִ֖ים בְּעָ֑ר
in Ar   the dwellers   and the Moabites

עַד אֲשֶׁר־אֶעֱבֹר אֶת־הַיַּרְדֵּן אֶל־הָאָרֶץ
the land - unto   the Jordan - that   I pass - which   till

אֲשֶׁר־יְהֹוָה אֱלֹהֵינוּ נֹתֵן לָנוּ׃
to us   gives   our Elohim   ihvh - which

29 (As the children of Esau which dwell in Seir, and the Moabites which dwell in Ar, did unto me;) until I shall pass over Jordan into the land which the LORD our God giveth us.

וְלֹא אָבָה סִיחֹן מֶלֶךְ חֶשְׁבּוֹן הַעֲבִרֵנוּ בּוֹ
in him   the pass us   Heshbon   king   Sihon   allowed   and not

כִּי־הִקְשָׁה יְהֹוָה אֱלֹהֶיךָ אֶת־רוּחוֹ וְאִמֵּץ אֶת־לְבָבוֹ
heart his - that   and made obstinate   his spirit - that   your Elohim   ihvh   hardened - like

לְמַעַן תִּתּוֹ בְיָדְךָ כַּיּוֹם הַזֶּה׃
the this   like day   in your hand   give him   to end

30 But Sihon king of Heshbon would not let us pass by him: for the LORD thy God hardened his spirit, and made his heart obstinate, that he might deliver him into thy hand, as appeareth this day.

ס

[ששי]

וַיֹּאמֶר יְהֹוָה אֵלַי רְאֵה הַחִלֹּתִי תֵּת לְפָנֶיךָ אֶת־סִיחֹן
Sihon - that   before you   give   the I began   see   unto me   ihvh   and he said

וְאֶת־אַרְצוֹ הָחֵל רָשׁ לָרֶשֶׁת אֶת־אַרְצוֹ׃
his land - that   to possess   evict   begin   his land - and that

31 And the LORD said unto me, Behold, I have begun to give Sihon and his land before thee: begin to possess, that thou mayest inherit his land.

וַיֵּצֵא סִיחֹן לִקְרָאתֵנוּ הוּא
he   to meet us   Sihon   and he came out

וְכָל־עַמּוֹ לַמִּלְחָמָה יָהְצָה׃
Jahaz   in war   his people - and all

32 Then Sihon came out against us, he and all his people, to fight at Jahaz.

וַיִּתְּנֵהוּ יְהֹוָה אֱלֹהֵינוּ לְפָנֵינוּ
before us   our Elohim   ihvh   and he gave him

וַנַּךְ אֹתוֹ וְאֶת־בָּנוֹ [בָּנָיו] וְאֶת־כָּל־עַמּוֹ׃
his people - all - and that   his sons - and that   to him   and we struck

33 And the LORD our God delivered him before us; and we smote him, and his sons, and all his people.

DEVARIM - CHAPTER 3

וַנִּלְכֹּד אֶת־כָּל־עָרָיו בָּעֵת הַהִוא
and we took that - all - his cities in time the it

וַנַּחֲרֵם אֶת־כָּל־עִיר מְתִם וְהַנָּשִׁים וְהַטָּף
and we utterly destroyed that - all - city men and the women and the little ones

לֹא הִשְׁאַרְנוּ שָׂרִיד:
not they remained survivor

34 And we took all his cities at that time, and utterly destroyed the men, and the women, and the little ones, of every city, we left none to remain:

רַק הַבְּהֵמָה בָּזַזְנוּ לָנוּ
only the cattle in prey to us

וּשְׁלַל הֶעָרִים אֲשֶׁר לָכָדְנוּ:
and spoils the cities which we took

35 Only the cattle we took for a prey unto ourselves, and the spoil of the cities which we took.

מֵעֲרֹעֵר אֲשֶׁר עַל־שְׂפַת־נַחַל אַרְנֹן
from Aroer which upon - beach - river Arnon

וְהָעִיר אֲשֶׁר בַּנַּחַל וְעַד־הַגִּלְעָד
and the city which in river and till - the Gilead

לֹא הָיְתָה קִרְיָה אֲשֶׁר שָׂגְבָה מִמֶּנּוּ
not it was town which too strong from us

אֶת־הַכֹּל נָתַן יְהוָה אֱלֹהֵינוּ לְפָנֵינוּ:
that - the all he gave ihvh our Elohim before us

36 From Aroer, which is by the brink of the river of Arnon, and from the city that is by the river, even unto Gilead, there was not one city too strong for us: the LORD our God delivered all unto us:

רַק אֶל־אֶרֶץ בְּנֵי־עַמּוֹן לֹא קָרָבְתָּ כָּל־יַד נַחַל יַבֹּק
only unto - land sons - Ammon not you near all - side river Jabbok

וְעָרֵי הָהָר וְכֹל אֲשֶׁר־צִוָּה יְהוָה אֱלֹהֵינוּ:
and cities the mountains and all which - commanded ihvh our Elohim

37 Only unto the land of the children of Ammon thou camest not, nor unto any place of the river Jabbok, nor unto the cities in the mountains, nor unto whatsoever the LORD our God forbad us.

CHAPTER 3

ספר דברים פרק ג

וַנֵּפֶן וַנַּעַל דֶּרֶךְ הַבָּשָׁן
and we turned and we footed way the Bashan

וַיֵּצֵא עוֹג מֶלֶךְ־הַבָּשָׁן לִקְרָאתֵנוּ
הוּא וְכָל־עַמּוֹ לַמִּלְחָמָה אֶדְרֶעִי׃

1 Then we turned, and went up the way to Bashan: and Og the king of Bashan came out against us, he and all his people, to battle at Edrei.

וַיֹּאמֶר יְהוָה אֵלַי אַל־תִּירָא אֹתוֹ כִּי בְיָדְךָ נָתַתִּי אֹתוֹ
וְאֶת־כָּל־עַמּוֹ וְאֶת־אַרְצוֹ וְעָשִׂיתָ לּוֹ
כַּאֲשֶׁר עָשִׂיתָ לְסִיחֹן מֶלֶךְ הָאֱמֹרִי אֲשֶׁר יוֹשֵׁב בְּחֶשְׁבּוֹן׃

2 And the LORD said unto me, Fear him not: for I will deliver him, and all his people, and his land, into thy hand; and thou shalt do unto him as thou didst unto Sihon king of the Amorites, which dwelt at Heshbon.

3 So the LORD our God delivered into our hands Og also, the king of Bashan, and all his people: and we smote him until none was left to him remaining.

4 And we took all his cities at that time, there was not a city which we took not from them, threescore cities, all the region of Argob, the kingdom of Og in Bashan.

כָּל־אֵלֶּה עָרִים בְּצֻרֹת חוֹמָה גְבֹהָה דְּלָתַיִם וּבְרִיחַ
לְבַד מֵעָרֵי הַפְּרָזִי הַרְבֵּה מְאֹד׃

5 All these cities were fenced with high walls, gates, and bars; beside unwalled towns a great many.

וַנַּחֲרֵם	אוֹתָם	כַּאֲשֶׁר	עָשִׂינוּ	לְסִיחֹן	מֶלֶךְ	חֶשְׁבּוֹן
and we utterly destroyed	to them	when	we did	to Sihon	king	Heshbon

הַחֲרֵם	כָּל־עִיר	מְתִם	הַנָּשִׁים	וְהַטָּף׃
the utterly destroying	city - all	dead	the women	and the little ones

6 And we utterly destroyed them, as we did unto Sihon king of Heshbon, utterly destroying the men, women, and children, of every city.

וְכָל־הַבְּהֵמָה	וּשְׁלַל	הֶעָרִים	בַּזּוֹנוּ	לָנוּ׃
the cattle - and all	and plunder	the cities	we took prey	to us

7 But all the cattle, and the spoil of the cities, we took for a prey to ourselves.

וַנִּקַּח	בָּעֵת	הַהִוא	אֶת־הָאָרֶץ	מִיַּד	שְׁנֵי	מַלְכֵי	הָאֱמֹרִי
and we took	in time	the it	the land - that	from hand	two	kings	the Amorites

אֲשֶׁר	בְּעֵבֶר	הַיַּרְדֵּן	מִנַּחַל	אַרְנֹן	עַד־הַר	חֶרְמוֹן׃
which	in side	the Jordan	from river	Arnon	mountain - till	Hermon

8 And we took at that time out of the hand of the two kings of the Amorites the land that was on this side Jordan, from the river of Arnon unto mount Hermon;

צִידֹנִים	יִקְרְאוּ	לְחֶרְמוֹן	שִׂרְיֹן	וְהָאֱמֹרִי	יִקְרְאוּ־לוֹ	שְׂנִיר׃
Sidonians	they call	to Hermon	Sirion	and the Amorites	to it - they call	Shenir

9 (Which Hermon the Sidonians call Sirion; and the Amorites call it Shenir;)

כֹּל	עָרֵי	הַמִּישֹׁר	וְכָל־הַגִּלְעָד
all	cities	the plain	the Gilead - and all

וְכָל־הַבָּשָׁן	עַד־סַלְכָה	וְאֶדְרֶעִי
the Bashan - and all	Salchah - till	and Edrei

עָרֵי	מַמְלֶכֶת	עוֹג	בַּבָּשָׁן׃
cities	kingdom	Og	in Bashan

10 All the cities of the plain, and all Gilead, and all Bashan, unto Salchah and Edrei, cities of the kingdom of Og in Bashan.

כִּי	רַק־עוֹג	מֶלֶךְ	הַבָּשָׁן	נִשְׁאַר	מִיֶּתֶר	הָרְפָאִים
like	Og - only	king	the Bashan	remained	from remnant	the giants

הִנֵּה	עַרְשׂוֹ	עֶרֶשׂ	בַּרְזֶל	הֲלֹה	הִוא	בְּרַבַּת	בְּנֵי	עַמּוֹן
here	his bed	bed	iron	the it	he	in Rabbath	son	Ammon

תֵּשַׁע	אַמּוֹת	אָרְכָּהּ	וְאַרְבַּע	אַמּוֹת	רָחְבָּהּ	בְּאַמַּת־אִישׁ׃
nine	cubits	length	and four	cubits	width	man - in forearm

11 For only Og king of Bashan remained of the remnant of giants; behold, his bedstead was a bedstead of iron; is it not in Rabbath of the children of Ammon? nine cubits was

the length thereof, and four cubits the breadth of it, after the cubit of a man.

וְאֶת־הָאָרֶץ הַזֹּאת יָרַשְׁנוּ בָּעֵת הַהִוא
the it in time we possessed the this the land - and that

מֵעֲרֹעֵר אֲשֶׁר־עַל־נַחַל אַרְנֹן וַחֲצִי הַר־הַגִּלְעָד
the Gilead - mountain and half Arnon river - upon - which from Aroer

וְעָרָיו נָתַתִּי לָרֻאוּבֵנִי וְלַגָּדִי׃
and to Gadites to Reubenites I gave and his cities

12 And this land, which we possessed at that time, from Aroer, which is by the river Arnon, and half mount Gilead, and the cities thereof, gave I unto the Reubenites and to the Gadites.

וְיֶתֶר הַגִּלְעָד וְכָל־הַבָּשָׁן מַמְלֶכֶת עוֹג
Og from kingdom the Bashan - and all the Gilead and remainder

נָתַתִּי לַחֲצִי שֵׁבֶט הַמְנַשֶּׁה
the Manasseh tribe to half I gave

כָּל חֶבֶל הָאַרְגֹּב לְכָל־הַבָּשָׁן הַהוּא יִקָּרֵא אֶרֶץ רְפָאִים׃
giants land it was called the it the Bashan - to all the Argob region all

13 And the rest of Gilead, and all Bashan, being the kingdom of Og, gave I unto the half tribe of Manasseh; all the region of Argob, with all Bashan, which was called the land of giants.

יָאִיר בֶּן־מְנַשֶּׁה לָקַח אֶת־כָּל־חֶבֶל
region - all - that took Manasseh - son Jair

אַרְגֹּב עַד־גְּבוּל הַגְּשׁוּרִי וְהַמַּעֲכָתִי
and the Maachathi the Geshuri border - till Argob

וַיִּקְרָא אֹתָם עַל־שְׁמוֹ אֶת־הַבָּשָׁן חַוֺּת יָאִיר עַד הַיּוֹם הַזֶּה׃
the this the day till jair havoth the Bashan - that his name - upon to them and he called

14 Jair the son of Manasseh took all the country of Argob unto the coasts of Geshuri and Maachathi; and called them after his own name, Bashan-havoth-jair, unto this day.

[שביעי]

וּלְמָכִיר נָתַתִּי אֶת־הַגִּלְעָד׃
the Gilead - that I gave and to Machir

15 And I gave Gilead unto Machir.

וְלָרֻאוּבֵנִי וְלַגָּדִי נָתַתִּי מִן־הַגִּלְעָד
the Gilead - from I gave and to Gadites and to Reubenites

וְעַד־נַחַל אַרְנֹן תּוֹךְ הַנַּחַל וּגְבֻל
and border the river midst Arnon river - and till

וְעַד יַבֹּק הַנַּחַל גְּבוּל בְּנֵי עַמּוֹן:
    Ammon sons border the river Jabbok and till

16 And unto the Reubenites and unto the Gadites I gave from Gilead even unto the river Arnon half the valley, and the border even unto the river Jabbok, which is the border of the children of Ammon;

וְהָעֲרָבָה וְהַיַּרְדֵּן וּגְבֻל מִכִּנֶּרֶת
from Chinnereth and border and the Jordan and the plain

וְעַד יָם הָעֲרָבָה יָם הַמֶּלַח תַּחַת אַשְׁדֹּת הַפִּסְגָּה מִזְרָחָה:
from east the pisgah Ashdoth below the Salt Sea the plain Sea and till

17 The plain also, and Jordan, and the coast thereof, from Chinnereth even unto the sea of the plain, even the salt sea, under Ashdoth-pisgah eastward.

וָאֲצַו אֶתְכֶם בָּעֵת הַהִוא לֵאמֹר
to say the it in time that you and I commanded

יְהוָה אֱלֹהֵיכֶם נָתַן לָכֶם אֶת־הָאָרֶץ הַזֹּאת לְרִשְׁתָּהּ
to possess it the this the land - that to you gave your Elohim ihvh

חֲלוּצִים תַּעַבְרוּ לִפְנֵי אֲחֵיכֶם בְּנֵי־יִשְׂרָאֵל כָּל־בְּנֵי־חָיִל:
able - sons - all Israel - sons your brothers before you will pass it armed ones

18 And I commanded you at that time, saying, The LORD your God hath given you this land to possess it: ye shall pass over armed before your brethren the children of Israel, all that are meet for the war.

רַק נְשֵׁיכֶם וְטַפְּכֶם וּמִקְנֵכֶם יָדַעְתִּי כִּי־מִקְנֶה רַב לָכֶם
to you much cattle - like I Know and your cattle and your little ones your wives only

יֵשְׁבוּ בְּעָרֵיכֶם אֲשֶׁר נָתַתִּי לָכֶם:
to you I gave which in your cities they dwell

19 But your wives, and your little ones, and your cattle, (for I know that ye have much cattle,) shall abide in your cities which I have given you;

[מפטיר]

עַד אֲשֶׁר־יָנִיחַ יְהוָה לַאֲחֵיכֶם כָּכֶם
like you to your brothers ihvh he gives rest - which till

וְיָרְשׁוּ גַם־הֵם אֶת־הָאָרֶץ אֲשֶׁר יְהוָה אֱלֹהֵיכֶם נֹתֵן לָהֶם
to them gave your Elohim ihvh which the land - that them - also and they possess

בְּעֵבֶר הַיַּרְדֵּן וְשַׁבְתֶּם אִישׁ לִירֻשָּׁתוֹ אֲשֶׁר נָתַתִּי לָכֶם:
to you I gave which to his possession each and you return the Jordan in passing

20 Until the LORD have given rest unto your brethren, as well as unto you, and until they also possess the land which the LORD your God hath given them beyond Jordan: and then shall ye return every man unto his possession, which I have given you.

וְאֶת־יְהוֹשׁוּעַ צִוֵּיתִי בָּעֵת הַהִוא לֵאמֹר
עֵינֶיךָ הָרֹאֹת אֵת כָּל־אֲשֶׁר עָשָׂה
יְהוָה אֱלֹהֵיכֶם לִשְׁנֵי הַמְּלָכִים הָאֵלֶּה
כֵּן־יַעֲשֶׂה יְהוָה לְכָל־הַמַּמְלָכוֹת אֲשֶׁר אַתָּה עֹבֵר שָׁמָּה׃

21 And I commanded Joshua at that time, saying, Thine eyes have seen all that the LORD your God hath done unto these two kings: so shall the LORD do unto all the kingdoms whither thou passest.

לֹא תִּירָאוּם כִּי יְהוָה אֱלֹהֵיכֶם הוּא הַנִּלְחָם לָכֶם׃

22 Ye shall not fear them: for the LORD your God he shall fight for you.

ס ס ס

Vetchanan

Chapter 3 cont

[פרשת ואתחנן]

וָאֶתְחַנַּן אֶל־יְהוָה בָּעֵת הַהִוא לֵאמֹר:

and I pleaded — ihvh - unto — in time — the it — to say

23 And I besought the LORD at that time, saying,

אֲדֹנָי יֱהוִה אַתָּה הַחִלּוֹתָ

Adoni — ihvh — you — the you began

לְהַרְאוֹת אֶת־עַבְדְּךָ אֶת־גָּדְלְךָ וְאֶת־יָדְךָ הַחֲזָקָה

to the show — that - your servant — that - your greatness — and that - your hand — the strong

אֲשֶׁר מִי־אֵל בַּשָּׁמַיִם וּבָאָרֶץ

which — what - El — in heaven — and in earth

אֲשֶׁר־יַעֲשֶׂה כְמַעֲשֶׂיךָ וְכִגְבוּרֹתֶךָ:

which - he does — like your deeds — and your might

24 O Lord GOD, thou hast begun to shew thy servant thy greatness, and thy mighty hand: for what God is there in heaven or in earth, that can do according to thy works, and according to thy might?

אֶעְבְּרָה־נָּא וְאֶרְאֶה אֶת־הָאָרֶץ הַטּוֹבָה

now - let me pass over — and I see — that - the land — the good

אֲשֶׁר בְּעֵבֶר הַיַּרְדֵּן הָהָר הַטּוֹב הַזֶּה וְהַלְּבָנֹן:

which — in beyond — the Jordan — the mountain — the good — the this — and the Lebanon

25 I pray thee, let me go over, and see the good land that is beyond Jordan, that goodly mountain, and Lebanon.

וַיִּתְעַבֵּר יְהוָה בִּי לְמַעַנְכֶם

and he was wroth — ihvh — in me — to sake of you

וְלֹא שָׁמַע אֵלַי וַיֹּאמֶר יְהוָה אֵלַי

and not — he listened — unto me — and he said — ihvh — unto me

רַב־לָךְ אַל־תּוֹסֶף דַּבֵּר אֵלַי עוֹד בַּדָּבָר הַזֶּה:

much - to you — don't you repeat — speak — unto me — more — in matter — the this

26 But the LORD was wroth with me for your sakes, and would not hear me: and the LORD said unto me, Let it suffice thee; speak no more unto me of this matter.

עֲלֵה רֹאשׁ הַפִּסְגָּה וְשָׂא עֵינֶיךָ

ascend — top — the Pisgah — and lift — eyes your

יָמָּה וְצָפֹנָה וְתֵימָנָה וּמִזְרָחָה

to sea — and to north — and to south — and to east

וּרְאֵ֣ה בְעֵינֶ֔יךָ כִּי־לֹ֥א תַעֲבֹ֖ר אֶת־הַיַּרְדֵּ֥ן הַזֶּֽה׃
the this   the Jordan - that   you will pass   not - like   in your eyes   and look

27 Get thee up into the top of Pisgah, and lift up thine eyes westward, and northward, and southward, and eastward, and behold it with thine eyes: for thou shalt not go over this Jordan.

וְצַ֥ו אֶת־יְהוֹשֻׁ֖עַ וְחַזְּקֵ֣הוּ וְאַמְּצֵ֑הוּ
and strengthen him   and encourage him   Joshua - that   and command

כִּי־ה֣וּא יַעֲבֹ֗ר לִפְנֵי֙ הָעָ֣ם הַזֶּ֔ה
the this   the people   before   he will pass   he - like

וְהוּא֙ יַנְחִ֣יל אוֹתָ֔ם אֶת־הָאָ֖רֶץ אֲשֶׁ֥ר תִּרְאֶֽה׃
you will see   which   the land - that   to them   he will inherit   and he

28 But charge Joshua, and encourage him, and strengthen him: for he shall go over before this people, and he shall cause them to inherit the land which thou shalt see.

וַנֵּ֣שֶׁב בַּגָּ֔יְא מ֖וּל בֵּ֥ית פְּעֽוֹר׃
peor   Beth   over by   in the valley   and we stayed

29 So we abode in the valley over against Beth-peor.

Chapter 4

ספר דברים פרק ד

וְעַתָּ֣ה יִשְׂרָאֵ֗ל שְׁמַ֤ע אֶל־הַֽחֻקִּים֙
the statutes - unto   listen   Israel   and now

וְאֶל־הַמִּשְׁפָּטִ֔ים אֲשֶׁ֧ר אָנֹכִ֛י מְלַמֵּ֥ד אֶתְכֶ֖ם
that you   teaching   I am   which   the judgments - and unto

לַעֲשׂ֑וֹת לְמַ֣עַן תִּֽחְי֗וּ וּבָאתֶם֙
and you go   you live   to end   to do

וִֽירִשְׁתֶּ֣ם אֶת־הָאָ֔רֶץ אֲשֶׁ֧ר יְהֹוָ֛ה אֱלֹהֵ֥י אֲבֹתֵיכֶ֖ם נֹתֵ֥ן לָכֶֽם׃
to you   gives   your fathers   Elohim   ihvh   which   the land - that   and you possess

1 Now therefore hearken, O Israel, unto the statutes and unto the judgments, which I teach you, for to do them, that ye may live, and go in and possess the land which the LORD God of your fathers giveth you.

לֹ֣א תֹסִ֗פוּ עַל־הַדָּבָר֙ אֲשֶׁ֤ר אָנֹכִי֙ מְצַוֶּ֣ה אֶתְכֶ֔ם
that you   commanding   I am   which   the word - upon   you add it   not

וְלֹ֥א תִגְרְע֖וּ מִמֶּ֑נּוּ לִשְׁמֹ֗ר אֶת־מִצְוֺת֙ יְהֹוָ֣ה אֱלֹֽהֵיכֶ֔ם
your Elohim   ihvh   commandments - that   to heed   from it   you subtract it   and not

אֲשֶׁ֥ר אָנֹכִ֖י מְצַוֶּ֥ה אֶתְכֶֽם׃
that you   commanding   I am   which

2 Ye shall not add unto the word which I command you, neither shall ye diminish ought

from it, that ye may keep the commandments of the LORD your God which I command you.

עֵינֵיכֶם הָרֹאוֹת אֵת אֲשֶׁר־עָשָׂה יְהֹוָה בְּבַעַל פְּעוֹר
peor　in Baal　ihvh　he did - which　that　the seeing ones　your eyes

כִּי כָל־הָאִישׁ אֲשֶׁר הָלַךְ אַחֲרֵי בַעַל־פְּעוֹר
peor - Baal　after　went　which　the man - all　like

הִשְׁמִידוֹ יְהֹוָה אֱלֹהֶיךָ מִקִּרְבֶּךָ׃
among you　your Elohim　ihvh　his destruction

3 Your eyes have seen what the LORD did because of Baal-peor: for all the men that followed Baal-peor, the LORD thy God hath destroyed them from among you.

וְאַתֶּם הַדְּבֵקִים בַּיהֹוָה אֱלֹהֵיכֶם חַיִּים כֻּלְּכֶם הַיּוֹם׃
the day　all you　alive ones　your Elohim　in ihvh　the clinging ones　and you

4 But ye that did cleave unto the LORD your God are alive every one of you this day.

[שני]

רְאֵה לִמַּדְתִּי אֶתְכֶם חֻקִּים וּמִשְׁפָּטִים
and judgments　statutes　that you　I taught　see

כַּאֲשֶׁר צִוַּנִי יְהֹוָה אֱלֹהָי לַעֲשׂוֹת כֵּן בְּקֶרֶב הָאָרֶץ
the land　in near　thus　to do　my Elohim　ihvh　he commanded me　which

אֲשֶׁר אַתֶּם בָּאִים שָׁמָּה לְרִשְׁתָּהּ׃
to possess her　to there　coming ones　you　which

5 Behold, I have taught you statutes and judgments, even as the LORD my God commanded me, that ye should do so in the land whither ye go to possess it.

6 Keep therefore and do them; for this is your wisdom and your understanding in the sight of the nations, which shall hear all these statutes, and say, Surely this great nation is a wise and understanding people.

7 For what nation is there so great, who hath God so nigh unto them, as the LORD our God is in all things that we call upon him for?

וּמִ֚י גּ֣וֹי גָּד֔וֹל אֲשֶׁר־ל֛וֹ חֻקִּ֥ים וּמִשְׁפָּטִ֖ים צַדִּיקִ֑ם
and what nation great to him - which statutes and judgments righteous ones

כְּכֹל֙ הַתּוֹרָ֣ה הַזֹּ֔את אֲשֶׁ֧ר אָנֹכִ֛י נֹתֵ֥ן לִפְנֵיכֶ֖ם הַיּֽוֹם׃
like all the law the this which I am giving before you the day

8 And what nation is there so great, that hath statutes and judgments so righteous as all this law, which I set before you this day?

רַ֡ק הִשָּׁ֣מֶר לְךָ֩ וּשְׁמֹ֨ר נַפְשְׁךָ֜ מְאֹ֗ד
only be heeding to you and heed your soul greatly

פֶּן־תִּשְׁכַּ֣ח אֶת־הַדְּבָרִ֡ים אֲשֶׁר־רָא֣וּ עֵינֶ֗יךָ
lest you forget that - the matters which - you saw your eyes

וּפֶן־יָס֨וּרוּ מִלְּבָ֣בְךָ֔ כֹּ֖ל יְמֵ֣י חַיֶּ֑יךָ
and thus - they depart from your heart all days your life

וְהוֹדַעְתָּ֥ם לְבָנֶ֖יךָ וְלִבְנֵ֥י בָנֶֽיךָ׃
and you teach them to your sons and to sons your sons

9 Only take heed to thyself, and keep thy soul diligently, lest thou forget the things which thine eyes have seen, and lest they depart from thy heart all the days of thy life: but teach them thy sons, and thy sons' sons;

י֗וֹם אֲשֶׁ֨ר עָמַ֜דְתָּ לִפְנֵ֨י יְהוָ֤ה אֱלֹהֶ֙יךָ֙ בְּחֹרֵ֔ב
day which you stood before ihvh your Elohim in Horeb

בֶּאֱמֹ֨ר יְהוָ֜ה אֵלַ֗י הַקְהֶל־לִי֙ אֶת־הָעָ֔ם
in saying ihvh unto me the assemble - to me that - the people

וְאַשְׁמִעֵ֖ם אֶת־דְּבָרָ֑י אֲשֶׁ֨ר יִלְמְד֜וּן לְיִרְאָ֣ה אֹתִ֗י כָּל־הַיָּמִ֗ים
and I make hear them my speaking - that which they learn them to fear to me all - the days

אֲשֶׁ֨ר הֵ֤ם חַיִּים֙ עַל־הָ֣אֲדָמָ֔ה וְאֶת־בְּנֵיהֶ֖ם יְלַמֵּדֽוּן׃
which they alive ones upon - the land and that - their sons they teach them

10 Specially the day that thou stoodest before the LORD thy God in Horeb, when the LORD said unto me, Gather me the people together, and I will make them hear my words, that they may learn to fear me all the days that they shall live upon the earth, and that they may teach their children.

וַתִּקְרְב֥וּן וַתַּעַמְד֖וּן תַּ֣חַת הָהָ֑ר
and you neared and you stood under the mountain

וְהָהָ֞ר בֹּעֵ֤ר בָּאֵשׁ֙ עַד־לֵ֣ב הַשָּׁמַ֔יִם חֹ֖שֶׁךְ עָנָ֥ן וַעֲרָפֶֽל׃
and the mountain burned in fire till - heart the heavens black cloud and darkness

11 And ye came near and stood under the mountain; and the mountain burned with fire

unto the midst of heaven, with darkness, clouds, and thick darkness.

וַיְדַבֵּ֨ר יְהֹוָ֧ה אֲלֵיכֶ֛ם מִתּ֥וֹךְ הָאֵ֖שׁ
and he spoke ihvh unto you from middle the fire

ק֣וֹל דְּבָרִים֙ אַתֶּ֣ם שֹׁמְעִ֔ים וּתְמוּנָ֛ה אֵינְכֶ֥ם רֹאִ֖ים זוּלָתִ֥י קֽוֹל׃
sound speakings you hearing ones and form not you seeing ones except voice

12 And the LORD spake unto you out of the midst of the fire: ye heard the voice of the words, but saw no similitude; only ye heard a voice.

וַיַּגֵּ֨ד לָכֶ֜ם אֶת־בְּרִית֗וֹ אֲשֶׁ֨ר צִוָּ֤ה אֶתְכֶם֙ לַעֲשׂ֔וֹת
and he declared to you his covenant - that which he commanded that you to do

עֲשֶׂ֖רֶת הַדְּבָרִ֑ים וַֽיִּכְתְּבֵ֔ם עַל־שְׁנֵ֖י לֻח֥וֹת אֲבָנִֽים׃
ten the speakings and he wrote them upon - two tablets stones

13 And he declared unto you his covenant, which he commanded you to perform, even ten commandments; and he wrote them upon two tables of stone.

וְאֹתִ֞י צִוָּ֤ה יְהֹוָה֙ בָּעֵ֣ת הַהִ֔וא
and to me he commanded ihvh in time the she

לְלַמֵּ֣ד אֶתְכֶ֔ם חֻקִּ֖ים וּמִשְׁפָּטִ֑ים
to teach that you decrees and laws

לַעֲשֹׂתְכֶ֣ם אֹתָ֔ם בָּאָ֕רֶץ אֲשֶׁ֥ר אַתֶּ֛ם עֹבְרִ֥ים שָׁ֖מָּה לְרִשְׁתָּֽהּ׃
to do you to them in land which you passing ones to there to possess her

14 And the LORD commanded me at that time to teach you statutes and judgments, that ye might do them in the land whither ye go over to possess it.

וְנִשְׁמַרְתֶּ֥ם מְאֹ֖ד לְנַפְשֹׁתֵיכֶ֑ם
and you heed greatly to your souls

כִּ֣י לֹ֤א רְאִיתֶם֙ כָּל־תְּמוּנָ֔ה
like not you saw all - likeness

בְּי֗וֹם דִּבֶּ֨ר יְהֹוָ֧ה אֲלֵיכֶ֛ם בְּחֹרֵ֖ב מִתּ֥וֹךְ הָאֵֽשׁ׃
in day spoke ihvh unto you at Horeb from midst the fire

15 Take ye therefore good heed unto yourselves; for ye saw no manner of similitude on the day that the LORD spake unto you in Horeb out of the midst of the fire:

פֶּ֨ן־תַּשְׁחִת֔וּן וַעֲשִׂיתֶ֥ם לָכֶ֛ם פֶּ֖סֶל
thus - you corrupted and you did to them idol

תְּמוּנַ֣ת כָּל־סָ֑מֶל תַּבְנִ֕ית זָכָ֖ר א֥וֹ נְקֵבָֽה׃
form all - figure model man or woman

16 Lest ye corrupt yourselves, and make you a graven image, the similitude of any figure, the likeness of male or female,

תַּבְנִית כָּל־בְּהֵמָה אֲשֶׁר בָּאָרֶץ
form / beast - all / which / in earth

תַּבְנִית כָּל־צִפּוֹר כָּנָף אֲשֶׁר תָּעוּף בַּשָּׁמָיִם:
form / bird - all / wing / which / she flies / in skies

17 The likeness of any beast that is on the earth, the likeness of any winged fowl that flieth in the air,

תַּבְנִית כָּל־רֹמֵשׂ בָּאֲדָמָה
form / one moving - all / in ground

תַּבְנִית כָּל־דָּגָה אֲשֶׁר־בַּמַּיִם מִתַּחַת לָאָרֶץ:
form / fish - all / in waters - which / from under / to earth

18 The likeness of any thing that creepeth on the ground, the likeness of any fish that is in the waters beneath the earth:

וּפֶן־תִּשָּׂא עֵינֶיךָ הַשָּׁמַיְמָה
you lift - and thus / your eyes / the skies

וְרָאִיתָ אֶת־הַשֶּׁמֶשׁ וְאֶת־הַיָּרֵחַ וְאֶת־הַכּוֹכָבִים
and you see / the sun - that / the moon - and that / the stars - and that

כֹּל צְבָא הַשָּׁמַיִם וְנִדַּחְתָּ וְהִשְׁתַּחֲוִיתָ לָהֶם
all / host / the heavens / and you enticed / and you bow down / to them

וַעֲבַדְתָּם אֲשֶׁר חָלַק יְהֹוָה אֱלֹהֶיךָ אֹתָם
and you served them / which / portion / ihvh / your elohim / to them

לְכֹל הָעַמִּים תַּחַת כָּל־הַשָּׁמָיִם:
to all / the nations / under / the heavens - all

19 And lest thou lift up thine eyes unto heaven, and when thou seest the sun, and the moon, and the stars, even all the host of heaven, shouldest be driven to worship them, and serve them, which the LORD thy God hath divided unto all nations under the whole heaven.

וְאֶתְכֶם לָקַח יְהֹוָה
and that you / took / ihvh

וַיּוֹצִא אֶתְכֶם מִכּוּר הַבַּרְזֶל מִמִּצְרָיִם
and he brought out / that you / from furnace / the iron / from Egypt

לִהְיוֹת לוֹ לְעַם נַחֲלָה כַּיּוֹם הַזֶּה:
to be / to him / to people / inheritance / like day / the this

20 But the LORD hath taken you, and brought you forth out of the iron furnace, even out of Egypt, to be unto him a people of inheritance, as ye are this day.

וַיהֹוָה הִתְאַנַּף־בִּי עַל־דִּבְרֵיכֶם
and ihvh / he became angry / in me - upon / you speakings

Vechanan - Chapter 4

וַיִּשָּׁבַע לְבִלְתִּי עָבְרִי אֶת־הַיַּרְדֵּן
the Jordan - that   to pass   without me   and he swore

וּלְבִלְתִּי־בֹא אֶל־הָאָרֶץ הַטּוֹבָה
the good   the land - unto   come - and without

אֲשֶׁר יְהֹוָה אֱלֹהֶיךָ נֹתֵן לְךָ נַחֲלָה:
inheritance   to you   giving   your Elohim   ihvh   which

21 Furthermore the LORD was angry with me for your sakes, and sware that I should not go over Jordan, and that I should not go in unto that good land, which the LORD thy God giveth thee for an inheritance:

כִּי אָנֹכִי מֵת בָּאָרֶץ הַזֹּאת אֵינֶנִּי עֹבֵר אֶת־הַיַּרְדֵּן
the Jordan - that   passing   without me   the this   and land   dying   I am   like

וְאַתֶּם עֹבְרִים וִירִשְׁתֶּם אֶת־הָאָרֶץ הַטּוֹבָה הַזֹּאת:
the this   the good   the land - that   and you will possess   passing ones   and you

22 But I must die in this land, I must not go over Jordan: but ye shall go over, and possess that good land.

הִשָּׁמְרוּ לָכֶם פֶּן־תִּשְׁכְּחוּ אֶת־בְּרִית יְהֹוָה אֱלֹהֵיכֶם
you Elohim   ihvh   covenant - that   you forget - thus   to you   be heedful

אֲשֶׁר כָּרַת עִמָּכֶם וַעֲשִׂיתֶם לָכֶם פֶּסֶל תְּמוּנַת
form   graven   to them   and you make   with you   he contracted   which

כֹּל אֲשֶׁר צִוְּךָ יְהֹוָה אֱלֹהֶיךָ:
your Elohim   ihvh   commanded   which   all

23 Take heed unto yourselves, lest ye forget the covenant of the LORD your God, which he made with you, and make you a graven image, or the likeness of any thing, which the LORD thy God hath forbidden thee.

כִּי יְהֹוָה אֱלֹהֶיךָ אֵשׁ אֹכְלָה הוּא אֵל קַנָּא:
jealous   El   he   consuming   fire   your Elohim   ihvh   like

24 For the LORD thy God is a consuming fire, even a jealous God.

פ

כִּי־תוֹלִיד בָּנִים וּבְנֵי בָנִים
sons   and sons   sons   you beget - like

וְנוֹשַׁנְתֶּם בָּאָרֶץ וְהִשְׁחַתֶּם וַעֲשִׂיתֶם פֶּסֶל תְּמוּנַת כֹּל
all   likeness   sculpture   and you make   and you be corrupt   in land   and you remain

וַעֲשִׂיתֶם הָרַע בְּעֵינֵי־יְהֹוָה אֱלֹהֶיךָ לְהַכְעִיסוֹ:
to his provoking   your Elohim   ihvh - in eyes   the evil   and you do

25 When thou shalt beget children, and children's children, and ye shall have remained long in the land, and shall corrupt yourselves, and make a graven image, or the likeness

of any thing, and shall do evil in the sight of the LORD thy God, to provoke him to anger:

הַעִידֹ֨תִי בָכֶ֣ם הַיּ֗וֹם אֶת־הַשָּׁמַ֛יִם וְאֶת־הָאָ֖רֶץ
the earth - and that   the heavens - that   the day   in you   I witness

כִּֽי־אָבֹ֣ד תֹּאבֵד֗וּן מַהֵר֙ מֵעַ֣ל הָאָ֔רֶץ
the land   from upon   quickly   you will perish   perish - like

אֲשֶׁ֨ר אַתֶּ֜ם עֹבְרִ֧ים אֶת־הַיַּרְדֵּ֛ן שָׁ֖מָּה לְרִשְׁתָּ֑הּ
to possess it   to there   the Jordan - that   passing ones   you   which

לֹֽא־תַאֲרִיכֻ֤ן יָמִים֙ עָלֶ֔יהָ כִּ֥י הִשָּׁמֵ֖ד תִּשָּׁמֵדֽוּן׃
you will be destroyed   cause to be destroyed   like   upon it   days   you prolong - not

26 I call heaven and earth to witness against you this day, that ye shall soon utterly perish from off the land whereunto ye go over Jordan to possess it; ye shall not prolong your days upon it, but shall utterly be destroyed.

וְהֵפִ֧יץ יְהוָ֛ה אֶתְכֶ֖ם בָּעַמִּ֑ים
in peoples   that you   ihvh   and will scatter

וְנִשְׁאַרְתֶּם֙ מְתֵ֣י מִסְפָּ֔ר בַּגּוֹיִ֕ם
in nations   number   few ones   and you will remain

אֲשֶׁ֨ר יְנַהֵ֧ג יְהוָ֛ה אֶתְכֶ֖ם שָֽׁמָּה׃
to there   that you   ihvh   he will drive   which

27 And the LORD shall scatter you among the nations, and ye shall be left few in number among the heathen, whither the LORD shall lead you.

וַעֲבַדְתֶּם־שָׁ֣ם אֱלֹהִ֔ים מַעֲשֵׂ֖ה יְדֵ֣י אָדָ֑ם
man   hands   made   gods   there - and you will serve

עֵ֣ץ וָאֶ֔בֶן אֲשֶׁ֥ר לֹֽא־יִרְאוּן֙
they see - not   which   and stone   wood

וְלֹ֣א יִשְׁמְע֔וּן וְלֹ֥א יֹאכְל֖וּן וְלֹ֥א יְרִיחֻֽן׃
they smell   and not   they eat   and not   they hear   and not

28 And there ye shall serve gods, the work of men's hands, wood and stone, which neither see, nor hear, nor eat, nor smell.

וּבִקַּשְׁתֶּ֥ם מִשָּׁ֛ם אֶת־יְהוָ֖ה אֱלֹהֶ֑יךָ
your Elohim   ihvh - that   from there   and you seek

וּמָצָ֑אתָ כִּ֣י תִדְרְשֶׁ֔נּוּ בְּכָל־לְבָבְךָ֖ וּבְכָל־נַפְשֶֽׁךָ׃
soul your - and in all   your heart - in all   you seek him   like   and you will find

29 But if from thence thou shalt seek the LORD thy God, thou shalt find him, if thou seek him with all thy heart and with all thy soul.

Vechanan - Chapter 4

בַּצַּ֣ר לְךָ֔ וּמְצָא֕וּךָ כֹּ֖ל הַדְּבָרִ֣ים הָאֵ֑לֶּה
the these   the matters   all   and finds you   to you   in distress

בְּאַחֲרִית֙ הַיָּמִ֔ים וְשַׁבְתָּ֙ עַד־יְהוָ֣ה אֱלֹהֶ֔יךָ וְשָׁמַעְתָּ֖ בְּקֹלֽוֹ׃
in his voice   and you will obey   your Elohim   ihvh - till   and you will return   the days   in afterwards

30 When thou art in tribulation, and all these things are come upon thee, even in the latter days, if thou turn to the LORD thy God, and shalt be obedient unto his voice;

כִּ֣י אֵ֤ל רַחוּם֙ יְהוָ֣ה אֱלֹהֶ֔יךָ
your Elohim   ihvh   merciful   El   like

לֹ֥א יַרְפְּךָ֖ וְלֹ֣א יַשְׁחִיתֶ֑ךָ
he will destroy you   and not   he will abandon you   not

וְלֹ֤א יִשְׁכַּח֙ אֶת־בְּרִ֣ית אֲבֹתֶ֔יךָ אֲשֶׁ֥ר נִשְׁבַּ֖ע לָהֶֽם׃
to them   he swore   which   your fathers   covenant - that   he will forget   and not

31 (For the LORD thy God is a merciful God;) he will not forsake thee, neither destroy thee, nor forget the covenant of thy fathers which he sware unto them.

כִּ֣י שְׁאַל־נָא֩ לְיָמִ֨ים רִֽאשֹׁנִ֜ים
first ones   to days   now - ask   like

אֲשֶׁר־הָי֣וּ לְפָנֶ֗יךָ לְמִן־הַיּוֹם֙
the day - to same   before you   it was - which

אֲשֶׁר֩ בָּרָ֨א אֱלֹהִ֤ים ׀ אָדָם֙ עַל־הָאָ֔רֶץ
the earth - upon   Adam   Elohim   created   which

וּלְמִקְצֵ֥ה הַשָּׁמַ֖יִם וְעַד־קְצֵ֣ה הַשָּׁמָ֑יִם הֲנִֽהְיָ֗ה
the it will be   the heavens   half - and till   the heavens   and to end

כַּדָּבָ֤ר הַגָּדוֹל֙ הַזֶּ֔ה א֖וֹ הֲנִשְׁמַ֥ע כָּמֹֽהוּ׃
like it   the heard   or   the this   the big   like matter

32 For ask now of the days that are past, which were before thee, since the day that God created man upon the earth, and ask from the one side of heaven unto the other, whether there hath been any such thing as this great thing is, or hath been heard like it?

הֲשָׁ֣מַֽע עָם֩ ק֨וֹל אֱלֹהִ֜ים מְדַבֵּ֧ר מִתּוֹךְ־הָאֵ֛שׁ
the fire - from midst   from speaking   Elohim   voice   people   the hear

כַּאֲשֶׁר־שָׁמַ֥עְתָּ אַתָּ֖ה וַיֶּֽחִי׃
and live   you   you heard - when

33 Did ever people hear the voice of God speaking out of the midst of the fire, as thou hast heard, and live?

א֣וֹ ׀ הֲנִסָּ֣ה אֱלֹהִ֗ים לָבוֹא֩ לָקַ֨חַת ל֥וֹ גוֹי֙ מִקֶּ֣רֶב גּ֔וֹי
nation   from near   nation   to you   to take   to come   Elohim   the journey   or

בְּמַסֹּת בְּאֹתֹת וּבְמוֹפְתִים
and in wonders · in signs · in temptations

וּבְמִלְחָמָה וּבְיָד חֲזָקָה וּבִזְרוֹעַ נְטוּיָה
stretched out · and in arm · might · and in hand · and in war

וּבְמוֹרָאִים גְּדֹלִים כְּכֹל אֲשֶׁר־עָשָׂה לָכֶם
to them · did - which · like all · great ones · and in terrors

יְהֹוָה אֱלֹהֵיכֶם בְּמִצְרַיִם לְעֵינֶיךָ׃
to your eyes · in Egypt · your Elohim · ihvh

34 Or hath God assayed to go and take him a nation from the midst of another nation, by temptations, by signs, and by wonders, and by war, and by a mighty hand, and by a stretched out arm, and by great terrors, according to all that the LORD your God did for you in Egypt before your eyes?

אַתָּה הָרְאֵתָ לָדַעַת
to know · the you saw · you

כִּי יְהֹוָה הוּא הָאֱלֹהִים אֵין עוֹד מִלְבַדּוֹ׃
beside him · still · isn't · the Elohim · it · ihvh · like

35 Unto thee it was shewed, that thou mightest know that the LORD he is God; there is none else beside him.

מִן־הַשָּׁמַיִם הִשְׁמִיעֲךָ אֶת־קֹלוֹ
his voice - that · caused you to hear · the heavens - from

לְיַסְּרֶךָ וְעַל־הָאָרֶץ הֶרְאֲךָ אֶת־אִשּׁוֹ הַגְּדוֹלָה
the great · his fire - that · showed you · the earth - upon · to instruct you

וּדְבָרָיו שָׁמַעְתָּ מִתּוֹךְ הָאֵשׁ׃
the fire · from midst · you heard · and his speakings

36 Out of heaven he made thee to hear his voice, that he might instruct thee: and upon earth he shewed thee his great fire; and thou heardest his words out of the midst of the fire.

וְתַחַת כִּי אָהַב אֶת־אֲבֹתֶיךָ וַיִּבְחַר בְּזַרְעוֹ אַחֲרָיו
after him · in his seed · and he chose · your fathers - that · loved · like · and under

וַיּוֹצִאֲךָ בְּפָנָיו בְּכֹחוֹ הַגָּדֹל מִמִּצְרָיִם׃
from Egypt · the big · in his might · in presence · and he brought out you

37 And because he loved thy fathers, therefore he chose their seed after them, and brought thee out in his sight with his mighty power out of Egypt;

לְהוֹרִישׁ גּוֹיִם גְּדֹלִים וַעֲצֻמִים מִמְּךָ מִפָּנֶיךָ
from your presence · from you · and mighty · great ones · nations · to drive out

Vechanan - Chapter 4

לַהֲבִיאֲךָ לָתֶת־לְךָ אֶת־אַרְצָם נַחֲלָה כַּיּוֹם הַזֶּה:
the this   like day   inheritance   their land - that   to you - to give   to bring you

38 To drive out nations from before thee greater and mightier than thou art, to bring thee in, to give thee their land for an inheritance, as it is this day.

וְיָדַעְתָּ הַיּוֹם וַהֲשֵׁבֹתָ אֶל־לְבָבֶךָ
you heart - unto   and the consider   the day   you know

כִּי יְהוָה הוּא הָאֱלֹהִים בַּשָּׁמַיִם מִמַּעַל
from above   in heaven   the Elohim   he   ihvh   like

וְעַל־הָאָרֶץ מִתָּחַת אֵין עוֹד:
other   isn't   from beneath   the earth - and upon

39 Know therefore this day, and consider it in thine heart, that the LORD he is God in heaven above, and upon the earth beneath: there is none else.

וְשָׁמַרְתָּ אֶת־חֻקָּיו וְאֶת־מִצְוֺתָיו
his commandments - and that   his statutes - that   and you listened

אֲשֶׁר אָנֹכִי מְצַוְּךָ הַיּוֹם אֲשֶׁר יִיטַב לְךָ וּלְבָנֶיךָ אַחֲרֶיךָ
after you   and to your sons   to you   it will be good   which   the day   commanding you   I am   which

וּלְמַעַן תַּאֲרִיךְ יָמִים עַל־הָאֲדָמָה
the earth - upon   days   you prolong   and to end

אֲשֶׁר יְהוָה אֱלֹהֶיךָ נֹתֵן לְךָ כָּל־הַיָּמִים:
the days - all   to you   given   your Elohim   ihvh   which

40 Thou shalt keep therefore his statutes, and his commandments, which I command thee this day, that it may go well with thee, and with thy children after thee, and that thou mayest prolong thy days upon the earth, which the LORD thy God giveth thee, for ever.

פ

[שלישי]

אָז יַבְדִּיל מֹשֶׁה שָׁלֹשׁ עָרִים בְּעֵבֶר הַיַּרְדֵּן מִזְרְחָה שָׁמֶשׁ:
sun   toward   rise of   the Jordan   in east   cities   three   Moses   he set aside   then

41 Then Moses severed three cities on this side Jordan toward the sun rising;

לָנֻס שָׁמָּה רוֹצֵחַ אֲשֶׁר יִרְצַח אֶת־רֵעֵהוּ בִּבְלִי־דַעַת
and he knowledge   without   neighbor his   that   he killed   which   one killing   to there   to flee

וְהוּא לֹא־שֹׂנֵא לוֹ מִתְּמֹל שִׁלְשֹׁם
previously   from before   to him   malice   not   and it

וְנָס אֶל־אַחַת מִן־הֶעָרִים הָאֵל וָחָי:
and he would live   the these   the cities   from   one unto   and he could flee

42 That the slayer might flee thither, which should kill his neighbour unawares, and hated him not in times past; and that fleeing unto one of these cities he might live:

אֶת־בֶּצֶר בַּמִּדְבָּר בְּאֶרֶץ הַמִּישֹׁר לָראוּבֵנִי
Bezer that in desert in land the plateau to Reubenite

וְאֶת־רָאמֹת בַּגִּלְעָד לַגָּדִי
Ramoth and that in Gilead to Gadite

וְאֶת־גּוֹלָן בַּבָּשָׁן לַמְנַשִּׁי׃
Golan and that in Bashan for Manasite

43 Namely, Bezer in the wilderness, in the plain country, of the Reubenites; and Ramoth in Gilead, of the Gadites; and Golan in Bashan, of the Manassites.

וְזֹאת הַתּוֹרָה אֲשֶׁר־שָׂם מֹשֶׁה לִפְנֵי בְּנֵי יִשְׂרָאֵל׃
and this the torah which he set Moses before sons Israel

44 And this is the law which Moses set before the children of Israel:

אֵלֶּה הָעֵדֹת וְהַחֻקִּים וְהַמִּשְׁפָּטִים
these the stipulations and the decrees and the laws which

אֲשֶׁר דִּבֶּר מֹשֶׁה אֶל־בְּנֵי יִשְׂרָאֵל בְּצֵאתָם מִמִּצְרָיִם׃
which he spoke Moses unto sons Israel when to come them from Egypt

45 These are the testimonies, and the statutes, and the judgments, which Moses spake unto the children of Israel, after they came forth out of Egypt,

בְּעֵבֶר הַיַּרְדֵּן בַּגַּיְא מוּל בֵּית פְּעוֹר
in east the Jordan in valley near Beth Peor

בְּאֶרֶץ סִיחֹן מֶלֶךְ הָאֱמֹרִי אֲשֶׁר יוֹשֵׁב בְּחֶשְׁבּוֹן
in land Sihon king the Amorite which reigning in Hesbon

אֲשֶׁר הִכָּה מֹשֶׁה וּבְנֵי יִשְׂרָאֵל בְּצֵאתָם מִמִּצְרָיִם׃
which he defeated Moses and sons Israel in to come them from Egypt

46 On this side Jordan, in the valley over against Beth-peor, in the land of Sihon king of the Amorites, who dwelt at Heshbon, whom Moses and the children of Israel smote, after they were come forth out of Egypt:

וַיִּירְשׁוּ אֶת־אַרְצוֹ
and they possessed that- his land

וְאֶת־אֶרֶץ עוֹג מֶלֶךְ־הַבָּשָׁן שְׁנֵי מַלְכֵי הָאֱמֹרִי
and that - land Og king - the Bashan two kings the Amorite

אֲשֶׁר בְּעֵבֶר הַיַּרְדֵּן מִזְרַח שָׁמֶשׁ׃
which in east the Jordan rise sun

47 And they possessed his land, and the land of Og king of Bashan, two kings of the Amorites, which were on this side Jordan toward the sun rising;

מֵעֲרֹעֵר אֲשֶׁר עַל־שְׂפַת־נַחַל אַרְנֹן
    Arnon   Gorge - rim - upon   which   from Aroer

וְעַד־הַר שִׂיאֹן הוּא חֶרְמוֹן׃
    Hermon   it   Sion   mount - and till

48 From Aroer, which is by the bank of the river Arnon, even unto mount Sion, which is Hermon,

וְכָל־הָעֲרָבָה עֵבֶר הַיַּרְדֵּן מִזְרָחָה
    from east   the Jordan   past   the plain - and all

וְעַד יָם הָעֲרָבָה תַּחַת אַשְׁדֹּת הַפִּסְגָּה׃
    the Pisgah   slopes   below   the plain   Sea   and till

49 And all the plain on this side Jordan eastward, even unto the sea of the plain, under the springs of Pisgah.

פ

Chapter 5

ספר דברים פרק ה

[רביעי]

וַיִּקְרָא מֹשֶׁה אֶל־כָּל־יִשְׂרָאֵל וַיֹּאמֶר אֲלֵהֶם
    unto them   and he said   Israel - all - unto   Moses   and he called

שְׁמַע יִשְׂרָאֵל אֶת־הַחֻקִּים וְאֶת־הַמִּשְׁפָּטִים
    the judgments - and that   the statutes - that   Israel   hear

אֲשֶׁר אָנֹכִי דֹּבֵר בְּאָזְנֵיכֶם הַיּוֹם
    the day   in your ears   speaking   I am   which

וּלְמַדְתֶּם אֹתָם וּשְׁמַרְתֶּם לַעֲשֹׂתָם׃
    to do them   and you heed them   to them   and you learn

1 And Moses called all Israel, and said unto them, Hear, O Israel, the statutes and judgments which I speak in your ears this day, that ye may learn them, and keep, and do them.

יְהוָֹה אֱלֹהֵינוּ כָּרַת עִמָּנוּ בְּרִית בְּחֹרֵב׃
    at Horeb   covenant   with us   cut   our Elohim   ihvh

2 The LORD our God made a covenant with us in Horeb.

לֹא אֶת־אֲבֹתֵינוּ כָּרַת יְהוָֹה אֶת־הַבְּרִית הַזֹּאת
    the this   the covenant - that   ihvh   cut   our fathers - that   not

כִּי אִתָּנוּ אֲנַחְנוּ אֵלֶּה פֹה הַיּוֹם כֻּלָּנוּ חַיִּים׃
    alive ones   all us   the day   here   these   we   with us   like

3 The LORD made not this covenant with our fathers, but with us, even us, who are all

of us here alive this day.

פָּנִ֥ים בְּפָנִ֖ים דִּבֶּ֧ר יְהֹוָ֛ה עִמָּכֶ֖ם בָּהָ֖ר מִתּ֥וֹךְ הָאֵֽשׁ׃
the fire   midst   in mountain   with you   ihvh   spoke   in faces   faces

4 The LORD talked with you face to face in the mount out of the midst of the fire,

אָנֹכִ֞י עֹמֵ֧ד בֵּין־יְהֹוָ֛ה וּבֵינֵיכֶ֖ם בָּעֵ֣ת הַהִ֑וא
the it   in time   and between you   ihvh - between   stood   I am

לְהַגִּ֥יד לָכֶ֖ם אֶת־דְּבַ֣ר יְהֹוָ֑ה
ihvh   speak - that   to you   to the tell

כִּ֧י יְרֵאתֶ֛ם מִפְּנֵ֥י הָאֵ֖שׁ
the fire   from presence   you were afraid   like

וְלֹֽא־עֲלִיתֶ֥ם בָּהָ֖ר לֵאמֹֽר׃
to say   in mountain   you ascended - and not

5 (I stood between the LORD and you at that time, to shew you the word of the LORD: for ye were afraid by reason of the fire, and went not up into the mount;) saying,

ס

פ פ פ

אָנֹכִי֙ יְהֹוָ֣ה אֱלֹהֶ֔יךָ
your Elohim   ihvh   I am

אֲשֶׁ֧ר הוֹצֵאתִ֛יךָ מֵאֶ֥רֶץ מִצְרַ֖יִם מִבֵּ֥ית עֲבָדִֽים׃
slaveries   from house   Egypt   from land   I brought out you   which

6 I am the LORD thy God, which brought thee out of the land of Egypt, from the house of bondage.

לֹֽא־יִהְיֶ֥ה לְךָ֛ אֱלֹהִ֥ים אֲחֵרִ֖ים עַל־פָּנָֽי׃
my face - upon   other ones   Elohim   to you   he will be - not

7 Thou shalt have none other gods before me.

form - all   idol   to you   you will make - not

אֲשֶׁ֤ר בַּשָּׁמַ֙יִם֙ מִמַּ֔עַל וַאֲשֶׁ֥ר בָּאָ֖רֶץ מִתָּ֑חַת
from beneath   in earth   and which   from above   in heavens   which

וַאֲשֶׁ֥ר בַּמַּ֖יִם מִתַּ֥חַת לָאָֽרֶץ׃
to earth   from below   in waters   and which

8 Thou shalt not make thee any graven image, or any likeness of any thing that is in heaven above, or that is in the earth beneath, or that is in the waters beneath the earth:

לֹא־תִשְׁתַּחֲוֶה לָהֶם וְלֹא תָעָבְדֵם
    you will serve them   and not   to them   you will bow - not

כִּי אָנֹכִי יְהוָה אֱלֹהֶיךָ אֵל קַנָּא
    jealous   El   your Elohim   ihvh   I am   like

פֹּקֵד עֲוֺן אָבוֹת עַל־בָּנִים וְעַל־שִׁלֵּשִׁים וְעַל־רִבֵּעִים לְשֹׂנְאָי׃
to my haters fourth ones - and upon third ones - and upon sons - upon fathers iniquity visiting

9 Thou shalt not bow down thyself unto them, nor serve them: for I the LORD thy God am a jealous God, visiting the iniquity of the fathers upon the children unto the third and fourth generation of them that hate me,

וְעֹשֶׂה חֶסֶד לַאֲלָפִים לְאֹהֲבַי וּלְשֹׁמְרֵי מִצְוֺתָו [מִצְוֺתָי]׃
  my commandments and to ones heeding to ones loving me to thousands mercy and doing

10 And shewing mercy unto thousands of them that love me and keep my commandments.

ס

לֹא תִשָּׂא אֶת־שֵׁם־יְהוָה אֱלֹהֶיךָ לַשָּׁוְא
    to falsehood your Elohim ihvh - name - that your will lift not

כִּי לֹא יְנַקֶּה יְהוָה אֵת אֲשֶׁר־יִשָּׂא אֶת־שְׁמוֹ לַשָּׁוְא׃
  to falsehood his name - that he lifts - which that ihvh he will be innocent not like

11 Thou shalt not take the name of the LORD thy God in vain: for the LORD will not hold him guiltless that taketh his name in vain.

ס

שָׁמוֹר אֶת־יוֹם הַשַּׁבָּת לְקַדְּשׁוֹ כַּאֲשֶׁר צִוְּךָ יְהוָה אֱלֹהֶיךָ׃
 your Elohim ihvh commanded you when to holy him the Sabbath day - that to heed

12 Keep the sabbath day to sanctify it, as the LORD thy God hath commanded thee.

שֵׁשֶׁת יָמִים תַּעֲבֹד וְעָשִׂיתָ כָּל־מְלַאכְתֶּךָ׃
    your work - all and you will do you will labor days six

13 Six days thou shalt labour, and do all thy work:

וְיוֹם הַשְּׁבִיעִי שַׁבָּת לַיהוָה אֱלֹהֶיךָ
    your Elohim to ihvh Sabbath the seventh and day

לֹא־תַעֲשֶׂה כָל־מְלָאכָה
    work - all you will do - not

אַתָּה וּבִנְךָ־וּבִתֶּךָ וְעַבְדְּךָ־וַאֲמָתֶךָ
 and your maid - and your man servant and your daughter - and your sons you

וְשׁוֹרְךָ וַחֲמֹרְךָ וְכָל־בְּהֶמְתֶּךָ
    your cattle - and all and your donkey and your ox

וְגֵרְךָ֙ אֲשֶׁ֣ר בִּשְׁעָרֶ֔יךָ
and your stranger   which   in your gates

לְמַ֗עַן יָנ֛וּחַ עַבְדְּךָ֥ וַאֲמָתְךָ֖ כָּמֽוֹךָ׃
to end   he rest   your man servant   and your maid   like you

14 But the seventh day is the sabbath of the LORD thy God: in it thou shalt not do any work, thou, nor thy son, nor thy daughter, nor thy manservant, nor thy maidservant, nor thine ox, nor thine ass, nor any of thy cattle, nor thy stranger that is within thy gates; that thy manservant and thy maidservant may rest as well as thou.

וְזָכַרְתָּ֞ כִּ֣י־עֶ֤בֶד הָיִ֙יתָ֙ בְּאֶ֣רֶץ מִצְרַ֔יִם
and you remember   like   slave   you were   in land   Egypt

וַיֹּצִ֨אֲךָ֜ יְהֹוָ֤ה אֱלֹהֶ֙יךָ֙
and brought you out   ihvh   your Elohim

מִשָּׁ֔ם בְּיָ֥ד חֲזָקָ֖ה וּבִזְרֹ֣עַ נְטוּיָ֑ה
from there   in hand   mighty   and with arm   out stretched

עַל־כֵּ֗ן צִוְּךָ֙ יְהֹוָ֣ה אֱלֹהֶ֔יךָ לַעֲשׂ֖וֹת אֶת־י֥וֹם הַשַּׁבָּֽת׃
upon - thus   commanded you   ihvh   your Elohim   to do   that - day   the Sabbath

15 And remember that thou wast a servant in the land of Egypt, and that the LORD thy God brought thee out thence through a mighty hand and by a stretched out arm: therefore the LORD thy God commanded thee to keep the sabbath day.

ס

כַּבֵּ֤ד אֶת־אָבִ֙יךָ֙ וְאֶת־אִמֶּ֔ךָ
honor   that - your father   and that - your mother

כַּאֲשֶׁ֥ר צִוְּךָ֖ יְהֹוָ֣ה אֱלֹהֶ֑יךָ לְמַ֣עַן ׀ יַאֲרִיכֻ֣ן יָמֶ֗יךָ
when   commanded you   ihvh   your Elohim   to end   they prolong   your days

וּלְמַ֙עַן֙ יִ֣יטַב לָ֔ךְ עַ֚ל הָֽאֲדָמָ֔ה אֲשֶׁר־יְהֹוָ֥ה אֱלֹהֶ֖יךָ נֹתֵ֥ן לָֽךְ׃
and to end   it will be good   to you   upon   the ground   ihvh - which   your Elohim   gives   to you

16 Honour thy father and thy mother, as the LORD thy God hath commanded thee; that thy days may be prolonged, and that it may go well with thee, in the land which the LORD thy God giveth thee.

ס

לֹ֥א תִרְצָֽח׃
not   you murder

17 Thou shalt not kill.

ס

וְלֹ֖א תִנְאָֽף׃
and not   you commit adultery

18 Neither shalt thou commit adultery.

ס

וְלֹא תִּגְנֹב
you steal — and not

19 Neither shalt thou steal.

ס

וְלֹא־תַעֲנֶה בְרֵעֲךָ עֵד שָׁוְא׃
falsehood — till — in your neighbor — you witness - and not

20 Neither shalt thou bear false witness against thy neighbour.

ס

וְלֹא תַחְמֹד אֵשֶׁת רֵעֶךָ
your neighbor — wife — you covet — and not

ס

וְלֹא תִתְאַוֶּה בֵּית רֵעֶךָ
your neighbor — house — you desire — and not

שָׂדֵהוּ וְעַבְדּוֹ וַאֲמָתוֹ שׁוֹרוֹ וַחֲמֹרוֹ וְכֹל אֲשֶׁר לְרֵעֶךָ׃
to your neighbor — which — and all — and his donkey — his ox — and his maid — and his manservant — his field

21 Neither shalt thou desire thy neighbour's wife, neither shalt thou covet thy neighbour's house, his field, or his manservant, or his maidservant, his ox, or his ass, or any thing that is thy neighbour's.

ס

[חמישי]

אֶת־הַדְּבָרִים הָאֵלֶּה דִּבֶּר יְהוָה אֶל־כָּל־קְהַלְכֶם בָּהָר
in mountain — your assembly - all - unto — ihvh — he spoke — the these — the speakings - that

מִתּוֹךְ הָאֵשׁ הֶעָנָן וְהָעֲרָפֶל קוֹל גָּדוֹל וְלֹא יָסָף
he added — and not — great — voice — and the darkness — the cloud — the fire — midst

וַיִּכְתְּבֵם עַל־שְׁנֵי לֻחֹת אֲבָנִים וַיִּתְּנֵם אֵלָי׃
unto me — and he gave them — stones — tablets — two - upon — and he wrote them

22 These words the LORD spake unto all your assembly in the mount out of the midst of the fire, of the cloud, and of the thick darkness, with a great voice: and he added no more. And he wrote them in two tables of stone, and delivered them unto me.

וַיְהִי כְּשָׁמְעֲכֶם אֶת־הַקּוֹל מִתּוֹךְ הַחֹשֶׁךְ וְהָהָר בֹּעֵר בָּאֵשׁ
in fire — blazing — and the mountain — the darkness — midst — the voice - that — like you heard — and it was

וַתִּקְרְב֣וּן אֵלַ֔י כָּל־רָאשֵׁ֥י שִׁבְטֵיכֶ֖ם וְזִקְנֵיכֶ֑ם
and your elders   your tribes   heads - all   unto me   and you came near

23 And it came to pass, when ye heard the voice out of the midst of the darkness, (for the mountain did burn with fire,) that ye came near unto me, even all the heads of your tribes, and your elders;

וַתֹּאמְר֗וּ הֵ֣ן הֶרְאָ֜נוּ יְהוָ֤ה אֱלֹהֵ֙ינוּ
our Elohim   ihvh   the showed us   thus   and you said it

אֶת־כְּבֹד֣וֹ וְאֶת־גָּדְל֔וֹ וְאֶת־קֹל֥וֹ
his voice - and that   his greatness - and that   his glory that

שָׁמַ֖עְנוּ מִתּ֣וֹךְ הָאֵ֑שׁ הַיּ֥וֹם הַזֶּ֖ה
the this   the day   the fire   midst   we heard

רָאִ֕ינוּ כִּֽי־יְדַבֵּ֧ר אֱלֹהִ֛ים אֶת־הָֽאָדָ֖ם וָחָֽי׃
and he lives   the Adam - that   Elohim   he speaks - like   we saw

24 And ye said, Behold, the LORD our God hath shewed us his glory and his greatness, and we have heard his voice out of the midst of the fire: we have seen this day that God doth talk with man, and he liveth.

וְעַתָּה֙ לָ֣מָּה נָמ֔וּת
we die   why   and now

כִּ֣י תֹֽאכְלֵ֔נוּ הָאֵ֥שׁ הַגְּדֹלָ֖ה הַזֹּ֑את אִם־יֹסְפִ֣ים ׀ אֲנַ֗חְנוּ
we   continuing ones - if   the this   the great   the fire   it will consume us   like

לִ֠שְׁמֹעַ אֶת־ק֨וֹל יְהוָ֧ה אֱלֹהֵ֛ינוּ ע֖וֹד וָמָֽתְנוּ׃
and we will die   still   our Elohim   ihvh   voice - that   to hear

25 Now therefore why should we die? for this great fire will consume us: if we hear the voice of the LORD our God any more, then we shall die.

כִּ֣י מִ֣י כָל־בָּשָׂ֡ר אֲשֶׁ֣ר שָׁמַ֣ע ק֣וֹל אֱלֹהִים֩ חַיִּ֜ים
living   Elohim   voice   heard   which   flesh - all   who   like

מְדַבֵּ֧ר מִתּוֹךְ־הָאֵ֛שׁ כָּמֹ֖נוּ וַיֶּֽחִי׃
and lived   like we   the fire - midst   speaking

26 For who is there of all flesh, that hath heard the voice of the living God speaking out of the midst of the fire, as we have, and lived?

קְרַ֤ב אַתָּה֙ וּֽשֲׁמָ֔ע אֵ֛ת כָּל־אֲשֶׁ֥ר יֹאמַ֖ר יְהוָ֣ה אֱלֹהֵ֑ינוּ
our Elohim   ihvh   says   which - all   that   and hear   you   near

אֵלֵ֙ינוּ֙ אֵ֣ת כָּל־אֲשֶׁ֧ר יְדַבֵּ֛ר יְהוָ֥ה אֱלֹהֵ֖ינוּ
our Elohim   ihvh   speaks   which - all   that   unto us

וְאַ֣תְּ ׀ תְּדַבֵּ֣ר אֵלֵ֗ינוּ וְשָׁמַ֖עְנוּ וְעָשִֽׂינוּ׃
and we will do   and we will listen   unto you   you will speak   and you

27 Go thou near, and hear all that the LORD our God shall say: and speak thou unto us all that the LORD our God shall speak unto thee; and we will hear it, and do it.

וַיִּשְׁמַ֤ע יְהוָה֙ אֶת־ק֣וֹל דִּבְרֵיכֶ֔ם בְּדַבֶּרְכֶ֖ם אֵלָ֑י
unto me   in you speaking   your speaking   sound - that   ihvh   and he heard

וַיֹּ֨אמֶר יְהוָ֜ה אֵלַ֗י שָׁ֠מַעְתִּי אֶת־ק֨וֹל דִּבְרֵ֜י הָעָ֤ם הַזֶּה֙
the this   the people   speakings   sound - that   I heard   unto me   ihvh   and he said

אֲשֶׁ֣ר דִּבְּר֣וּ אֵלֶ֔יךָ הֵיטִ֖יבוּ כָּל־אֲשֶׁ֥ר דִּבֵּֽרוּ׃
they spoke   which - all   they were good   unto you   they spoke   which

28 And the LORD heard the voice of your words, when ye spake unto me; and the LORD said unto me, I have heard the voice of the words of this people, which they have spoken unto thee: they have well said all that they have spoken.

מִֽי־יִתֵּ֡ן וְהָיָה֩ לְבָבָ֨ם זֶ֜ה לָהֶ֗ם לְיִרְאָ֥ה אֹתִ֛י
to me   to fear   to them   this   their heart   and it be   he gives - who

וְלִשְׁמֹ֥ר אֶת־כָּל־מִצְוֹתַ֖י כָּל־הַיָּמִ֑ים
the days - all   my commandments - all - that   and to heed

לְמַ֨עַן יִיטַ֥ב לָהֶ֛ם וְלִבְנֵיהֶ֖ם לְעֹלָֽם׃
forever   and to their sons   to them   it will be good   to end

29 O that there were such an heart in them, that they would fear me, and keep all my commandments always, that it might be well with them, and with their children for ever!

לֵ֖ךְ אֱמֹ֣ר לָהֶ֑ם שׁ֥וּבוּ לָכֶ֖ם לְאָהֳלֵיכֶֽם׃
to your tents   to you   you return   to them   say   go

30 Go say to them, Get you into your tents again.

וְאַתָּ֗ה פֹּה֙ עֲמֹ֣ד עִמָּדִ֔י
with me   stand   here   and you

וַאֲדַבְּרָ֣ה אֵלֶ֗יךָ אֵ֧ת כָּל־הַמִּצְוָ֛ה וְהַחֻקִּ֥ים
and the statutes   the commandment - all   that   unto you   and I will speak

וְהַמִּשְׁפָּטִ֖ים אֲשֶׁ֣ר תְּלַמְּדֵ֑ם
you will teach them   which   and the judgments

וְעָשׂ֣וּ בָאָ֔רֶץ אֲשֶׁ֧ר אָנֹכִ֛י נֹתֵ֥ן לָהֶ֖ם לְרִשְׁתָּֽהּ׃
to possess it   to them   giving   I am   which   in land   and they will do

31 But as for thee, stand thou here by me, and I will speak unto thee all the commandments, and the statutes, and the judgments, which thou shalt teach them, that they may do them in the land which I give them to possess it.

וּשְׁמַרְתֶּ֣ם לַעֲשׂ֔וֹת כַּאֲשֶׁ֥ר צִוָּ֛ה יְהוָ֥ה אֱלֹהֵיכֶ֖ם אֶתְכֶ֑ם
that you   your Elohim   ihvh   he commanded   when   to do   and you will heed

לֹא תָסֻרוּ יָמִין וּשְׂמֹאל׃
or left   right   your turn   not

32 Ye shall observe to do therefore as the LORD your God hath commanded you: ye shall not turn aside to the right hand or to the left.

בְּכָל־הַדֶּרֶךְ אֲשֶׁר צִוָּה יְהֹוָה אֱלֹהֵיכֶם אֶתְכֶם
that you   your Elohim   ihvh   commanded   which   the way - in all

תֵּלֵכוּ לְמַעַן תִּחְיוּן וְטוֹב לָכֶם
to you   and good   you will live   to end   you walk it

וְהַאֲרַכְתֶּם יָמִים בָּאָרֶץ אֲשֶׁר תִּירָשׁוּן׃
you will possess   which   in land   days   and the prolong you

33 Ye shall walk in all the ways which the LORD your God hath commanded you, that ye may live, and that it may be well with you, and that ye may prolong your days in the land which ye shall possess.

Chapter 6

ספר דברים פרק ו

וְזֹאת הַמִּצְוָה הַחֻקִּים וְהַמִּשְׁפָּטִים
and the judgments   the statutes   the command   and this

אֲשֶׁר צִוָּה יְהֹוָה אֱלֹהֵיכֶם לְלַמֵּד אֶתְכֶם לַעֲשׂוֹת בָּאָרֶץ
in land   to do   that you   to teach   your Elohim   ihvh   commanded   which

אֲשֶׁר אַתֶּם עֹבְרִים שָׁמָּה לְרִשְׁתָּהּ׃
to possess it   to there   passing ones   to you   which

1 Now these are the commandments, the statutes, and the judgments, which the LORD your God commanded to teach you, that ye might do them in the land whither ye go to possess it:

לְמַעַן תִּירָא אֶת־יְהֹוָה אֱלֹהֶיךָ
your Elohim   ihvh - that   you will fear   to end

לִשְׁמֹר אֶת־כָּל־חֻקֹּתָיו וּמִצְוֹתָיו
and his commandments   his statutes - all - that   to heed

אֲשֶׁר אָנֹכִי מְצַוֶּךָ אַתָּה וּבִנְךָ וּבֶן־בִּנְךָ
your son - and son   and your sons   you   commanding you   I am   which

כֹּל יְמֵי חַיֶּיךָ וּלְמַעַן יַאֲרִכֻן יָמֶיךָ׃
your days   they will be prolonged   and to end   your lives   days   all

2 That thou mightest fear the LORD thy God, to keep all his statutes and his commandments, which I command thee, thou, and thy son, and thy son's son, all the days of thy life; and that thy days may be prolonged.

Vechanan - Chapter 6

וְשָׁמַעְתָּ֤ יִשְׂרָאֵל֙ וְשָׁמַרְתָּ֣ לַעֲשׂ֔וֹת

to do   and you heed   Israel   and you hear

אֲשֶׁר֙ יִיטַ֣ב לְךָ֔ וַאֲשֶׁ֥ר תִּרְבּ֖וּן מְאֹ֑ד

greatly   it will increase   and which   to you   it will be good   which

כַּאֲשֶׁר֩ דִּבֶּ֨ר יְהוָ֜ה אֱלֹהֵ֧י אֲבֹתֶ֛יךָ לָ֖ךְ

to you   your fathers   your Elohim   ihvh   spoke   when

אֶ֛רֶץ זָבַ֥ת חָלָ֖ב וּדְבָֽשׁ׃

and honey   milk   flowing   land

3 Hear therefore, O Israel, and observe to do it; that it may be well with thee, and that ye may increase mightily, as the LORD God of thy fathers hath promised thee, in the land that floweth with milk and honey.

פ

[ששי]

שְׁמַ֖ע יִשְׂרָאֵ֑ל יְהוָ֥ה אֱלֹהֵ֖ינוּ יְהוָ֥ה ׀ אֶחָֽד׃

one   ihvh   our Elohim   ihvh   Israel   hear

4 Hear, O Israel: The LORD our God is one LORD:

וְאָ֣הַבְתָּ֔ אֵ֖ת יְהוָ֣ה אֱלֹהֶ֑יךָ

your Elohim   ihvh   that   and you will love

בְּכָל־לְבָבְךָ֥ וּבְכָל־נַפְשְׁךָ֖ וּבְכָל־מְאֹדֶֽךָ׃

your being - and in all   your soul - and in all   your heart - in all

5 And thou shalt love the LORD thy God with all thine heart, and with all thy soul, and with all thy might.

וְהָי֞וּ הַדְּבָרִ֣ים הָאֵ֗לֶּה אֲשֶׁ֨ר אָנֹכִ֧י מְצַוְּךָ֛ הַיּ֖וֹם עַל־לְבָבֶֽךָ׃

your heart - upon   the day   commanding you   I am   which   the these   the speakings   and it be

6 And these words, which I command thee this day, shall be in thine heart:

וְשִׁנַּנְתָּ֣ם לְבָנֶ֔יךָ וְדִבַּרְתָּ֖ בָּ֑ם בְּשִׁבְתְּךָ֤ בְּבֵיתֶ֨ךָ֙

in your house   in your sit sitting   in them   and you speak   to your sons   and you repeat

וּבְלֶכְתְּךָ֣ בַדֶּ֔רֶךְ וּֽבְשָׁכְבְּךָ֖ וּבְקוּמֶֽךָ׃

and in your getting up   and in your lying down   in way   and in your walking

7 And thou shalt teach them diligently unto thy children, and shalt talk of them when thou sittest in thine house, and when thou walkest by the way, and when thou liest down, and when thou risest up.

וּקְשַׁרְתָּ֥ם לְא֖וֹת עַל־יָדֶ֑ךָ וְהָי֥וּ לְטֹטָפֹ֖ת בֵּ֥ין עֵינֶֽיךָ׃

your eyes   between   to frontlets   and they be   your hand - upon   to sign   and you bind them

8 And thou shalt bind them for a sign upon thine hand, and they shall be as frontlets

between thine eyes.

וּכְתַבְתָּם עַל־מְזֻזוֹת בֵּיתֶךָ וּבִשְׁעָרֶיךָ׃
and you write them door post - upon your house and in your gates

9 And thou shalt write them upon the posts of thy house, and on thy gates.

ס

וְהָיָה כִּי־יְבִיאֲךָ יְהוָה אֱלֹהֶיךָ אֶל־הָאָרֶץ
and it will be like - he brings you ihvh your Elohim unto - the land

אֲשֶׁר נִשְׁבַּע לַאֲבֹתֶיךָ לְאַבְרָהָם לְיִצְחָק וּלְיַעֲקֹב
which he swore to your fathers to Abraham to Isaac and to Jacob

לָתֶת לָךְ עָרִים גְּדֹלֹת וְטֹבֹת אֲשֶׁר לֹא־בָנִיתָ׃
to give to you cities large ones and good ones which not - you built

10 And it shall be, when the LORD thy God shall have brought thee into the land which he sware unto thy fathers, to Abraham, to Isaac, and to Jacob, to give thee great and goodly cities, which thou buildedst not,

וּבָתִּים מְלֵאִים כָּל־טוּב אֲשֶׁר לֹא־מִלֵּאתָ
and houses full ones all - good which not - you filled

וּבֹרֹת חֲצוּבִים אֲשֶׁר לֹא־חָצַבְתָּ כְּרָמִים וְזֵיתִים
and wells dug ones which not - you dug vineyards and olive groves

אֲשֶׁר לֹא־נָטָעְתָּ וְאָכַלְתָּ וְשָׂבָעְתָּ׃
which not - you planted and you eat and you full

11 And houses full of all good things, which thou filledst not, and wells digged, which thou diggedst not, vineyards and olive trees, which thou plantedst not; when thou shalt have eaten and be full;

הִשָּׁמֶר לְךָ פֶּן־תִּשְׁכַּח אֶת־יְהוָה
be heeding to you lest - you forget that - ihvh

אֲשֶׁר הוֹצִיאֲךָ מֵאֶרֶץ מִצְרַיִם מִבֵּית עֲבָדִים׃
which brought out you from land Egypt from house slaveries

12 Then beware lest thou forget the LORD, which brought thee forth out of the land of Egypt, from the house of bondage.

אֶת־יְהוָה אֱלֹהֶיךָ תִּירָא
that - ihvh your Elohim you fear

וְאֹתוֹ תַעֲבֹד וּבִשְׁמוֹ תִּשָּׁבֵעַ׃
and to him you serve and in his name you swear

13 Thou shalt fear the LORD thy God, and serve him, and shalt swear by his name.

Vechanan - Chapter 6

לֹא תֵלְכוּן אַחֲרֵי אֱלֹהִים אֲחֵרִים
not you follow after elohim other ones

מֵאֱלֹהֵי הָעַמִּים אֲשֶׁר סְבִיבוֹתֵיכֶם׃
from elohim the people which surround you

14 Ye shall not go after other gods, of the gods of the people which are round about you;

כִּי אֵל קַנָּא יְהוָה אֱלֹהֶיךָ בְּקִרְבֶּךָ
like El jealous ihvh your Elohim in near you

פֶּן־יֶחֱרֶה אַף־יְהוָה אֱלֹהֶיךָ בָּךְ
thus he burns ihvh - anger your Elohim in you

וְהִשְׁמִידְךָ מֵעַל פְּנֵי הָאֲדָמָה׃
and destroys you from upon face the ground

15 (For the LORD thy God is a jealous God among you) lest the anger of the LORD thy God be kindled against thee, and destroy thee from off the face of the earth.

ס

לֹא תְנַסּוּ אֶת־יְהוָה אֱלֹהֵיכֶם כַּאֲשֶׁר נִסִּיתֶם בַּמַּסָּה׃
not you probe ihvh - that your Elohim when you probed in Massah

16 Ye shall not tempt the LORD your God, as ye tempted him in Massah.

שָׁמוֹר תִּשְׁמְרוּן אֶת־מִצְוֹת יְהוָה אֱלֹהֵיכֶם
to heed you heeded commandments - that ihvh your Elohim

וְעֵדֹתָיו וְחֻקָּיו אֲשֶׁר צִוָּךְ׃
and his testimonies and his statutes which commanded you

17 Ye shall diligently keep the commandments of the LORD your God, and his testimonies, and his statutes, which he hath commanded thee.

and you do the upright and the good in eyes ihvh to end it will be good to you

וּבָאתָ וְיָרַשְׁתָּ אֶת־הָאָרֶץ הַטֹּבָה
and you come and you possess the land that the good

אֲשֶׁר־נִשְׁבַּע יְהוָה לַאֲבֹתֶיךָ׃
swore - which ihvh to your fathers

18 And thou shalt do that which is right and good in the sight of the LORD: that it may be well with thee, and that thou mayest go in and possess the good land which the LORD sware unto thy fathers,

to thrust out your enemies - all - that from before you when spoke ihvh

19 To cast out all thine enemies from before thee, as the LORD hath spoken.

ס

כִּי־יִשְׁאָלְךָ֤ בִנְךָ֙ מָחָ֣ר לֵאמֹ֔ר מָ֣ה הָעֵדֹ֗ת וְהַֽחֻקִּים֙
he asks you - like   your son   tomorrow   to say   what   the testimonies   and the statutes

וְהַמִּשְׁפָּטִ֔ים אֲשֶׁ֥ר צִוָּ֛ה יְהֹוָ֥ה אֱלֹהֵ֖ינוּ אֶתְכֶֽם׃
and the judgments   which   commanded   ihvh   our Elohim   that you

20 And when thy son asketh thee in time to come, saying, What mean the testimonies, and the statutes, and the judgments, which the LORD our God hath commanded you?

וְאָמַרְתָּ֣ לְבִנְךָ֔ עֲבָדִ֛ים הָיִ֥ינוּ לְפַרְעֹ֖ה בְּמִצְרָ֑יִם
and you say   to your son   slaves   we were   to Pharaoh   in Egypt

וַיֹּצִיאֵ֧נוּ יְהֹוָ֛ה מִמִּצְרַ֖יִם בְּיָ֥ד חֲזָקָֽה׃
and he brought us out   ihvh   from Egypt   in hand   mighty

21 Then thou shalt say unto thy son, We were Pharaoh's bondmen in Egypt; and the LORD brought us out of Egypt with a mighty hand:

וַיִּתֵּ֣ן יְהֹוָ֡ה אוֹתֹ֣ת וּ֠מֹפְתִים גְּדֹלִ֨ים וְרָעִ֧ים
and gave   ihvh   signs   and wonders   great ones   and bad ones

בְּמִצְרַ֛יִם בְּפַרְעֹ֥ה וּבְכׇל־בֵּית֖וֹ לְעֵינֵֽינוּ׃
in Egypt   in Pharaoh   and in all - house his   to our eyes

22 And the LORD shewed signs and wonders, great and sore, upon Egypt, upon Pharaoh, and upon all his household, before our eyes:

וְאוֹתָ֖נוּ הוֹצִ֣יא מִשָּׁ֑ם לְמַ֙עַן֙ הָבִ֣יא אֹתָ֔נוּ
and to us   the come   to end   from there   he brought out   to us

לָ֤תֶת לָ֙נוּ֙ אֶת־הָאָ֔רֶץ אֲשֶׁ֥ר נִשְׁבַּ֖ע לַאֲבֹתֵֽינוּ׃
to give   to us   the land - that   which   he swore   to our fathers

23 And he brought us out from thence, that he might bring us in, to give us the land which he sware unto our fathers.

וַיְצַוֵּ֣נוּ יְהֹוָ֗ה לַעֲשׂוֹת֙ אֶת־כׇּל־הַחֻקִּ֣ים הָאֵ֔לֶּה
and commanded us   ihvh   to do   that - all - the decrees   the these

לְיִרְאָ֖ה אֶת־יְהֹוָ֣ה אֱלֹהֵ֑ינוּ
to fear   that - ihvh   our Elohim

לְט֥וֹב לָ֛נוּ כׇּל־הַיָּמִ֖ים לְחַיֹּתֵ֥נוּ כְּהַיּ֥וֹם הַזֶּֽה׃
to good   to us   all - the days   to keep us alive   like the day   the this

24 And the LORD commanded us to do all these statutes, to fear the LORD our God, for our good always, that he might preserve us alive, as it is at this day.

Vechanan - Chapter 7

וּצְדָקָה תִּהְיֶה־לָּנוּ
and righteousness — to us - it will be

כִּי־נִשְׁמֹר לַעֲשׂוֹת אֶת־כָּל־הַמִּצְוָה הַזֹּאת
we heed - like   to do   that - all - the commandment   the this

לִפְנֵי יְהוָה אֱלֹהֵינוּ כַּאֲשֶׁר צִוָּנוּ׃
before   ihvh   our Elohim   when   he commanded us

25 And it shall be our righteousness, if we observe to do all these commandments before the LORD our God, as he hath commanded us.

ס

Chapter 7

ספר דברים פרק ז

[שביעי]

כִּי יְבִיאֲךָ יְהוָה אֱלֹהֶיךָ
like   brings you   ihvh   your Elohim

אֶל־הָאָרֶץ אֲשֶׁר־אַתָּה בָא־שָׁמָּה לְרִשְׁתָּהּ
unto- the land   which - you   come- to there   to possess it

וְנָשַׁל גּוֹיִם־רַבִּים מִפָּנֶיךָ
and he eases out   many - nations   from before you

הַחִתִּי וְהַגִּרְגָּשִׁי וְהָאֱמֹרִי וְהַכְּנַעֲנִי
the Hittites   and the Girgashites   and the Amorites   and the Canaanites

וְהַפְּרִזִּי וְהַחִוִּי וְהַיְבוּסִי
and the Perizzites   and the Hivites   and the Jebusites

שִׁבְעָה גוֹיִם רַבִּים וַעֲצוּמִים מִמֶּךָּ׃
seven   nations   many ones   and mightier ones   from you

1 When the LORD thy God shall bring thee into the land whither thou goest to possess it, and hath cast out many nations before thee, the Hittites, and the Girgashites, and the Amorites, and the Canaanites, and the Perizzites, and the Hivites, and the Jebusites, seven nations greater and mightier than thou;

וּנְתָנָם יְהוָה אֱלֹהֶיךָ לְפָנֶיךָ
and gives them   ihvh   your Elohim   before you

וְהִכִּיתָם הַחֲרֵם תַּחֲרִים אֹתָם
and you smite them   the utterly destroy   you will utterly destroy   to them

לֹא־תִכְרֹת לָהֶם בְּרִית וְלֹא תְחָנֵּם׃
not - you cut   with them   covenant   and not   you show them mercy

2 And when the LORD thy God shall deliver them before thee; thou shalt smite them,

and utterly destroy them; thou shalt make no covenant with them, nor shew mercy unto them:

וְלֹא תִּתְחַתֵּן בָּם
and not you marry them (women) in them

בִּתְּךָ לֹא־תִתֵּן לִבְנוֹ וּבִתּוֹ לֹא־תִקַּח לִבְנֶךָ׃
your daughter you give - not to his son and his daughter you take - not to your son

3 Neither shalt thou make marriages with them; thy daughter thou shalt not give unto his son, nor his daughter shalt thou take unto thy son.

כִּי־יָסִיר אֶת־בִּנְךָ מֵאַחֲרַי וְעָבְדוּ אֱלֹהִים אֲחֵרִים
like - he will remove your son - that from following me and they will serve elohim other ones

וְחָרָה אַף־יְהוָה בָּכֶם וְהִשְׁמִידְךָ מַהֵר׃
and he will burn ihvh - anger in you and he will destroy you quickly

4 For they will turn away thy son from following me, that they may serve other gods: so will the anger of the LORD be kindled against you, and destroy thee suddenly.

כִּי אִם־כֹּה תַעֲשׂוּ לָהֶם מִזְבְּחֹתֵיהֶם תִּתֹּצוּ
like if - thus you do it to them their altars you will break down

וּמַצֵּבֹתָם תְּשַׁבֵּרוּ וַאֲשֵׁירֵהֶם תְּגַדֵּעוּן
and their sacred images you smash it and their happiness things you hack down

וּפְסִילֵיהֶם תִּשְׂרְפוּן בָּאֵשׁ׃
and their graven idols your burn in fire

5 But thus shall ye deal with them; ye shall destroy their altars, and break down their images, and cut down their groves, and burn their graven images with fire.

כִּי עַם קָדוֹשׁ אַתָּה לַיהוָה אֱלֹהֶיךָ
like people holy you to ihvh your Elohim

בְּךָ בָּחַר יְהוָה אֱלֹהֶיךָ לִהְיוֹת לוֹ לְעַם
in you chose ihvh your Elohim to be to him to people

סְגֻלָּה מִכֹּל הָעַמִּים אֲשֶׁר עַל־פְּנֵי הָאֲדָמָה׃
treasure from all the peoples which upon - faces the earth

6 For thou art an holy people unto the LORD thy God: the LORD thy God hath chosen thee to be a special people unto himself, above all people that are upon the face of the earth.

לֹא מֵרֻבְּכֶם מִכָּל־הָעַמִּים חָשַׁק יְהוָה בָּכֶם
not from many you the people - from all affection ihvh in you

וַיִּבְחַר בָּכֶם כִּי־אַתֶּם הַמְעַט מִכָּל־הָעַמִּים׃
and he chose in you like - you the fewest the people - from all

7 The LORD did not set his love upon you, nor choose you, because ye were more in

number than any people; for ye were the fewest of all people:

כִּי מֵאַהֲבַת יְהֹוָה אֶתְכֶם וּמִשָּׁמְרוֹ אֶת־הַשְּׁבֻעָה
like from love ihvh that you and from his heeding the oath - that

אֲשֶׁר נִשְׁבַּע לַאֲבֹתֵיכֶם הוֹצִיא יְהֹוָה אֶתְכֶם בְּיָד חֲזָקָה
which he swore to your fathers ihvh brought out that you in hand mighty

וַיִּפְדְּךָ מִבֵּית עֲבָדִים מִיַּד פַּרְעֹה מֶלֶךְ־מִצְרָיִם׃
and he redeemed you from house slaveries form hand Pharaoh Egypt - king

8 But because the LORD loved you, and because he would keep the oath which he had sworn unto your fathers, hath the LORD brought you out with a mighty hand, and redeemed you out of the house of bondmen, from the hand of Pharaoh king of Egypt.

[מפטיר]

וְיָדַעְתָּ כִּי־יְהֹוָה אֱלֹהֶיךָ הוּא הָאֱלֹהִים הָאֵל
and you know ihvh - like your Elohim he the Elohim the El

הַנֶּאֱמָן שֹׁמֵר הַבְּרִית
the faithful heeding the covenant

וְהַחֶסֶד לְאֹהֲבָיו וּלְשֹׁמְרֵי מִצְוֹתָו [מִצְוֹתָיו] לְאֶלֶף דּוֹר׃
and the mercy to his ones loving and to ones heeding his commandments to thousand generation

9 Know therefore that the LORD thy God, he is God, the faithful God, which keepeth covenant and mercy with them that love him and keep his commandments to a thousand generations;

וּמְשַׁלֵּם לְשֹׂנְאָיו אֶל־פָּנָיו לְהַאֲבִידוֹ
and repaying to ones hating him his face - unto to his destruction

לֹא יְאַחֵר לְשֹׂנְאוֹ אֶל־פָּנָיו יְשַׁלֶּם־לוֹ׃
not he will be slack to his hating ones his face - unto to him - he will pay

10 And repayeth them that hate him to their face, to destroy them: he will not be slack to him that hateth him, he will repay him to his face.

וְשָׁמַרְתָּ אֶת־הַמִּצְוָה
and you heed the commandment - that

וְאֶת־הַחֻקִּים וְאֶת־הַמִּשְׁפָּטִים
the statutes - and that the judgments - and that

אֲשֶׁר אָנֹכִי מְצַוְּךָ הַיּוֹם לַעֲשׂוֹתָם׃
which I am commanding you the day to do them

11 Thou shalt therefore keep the commandments, and the statutes, and the judgments, which I command thee this day, to do them.

פ פ פ

Ekev
Chapter 7 cont

[פרשת עקב]

וְהָיָ֣ה ׀ עֵ֣קֶב תִּשְׁמְע֗וּן אֵ֤ת הַמִּשְׁפָּטִים֙ הָאֵ֔לֶּה
and it will be   because   you hearken   that   the judgments   the these

וּשְׁמַרְתֶּ֥ם וַעֲשִׂיתֶ֖ם אֹתָ֑ם
and you are heeding   and you do   to them

וְשָׁמַר֩ יְהוָ֨ה אֱלֹהֶ֜יךָ לְךָ֗ אֶֽת־הַבְּרִית֙
and he will heed   ihvh   your Elohim   to you   the covenant - that

וְאֶת־הַחֶ֔סֶד אֲשֶׁ֥ר נִשְׁבַּ֖ע לַאֲבֹתֶֽיךָ׃
the mercy - and that   which   he swore   to your fathers

12 Wherefore it shall come to pass, if ye hearken to these judgments, and keep, and do them, that the LORD thy God shall keep unto thee the covenant and the mercy which he sware unto thy fathers:

וַאֲהֵ֣בְךָ֔ וּבֵרַכְךָ֖ וְהִרְבֶּ֑ךָ וּבֵרַ֣ךְ פְּרִֽי־בִטְנְךָ֣
and he will love you   and he will bless you   and he will increase you   and he will bless   your womb - fruit

וּפְרִֽי־אַדְמָתֶ֗ךָ דְּגָֽנְךָ֤ וְתִֽירֹשְׁךָ֙ וְיִצְהָרֶ֔ךָ שְׁגַר־אֲלָפֶ֖יךָ
and fruit - your ground   your grain   and your new wine   and your oil   your herd - drop of

וְעַשְׁתְּרֹ֣ת צֹאנֶ֑ךָ עַ֚ל הָֽאֲדָמָ֔ה
and cast ones   your flock   upon   the ground

אֲשֶׁר־נִשְׁבַּ֥ע לַאֲבֹתֶ֖יךָ לָ֥תֶת לָֽךְ׃
he swore - which   to your fathers   to give   to you

13 And he will love thee, and bless thee, and multiply thee: he will also bless the fruit of thy womb, and the fruit of thy land, thy corn, and thy wine, and thine oil, the increase of thy kine, and the flocks of thy sheep, in the land which he sware unto thy fathers to give thee.

בָּר֥וּךְ תִּֽהְיֶ֖ה מִכָּל־הָעַמִּ֑ים לֹא־יִהְיֶ֥ה בְךָ֛ עָקָ֖ר
blessed   you will be   the peoples - from all   will be - not   in you   childless man

וַעֲקָרָ֖ה וּבִבְהֶמְתֶּֽךָ׃
and childless woman   and in your livestock

14 Thou shalt be blessed above all people: there shall not be male or female barren among you, or among your cattle.

וְהֵסִ֧יר יְהוָ֛ה מִמְּךָ֖ כָּל־חֹ֑לִי
and he will remove   ihvh   form you   sickness - all

וְכָל־מַדְוֵי מִצְרַיִם הָרָעִים אֲשֶׁר יָדַעְתָּ
you knew   which   the evil ones   Egypt   languishes - and all

לֹא יְשִׂימָם בָּךְ וּנְתָנָם בְּכָל־שֹׂנְאֶיךָ׃
ones hating you - in all   and he will give them   in you   he will put them   not

15 And the LORD will take away from thee all sickness, and will put none of the evil diseases of Egypt, which thou knowest, upon thee; but will lay them upon all them that hate thee.

וְאָכַלְתָּ אֶת־כָּל־הָעַמִּים אֲשֶׁר יְהוָה אֱלֹהֶיךָ נֹתֵן לָךְ
to you   giving   your Elohim   ihvh   which   the peoples - all - that   and you consume

לֹא־תָחוֹס עֵינְךָ עֲלֵיהֶם
upon them   your eye   you pity - not

וְלֹא תַעֲבֹד אֶת־אֱלֹהֵיהֶם
their elohim - that   you serve   and not

כִּי־מוֹקֵשׁ הוּא לָךְ׃
to you   it   snare - like

16 And thou shalt consume all the people which the LORD thy God shall deliver thee; thine eye shall have no pity upon them: neither shalt thou serve their gods; for that will be a snare unto thee.

ס

כִּי תֹאמַר בִּלְבָבְךָ רַבִּים הַגּוֹיִם הָאֵלֶּה מִמֶּנִּי
from me   the these   the nations   much   in your heart   you say   like

אֵיכָה אוּכַל לְהוֹרִישָׁם׃
to drive out them   I able   how

17 If thou shalt say in thine heart, These nations are more than I; how can I dispossess them?

לֹא תִירָא מֵהֶם זָכֹר תִּזְכֹּר
you remember   remember   form them   you be afraid   not

אֵת אֲשֶׁר־עָשָׂה יְהוָה אֱלֹהֶיךָ לְפַרְעֹה וּלְכָל־מִצְרָיִם׃
Egypt - and to all   to Pharaoh   your Elohim   ihvh   he did - which   that

18 Thou shalt not be afraid of them: but shalt well remember what the LORD thy God did unto Pharaoh, and unto all Egypt;

הַמַּסֹּת הַגְּדֹלֹת אֲשֶׁר־רָאוּ עֵינֶיךָ
your eyes   they saw - which   the great ones   the trials

וְהָאֹתֹת וְהַמֹּפְתִים וְהַיָּד הַחֲזָקָה וְהַזְּרֹעַ הַנְּטוּיָה
out stretched   and the arm   the mighty   and the hand   and the wonders   and the signs

אֲשֶׁר הוֹצִאֲךָ יְהוָה אֱלֹהֶיךָ כֵּן־יַעֲשֶׂה יְהוָה אֱלֹהֶיךָ
which   brought out you   ihvh   your Elohim   thus - he will do   ihvh   your Elohim

לְכָל־הָעַמִּים אֲשֶׁר־אַתָּה יָרֵא מִפְּנֵיהֶם׃
the peoples - to all   which - you   fearing   from their presence

19 The great temptations which thine eyes saw, and the signs, and the wonders, and the mighty hand, and the stretched out arm, whereby the LORD thy God brought thee out: so shall the LORD thy God do unto all the people of whom thou art afraid.

וְגַם אֶת־הַצִּרְעָה יְשַׁלַּח יְהוָה אֱלֹהֶיךָ בָּם
and also   the hornet that   he will sent   ihvh   your elohim   in them

עַד־אֲבֹד הַנִּשְׁאָרִים וְהַנִּסְתָּרִים מִפָּנֶיךָ׃
until perish   the surviving ones   and the hiding ones   from your presence

20 Moreover the LORD thy God will send the hornet among them, until they that are left, and hide themselves from thee, be destroyed.

לֹא תַעֲרֹץ מִפְּנֵיהֶם כִּי־יְהוָה אֱלֹהֶיךָ בְּקִרְבֶּךָ
not   you be terrified   from their presence   like - ihvh   your Elohim   in near you

אֵל גָּדוֹל וְנוֹרָא׃
El   great   and awesome

21 Thou shalt not be affrighted at them: for the LORD thy God is among you, a mighty God and terrible.

וְנָשַׁל יְהוָה אֱלֹהֶיךָ אֶת־הַגּוֹיִם הָאֵל מִפָּנֶיךָ מְעַט מְעָט
and he will drive   ihvh   your Elohim   that - the nations   the those   from your presence   little   little

לֹא תוּכַל כַּלֹּתָם מַהֵר פֶּן־תִּרְבֶּה עָלֶיךָ חַיַּת הַשָּׂדֶה׃
not   you able   to eliminate them   quickly   lest - it will multiply   upon you   animal   the field

22 And the LORD thy God will put out those nations before thee by little and little: thou mayest not consume them at once, lest the beasts of the field increase upon thee.

וּנְתָנָם יְהוָה אֱלֹהֶיךָ לְפָנֶיךָ
and he will give them   ihvh   your Elohim   to your presence

וְהָמָם מְהוּמָה גְדֹלָה עַד הִשָּׁמְדָם׃
and he will wear away them   perplexing   great   till   destroying them

23 But the LORD thy God shall deliver them unto thee, and shall destroy them with a mighty destruction, until they be destroyed.

וְנָתַן מַלְכֵיהֶם בְּיָדֶךָ
and he will give   their kings   in your hand

וְהַאֲבַדְתָּ אֶת־שְׁמָם מִתַּחַת הַשָּׁמָיִם
and you will destroy   that - their name   from under   the heavens

Ekev - Chapter 8

לֹא־יִתְיַצֵּב אִישׁ בְּפָנֶיךָ עַד הִשְׁמִדְךָ אֹתָם:
to them   you destroyed   till   in your face   each   he will stand - not

24 And he shall deliver their kings into thine hand, and thou shalt destroy their name from under heaven: there shall no man be able to stand before thee, until thou have destroyed them.

פְּסִילֵי אֱלֹהֵיהֶם תִּשְׂרְפוּן בָּאֵשׁ
in fire   you burn   their Elohim   images

לֹא־תַחְמֹד כֶּסֶף וְזָהָב עֲלֵיהֶם
upon them   and gold   silver   you covet - not

וְלָקַחְתָּ לָךְ פֶּן תִּוָּקֵשׁ בּוֹ
in it   you snared   lest   to you   and you take

כִּי תוֹעֲבַת יְהוָה אֱלֹהֶיךָ הוּא:
it   your Elohim   ihvh   abomination   like

25 The graven images of their gods shall ye burn with fire: thou shalt not desire the silver or gold that is on them, nor take it unto thee, lest thou be snared therein: for it is an abomination to the LORD thy God.

וְלֹא־תָבִיא תוֹעֵבָה אֶל־בֵּיתֶךָ
your house - unto   abomination   you bring - and not

וְהָיִיתָ חֵרֶם כָּמֹהוּ שַׁקֵּץ תְּשַׁקְּצֶנּוּ
you will abominate it   abominate   like it   cursed   and you be

וְתַעֵב תְּתַעֲבֶנּוּ כִּי־חֵרֶם הוּא:
it   cursed - like   you abhor it   and abhor

פ

26 Neither shalt thou bring an abomination into thine house, lest thou be a cursed thing like it: but thou shalt utterly detest it, and thou shalt utterly abhor it; for it is a cursed thing.

Chapter 8

ספר דברים פרק ח

כָּל־הַמִּצְוָה אֲשֶׁר אָנֹכִי מְצַוְּךָ הַיּוֹם תִּשְׁמְרוּן לַעֲשׂוֹת
to do   you heed   the day   commanded you   I am   which   the commandments - all

לְמַעַן תִּחְיוּן וּרְבִיתֶם וּבָאתֶם
and you come   and you multiply   you live   to end

וִירִשְׁתֶּם אֶת־הָאָרֶץ אֲשֶׁר־נִשְׁבַּע יְהוָה לַאֲבֹתֵיכֶם:
to your fathers   ihvh   he promised - which   the land - that   and you possess

1 All the commandments which I command thee this day shall ye observe to do, that ye may live, and multiply, and go in and possess the land which the LORD sware unto your

fathers.

וְזָכַרְתָּ֗ אֶת־כָּל־הַדֶּ֙רֶךְ֙
and you remember   that - all - the way

אֲשֶׁ֨ר הוֹלִֽיכֲךָ֜ יְהוָ֧ה אֱלֹהֶ֛יךָ זֶ֛ה אַרְבָּעִ֥ים שָׁנָ֖ה בַּמִּדְבָּ֑ר
which   he caused you go   ihvh   your Elohim   this   forty   year   in desert

לְמַ֨עַן עַנֹּֽתְךָ֜ לְנַסֹּֽתְךָ֗ לָדַ֜עַת אֶת־אֲשֶׁ֧ר בִּֽלְבָבְךָ֛
to end   you humbled   to test you   to know   that - which   in your heart

הֲתִשְׁמֹ֥ר מִצְוֺתָ֖יו [מִצְוֺתָ֖יו] אִם־לֹֽא׃
the heed   his commandments   not - if

2 And thou shalt remember all the way which the LORD thy God led thee these forty years in the wilderness, to humble thee, and to prove thee, to know what was in thine heart, whether thou wouldest keep his commandments, or no.

וַֽיְעַנְּךָ֮ וַיַּרְעִבֶ֒ךָ֒ וַיַּֽאֲכִֽלְךָ֤ אֶת־הַמָּן֙
and he humbled you   and he suffered you   and he fed you   that - the manna

אֲשֶׁ֣ר לֹא־יָדַ֔עְתָּ וְלֹ֥א יָדְע֖וּן אֲבֹתֶ֑יךָ
which   not - you knew   and not   they knew   your fathers

לְמַ֣עַן הוֹדִֽיעֲךָ֗ כִּ֠י לֹ֣א עַל־הַלֶּ֤חֶם לְבַדּוֹ֙ יִחְיֶ֣ה הָֽאָדָ֔ם
to end   teaching you   like   not   upon - the bread   it alone   he lives   the man

כִּ֛י עַל־כָּל־מוֹצָ֥א פִֽי־יְהוָ֖ה יִֽחְיֶ֥ה הָאָדָֽם׃
like   upon - all - coming out   mouth - ihvh   he lives   the man

3 And he humbled thee, and suffered thee to hunger, and fed thee with manna, which thou knewest not, neither did thy fathers know; that he might make thee know that man doth not live by bread only, but by every word that proceedeth out of the mouth of the LORD doth man live.

שִׂמְלָ֨תְךָ֜ לֹ֤א בָֽלְתָה֙ מֵֽעָלֶ֔יךָ
your clothing   not   wore out   from upon you

וְרַגְלְךָ֖ לֹ֣א בָצֵ֑קָה זֶ֖ה אַרְבָּעִ֥ים שָׁנָֽה׃
and your foot   not   swelled   this   forty   year

4 Thy raiment waxed not old upon thee, neither did thy foot swell, these forty years.

וְיָדַעְתָּ֖ עִם־לְבָבֶ֑ךָ
and you know   with - your heart

כִּ֗י כַּאֲשֶׁ֨ר יְיַסֵּ֥ר אִ֖ישׁ אֶת־בְּנ֑וֹ
like   when   he disciplines   man   that - his son

יְהוָ֥ה אֱלֹהֶ֖יךָ מְיַסְּרֶֽךָּ׃
ihvh   your Elohim   from disciplining you

5 Thou shalt also consider in thine heart, that, as a man chasteneth his son, so the

LORD thy God chasteneth thee.

וְשָׁמַרְתָּ אֶת־מִצְוֹת יְהֹוָה אֱלֹהֶיךָ
and you heed   commandments - that   ihvh   your Elohim

לָלֶכֶת בִּדְרָכָיו וּלְיִרְאָה אֹתוֹ:
to walk   in his ways   and to fear   to him

6 Therefore thou shalt keep the commandments of the LORD thy God, to walk in his ways, and to fear him.

כִּי יְהֹוָה אֱלֹהֶיךָ מְבִיאֲךָ אֶל־אֶרֶץ טוֹבָה
like   ihvh   your Elohim   bringing you   land - unto   good

אֶרֶץ נַחֲלֵי מַיִם עֲיָנֹת
land   brooks   waters   streams

וּתְהֹמֹת יֹצְאִים בַּבִּקְעָה וּבָהָר:
and springs   coming out ones   in valley   and in mountain

7 For the LORD thy God bringeth thee into a good land, a land of brooks of water, of fountains and depths that spring out of valleys and hills;

אֶרֶץ חִטָּה וּשְׂעֹרָה
land   wheat   and barley

וְגֶפֶן וּתְאֵנָה וְרִמּוֹן אֶרֶץ־זֵית שֶׁמֶן וּדְבָשׁ:
and vine   and fig tree   and pomegranate   olive - land   oil   and honey

8 A land of wheat, and barley, and vines, and fig trees, and pomegranates; a land of oil olive, and honey;

אֶרֶץ אֲשֶׁר לֹא בְמִסְכֵּנֻת תֹּאכַל־בָּהּ לֶחֶם
land   which   not   in scarcity   in it - you will eat   bread

לֹא־תֶחְסַר כֹּל בָּהּ אֶרֶץ אֲשֶׁר אֲבָנֶיהָ בַרְזֶל
you will lack - not   all   in it   land   which   its rocks   iron

וּמֵהֲרָרֶיהָ תַּחְצֹב נְחֹשֶׁת:
and from its mountains   you dig   copper

9 A land wherein thou shalt eat bread without scarceness, thou shalt not lack any thing in it; a land whose stones are iron, and out of whose hills thou mayest dig brass.

וְאָכַלְתָּ וְשָׂבָעְתָּ
and you eat   and you full

וּבֵרַכְתָּ אֶת־יְהֹוָה אֱלֹהֶיךָ עַל־הָאָרֶץ הַטֹּבָה אֲשֶׁר נָתַן־לָךְ:
and you will bless   ihvh - that   your Elohim   the land - upon   the good   which   to you - he gives

10 When thou hast eaten and art full, then thou shalt bless the LORD thy God for the good land which he hath given thee.

[שֵׁנִי]

הִשָּׁ֣מֶר לְךָ֔ פֶּן־תִּשְׁכַּ֖ח אֶת־יְהוָ֣ה אֱלֹהֶ֑יךָ לְבִלְתִּ֨י שְׁמֹ֤ר מִצְוֺתָיו֙
his commands heeding without your Elohim ihvh - that you forget - lest to you heed

וּמִשְׁפָּטָ֣יו וְחֻקֹּתָ֔יו אֲשֶׁ֛ר אָנֹכִ֥י מְצַוְּךָ֖ הַיּֽוֹם׃
the day commanding you I am which and his statutes and his judgments

11 Beware that thou forget not the LORD thy God, in not keeping his commandments, and his judgments, and his statutes, which I command thee this day:

פֶּן־תֹּאכַ֖ל וְשָׂבָ֑עְתָּ וּבָתִּ֥ים טֹבִ֛ים תִּבְנֶ֖ה וְיָשָֽׁבְתָּ׃
and you dwelt you built good ones and houses and you satisfied you eat - lest

12 Lest when thou hast eaten and art full, and hast built goodly houses, and dwelt therein;

וּבְקָֽרְךָ֤ וְצֹֽאנְךָ֙ יִרְבְּיֻ֔ן
they multiply and your flocks and in your herds

וְכֶ֤סֶף וְזָהָב֙ יִרְבֶּה־לָּ֔ךְ וְכֹ֥ל אֲשֶׁר־לְךָ֖ יִרְבֶּֽה׃
it multiplies to you - which and all to you - it increases and gold and silver

13 And when thy herds and thy flocks multiply, and thy silver and thy gold is multiplied, and all that thou hast is multiplied;

וְרָ֖ם לְבָבֶ֑ךָ וְשָֽׁכַחְתָּ֙ אֶת־יְהוָ֣ה אֱלֹהֶ֔יךָ
your Elohim ihvh - that and you forget your heart and high

הַמּוֹצִֽיאֲךָ֛ מֵאֶ֥רֶץ מִצְרַ֖יִם מִבֵּ֥ית עֲבָדִֽים׃
slaveries from house Egypt form land the one bringing out you

14 Then thine heart be lifted up, and thou forget the LORD thy God, which brought thee forth out of the land of Egypt, from the house of bondage;

הַמּוֹלִֽיכֲךָ֙ בַּמִּדְבָּ֣ר הַגָּדֹ֔ל
the great in wilderness the leading you

וְהַנּוֹרָ֗א נָחָ֤שׁ ׀ שָׂרָף֙ וְעַקְרָ֔ב וְצִמָּא֖וֹן
and drought and scorpion venomous snake and the awsome

אֲשֶׁ֣ר אֵֽין־מָ֑יִם הַמּוֹצִ֤יא לְךָ֙ מַ֔יִם מִצּ֖וּר הַֽחַלָּמִֽישׁ׃
the flint rock from rock waters to you the bringing out waters - isn't where

15 Who led thee through that great and terrible wilderness, wherein were fiery serpents, and scorpions, and drought, where there was no water; who brought thee forth water out of the rock of flint;

הַמַּֽאֲכִֽלְךָ֥ מָן֙ בַּמִּדְבָּ֔ר אֲשֶׁ֥ר לֹא־יָדְע֖וּן אֲבֹתֶ֑יךָ
your fathers you knew - not which in wilderness manna the feeding you

לְמַ֣עַן עַנֹּֽתְךָ֗ וּלְמַ֙עַן֙ נַסֹּתֶ֔ךָ לְהֵיטִֽבְךָ֖ בְּאַחֲרִיתֶֽךָ׃
in your afterwards to your benefit prove you and to end humbled you to end

16 Who fed thee in the wilderness with manna, which thy fathers knew not, that he might humble thee, and that he might prove thee, to do thee good at thy latter end;

וְאָמַרְתָּ֖ בִּלְבָבֶ֑ךָ כֹּחִי֙ וְעֹ֣צֶם יָדִ֔י עָ֥שָׂה לִ֖י אֶת־הַחַ֥יִל הַזֶּֽה:
the this   the wealth - that   to me   did   my hand   and might   my power   in your heart   and you may say

17 And thou say in thine heart, My power and the might of mine hand hath gotten me this wealth.

וְזָֽכַרְתָּ֙ אֶת־יְהוָ֣ה אֱלֹהֶ֔יךָ
your Elohim   ihvh - that   and you remember

כִּ֣י ה֗וּא הַנֹּתֵ֥ן לְךָ֛ כֹּ֖חַ לַעֲשׂ֣וֹת חָ֑יִל
wealth   to do   power   to you   the one giving   he   like

לְמַ֨עַן הָקִ֧ים אֶת־בְּרִית֛וֹ
his covenant - that   to establish   to end

אֲשֶׁר־נִשְׁבַּ֥ע לַאֲבֹתֶ֖יךָ כַּיּ֥וֹם הַזֶּֽה:
the this   like day   to your fathers   he swore - which

18 But thou shalt remember the LORD thy God: for it is he that giveth thee power to get wealth, that he may establish his covenant which he sware unto thy fathers, as it is this day.

פ

וְהָיָ֗ה אִם־שָׁכֹ֤חַ תִּשְׁכַּח֙ אֶת־יְהוָ֣ה אֱלֹהֶ֔יךָ
your Elohim   ihvh - that   you forget   forget - if   and it will be

וְהָֽלַכְתָּ֗ אַחֲרֵי֙ אֱלֹהִ֣ים אֲחֵרִ֔ים
other ones   elohim   after   and you go

וַעֲבַדְתָּ֖ם וְהִשְׁתַּחֲוִ֣יתָ לָהֶ֑ם
to them   and you bow down   and you serve them

הַעִדֹ֤תִי בָכֶם֙ הַיּ֔וֹם כִּ֥י אָבֹ֖ד תֹּאבֵדֽוּן:
you will perish   to perish   like   the day   in you   the I testify

19 And it shall be, if thou do at all forget the LORD thy God, and walk after other gods, and serve them, and worship them, I testify against you this day that ye shall surely perish.

כַּגּוֹיִ֗ם אֲשֶׁ֤ר יְהוָה֙ מַאֲבִ֣יד מִפְּנֵיכֶ֔ם
from before you   destroying   ihvh   which   like nations

כֵּ֖ן תֹּאבֵד֑וּן עֵ֚קֶב לֹ֣א תִשְׁמְע֔וּן בְּק֖וֹל יְהוָ֥ה אֱלֹהֵיכֶֽם:
your Elohim   ihvh   to voice   you hear   not   because   you will perish   thus

20 As the nations which the LORD destroyeth before your face, so shall ye perish; because ye would not be obedient unto the voice of the LORD your God.

פ

Chapter 9

ספר דברים פרק ט

שְׁמַע יִשְׂרָאֵל אַתָּה עֹבֵר הַיּוֹם אֶת־הַיַּרְדֵּן
hear   Israel   you   passing   the day   the Jordan - that

לָבֹא לָרֶשֶׁת גּוֹיִם גְּדֹלִים וַעֲצֻמִים מִמֶּךָּ
to come   to possess   nations   greater ones   and mightier ones   from you

עָרִים גְּדֹלֹת וּבְצֻרֹת בַּשָּׁמָיִם:
cities   great ones   and walls   in heavens

1 Hear, O Israel: Thou art to pass over Jordan this day, to go in to possess nations greater and mightier than thyself, cities great and fenced up to heaven,

עַם־גָּדוֹל וָרָם בְּנֵי עֲנָקִים אֲשֶׁר אַתָּה יָדַעְתָּ
great - people   and tall   sons   Anakims   which   you   you know

וְאַתָּה שָׁמַעְתָּ מִי יִתְיַצֵּב לִפְנֵי בְּנֵי־עֲנָק:
and you   you heard   who   he can stand   before   Anak - sons

2 A people great and tall, the children of the Anakims, whom thou knowest, and of whom thou hast heard say, Who can stand before the children of Anak!

וְיָדַעְתָּ הַיּוֹם כִּי יְהוָה אֱלֹהֶיךָ הוּא־הָעֹבֵר לְפָנֶיךָ
and you know   the day   like   ihvh   your Elohim   the one passing - he   before you

אֵשׁ אֹכְלָה הוּא יַשְׁמִידֵם וְהוּא יַכְנִיעֵם לְפָנֶיךָ
fire   consumes   he   he will destroy them   and he   he will bring down them   before you

וְהוֹרַשְׁתָּם וְהַאֲבַדְתָּם מַהֵר כַּאֲשֶׁר דִּבֶּר יְהוָה לָךְ:
and you will drive out them   and you will destroy them   quickly   when   spoke   ihvh   to you

3 Understand therefore this day, that the LORD thy God is he which goeth over before thee; as a consuming fire he shall destroy them, and he shall bring them down before thy face: so shalt thou drive them out, and destroy them quickly, as the LORD hath said unto thee.

[שלישי]

אַל־תֹּאמַר בִּלְבָבְךָ בַּהֲדֹף יְהוָה אֱלֹהֶיךָ אֹתָם מִלְּפָנֶיךָ
you say - don't   in your heart   in thrust   ihvh   your Elohim   to them   from before you

לֵאמֹר בְּצִדְקָתִי הֱבִיאַנִי יְהוָה לָרֶשֶׁת אֶת־הָאָרֶץ הַזֹּאת
to say   in my righteousness   he brought me   ihvh   to possess   the land that   the this

וּבְרִשְׁעַת הַגּוֹיִם הָאֵלֶּה יְהוָה מוֹרִישָׁם מִפָּנֶיךָ:
and in wickedness   the nations   the these   ihvh   driving them   from your prescence

4 Speak not thou in thine heart, after that the LORD thy God hath cast them out from before thee, saying, For my righteousness the LORD hath brought me in to possess this land: but for the wickedness of these nations the LORD doth drive them out from

before thee.

לֹא בְּצִדְקָתְךָ וּבְיֹשֶׁר לְבָבְךָ
not in your righteousness and in uprightness your heart

אַתָּה בָא לָרֶשֶׁת אֶת־אַרְצָם
you come to possess that - their land

כִּי בְּרִשְׁעַת הַגּוֹיִם הָאֵלֶּה יְהוָה אֱלֹהֶיךָ מוֹרִישָׁם מִפָּנֶיךָ
like in wickedness the nations the these ihvh your Elohim dirves them from your prescence

וּלְמַעַן הָקִים אֶת־הַדָּבָר אֲשֶׁר נִשְׁבַּע יְהוָה לַאֲבֹתֶיךָ
and to end confirm that - the matter which swore ihvh to your fathers

לְאַבְרָהָם לְיִצְחָק וּלְיַעֲקֹב׃
to Abraham to Isacc and to Jacob

5 Not for thy righteousness, or for the uprightness of thine heart, dost thou go to possess their land: but for the wickedness of these nations the LORD thy God doth drive them out from before thee, and that he may perform the word which the LORD sware unto thy fathers, Abraham, Isaac, and Jacob.

וְיָדַעְתָּ כִּי לֹא בְצִדְקָתְךָ יְהוָה אֱלֹהֶיךָ נֹתֵן לְךָ
and you understand like not in your righteousness ihvh your Elohim giving to you

אֶת־הָאָרֶץ הַטּוֹבָה הַזֹּאת לְרִשְׁתָּהּ
that the land the good the this to possess her

כִּי עַם־קְשֵׁה־עֹרֶף אָתָּה׃
like people stiff neck you

6 Understand therefore, that the LORD thy God giveth thee not this good land to possess it for thy righteousness; for thou art a stiff necked people.

זְכֹר אַל־תִּשְׁכַּח
remember don't - you forget

אֵת אֲשֶׁר־הִקְצַפְתָּ אֶת־יְהוָה אֱלֹהֶיךָ בַּמִּדְבָּר
that which - you provoked that - ihvh your Elohim in wilderness

לְמִן־הַיּוֹם אֲשֶׁר־יָצָאתָ מֵאֶרֶץ מִצְרַיִם
to end - the day which - you came out from land Egypt

עַד־בֹּאֲכֶם עַד־הַמָּקוֹם הַזֶּה
until - you came till - the place the this

מַמְרִים הֱיִיתֶם עִם־יְהוָה׃
rebelling ones you were with - ihvh

7 Remember, and forget not, how thou provokedst the LORD thy God to wrath in the wilderness: from the day that thou didst depart out of the land of Egypt, until ye came unto this place, ye have been rebellious against the LORD.

וּבְחֹרֵב הִקְצַפְתֶּם אֶת־יְהֹוָה
ihvh - that   you aroused wrath   and in Horeb

וַיִּתְאַנַּף יְהֹוָה בָּכֶם לְהַשְׁמִיד אֶתְכֶם:
that you   to destroy   in you   ihvh   and he was angry

8 Also in Horeb ye provoked the LORD to wrath, so that the LORD was angry with you to have destroyed you.

בַּעֲלֹתִי הָהָרָה לָקַחַת לוּחֹת הָאֲבָנִים לוּחֹת הַבְּרִית
the covenant   tables   the stones   tablets   to take   the mountain   in my going up

אֲשֶׁר־כָּרַת יְהֹוָה עִמָּכֶם
with you   ihvh   he cut - which

וָאֵשֵׁב בָּהָר אַרְבָּעִים יוֹם וְאַרְבָּעִים לַיְלָה
night   and forty   day   forty   in mountain   and I dwelled

לֶחֶם לֹא אָכַלְתִּי וּמַיִם לֹא שָׁתִיתִי:
I drank   not   and water   I ate   not   bread

9 When I was gone up into the mount to receive the tables of stone, even the tables of the covenant which the LORD made with you, then I abode in the mount forty days and forty nights, I neither did eat bread nor drink water:

וַיִּתֵּן יְהֹוָה אֵלַי אֶת־שְׁנֵי לוּחֹת הָאֲבָנִים
the stones   tablets   two - that   to me   ihvh   and gave

כְּתֻבִים בְּאֶצְבַּע אֱלֹהִים
Elhom   in finger   written ones

וַעֲלֵיהֶם כְּכָל־הַדְּבָרִים אֲשֶׁר דִּבֶּר יְהֹוָה עִמָּכֶם
with you   ihvh   spoke   which   the speakings - like all   and upon them

בָּהָר מִתּוֹךְ הָאֵשׁ בְּיוֹם הַקָּהָל:
the assembly   in day   the fire   midst   in mountain

10 And the LORD delivered unto me two tables of stone written with the finger of God; and on them was written according to all the words, which the LORD spake with you in the mount out of the midst of the fire in the day of the assembly.

וַיְהִי מִקֵּץ אַרְבָּעִים יוֹם וְאַרְבָּעִים לָיְלָה
night   and forty   day   forty   from end   and it was

נָתַן יְהֹוָה אֵלַי אֶת־שְׁנֵי לֻחֹת הָאֲבָנִים לֻחוֹת הַבְּרִית:
the covenant   tablets   the stones   tablets   two - that   unto me   ihvh   gave

11 And it came to pass at the end of forty days and forty nights, that the LORD gave me the two tables of stone, even the tables of the covenant.

וַיֹּאמֶר יְהֹוָה אֵלַי קוּם רֵד מַהֵר מִזֶּה
from this   from mountain   descend   rise   unto me   ihvh   and he told

EKEV - CHAPTER 9

כִּי שִׁחֵת עַמְּךָ אֲשֶׁר הוֹצֵאתָ מִמִּצְרָיִם
like corrupted your people which you brought out from Egypt

סָרוּ מַהֵר מִן־הַדֶּרֶךְ אֲשֶׁר צִוִּיתִם עָשׂוּ לָהֶם מַסֵּכָה׃
they turned quickly from - the way which I commanded them they do to them graven image

12 And the LORD said unto me, Arise, get thee down quickly from hence; for thy people which thou hast brought forth out of Egypt have corrupted themselves; they are quickly turned aside out of the way which I commanded them; they have made them a molten image.

וַיֹּאמֶר יְהוָה אֵלַי לֵאמֹר
and he said ihvh unto me to say

רָאִיתִי אֶת־הָעָם הַזֶּה וְהִנֵּה עַם־קְשֵׁה־עֹרֶף הוּא׃
I saw that - the people the this and here people - hard - neck it

13 Furthermore the LORD spake unto me, saying, I have seen this people, and, behold, it is a stiffnecked people:

הֶרֶף מִמֶּנִּי וְאַשְׁמִידֵם
hold back from me and I will destroy them

וְאֶמְחֶה אֶת־שְׁמָם מִתַּחַת הַשָּׁמָיִם
and I will blot out that - their name from under the heaven

וְאֶעֱשֶׂה אוֹתְךָ לְגוֹי־עָצוּם וָרָב מִמֶּנּוּ׃
and I will make you to nation - mighty and many from him

14 Let me alone, that I may destroy them, and blot out their name from under heaven: and I will make of thee a nation mightier and greater than they.

וָאֵפֶן וָאֵרֵד מִן־הָהָר וְהָהָר בֹּעֵר בָּאֵשׁ
and I turned and I descended from - the mountain and the mountain blazing in fire

וּשְׁנֵי לוּחֹת הַבְּרִית עַל שְׁתֵּי יָדָי׃
and two tablets the covenant upon my two hands

15 So I turned and came down from the mount, and the mount burned with fire: and the two tables of the covenant were in my two hands.

וָאֵרֶא וְהִנֵּה חֲטָאתֶם לַיהוָה אֱלֹהֵיכֶם
and I looked and here you sinned to ihvh your Elhohim

עֲשִׂיתֶם לָכֶם עֵגֶל מַסֵּכָה
you made to you calf graven image

סַרְתֶּם מַהֵר מִן־הַדֶּרֶךְ אֲשֶׁר־צִוָּה יְהוָה אֶתְכֶם׃
you turned quickly from - the way which - commanded ihvh that you

16 And I looked, and, behold, ye had sinned against the LORD your God, and had made you a molten calf: ye had turned aside quickly out of the way which the LORD

had commanded you.

וָאֶתְפֹּשׂ בִּשְׁנֵי הַלֻּחֹת
and I held *in two* *the tablets*

וָאַשְׁלִכֵם מֵעַל שְׁתֵּי יָדָי וָאֲשַׁבְּרֵם לְעֵינֵיכֶם׃
and I cast them *from upon* *two* *my hands* *and I broke them* *to your eyes*

17 And I took the two tables, and cast them out of my two hands, and brake them before your eyes.

וָאֶתְנַפַּל לִפְנֵי יהוה כָּרִאשֹׁנָה
and I fell *before* *ihvh* *like first*

אַרְבָּעִים יוֹם וְאַרְבָּעִים לָיְלָה
forty *day* *and forty* *night*

לֶחֶם לֹא אָכַלְתִּי וּמַיִם לֹא שָׁתִיתִי
bread *not* *I ate* *and water* *not* *I drank*

עַל כָּל־חַטֹּאתְכֶם אֲשֶׁר חֲטָאתֶם
upon *all - your sin* *which* *you sinned*

לַעֲשׂוֹת הָרַע בְּעֵינֵי יהוה לְהַכְעִיסוֹ׃
to do *the evil* *in eyes* *ihvh* *to kindle his anger*

18 And I fell down before the LORD, as at the first, forty days and forty nights: I did neither eat bread, nor drink water, because of all your sins which ye sinned, in doing wickedly in the sight of the LORD, to provoke him to anger.

כִּי יָגֹרְתִּי מִפְּנֵי הָאַף וְהַחֵמָה
like *I shrank* *from presence* *the anger* *and the wrath*

אֲשֶׁר קָצַף יהוה עֲלֵיכֶם לְהַשְׁמִיד אֶתְכֶם
which *stirred wrath* *ihvh* *upon you* *to destroy* *that you*

וַיִּשְׁמַע יהוה אֵלַי גַּם בַּפַּעַם הַהִוא׃
and he listened *ihvh* *unto me* *also* *in [this] time* *the it*

19 For I was afraid of the anger and hot displeasure, wherewith the LORD was wroth against you to destroy you. But the LORD hearkened unto me at that time also.

וּבְאַהֲרֹן הִתְאַנַּף יהוה מְאֹד לְהַשְׁמִידוֹ
and in Aaron *he was angry* *ihvh* *very* *to his destruction*

וָאֶתְפַּלֵּל גַּם־בְּעַד אַהֲרֹן בָּעֵת הַהִוא׃
and I prayed *also - in side* *Aaron* *in time* *the it*

20 And the LORD was very angry with Aaron to have destroyed him: and I prayed for Aaron also the same time.

וְאֶת־חַטַּאתְכֶם אֲשֶׁר־עֲשִׂיתֶם אֶת־הָעֵגֶל לָקַחְתִּי
you sinful - and that *you made - which* *the calf - that* *I took*

Ekev - Chapter 9

וָאֶשְׂרֹף אֹתוֹ בָּאֵשׁ
        in fire   to it   and I burned

וָאֶכֹּת אֹתוֹ טָחוֹן הֵיטֵב עַד אֲשֶׁר־דַּק לְעָפָר
to dust soft - which until the fine grinding to it and I pounding

וָאַשְׁלִךְ אֶת־עֲפָרוֹ אֶל־הַנַּחַל הַיֹּרֵד מִן־הָהָר׃
the mountain - from the descending the stream - unto it's dust - that and I threw

21 And I took your sin, the calf which ye had made, and burnt it with fire, and stamped it, and ground it very small, even until it was as small as dust: and I cast the dust thereof into the brook that descended out of the mount.

וּבְתַבְעֵרָה וּבְמַסָּה וּבְקִבְרֹת הַתַּאֲוָה
Hattaavah and in Kibroth and in Massah and at Taberah

מַקְצִפִים הֱיִיתֶם אֶת־יְהוָה׃
ihvh - that you were provoking ones

22 And at Taberah, and at Massah, and at Kibroth-hattaavah, ye provoked the LORD to wrath.

וּבִשְׁלֹחַ יְהוָה אֶתְכֶם מִקָּדֵשׁ בַּרְנֵעַ לֵאמֹר
to say Barnea from Kadesh that you ihvh and in sending

עֲלוּ וּרְשׁוּ אֶת־הָאָרֶץ אֲשֶׁר נָתַתִּי לָכֶם
to you I gave which the land - that and you posess you go up

וַתַּמְרוּ אֶת־פִּי יְהוָה אֱלֹהֵיכֶם וְלֹא הֶאֱמַנְתֶּם לוֹ
to him you believed and not your Elohim ihvh mouth - that and you say

וְלֹא שְׁמַעְתֶּם בְּקֹלוֹ׃
in his voice you listened and not

23 Likewise when the LORD sent you from Kadesh-barnea, saying, Go up and possess the land which I have given you; then ye rebelled against the commandment of the LORD your God, and ye believed him not, nor hearkened to his voice.

מַמְרִים הֱיִיתֶם עִם־יְהוָה מִיּוֹם דַּעְתִּי אֶתְכֶם׃
that you I knew from day ihvh - with you were rebelling ones

24 Ye have been rebellious against the LORD from the day that I knew you.

וָאֶתְנַפַּל לִפְנֵי יְהוָה
ihvh before and I fell

אֵת אַרְבָּעִים הַיּוֹם וְאֶת־אַרְבָּעִים הַלָּיְלָה
the night forty - and that the day forty - that

אֲשֶׁר הִתְנַפָּלְתִּי כִּי־אָמַר יְהוָה לְהַשְׁמִיד אֶתְכֶם׃
that you to destroy ihvh said - like I caused to fall which

25 Thus I fell down before the LORD forty days and forty nights, as I fell down at the first; because the LORD had said he would destroy you.

וָאֶתְפַּלֵּל אֶל־יְהוָה וָאֹמַר אֲדֹנָי יְהוִה
ihvh   Adoni   and said   ihvh - unto   and I prayed

אַל־תַּשְׁחֵת עַמְּךָ וְנַחֲלָתְךָ אֲשֶׁר פָּדִיתָ בְּגָדְלֶךָ
in your greatness   you redeemed   which   and your inheritance   your people   you destroy - don't

אֲשֶׁר־הוֹצֵאתָ מִמִּצְרַיִם בְּיָד חֲזָקָה׃
mighty   in hand   from Egypt   you brought out - which

26 I prayed therefore unto the LORD, and said, O Lord GOD, destroy not thy people and thine inheritance, which thou hast redeemed through thy greatness, which thou hast brought forth out of Egypt with a mighty hand.

זְכֹר לַעֲבָדֶיךָ לְאַבְרָהָם לְיִצְחָק וּלְיַעֲקֹב
and to Jacob   to Isaac   to Abraham   to your servants   remember

אַל־תֵּפֶן אֶל־קְשִׁי הָעָם הַזֶּה
the this   the people   stubbornness - unto   you facing - don't

וְאֶל־רִשְׁעוֹ וְאֶל־חַטָּאתוֹ׃
his sin - and unto   his wickedness - and unto

27 Remember thy servants, Abraham, Isaac, and Jacob; look not unto the stubbornness of this people, nor to their wickedness, nor to their sin:

פֶּן־יֹאמְרוּ הָאָרֶץ אֲשֶׁר הוֹצֵאתָנוּ מִשָּׁם
from there   you brought out us   which   the land   they will say - lest

מִבְּלִי יְכֹלֶת יְהוָה לַהֲבִיאָם אֶל־הָאָרֶץ אֲשֶׁר־דִּבֶּר לָהֶם
to them   he spoke - which   the land - unto   to bring them   ihvh   able   from without

וּמִשִּׂנְאָתוֹ אוֹתָם הוֹצִיאָם לַהֲמִתָם בַּמִּדְבָּר׃
in wilderness   to kill them   brought out them   to them   and from his hateing

28 Lest the land whence thou broughtest us out say, Because the LORD was not able to bring them into the land which he promised them, and because he hated them, he hath brought them out to slay them in the wilderness.

וְהֵם עַמְּךָ וְנַחֲלָתְךָ
and your inheritance   your people   and they

אֲשֶׁר הוֹצֵאתָ בְּכֹחֲךָ הַגָּדֹל וּבִזְרֹעֲךָ הַנְּטוּיָה׃
the outstretched   and in your arm   the great   in your power   you brought out   which

29 Yet they are thy people and thine inheritance, which thou broughtest out by thy mighty power and by thy stretched out arm.

פ

Chapter 9

ספר דברים פרק י

[רביעי]

בָּעֵת הַהִוא אָמַר יְהֹוָה אֵלַי
in time / the it / said / ihvh / unto me

פְּסָל־לְךָ שְׁנֵי־לוּחֹת אֲבָנִים כָּרִאשֹׁנִים
to you - chisel out / tablets - two / stones / like first ones

וַעֲלֵה אֵלַי הָהָרָה וְעָשִׂיתָ לְּךָ אֲרוֹן עֵץ׃
and ascend / unto me / the mountain / and you make / to you / chest / wood

1 At that time the LORD said unto me, Hew thee two tables of stone like unto the first, and come up unto me into the mount, and make thee an ark of wood.

וְאֶכְתֹּב עַל־הַלֻּחֹת אֶת־הַדְּבָרִים
and I will write / the tablets - upon / the speakings - that

אֲשֶׁר הָיוּ עַל־הַלֻּחֹת הָרִאשֹׁנִים
which / they were / the tables - upon / the first ones

אֲשֶׁר שִׁבַּרְתָּ וְשַׂמְתָּם בָּאָרוֹן׃
which / you broke / and you put them / in chest

2 And I will write on the tables the words that were in the first tables which thou brakest, and thou shalt put them in the ark.

וָאַעַשׂ אֲרוֹן עֲצֵי שִׁטִּים
and I made / chest / woods / shittim

וָאֶפְסֹל שְׁנֵי־לֻחֹת אֲבָנִים כָּרִאשֹׁנִים
and I chiseled / tablets - two / stones / like first ones

וָאַעַל הָהָרָה וּשְׁנֵי הַלֻּחֹת בְּיָדִי׃
and I ascended / the mountain / and two / the tablets / in my hand

3 And I made an ark of shittim wood, and hewed two tables of stone like unto the first, and went up into the mount, having the two tables in mine hand.

וַיִּכְתֹּב עַל־הַלֻּחֹת כַּמִּכְתָּב הָרִאשׁוֹן
and he wrote / the tablets - upon / like writings / the first

אֵת עֲשֶׂרֶת הַדְּבָרִים אֲשֶׁר דִּבֶּר יְהֹוָה אֲלֵיכֶם בָּהָר
that / ten / the speakings / which / spoke / ihvh / unto you / in mountain

מִתּוֹךְ הָאֵשׁ בְּיוֹם הַקָּהָל וַיִּתְּנֵם יְהֹוָה אֵלָי׃
midst / the fire / in day / the assembly / and he gave them / ihvh / unto me

4 And he wrote on the tables, according to the first writing, the ten commandments, which the LORD spake unto you in the mount out of the midst of the fire in the day

of the assembly: and the LORD gave them unto me.

וָאֵ֙פֶן֙ וָאֵרֵ֣ד מִן־הָהָ֔ר
and I turned   and I descended   the mountain - from

וָאָשִׂם֙ אֶת־הַלֻּחֹ֔ת בָּאָר֖וֹן אֲשֶׁ֣ר עָשִׂ֑יתִי
and I put   the tablets - that   in chest   which   I made

וַיִּ֣הְיוּ שָׁ֔ם כַּאֲשֶׁ֥ר צִוַּ֖נִי יְהוָֽה׃
and they were   there   when   commanded me   ihvh

5 And I turned myself and came down from the mount, and put the tables in the ark which I had made; and there they be, as the LORD commanded me.

וּבְנֵ֣י יִשְׂרָאֵ֗ל נָסְע֛וּ מִבְּאֵרֹ֥ת בְּנֵי־יַעֲקָ֖ן
and sons   Israel   they travelled   from wells   Jaakan sons

מוֹסֵרָ֑ה שָׁ֣ם מֵ֤ת אַהֲרֹן֙ וַיִּקָּבֵ֣ר שָׁ֔ם
Mosera   there   and he was buried   Aaron   he died   there

וַיְכַהֵ֛ן אֶלְעָזָ֥ר בְּנ֖וֹ תַּחְתָּֽיו׃
and he be priest   Elizar   his son   in his place

6 And the children of Israel took their journey from Beeroth of the children of Jaakan to Mosera: there Aaron died, and there he was buried; and Eleazar his son ministered in the priest's office in his stead.

מִשָּׁ֥ם נָסְע֖וּ הַגֻּדְגֹּ֑דָה
from there   they travelled   the Gudgodah

וּמִן־הַגֻּדְגֹּ֣דָה יָטְבָ֔תָה אֶ֖רֶץ נַ֥חֲלֵי מָֽיִם׃
the Gudgodah - and from   Jotbath   land   streams   water

7 From thence they journeyed unto Gudgodah; and from Gudgodah to Jotbath, a land of rivers of waters.

בָּעֵ֣ת הַהִ֗וא הִבְדִּ֤יל יְהוָה֙ אֶת־שֵׁ֣בֶט הַלֵּוִ֔י
in time   the it   he divided   ihvh   tribe - that   the Levi

לָשֵׂ֖את אֶת־אֲר֣וֹן בְּרִית־יְהוָ֑ה לַעֲמֹד֩ לִפְנֵ֨י יְהוָ֤ה
to carry   chest - that   ihvh - covenant   to stand   before   ihvh

לְשָֽׁרְתוֹ֙ וּלְבָרֵ֣ךְ בִּשְׁמ֔וֹ עַ֖ד הַיּ֥וֹם הַזֶּֽה׃
to his misistering   and to bless   in his name   till   the day   the this

8 At that time the LORD separated the tribe of Levi, to bear the ark of the covenant of the LORD, to stand before the LORD to minister unto him, and to bless in his name, unto this day.

עַל־כֵּ֞ן לֹֽא־הָיָ֧ה לְלֵוִ֛י חֵ֖לֶק
this - upon   it is - not   to Levi   portion

וְנַחֲלָה עִם־אֶחָיו יְהוָה הוּא נַחֲלָתוֹ
his inheritance he ihvh his brothers - with and inheritance

כַּאֲשֶׁר דִּבֶּר יְהוָה אֱלֹהֶיךָ לוֹ׃
to him your Elohim ihvh spoke when

9 Wherefore Levi hath no part nor inheritance with his brethren; the LORD is his inheritance, according as the LORD thy God promised him.

וְאָנֹכִי עָמַדְתִּי בָהָר כַּיָּמִים הָרִאשֹׁנִים
the first ones like days in mountain I standing and I am

אַרְבָּעִים יוֹם וְאַרְבָּעִים לָיְלָה
night and forty day forty

וַיִּשְׁמַע יְהוָה אֵלַי גַּם בַּפַּעַם הַהִוא
the it in time also unto me ihvh and he listened

לֹא־אָבָה יְהוָה הַשְׁחִיתֶךָ׃
the destroy you ihvh he come - not

10 And I stayed in the mount, according to the first time, forty days and forty nights; and the LORD hearkened unto me at that time also, and the LORD would not destroy thee.

וַיֹּאמֶר יְהוָה אֵלַי קוּם לֵךְ לְמַסַּע לִפְנֵי הָעָם
the people before to journey to go rise to me ihvh and he said

וְיָבֹאוּ וְיִירְשׁוּ אֶת־הָאָרֶץ
the land - that and they possess and they come

אֲשֶׁר־נִשְׁבַּעְתִּי לַאֲבֹתָם לָתֵת לָהֶם׃
to them to give to their fathers I swore - which

11 And the LORD said unto me, Arise, take thy journey before the people, that they may go in and possess the land, which I sware unto their fathers to give unto them.

פ

[חמישי]

וְעַתָּה יִשְׂרָאֵל מָה יְהוָה אֱלֹהֶיךָ שֹׁאֵל מֵעִמָּךְ
from with you asking your Elohim ihvh what Israel and now

כִּי אִם־לְיִרְאָה אֶת־יְהוָה אֱלֹהֶיךָ לָלֶכֶת בְּכָל־דְּרָכָיו
his ways - in all to walk your Elohim ihvh - that to fear - with like

וּלְאַהֲבָה אֹתוֹ וְלַעֲבֹד אֶת־יְהוָה אֱלֹהֶיךָ
your Elohim ihvh that and to serve to him and to love

בְּכָל־לְבָבְךָ וּבְכָל־נַפְשֶׁךָ׃
your soul - and in all your heart - in all

12 And now, Israel, what doth the LORD thy God require of thee, but to fear the LORD thy God, to walk in all his ways, and to love him, and to serve the LORD thy God with all thy heart and with all thy soul,

לִשְׁמֹר אֶת־מִצְוֺת יְהֹוָה וְאֶת־חֻקֹּתָיו
his statutes - and that   ihvh   commands - that   to heed

אֲשֶׁר אָנֹכִי מְצַוְּךָ הַיּוֹם לְטוֹב לָךְ׃
to you   to good   the day   commanding you   I am   which

13 To keep the commandments of the LORD, and his statutes, which I command thee this day for thy good?

הֵן לַיהֹוָה אֱלֹהֶיךָ הַשָּׁמַיִם
the heaven   your Elohim   to ihvh   thus

וּשְׁמֵי הַשָּׁמַיִם הָאָרֶץ וְכָל־אֲשֶׁר־בָּהּ׃
in her - which - and all   the earth   the heavens   and heaven

14 Behold, the heaven and the heaven of heavens is the LORD'S thy God, the earth also, with all that therein is.

רַק בַּאֲבֹתֶיךָ חָשַׁק יְהֹוָה לְאַהֲבָה אוֹתָם
to them   to love   ihvh   attached   in your fathers   only

וַיִּבְחַר בְּזַרְעָם אַחֲרֵיהֶם בָּכֶם
in you   after them   in their seed   and he chose

מִכָּל־הָעַמִּים כַּיּוֹם הַזֶּה׃
the this   like day   the nations - from all

15 Only the LORD had a delight in thy fathers to love them, and he chose their seed after them, even you above all people, as it is this day.

וּמַלְתֶּם אֵת עָרְלַת לְבַבְכֶם
your heart   foreskin   that   and you circumcise

וְעָרְפְּכֶם לֹא תַקְשׁוּ עוֹד׃
again   you make hard   not   and your neck

16 Circumcise therefore the foreskin of your heart, and be no more stiffnecked.

כִּי יְהֹוָה אֱלֹהֵיכֶם הוּא אֱלֹהֵי הָאֱלֹהִים
the Elohim   Elohim   he   your Elohim   ihvh   like

וַאֲדֹנֵי הָאֲדֹנִים הָאֵל הַגָּדֹל הַגִּבֹּר וְהַנּוֹרָא
and the awesome   the mighty   the great   the El   the Aonim   and Adoni

אֲשֶׁר לֹא־יִשָּׂא פָנִים וְלֹא יִקַּח שֹׁחַד׃
bribe   he takes   and not   faces   he lifts - not   which

17 For the LORD your God is God of gods, and Lord of lords, a great God, a mighty, and a terrible, which regardeth not persons, nor taketh reward:

עֹשֶׂה מִשְׁפַּט יָתוֹם וְאַלְמָנָה
and widow fatherless judgment he does

וְאֹהֵב גֵּר לָתֶת לוֹ לֶחֶם וְשִׂמְלָה׃
and clothing bread to him to give stranger and loves

18 He doth execute the judgment of the fatherless and widow, and loveth the stranger, in giving him food and raiment.

וַאֲהַבְתֶּם אֶת־הַגֵּר
the stranger - that and you love

כִּי־גֵרִים הֱיִיתֶם בְּאֶרֶץ מִצְרָיִם׃
Egypt in land you were strangers - like

19 Love ye therefore the stranger: for ye were strangers in the land of Egypt.

אֶת־יְהוָה אֱלֹהֶיךָ תִּירָא אֹתוֹ תַעֲבֹד
you serve to him you fear your Elohim ihvh - that

וּבוֹ תִדְבָּק וּבִשְׁמוֹ תִּשָּׁבֵעַ׃
you swear oath and in his name you cleave and to him

20 Thou shalt fear the LORD thy God; him shalt thou serve, and to him shalt thou cleave, and swear by his name.

הוּא תְהִלָּתְךָ וְהוּא אֱלֹהֶיךָ
you Elohim and he your praise he

אֲשֶׁר־עָשָׂה אִתְּךָ אֶת־הַגְּדֹלֹת וְאֶת־הַנּוֹרָאֹת הָאֵלֶּה
the these the awesome ones - and that the great ones - that with you he did - which

אֲשֶׁר רָאוּ עֵינֶיךָ׃
your eyes they saw which

21 He is thy praise, and he is thy God, that hath done for thee these great and terrible things, which thine eyes have seen.

בְּשִׁבְעִים נֶפֶשׁ יָרְדוּ אֲבֹתֶיךָ מִצְרָיְמָה
into Egypt your fathers they descended soul in seventy

וְעַתָּה שָׂמְךָ יְהוָה אֱלֹהֶיךָ
your Elohim ihvh put you and now

כְּכוֹכְבֵי הַשָּׁמַיִם לָרֹב׃
to many the skies like stars

22 Thy fathers went down into Egypt with threescore and ten persons; and now the LORD thy God hath made thee as the stars of heaven for multitude.

Chapter 11

ספר דברים פרק יא

וְאָהַבְתָּ֖ אֵ֣ת יְהוָ֣ה אֱלֹהֶ֑יךָ וְשָׁמַרְתָּ֣ מִשְׁמַרְתּ֗וֹ
and you love *that* *ihvh* *your Elohim* *and you heed* *his requirement*

וְחֻקֹּתָ֥יו וּמִשְׁפָּטָ֖יו וּמִצְוֺתָ֑יו כָּל־הַיָּמִֽים׃
and his statutes *and his laws* *and his commands* *all - the days*

1 Therefore thou shalt love the LORD thy God, and keep his charge, and his statutes, and his judgments, and his commandments, alway.

וִֽידַעְתֶּם֮ הַיּוֹם֒ כִּ֣י לֹ֤א אֶת־בְּנֵיכֶם֙
and you remember *the day* *like* *not* *that - your sons*

אֲשֶׁ֣ר לֹא־יָדְע֔וּ וַאֲשֶׁ֖ר לֹא־רָא֑וּ
which *not - they knew* *and which* *not - they saw*

אֶת־מוּסַ֖ר יְהוָ֣ה אֱלֹהֵיכֶ֑ם אֶת־גָּדְל֕וֹ
that - discipline *ihvh* *your Elohim* *that - his greatness*

אֶת־יָדוֹ֙ הַחֲזָקָ֔ה וּזְרֹע֖וֹ הַנְּטוּיָֽה׃
that - his hand *the mighty* *and his arm* *the outstretched*

2 And know ye this day: for I speak not with your children which have not known, and which have not seen the chastisement of the LORD your God, his greatness, his mighty hand, and his stretched out arm,

וְאֶת־אֹתֹתָיו֙ וְאֶֽת־מַעֲשָׂ֔יו
and that - his signs *and that - his deeds*

אֲשֶׁ֥ר עָשָׂ֖ה בְּת֣וֹךְ מִצְרָ֑יִם
which *he did* *in midst* *Egypt*

לְפַרְעֹ֥ה מֶֽלֶךְ־מִצְרַ֖יִם וּלְכָל־אַרְצֽוֹ׃
to Pharaoh *king - Egypt* *and to all - his land*

3 And his miracles, and his acts, which he did in the midst of Egypt unto Pharaoh the king of Egypt, and unto all his land;

וַאֲשֶׁ֣ר עָשָׂה֩ לְחֵ֨יל מִצְרַ֜יִם לְסוּסָ֣יו וּלְרִכְבּ֗וֹ
and what *he did* *to army* *Egypt* *to his horses* *and to his chariots*

אֲשֶׁ֨ר הֵצִ֜יף אֶת־מֵ֤י יַם־סוּף֙ עַל־פְּנֵיהֶ֔ם בְּרָדְפָ֖ם אַחֲרֵיכֶ֑ם
which *he caused flow* *that - waters* *sea - end* *upon - their faces* *in their pursuing* *after you*

וַיְאַבְּדֵ֣ם יְהוָ֔ה עַ֖ד הַיּ֥וֹם הַזֶּֽה׃
and destroyed them *ihvh* *till* *the day* *to this*

4 And what he did unto the army of Egypt, unto their horses, and to their chariots; how he made the water of the Red sea to overflow them as they pursued after you, and how the LORD hath destroyed them unto this day;

Ekev - Chapter 11

וַאֲשֶׁ֧ר עָשָׂ֣ה לָכֶ֣ם בַּמִּדְבָּ֗ר עַד־בֹּאֲכֶ֖ם עַד־הַמָּק֥וֹם הַזֶּֽה׃
and which he did to you in desert till to come you till the place the this

5 And what he did unto you in the wilderness, until ye came into this place;

וַאֲשֶׁ֨ר עָשָׂ֜ה לְדָתָ֣ן וְלַאֲבִירָ֗ם בְּנֵ֣י אֱלִיאָ֖ב בֶּן־רְאוּבֵ֑ן
and which he did to Dathan and to Abram sons Eliab Reuben - son

אֲשֶׁ֨ר פָּצְתָ֤ה הָאָ֙רֶץ֙ אֶת־פִּ֔יהָ וַתִּבְלָעֵ֥ם
which opened the earth that - her mouth and swallowed them

וְאֶת־בָּתֵּיהֶ֖ם וְאֶת־אָהֳלֵיהֶ֑ם וְאֵ֤ת כָּל־הַיְקוּם֙
that - their house and that - their tents and that - all the substance

אֲשֶׁ֣ר בְּרַגְלֵיהֶ֔ם בְּקֶ֖רֶב כָּל־יִשְׂרָאֵֽל׃
which in their feet in midst all - Israel

6 And what he did unto Dathan and Abiram, the sons of Eliab, the son of Reuben: how the earth opened her mouth, and swallowed them up, and their households, and their tents, and all the substance that was in their possession, in the midst of all Israel:

כִּ֤י עֵֽינֵיכֶם֙ הָֽרֹאֹ֔ת אֶת־כָּל־מַעֲשֵׂ֥ה יְהוָ֖ה הַגָּדֹ֑ל אֲשֶׁ֥ר עָשָֽׂה׃
like your eyes the ones seeing that act - all ihvh the great which he did

7 But your eyes have seen all the great acts of the LORD which he did.

וּשְׁמַרְתֶּם֙ אֶת־כָּל־הַמִּצְוָ֔ה
and you observe that - all - the command

אֲשֶׁ֛ר אָנֹכִ֥י מְצַוְּךָ֖ הַיּ֑וֹם לְמַ֣עַן תֶּחֶזְק֗וּ
which I am commanding you the day to end you will be strong

וּבָאתֶם֙ וִֽירִשְׁתֶּ֣ם אֶת־הָאָ֔רֶץ
and you come and you possess that - the land

אֲשֶׁ֥ר אַתֶּ֛ם עֹבְרִ֥ים שָׁ֖מָּה לְרִשְׁתָּֽהּ׃
which you passing ones towards there to possess it

8 Therefore shall ye keep all the commandments which I command you this day, that ye may be strong, and go in and possess the land, whither ye go to possess it;

וּלְמַ֨עַן תַּאֲרִ֤יכוּ יָמִים֙ עַל־הָ֣אֲדָמָ֔ה
and to end you will live long in days upon - the land

אֲשֶׁר֩ נִשְׁבַּ֨ע יְהוָ֧ה לַאֲבֹתֵיכֶ֛ם
which swore ihvh to your fathers

לָתֵ֥ת לָהֶ֖ם וּלְזַרְעָ֑ם אֶ֛רֶץ זָבַ֥ת חָלָ֖ב וּדְבָֽשׁ׃
to give to them and to their seed land flowing milk and honey

9 And that ye may prolong your days in the land, which the LORD sware unto your fathers to give unto them and to their seed, a land that floweth with milk and honey.

ס

[ששי]

כִּי הָאָרֶץ אֲשֶׁר אַתָּה בָא־שָׁמָּה לְרִשְׁתָּהּ
like the land which you to there - come to possess it

לֹא כְאֶרֶץ מִצְרַיִם הִוא אֲשֶׁר יְצָאתֶם מִשָּׁם
not like land Egypt it which you came out from there

אֲשֶׁר תִּזְרַע אֶת־זַרְעֲךָ וְהִשְׁקִיתָ בְרַגְלְךָ כְּגַן הַיָּרָק׃
which you sowed seed your - that and you irrigated in your foot like garden the vegitation

10 For the land, whither thou goest in to possess it, is not as the land of Egypt, from whence ye came out, where thou sowedst thy seed, and wateredst it with thy foot, as a garden of herbs:

וְהָאָרֶץ אֲשֶׁר אַתֶּם עֹבְרִים שָׁמָּה לְרִשְׁתָּהּ
and the land which you passing there to possess

אֶרֶץ הָרִים וּבְקָעֹת לִמְטַר הַשָּׁמַיִם תִּשְׁתֶּה־מָּיִם׃
land mountains and valleys to rain the heavens water - it drinks

11 But the land, whither ye go to possess it, is a land of hills and valleys, and drinketh water of the rain of heaven:

אֶרֶץ אֲשֶׁר־יְהוָה אֱלֹהֶיךָ דֹּרֵשׁ אֹתָהּ
land which - ihvh your Elohim inquiring to you

תָּמִיד עֵינֵי יְהוָה אֱלֹהֶיךָ בָּהּ
continually eyes ihvh your Elhohim in her

מֵרֵשִׁית הַשָּׁנָה וְעַד אַחֲרִית שָׁנָה׃
from beginning the year and till end year

12 A land which the LORD thy God careth for: the eyes of the LORD thy God are always upon it, from the beginning of the year even unto the end of the year.

ס

וְהָיָה אִם־שָׁמֹעַ תִּשְׁמְעוּ אֶל־מִצְוֺתַי
and it will be listen - if you listen it unto - my commandments

אֲשֶׁר אָנֹכִי מְצַוֶּה אֶתְכֶם הַיּוֹם לְאַהֲבָה אֶת־יְהוָה אֱלֹהֵיכֶם
which I am commanding that you the day to love that - ihvh you Elohim

וּלְעָבְדוֹ בְּכָל־לְבַבְכֶם וּבְכָל־נַפְשְׁכֶם׃
and to serve him in all - you heart and in all - your soul

13 And it shall come to pass, if ye shall hearken diligently unto my commandments which I command you this day, to love the LORD your God, and to serve him with all your heart and with all your soul,

Ekev - Chapter 11

וְנָתַתִּי מְטַר־אַרְצְכֶם בְּעִתּוֹ יוֹרֶה וּמַלְקוֹשׁ
and I will give   rain - land you   in his season   first rain   and latter rain

וְאָסַפְתָּ דְגָנֶךָ וְתִירֹשְׁךָ וְיִצְהָרֶךָ׃
and you will gather   your grain   and new wine   and your oil

14 That I will give you the rain of your land in his due season, the first rain and the latter rain, that thou mayest gather in thy corn, and thy wine, and thine oil.

וְנָתַתִּי עֵשֶׂב בְּשָׂדְךָ לִבְהֶמְתֶּךָ וְאָכַלְתָּ וְשָׂבָעְתָּ׃
and I will give   grass   in your field   to your cattle   and you will eat   and you will be satisfied

15 And I will send grass in thy fields for thy cattle, that thou mayest eat and be full.

הִשָּׁמְרוּ לָכֶם פֶּן־יִפְתֶּה לְבַבְכֶם וְסַרְתֶּם
be heedful   to you   it turn - lest   your heart   and you depart

וַעֲבַדְתֶּם אֱלֹהִים אֲחֵרִים וְהִשְׁתַּחֲוִיתֶם לָהֶם׃
and you worship   elohim   other ones   and you will bow   to them

16 Take heed to yourselves, that your heart be not deceived, and ye turn aside, and serve other gods, and worship them;

וְחָרָה אַף־יְהוָה בָּכֶם וְעָצַר אֶת־הַשָּׁמַיִם
and will burn   ihvh - anger   in you   and he will shut   the heavens - that

וְלֹא־יִהְיֶה מָטָר וְהָאֲדָמָה לֹא תִתֵּן אֶת־יְבוּלָהּ
and not - it wil be   rain   and the ground   not   it give   its produce - that

וַאֲבַדְתֶּם מְהֵרָה מֵעַל הָאָרֶץ הַטֹּבָה אֲשֶׁר יְהוָה נֹתֵן לָכֶם׃
and you perish   quickly   from upon   the land   the good   which   ihvh   gives   to you

17 And then the LORD'S wrath be kindled against you, and he shut up the heaven, that there be no rain, and that the land yield not her fruit; and lest ye perish quickly from off the good land which the LORD giveth you.

וְשַׂמְתֶּם אֶת־דְּבָרַי אֵלֶּה עַל־לְבַבְכֶם וְעַל־נַפְשְׁכֶם
and you put   that - my speakings   these   upon - your heart   and upon - your soul

וּקְשַׁרְתֶּם אֹתָם לְאוֹת עַל־יֶדְכֶם
and you bind   to them   to sign   upon - your hand

וְהָיוּ לְטוֹטָפֹת בֵּין עֵינֵיכֶם׃
and they be   to frontlets   between   your eyes

18 Therefore shall ye lay up these my words in yo ur heart and in your soul, and bind them for a sign upon your hand, that they may be as frontlets between your eyes.

וְלִמַּדְתֶּם אֹתָם אֶת־בְּנֵיכֶם לְדַבֵּר בָּם בְּשִׁבְתְּךָ בְּבֵיתֶךָ
and you teach   to them   that - you sons   to speak   in them   to your siting   in your house

וּבְלֶכְתְּךָ בַדֶּרֶךְ וּבְשָׁכְבְּךָ וּבְקוּמֶךָ׃
and in your walking   in road   and in your lying down   and in your getting up

19 And ye shall teach them your children, speaking of them when thou sittest in thine house, and when thou walkest by the way, when thou liest down, and when thou risest up.

וּכְתַבְתָּ֛ם עַל־מְזוּז֥וֹת בֵּיתֶ֖ךָ וּבִשְׁעָרֶֽיךָ׃
and you write them   door posts - upon   your your house   and in your gates

20 And thou shalt write them upon the door posts of thine house, and upon thy gates:

לְמַ֨עַן יִרְבּ֜וּ יְמֵיכֶ֣ם וִימֵ֣י בְנֵיכֶ֗ם עַ֚ל הָ֣אֲדָמָ֔ה
to end   they will be many   your days   and day your sons   upon   the ground

אֲשֶׁ֨ר נִשְׁבַּ֧ע יְהוָ֛ה לַאֲבֹתֵיכֶ֖ם
which   swore   ihvh   to your fathers

לָתֵ֣ת לָהֶ֑ם כִּימֵ֥י הַשָּׁמַ֖יִם עַל־הָאָֽרֶץ׃
to give   to them   like days   the heaven   the earth - upon

21 That your days may be multiplied, and the days of your children, in the land which the LORD sware unto your fathers to give them, as the days of heaven upon the earth.

ס

[שביעי] [מפטיר]

כִּי֩ אִם־שָׁמֹ֨ר תִּשְׁמְר֜וּן אֶת־כָּל־הַמִּצְוָ֣ה הַזֹּ֗את
like   heed - if   you heed it   that - all - the commandments   the this

אֲשֶׁ֧ר אָנֹכִ֛י מְצַוֶּ֥ה אֶתְכֶ֖ם לַעֲשׂתָ֑הּ
which   I am   commanding   that you   to do them

לְאַהֲבָ֞ה אֶת־יְהוָ֤ה אֱלֹהֵיכֶם֙
to love   ihvh - that   your Elohim

לָלֶ֥כֶת בְּכָל־דְּרָכָ֖יו וּלְדָבְקָה־בֽוֹ׃
to walk   in all - his ways   and to cleave - in him

22 For if ye shall diligently keep all these commandments which I command you, to do them, to love the LORD your God, to walk in all his ways, and to cleave unto him;

וְהוֹרִ֧ישׁ יְהוָ֛ה אֶת־כָּל־הַגּוֹיִ֥ם הָאֵ֖לֶּה מִלִּפְנֵיכֶ֑ם
and will drive out   ihvh   that - all - the nations   the these   from before you

וִֽירִשְׁתֶּ֣ם גּוֹיִ֔ם גְּדֹלִ֥ים וַעֲצֻמִ֖ים מִכֶּֽם׃
and you will possess   nations   greater ones   and mighty ones   from you

23 Then will the LORD drive out all these nations from before you, and ye shall possess greater nations and mightier than yourselves.

כָּל־הַמָּק֗וֹם אֲשֶׁ֨ר תִּדְרֹ֧ךְ כַּֽף־רַגְלְכֶ֛ם בּ֖וֹ
the place- all   which   she drives   your foot - sole   in it

Ekev - Chapter 11

לָכֶ֣ם יִהְיֶ֔ה מִן־הַמִּדְבָּ֨ר וְהַלְּבָנ֜וֹן מִן־הַנָּהָ֣ר נְהַר־פְּרָ֗ת
to you · it will be · the wilderness - from · and the Lebanon · the river - from · Euphrates - river

וְעַד֙ הַיָּ֣ם הָאַחֲר֔וֹן יִהְיֶ֖ה גְּבֻלְכֶֽם׃
and till · the sea · afterwards · it will be · your borders

24 Every place whereon the soles of your feet shall tread shall be yours: from the wilderness and Lebanon, from the river, the river Euphrates, even unto the uttermost sea shall your coast be.

לֹא־יִתְיַצֵּ֥ב אִ֖ישׁ בִּפְנֵיכֶ֑ם
not - he will stand · man · in before you

פַּחְדְּכֶ֣ם וּמֽוֹרַאֲכֶ֗ם יִתֵּ֣ן ׀ יְהוָ֣ה אֱלֹֽהֵיכֶ֗ם עַל־פְּנֵ֤י כָל־הָאָ֨רֶץ֙
your terror · and your fear · he gives · · your Elohim · upon - face · all - the land

אֲשֶׁ֣ר תִּדְרְכוּ־בָ֔הּ כַּאֲשֶׁ֖ר דִּבֶּ֥ר לָכֶֽם׃
which · in - you drive it · when · he spoke · to you

25 There shall no man be able to stand before you: for the LORD your God shall lay the fear of you and the dread of you upon all the land that ye shall tread upon, as he hath said unto you.

ס ס ס

Rehei

Chapter 11 cont

[פרשת ראה]

רְאֵה אָנֹכִי נֹתֵן לִפְנֵיכֶם הַיּוֹם בְּרָכָה וּקְלָלָה:
see   I am   giving   before you   the day   blessing   and curse

26 Behold, I set before you this day a blessing and a curse;

אֶת־הַבְּרָכָה אֲשֶׁר תִּשְׁמְעוּ אֶל־מִצְוֹת יְהוָה אֱלֹהֵיכֶם
that - the blessing   which   you heed it   commandments - unto   ihvh   your Elohim

אֲשֶׁר אָנֹכִי מְצַוֶּה אֶתְכֶם הַיּוֹם:
that   I am   commanding   that you   the day

27 A blessing, if ye obey the commandments of the LORD your God, which I command you this day:

וְהַקְּלָלָה אִם־לֹא תִשְׁמְעוּ אֶל־מִצְוֹת יְהוָה אֱלֹהֵיכֶם
and the curse   if - not   you heed it   commandments - unto   ihvh   your Elohim

וְסַרְתֶּם מִן־הַדֶּרֶךְ אֲשֶׁר אָנֹכִי מְצַוֶּה אֶתְכֶם הַיּוֹם
and you turn   from - the way   which   I am   commanding   that you   the day

לָלֶכֶת אַחֲרֵי אֱלֹהִים אֲחֵרִים אֲשֶׁר לֹא־יְדַעְתֶּם:
to go   after   elohim   other ones   which   not - you knew

28 And a curse, if ye will not obey the commandments of the LORD your God, but turn aside out of the way which I command you this day, to go after other gods, which ye have not known.

ס

וְהָיָה כִּי יְבִיאֲךָ יְהוָה אֱלֹהֶיךָ אֶל־הָאָרֶץ
and it will be   like   brings you   ihvh   your Elohim   unto - the land

אֲשֶׁר־אַתָּה בָא־שָׁמָּה לְרִשְׁתָּהּ
which - you   come - to there   to possess it

וְנָתַתָּה אֶת־הַבְּרָכָה עַל־הַר גְּרִזִים
and you give   that - the blessing   upon - mountain   Gerizim

וְאֶת־הַקְּלָלָה עַל־הַר עֵיבָל:
that - the curse   upon - mountain   Ebal

29 And it shall come to pass, when the LORD thy God hath brought thee in unto the land whither thou goest to possess it, that thou shalt put the blessing upon mount Gerizim, and the curse upon mount Ebal.

הֲלֹא־הֵמָּה בְּעֵבֶר הַיַּרְדֵּן אַחֲרֵי דֶּרֶךְ מְבוֹא הַשָּׁמֶשׁ
not - they are   in across   the Jordan   after   way   sets   the sun

בְּאֶרֶץ הַכְּנַעֲנִי הַיֹּשֵׁב בָּעֲרָבָה מוּל הַגִּלְגָּל אֵצֶל אֵלוֹנֵי מֹרֶה:
Moreh   plains   side of   the Gilgal   vicinity   in Arabah   the dwelling   the Canaanite   in land

30 Are they not on the other side Jordan, by the way where the sun goeth down, in the land of the Canaanites, which dwell in the champaign over against Gilgal, beside the plains of Moreh?

כִּי אַתֶּם עֹבְרִים אֶת־הַיַּרְדֵּן לָבֹא לָרֶשֶׁת אֶת־הָאָרֶץ
the land - that   to possess   to come   the Jordan - that   passing ones   you   like

אֲשֶׁר־יְהוָה אֱלֹהֵיכֶם נֹתֵן לָכֶם
to you   given   your Elohim   ihvh - which

וִירִשְׁתֶּם אֹתָהּ וִישַׁבְתֶּם־בָּהּ:
in it - and you dwell   to it   and you possess

31 For ye shall pass over Jordan to go in to possess the land which the LORD your God giveth you, and ye shall possess it, and dwell therein.

וּשְׁמַרְתֶּם לַעֲשׂוֹת אֵת כָּל־הַחֻקִּים
the statutes - all   that   to do   and you will heed

וְאֶת־הַמִּשְׁפָּטִים אֲשֶׁר אָנֹכִי נֹתֵן לִפְנֵיכֶם הַיּוֹם:
the day   before you   giving   I am   which   the judgments - and that

32 And ye shall observe to do all the statutes and judgments which I set before you this day.

Chapter 12

ספר דברים פרק יב

אֵלֶּה הַחֻקִּים וְהַמִּשְׁפָּטִים אֲשֶׁר תִּשְׁמְרוּן לַעֲשׂוֹת בָּאָרֶץ
in land   to do   you will heed   which   and the judgments   the statutes   these

אֲשֶׁר נָתַן יְהוָה אֱלֹהֵי אֲבֹתֶיךָ לָךְ
to you   your fathers   Elohim   ihvh   gave   which

לְרִשְׁתָּהּ כָּל־הַיָּמִים אֲשֶׁר־אַתֶּם חַיִּים עַל־הָאֲדָמָה:
the ground - upon   alive   that you - which   the days - all   to possess her

1 These are the statutes and judgments, which ye shall observe to do in the land, which the LORD God of thy fathers giveth thee to possess it, all the days that ye live upon the earth.

אַבֵּד תְּאַבְּדוּן אֶת־כָּל־הַמְּקֹמוֹת אֲשֶׁר עָבְדוּ־שָׁם הַגּוֹיִם
the nations   there - they served   which   the places - all - that   you will destroy   destroy

אֲשֶׁר אַתֶּם יֹרְשִׁים אֹתָם אֶת־אֱלֹהֵיהֶם
your Elohim - that   to them   possessing ones   you   which

עַל־הֶהָרִים הָרָמִים וְעַל־הַגְּבָעוֹת וְתַחַת כָּל־עֵץ רַעֲנָן:
flourishing   tree all   and under   the hills - and upon   the high ones   the mountains - upon

2 Ye shall utterly destroy all the places, wherein the nations which ye shall possess served their gods, upon the high mountains, and upon the hills, and under every green tree:

וְנִתַּצְתֶּם אֶת־מִזְבְּחֹתָם וְשִׁבַּרְתֶּם אֶת־מַצֵּבֹתָם
their pillars - that and you smash their altars - that and you break down

וַאֲשֵׁרֵיהֶם תִּשְׂרְפוּן בָּאֵשׁ
in fire you burn and their happiness

וּפְסִילֵי אֱלֹהֵיהֶם תְּגַדֵּעוּן
you chop down their elohim and idols

וְאִבַּדְתֶּם אֶת־שְׁמָם מִן־הַמָּקוֹם הַהוּא׃
the that the place - from their names - that and you wipe out

3 And ye shall overthrow their altars, and break their pillars, and burn their groves with fire; and ye shall hew down the graven images of their gods, and destroy the names of them out of that place.

לֹא־תַעֲשׂוּן כֵּן לַיהוָה אֱלֹהֵיכֶם׃
your Elohim to ihvh thus you will do - not

4 Ye shall not do so unto the LORD your God.

כִּי אִם־אֶל־הַמָּקוֹם אֲשֶׁר־יִבְחַר יְהוָה אֱלֹהֵיכֶם
your Elohim ihvh he will choose - which the place - unto - with like

מִכָּל־שִׁבְטֵיכֶם לָשׂוּם אֶת־שְׁמוֹ שָׁם
there his name - that to put your tribes - from all

לְשִׁכְנוֹ תִדְרְשׁוּ וּבָאתָ שָׁמָּה׃
to there and you come you will seek to his dwelling

5 But unto the place which the LORD your God shall choose out of all your tribes to put his name there, even unto his habitation shall ye seek, and thither thou shalt come:

וַהֲבֵאתֶם שָׁמָּה עֹלֹתֵיכֶם וְזִבְחֵיכֶם
and your sacrifices your burnt offerings to there and will you bring

וְאֵת מַעְשְׂרֹתֵיכֶם וְאֵת תְּרוּמַת יֶדְכֶם
your hand heave offering and that your tithes and that

וְנִדְרֵיכֶם וְנִדְבֹתֵיכֶם וּבְכֹרֹת בְּקַרְכֶם וְצֹאנְכֶם׃
and your flock your herd and first born ones and your free will offerings and your vows

6 And thither ye shall bring your burnt offerings, and your sacrifices, and your tithes, and heave offerings of your hand, and your vows, and your freewill offerings, and the firstlings of your herds and of your flocks:

וַאֲכַלְתֶּם־שָׁם לִפְנֵי יְהוָה אֱלֹהֵיכֶם
your Elohim ihvh before there - and you eat

וּשְׂמַחְתֶּם בְּכֹל מִשְׁלַח יֶדְכֶם אַתֶּם וּבָתֵּיכֶם
and household   you   you hand   your handiwork   in all   and you be happy

אֲשֶׁר בֵּרַכְךָ יְהֹוָה אֱלֹהֶיךָ:
your Elohim   ihvh   blessed you   which

7 And there ye shall eat before the LORD your God, and ye shall rejoice in all that ye put your hand unto, ye and your households, wherein the LORD thy God hath blessed thee.

לֹא תַעֲשׂוּן כְּכֹל אֲשֶׁר אֲנַחְנוּ עֹשִׂים פֹּה הַיּוֹם
the day   here   doing ones   we   which   like all   you do   not

אִישׁ כָּל־הַיָּשָׁר בְּעֵינָיו:
in his eyes   the upright - all   man

8 Ye shall not do after all the things that we do here this day, every man whatsoever is right in his own eyes.

כִּי לֹא־בָאתֶם עַד־עָתָּה אֶל־הַמְּנוּחָה
the resting place - unto   now - till   you come - not   like

וְאֶל־הַנַּחֲלָה אֲשֶׁר־יְהֹוָה אֱלֹהֶיךָ נֹתֵן לָךְ:
to you   gives   your Elohim   ihvh - which   the inheritance - and unto

9 For ye are not as yet come to the rest and to the inheritance, which the LORD your God giveth you.

וַעֲבַרְתֶּם אֶת־הַיַּרְדֵּן וִישַׁבְתֶּם בָּאָרֶץ
in land   and you will dwell   the Jordan - that   and you will pass

אֲשֶׁר־יְהֹוָה אֱלֹהֵיכֶם מַנְחִיל אֶתְכֶם
that you   bequeaths   your Elohim   ihvh - which

וְהֵנִיחַ לָכֶם מִכָּל־אֹיְבֵיכֶם מִסָּבִיב וִישַׁבְתֶּם־בֶּטַח:
safely - and you will dwell   from around   your enemies - from all   to you   and he gives rest

10 But *when* ye go over Jordan, and dwell in the land which the LORD your God giveth you to inherit, and *when* he giveth you rest from all your enemies round about, so that ye dwell in safety;

[שני]

וְהָיָה הַמָּקוֹם
the place   and it will be

אֲשֶׁר־יִבְחַר יְהֹוָה אֱלֹהֵיכֶם בּוֹ לְשַׁכֵּן שְׁמוֹ שָׁם
there   his name   to dwell   in him   your Elohim   ihvh   he will choose - which

שָׁמָּה תָבִיאוּ אֵת כָּל־אֲשֶׁר אָנֹכִי מְצַוֶּה אֶתְכֶם
that you   commanding   I am   which - all   that   you bring   to there

עוֹלֹתֵיכֶם֙ וְזִבְחֵיכֶ֔ם מַעְשְׂרֹ֣תֵיכֶ֔ם וּתְרֻמַ֖ת יֶדְכֶ֑ם
your burnt offerings and your sacrifices your tithes and heave offerings your hand

וְכֹל֙ מִבְחַ֣ר נִדְרֵיכֶ֔ם אֲשֶׁ֥ר תִּדְּר֖וּ לַיהוָֽה׃
and all choice your vow offerings which you vowed to ihvh

11 Then there shall be a place which the LORD your God shall choose to cause his name to dwell there; thither shall ye bring all that I command you; your burnt offerings, and your sacrifices, your tithes, and the heave offering of your hand, and all your choice vows which ye vow unto the LORD:

וּשְׂמַחְתֶּ֗ם לִפְנֵי֙ יְהוָ֣ה אֱלֹֽהֵיכֶ֔ם אַתֶּ֑ם
and you will rejoice before ihvh your Elohim that you

וּבְנֵיכֶ֣ם וּבְנֹתֵיכֶ֔ם וְעַבְדֵיכֶ֖ם וְאַמְהֹתֵיכֶ֑ם
and your sons and your daughters and your menservants and your maidservants

וְהַלֵּוִי֙ אֲשֶׁ֣ר בְּשַׁעֲרֵיכֶ֔ם
and the Levite which in gates you

כִּ֣י אֵ֥ין ל֛וֹ חֵ֥לֶק וְנַחֲלָ֖ה אִתְּכֶֽם׃
like isn't to him allotment and inheritance with you

12 And ye shall rejoice before the LORD your God, ye, and your sons, and your daughters, and your menservants, and your maidservants, and the Levite that is within your gates; forasmuch as he hath no part nor inheritance with you.

הִשָּׁ֣מֶר לְךָ֔ פֶּֽן־תַּעֲלֶ֖ה עֹלֹתֶ֑יךָ בְּכָל־מָק֖וֹם אֲשֶׁ֥ר תִּרְאֶֽה׃
cause to heed to you lest - you sacrifice your burnt offerings place - in all which you see

13 Take heed to thyself that thou offer not thy burnt offerings in every place that thou seest:

כִּ֣י אִם־בַּמָּק֗וֹם אֲשֶׁר־יִבְחַ֤ר יְהוָה֙ בְּאַחַ֣ד שְׁבָטֶ֔יךָ
like if - in place which - he will choose ihvh in one your tribes

שָׁ֖ם תַּעֲלֶ֣ה עֹלֹתֶ֑יךָ וְשָׁ֣ם תַּעֲשֶׂ֗ה כֹּ֚ל אֲשֶׁ֣ר אָנֹכִ֖י מְצַוֶּֽךָּ׃
there you offer your burnt offerings and there you do all which I am commanding you

14 But in the place which the LORD shall choose in one of thy tribes, there thou shalt offer thy burnt offerings, and there thou shalt do all that I command thee.

רַק֩ בְּכָל־אַוַּ֨ת נַפְשְׁךָ֜ תִּזְבַּ֣ח
only want - in all your soul you slaughter

וְאָכַלְתָּ֣ בָשָׂ֔ר כְּבִרְכַּ֛ת יְהוָ֥ה אֱלֹהֶ֖יךָ
and you eat meat like blessing ihvh your Elohim

אֲשֶׁ֥ר נָֽתַן־לְךָ֖ בְּכָל־שְׁעָרֶ֑יךָ הַטָּמֵ֧א
which he gives - to you your gates - in all the unclean

וְהַטָּהוֹר יֹאכְלֶנּוּ כַּצְּבִי וְכָאַיָּל:
and like deer | like gazelle | he may eat it | and the clean

15 Notwithstanding thou mayest kill and eat flesh in all thy gates, whatsoever thy soul lusteth after, according to the blessing of the LORD thy God which he hath given thee: the unclean and the clean may eat thereof, as of the roebuck, and as of the hart.

רַק הַדָּם לֹא תֹאכֵלוּ
you will eat | not | the blood | only

עַל־הָאָרֶץ תִּשְׁפְּכֶנּוּ כַּמָּיִם:
like water | you pour it | the ground - upon

16 Only ye shall not eat the blood; ye shall pour it upon the earth as water.

לֹא־תוּכַל לֶאֱכֹל בִּשְׁעָרֶיךָ מַעְשַׂר דְּגָנְךָ
your grain | tithe | in your gates | to eat | you able - not

וְתִירֹשְׁךָ וְיִצְהָרֶךָ וּבְכֹרֹת בְּקָרְךָ וְצֹאנֶךָ
and your flock | your herd | and ones first born | and oil your | and your grape juice

וְכָל־נְדָרֶיךָ אֲשֶׁר תִּדֹּר וְנִדְבֹתֶיךָ וּתְרוּמַת יָדֶךָ:
your hand | and heave offering | and your free will offerings | you vowed | which | your vows - and all

17 Thou mayest not eat within thy gates the tithe of thy corn, or of thy wine, or of thy oil, or the firstlings of thy herds or of thy flock, nor any of thy vows which thou vowest, nor thy freewill offerings, or heave offering of thine hand:

כִּי אִם־לִפְנֵי יְהוָה אֱלֹהֶיךָ תֹּאכְלֶנּוּ
you eat it | your Elohim | ihvh | before - if | like

בַּמָּקוֹם אֲשֶׁר יִבְחַר יְהוָה אֱלֹהֶיךָ בּוֹ
in him | your Elohim | ihvh | he will choose | which | in place

אַתָּה וּבִנְךָ וּבִתֶּךָ וְעַבְדְּךָ וַאֲמָתֶךָ
and your maidservant | and your manservant | and your daughter | and your son | you

וְהַלֵּוִי אֲשֶׁר בִּשְׁעָרֶיךָ
in your gates | which | and the Levite

וְשָׂמַחְתָּ לִפְנֵי יְהוָה אֱלֹהֶיךָ בְּכֹל מִשְׁלַח יָדֶךָ:
your hand | undertaking | in all | your Elohim | ihvh | before | and you rejoice

18 But thou must eat them before the LORD thy God in the place which the LORD thy God shall choose, thou, and thy son, and thy daughter, and thy manservant, and thy maidservant, and the Levite that is within thy gates: and thou shalt rejoice before the LORD thy God in all that thou puttest thine hands unto.

הִשָּׁמֶר לְךָ פֶּן־תַּעֲזֹב אֶת־הַלֵּוִי
the Levite - that | you neglect - lest | to you | cause to heed

כָּל־יָמֶיךָ עַל־אַדְמָתֶךָ׃
your ground - upon   your days - all

19 Take heed to thyself that thou forsake not the Levite as long as thou livest upon the earth.

ס

כִּי־יַרְחִיב יְהוָה אֱלֹהֶיךָ אֶת־גְּבֻלְךָ
your territory - that   your Elohim   ihvh   he widens - like

כַּאֲשֶׁר דִּבֶּר־לָךְ וְאָמַרְתָּ אֹכְלָה בָשָׂר
meat   I eat   and you say   to you - he spoke   when

כִּי־תְאַוֶּה נַפְשְׁךָ לֶאֱכֹל בָּשָׂר
meat   to eat   your soul   it yearns - like

בְּכָל־אַוַּת נַפְשְׁךָ תֹּאכַל בָּשָׂר׃
meat   you eat   your soul   yearning - in all

20 When the LORD thy God shall enlarge thy border, as he hath promised thee, and thou shalt say, I will eat flesh, because thy soul longeth to eat flesh; thou mayest eat flesh, whatsoever thy soul lusteth after.

כִּי־יִרְחַק מִמְּךָ הַמָּקוֹם אֲשֶׁר יִבְחַר יְהוָה אֱלֹהֶיךָ
your Elohim   ihvh   he chooses   which   the place   from you   he is far - like

לָשׂוּם שְׁמוֹ שָׁם וְזָבַחְתָּ מִבְּקָרְךָ וּמִצֹּאנְךָ
and from your flock   from your herd   and you will slaughter   there   his name   to put

אֲשֶׁר נָתַן יְהוָה לָךְ כַּאֲשֶׁר צִוִּיתִךָ
I commanded you   when   to you   ihvh   he gave   which

וְאָכַלְתָּ בִּשְׁעָרֶיךָ בְּכֹל אַוַּת נַפְשֶׁךָ׃
your soul   yearning   in all   in your gates   and you eat

21 If the place which the LORD thy God hath chosen to put his name there be too far from thee, then thou shalt kill of thy herd and of thy flock, which the LORD hath given thee, as I have commanded thee, and thou shalt eat in thy gates whatsoever thy soul lusteth after.

אַךְ כַּאֲשֶׁר יֵאָכֵל אֶת־הַצְּבִי וְאֶת־הָאַיָּל
the deer - and that   the gazelle - that   he is eaten   when   only

כֵּן תֹּאכְלֶנּוּ הַטָּמֵא וְהַטָּהוֹר יַחְדָּו יֹאכְלֶנּוּ׃
he will eat them   together   and the clean   the unclean   you eat it   thus

22 Even as the roebuck and the hart is eaten, so thou shalt eat them: the unclean and the clean shall eat of them alike.

רַק חֲזַק לְבִלְתִּי אֲכֹל הַדָּם
the blood   eat   to not   be strong   only

Rehei - Chapter 12

כִּי הַדָּם הוּא הַנֶּפֶשׁ
the soul — it — the blood — like

וְלֹא־תֹאכַל הַנֶּפֶשׁ עִם־הַבָּשָׂר׃
the meat - with — the soul — you eat - and not

23 Only be sure that thou eat not the blood: for the blood is the life; and thou mayest not eat the life with the flesh.

לֹא תֹאכְלֶנּוּ עַל־הָאָרֶץ תִּשְׁפְּכֶנּוּ כַּמָּיִם׃
like water — you pour it — the earth - upon — you will eat it — not

24 Thou shalt not eat it; thou shalt pour it upon the earth as water.

לֹא תֹאכְלֶנּוּ לְמַעַן יִיטַב לְךָ
to you — it will be good — to end — you eat it — not

וּלְבָנֶיךָ אַחֲרֶיךָ כִּי־תַעֲשֶׂה הַיָּשָׁר בְּעֵינֵי יְהוָה׃
ihvh — in eyes — the upright — you will do - like — after you — and to your sons

25 Thou shalt not eat it; that it may go well with thee, and with thy children after thee, when thou shalt do that which is right in the sight of the LORD.

רַק קָדָשֶׁיךָ אֲשֶׁר־יִהְיוּ לְךָ וּנְדָרֶיךָ
and your vowed — to you — they are - which — your holiness — only

תִּשָּׂא וּבָאתָ אֶל־הַמָּקוֹם אֲשֶׁר־יִבְחַר יְהוָה׃
ihvh — he will choose - which — the place- unto — and you go — you carry

26 Only thy holy things which thou hast, and thy vows, thou shalt take, and go unto the place which the LORD shall choose.

וְעָשִׂיתָ עֹלֹתֶיךָ הַבָּשָׂר
the meat — your burnt offerings — and you make

וְהַדָּם עַל־מִזְבַּח יְהוָה אֱלֹהֶיךָ
your Elohim — ihvh — altar - upon — and the blood

וְדַם־זְבָחֶיךָ יִשָּׁפֵךְ עַל־מִזְבַּח יְהוָה אֱלֹהֶיךָ
your Elohim — ihvh — altar - upon — he must pour — your sacrifices - and blood

וְהַבָּשָׂר תֹּאכֵל׃
you will eat — and the meat

27 And thou shalt offer thy burnt offerings, the flesh and the blood, upon the altar of the LORD thy God: and the blood of thy sacrifices shall be poured out upon the altar of the LORD thy God, and thou shalt eat the flesh.

שְׁמֹר וְשָׁמַעְתָּ אֵת כָּל־הַדְּבָרִים הָאֵלֶּה
the these — the speaking - all — that — and you obey — heed

אֲשֶׁר אָנֹכִי מְצַוֶּךָּ לְמַעַן יִיטַב לְךָ
to you — it be good — to end — commanding you — I am — which

וּלְבָנֶיךָ אַחֲרֶיךָ עַד־עוֹלָם
and to your sons   after you   till - forever

כִּי תַעֲשֶׂה הַטּוֹב וְהַיָּשָׁר בְּעֵינֵי יְהוָה אֱלֹהֶיךָ׃
like you will do the good and the upright in eyes ihvh your Elohim

28 Observe and hear all these words which I command thee, that it may go well with thee, and with thy children after thee for ever, when thou doest that which is good and right in the sight of the LORD thy God.

ס

[שְׁלִישִׁי]

כִּי־יַכְרִית יְהוָה אֱלֹהֶיךָ אֶת־הַגּוֹיִם
like - he will cut off ihvh your Elohim that - the nations

אֲשֶׁר אַתָּה בָא־שָׁמָּה לָרֶשֶׁת אוֹתָם מִפָּנֶיךָ
which you come - to there to possess to them from before you

וְיָרַשְׁתָּ אֹתָם וְיָשַׁבְתָּ בְּאַרְצָם׃
drive out it you and you settle it in their land

29 When the LORD thy God shall cut off the nations from before thee, whither thou goest to possess them, and thou succeedest them, and dwellest in their land;

הִשָּׁמֶר לְךָ פֶּן־תִּנָּקֵשׁ אַחֲרֵיהֶם אַחֲרֵי הִשָּׁמְדָם מִפָּנֶיךָ
cause to heed to you lest - you ensnared after them after caused destroyed them from before you

וּפֶן־תִּדְרֹשׁ לֵאלֹהֵיהֶם לֵאמֹר
and lest - you inquire to their elohim to say

אֵיכָה יַעַבְדוּ הַגּוֹיִם הָאֵלֶּה אֶת־אֱלֹהֵיהֶם
how they serve the nations the these that - their elohim

וְאֶעֱשֶׂה־כֵּן גַּם־אָנִי׃
and I do - thus also - I

30 Take heed to thyself that thou be not snared by following them, after that they be destroyed from before thee; and that thou inquire not after their gods, saying, How did these nations serve their gods? even so will I do likewise.

לֹא־תַעֲשֶׂה כֵן לַיהוָה אֱלֹהֶיךָ
not - you do thus to ihvh your Elohim

כִּי כָל־תּוֹעֲבַת יְהוָה
like all - abomination ihvh

אֲשֶׁר שָׂנֵא עָשׂוּ לֵאלֹהֵיהֶם
which he hates they do to their elohim

כִּי גַם אֶת־בְּנֵיהֶם
their sons - that   also   like

וְאֶת־בְּנֹתֵיהֶם יִשְׂרְפוּ בָאֵשׁ לֵאלֹהֵיהֶם׃
to their elohim   in fire   they burned   their daughters - and that

31 Thou shalt not do so unto the LORD thy God: for every abomination to the LORD, which he hateth, have they done unto their gods; for even their sons and their daughters they have burnt in the fire to their gods.

ספר דברים פרק יג

אֵת כָּל־הַדָּבָר אֲשֶׁר אָנֹכִי מְצַוֶּה אֶתְכֶם אֹתוֹ
to it   that you   commanding   I am   which   the matter - all   that

תִּשְׁמְרוּ לַעֲשׂוֹת לֹא־תֹסֵף עָלָיו וְלֹא תִגְרַע מִמֶּנּוּ׃
from it   you take away   and not   upon it   you add - not   to do   you heed it

32 What thing soever I command you, observe to do it: thou shalt not add thereto, nor diminish from it.

פ

Chapter 13

כִּי־יָקוּם בְּקִרְבְּךָ נָבִיא אוֹ חֹלֵם חֲלוֹם
dream   one dreaming   or   prophet   in among you   he rises - like

וְנָתַן אֵלֶיךָ אוֹת אוֹ מוֹפֵת׃
wonder   or   sign   unto you   and gives

1 If there arise among you a prophet, or a dreamer of dreams, and giveth thee a sign or a wonder,

וּבָא הָאוֹת וְהַמּוֹפֵת אֲשֶׁר־דִּבֶּר אֵלֶיךָ
to you   he spoke - which   and the wonder   the sign   and come

אֲשֶׁר לֵאמֹר נֵלְכָה אַחֲרֵי אֱלֹהִים אֲחֵרִים לֹא־יְדַעְתָּם
you knew them - not   other ones   elohim ones   after   we go   to say   which

וְנָעָבְדֵם׃
and we serve them

2 And the sign or the wonder come to pass, whereof he spake unto thee, saying, Let us go after other gods, which thou hast not known, and let us serve them;

לֹא תִשְׁמַע אֶל־דִּבְרֵי הַנָּבִיא הַהוּא
the it   the prophet   speakings - unto   you hear   not

אוֹ אֶל־חוֹלֵם הַחֲלוֹם הַהוּא
the vvit   the dream   one dreaming - unto   or

כִּי מְנַסֶּה יְהוָה אֱלֹהֵיכֶם אֶתְכֶם
    that you   your Elohim   ihvh   testing   like

לָדַעַת הֲיִשְׁכֶם אֹהֲבִים אֶת־יְהוָה אֱלֹהֵיכֶם
    your Elohim   ihvh - that   loving ones   the it is you   to know

בְּכָל־לְבַבְכֶם וּבְכָל־נַפְשְׁכֶם׃
    your soul - and in all   your heart - in all

3 Thou shalt not hearken unto the words of that prophet, or that dreamer of dreams: for the LORD your God proveth you, to know whether ye love the LORD your God with all your heart and with all your soul.

אַחֲרֵי יְהוָה אֱלֹהֵיכֶם תֵּלֵכוּ וְאֹתוֹ תִירָאוּ
    you fear   and to him   you go   your Elohim   ihvh   after

וְאֶת־מִצְוֺתָיו תִּשְׁמֹרוּ וּבְקֹלוֹ תִשְׁמָעוּ
    you hear it   and in his voice   you heed it   his commandments - and that

וְאֹתוֹ תַעֲבֹדוּ וּבוֹ תִדְבָּקוּן׃
    you will cling   and in him   you will serve him   and to him

4 Ye shall walk after the LORD your God, and fear him, and keep his commandments, and obey his voice, and ye shall serve him, and cleave unto him.

וְהַנָּבִיא הַהוּא אוֹ חֹלֵם הַחֲלוֹם הַהוּא יוּמָת
    he is killed   the it   the dream   one dreaming   or   the he   and the prophet

כִּי דִבֶּר־סָרָה עַל־יְהוָה אֱלֹהֵיכֶם
    your Elohim   ihvh - upon   rebellion - spoke   like

הַמּוֹצִיא אֶתְכֶם מֵאֶרֶץ מִצְרַיִם
    Egypt   from land   that you   the one bringing out

וְהַפֹּדְךָ מִבֵּית עֲבָדִים לְהַדִּיחֲךָ מִן־הַדֶּרֶךְ
    the way - from   to induce you   servants   from house   and the one ransoming you

אֲשֶׁר צִוְּךָ יְהוָה אֱלֹהֶיךָ לָלֶכֶת בָּהּ
    in it   to walk   your Elohim   ihvh   commanded you   which

וּבִעַרְתָּ הָרָע מִקִּרְבֶּךָ׃
    from within you   the bad   and you eradicate

5 And that prophet, or that dreamer of dreams, shall be put to death; because he hath spoken to turn you away from the LORD your God, which brought you out of the land of Egypt, and redeemed you out of the house of bondage, to thrust thee out of the way which the LORD thy God commanded thee to walk in. So shalt thou put the evil away from the midst of thee.

ס

Rehei - Chapter 13

כִּי יְסִיתְךָ אָחִיךָ בֶן־אִמֶּךָ אוֹ־בִנְךָ אוֹ־בִתְּךָ
like he inciting you your brother your mother - son or - your son or - your daughter

אוֹ אֵשֶׁת חֵיקֶךָ אוֹ רֵעֲךָ אֲשֶׁר כְּנַפְשְׁךָ
or woman your bosom or your neighbor which like your soul

בַּסֵּתֶר לֵאמֹר נֵלְכָה וְנַעַבְדָה אֱלֹהִים אֲחֵרִים
in concealment to say we go and we serve elohim other ones

אֲשֶׁר לֹא יָדַעְתָּ אַתָּה וַאֲבֹתֶיךָ׃
which not you known you and your fathers

6 If thy brother, the son of thy mother, or thy son, or thy daughter, or the wife of thy bosom, or thy friend, which is as thine own soul, entice thee secretly, saying, Let us go and serve other gods, which thou hast not known, thou, nor thy fathers;

מֵאֱלֹהֵי הָעַמִּים אֲשֶׁר סְבִיבֹתֵיכֶם הַקְּרֹבִים אֵלֶיךָ
from elohims the peoples which around you the near ones unto you

אוֹ הָרְחֹקִים מִמֶּךָּ מִקְצֵה הָאָרֶץ וְעַד־קְצֵה הָאָרֶץ׃
or the far ones from you from end the land and till - end the land

7 Namely, of the gods of the people which are round about you, nigh unto thee, or far off from thee, from the one end of the earth even unto the other end of the earth;

לֹא־תֹאבֶה לוֹ וְלֹא תִשְׁמַע אֵלָיו
you comply - not to him and not you listen unto him

וְלֹא־תָחוֹס עֵינְךָ עָלָיו וְלֹא־תַחְמֹל
you spare - and not upon him your eye it must pity - and not

וְלֹא־תְכַסֶּה עָלָיו׃
upon him you cover - and not

8 Thou shalt not consent unto him, nor hearken unto him; neither shall thine eye pity him, neither shalt thou spare, neither shalt thou conceal him:

כִּי הָרֹג תַּהַרְגֶנּוּ יָדְךָ תִּהְיֶה־בּוֹ בָרִאשׁוֹנָה לַהֲמִיתוֹ
like kill you kill him your hand on him - it must be in first to the death him

וְיַד כָּל־הָעָם בָּאַחֲרֹנָה׃
and hand the people - all in afterwards

9 But thou shalt surely kill him; thine hand shall be first upon him to put him to death, and afterwards the hand of all the people.

וּסְקַלְתּוֹ בָאֲבָנִים וָמֵת
and stone him in stones and he dies

הַמּוֹצִיאֲךָ מֵאֶרֶץ מִצְרַיִם מִבֵּית עֲבָדִים׃
   slaveries from house Egypt from land the one bringing you

10 And thou shalt stone him with stones, that he die; because he hath sought to thrust thee away from the LORD thy God, which brought thee out of the land of Egypt, from the house of bondage.

וְכָל־יִשְׂרָאֵל יִשְׁמְעוּ וְיִרָאוּן
  and fear they will hear Israel - and all

וְלֹא־יוֹסִפוּ לַעֲשׂוֹת כַּדָּבָר הָרָע הַזֶּה בְּקִרְבֶּךָ׃
in among you the this the evil like matter to do they will repeat - and not

11 And all Israel shall hear, and fear, and shall do no more any such wickedness as this is among you.

ס

כִּי־תִשְׁמַע בְּאַחַת עָרֶיךָ אֲשֶׁר יְהוָה אֱלֹהֶיךָ נֹתֵן לְךָ
to you giver your Elohim ihvh which your cities about one you hear - like

לָשֶׁבֶת שָׁם לֵאמֹר׃
to say there to live

12 If thou shalt hear say in one of thy cities, which the LORD thy God hath given thee to dwell there, saying,

יָצְאוּ אֲנָשִׁים בְּנֵי־בְלִיַּעַל מִקִּרְבֶּךָ
from among you Belial - sons men they went out

וַיַּדִּיחוּ אֶת־יֹשְׁבֵי עִירָם לֵאמֹר
to say their city dwelling ones - that and they induced

נֵלְכָה וְנַעַבְדָה אֱלֹהִים אֲחֵרִים אֲשֶׁר לֹא־יְדַעְתֶּם׃
you knew - not which other ones elohim let us serve let us go

13 Certain men, the children of Belial, are gone out from among you, and have withdrawn the inhabitants of their city, saying, Let us go and serve other gods, which ye have not known;

וְדָרַשְׁתָּ וְחָקַרְתָּ וְשָׁאַלְתָּ הֵיטֵב
the best and you ask and you probe and you inquire

וְהִנֵּה אֱמֶת נָכוֹן הַדָּבָר נֶעֶשְׂתָה
it was done the matter certain true and here

הַתּוֹעֵבָה הַזֹּאת בְּקִרְבֶּךָ׃
in among you the this the abomination

14 Then shalt thou inquire, and make search, and ask diligently; and, behold, if it be truth, and the thing certain, that such abomination is wrought among you;

הַכֵּ֤ה תַכֶּה֙ אֶת־יֹשְׁבֵ֜י הָעִ֥יר הַהִ֛וא לְפִי־חָ֖רֶב הַחֲרֵ֣ם אֹתָ֑הּ
to it   the doom   sword - to edge   the it   the city   ones dwelling - that   you kill   to kill

וְאֶת־כָּל־אֲשֶׁר־בָּ֥הּ וְאֶת־בְּהֶמְתָּ֖הּ לְפִי־חָֽרֶב׃
sword - with edge   it's cattle - and that   in it - which - all - and that

15 Thou shalt surely smite the inhabitants of that city with the edge of the sword, destroying it utterly, and all that is therein, and the cattle thereof, with the edge of the sword.

וְאֶת־כָּל־שְׁלָלָ֗הּ תִּקְבֹּץ֙ אֶל־תּ֣וֹךְ רְחֹבָ֔הּ
it's street   middle - unto   you gather   booty - all - and that

וְשָׂרַפְתָּ֨ בָאֵ֜שׁ אֶת־הָעִ֤יר
the city - that   in fire   and you burn

וְאֶת־כָּל־שְׁלָלָהּ֙ כָּלִ֔יל לַיהוָ֖ה אֱלֹהֶ֑יךָ
your Elohim   to ihvh   all offering   booty - all - and that

וְהָיְתָה֙ תֵּ֣ל עוֹלָ֔ם לֹ֥א תִבָּנֶ֖ה עֽוֹד׃
again   it be rebuilt   not   forever   ruin   and it will be

16 And thou shalt gather all the spoil of it into the midst of the street thereof, and shalt burn with fire the city, and all the spoil thereof every whit, for the LORD thy God: and it shall be an heap for ever; it shall not be built again.

וְלֹֽא־יִדְבַּ֧ק בְּיָדְךָ֛ מְא֖וּמָה מִן־הַחֵ֑רֶם
the condemned - from   anything   in your hand   he will cling - and not

לְמַעַן֩ יָשׁ֨וּב יְהוָ֜ה מֵחֲר֣וֹן אַפּ֗וֹ
his anger   form fierceness   ihvh   he will return   to end

וְנָֽתַן־לְךָ֤ רַחֲמִים֙ וְרִֽחַמְךָ֔
and have compassion on you   mercies   to you - and will give

וְהִרְבֶּ֕ךָ כַּאֲשֶׁ֥ר נִשְׁבַּ֖ע לַאֲבֹתֶֽיךָ׃
to your fathers   he swore   when   as will increase you

17 And there shall cleave nought of the cursed thing to thine hand: that the LORD may turn from the fierceness of his anger, and shew thee mercy, and have compassion upon thee, and multiply thee, as he hath sworn unto thy fathers;

כִּ֣י תִשְׁמַ֗ע בְּקוֹל֙ יְהוָ֣ה אֱלֹהֶ֔יךָ לִשְׁמֹר֙ אֶת־כָּל־מִצְוֹתָ֔יו
commands his - all - that   to heed   your Elohim   ihvh   in voice   you hear   like

אֲשֶׁ֛ר אָנֹכִ֥י מְצַוְּךָ֖ הַיּ֑וֹם לַעֲשׂוֹת֙
to do   the day   commanding you   I am   which

הַיָּשָׁ֕ר בְּעֵינֵ֖י יְהוָ֥ה אֱלֹהֶֽיךָ׃
your Elohim   ihvh   in eyes   the upright

18 When thou shalt hearken to the voice of the LORD thy God, to keep all his com-

mandments which I command thee this day, to do that which is right in the eyes of the LORD thy God.

ס

Chapter 14

ספר דברים פרק יד

[רביעי]

בָּנִים אַתֶּם לַיהוָה אֱלֹהֵיכֶם
sons   you   to ihvh   your Elohim

לֹא תִתְגֹּדְדוּ וְלֹא־תָשִׂימוּ קָרְחָה בֵּין עֵינֵיכֶם לָמֵת׃
not   you cut yourselves   and not - you put   baldness   between   your eyes   to dead one

1 Ye are the children of the LORD your God: ye shall not cut yourselves, nor make any baldness between your eyes for the dead.

כִּי עַם קָדוֹשׁ אַתָּה לַיהוָה אֱלֹהֶיךָ
like   people   holy   you   to ihvh   your Elohim

וּבְךָ בָּחַר יְהוָה לִהְיוֹת לוֹ לְעַם
and in you   he chose   ihvh   to be   to him   to people

סְגֻלָּה מִכֹּל הָעַמִּים אֲשֶׁר עַל־פְּנֵי הָאֲדָמָה׃
special   from all   the peoples   which   upon - face   the earth

2 For thou art an holy people unto the LORD thy God, and the LORD hath chosen thee to be a peculiar people unto himself, above all the nations that are upon the earth.

ס

לֹא תֹאכַל כָּל־תּוֹעֵבָה׃
not   you eat   all - abominable thing

3 Thou shalt not eat any abominable thing.

זֹאת הַבְּהֵמָה אֲשֶׁר תֹּאכֵלוּ
this   the animal   which   you may eat

שׁוֹר שֵׂה כְשָׂבִים וְשֵׂה עִזִּים׃
ox   flock   sheep   and flock   goats

4 These are the beasts which ye shall eat: the ox, the sheep, and the goat,

אַיָּל וּצְבִי וְיַחְמוּר וְאַקּוֹ וְדִישֹׁן וּתְאוֹ וָזָמֶר׃
deer   and gazelle   and roe deer   and wild goat   and ibex   and antelope   and mountain sheep

5 The hart, and the roebuck, and the fallow deer, and the wild goat, and the pygarg, and the wild ox, and the chamois.

וְכָל־בְּהֵמָה מַפְרֶסֶת פַּרְסָה וְשֹׁסַעַת שֶׁסַע שְׁתֵּי פְרָסוֹת
hoofs   two   cleft and dividing hoof bisecting animal - and all

מַעֲלַת גֵּרָה בַּבְּהֵמָה אֹתָהּ תֹּאכֵלוּ׃
you may eat   to it   in animal   cud   bringing up

6 And every beast that parteth the hoof, and cleaveth the cleft into two claws, and cheweth the cud among the beasts, that ye shall eat.

אַךְ אֶת־זֶה לֹא תֹאכְלוּ מִמַּעֲלֵי הַגֵּרָה
the cud from bringing up you will eat not this - that however

וּמִמַּפְרִיסֵי הַפַּרְסָה הַשְּׁסוּעָה
the being cloven   the hoof   and from ones bisecting

אֶת־הַגָּמָל וְאֶת־הָאַרְנֶבֶת וְאֶת־הַשָּׁפָן
the coney - and that   the rabbit - and that   that - the camel that

כִּי־מַעֲלֵה גֵרָה הֵמָּה וּפַרְסָה לֹא הִפְרִיסוּ
they bisect   not   and hoof   they   cud   bringing up - like

טְמֵאִים הֵם לָכֶם׃
to you   they   unclean ones

7 Nevertheless these ye shall not eat of them that chew the cud, or of them that divide the cloven hoof; as the camel, and the hare, and the coney: for they chew the cud, but divide not the hoof; therefore they are unclean unto you.

וְאֶת־הַחֲזִיר כִּי־מַפְרִיס פַּרְסָה הוּא וְלֹא גֵרָה
cud   and not   he   hoof bisecting - like   the pig - and that

טָמֵא הוּא לָכֶם מִבְּשָׂרָם לֹא תֹאכֵלוּ
you eat it   not   from meat of them   to you   he   unclean

וּבְנִבְלָתָם לֹא תִגָּעוּ׃
you touch   not   and in carcass them

8 And the swine, because it divideth the hoof, yet cheweth not the cud, it is unclean unto you: ye shall not eat of their flesh, nor touch their dead carcase.

ס

אֶת־זֶה תֹּאכְלוּ מִכֹּל אֲשֶׁר בַּמָּיִם
in waters   which   from all   you will eat   this - that

כֹּל אֲשֶׁר־לוֹ סְנַפִּיר וְקַשְׂקֶשֶׂת תֹּאכֵלוּ׃
you may eat   and scales   fin   to it - which   all

9 These ye shall eat of all that are in the waters: all that have fins and scales shall ye eat:

וְכֹל אֲשֶׁר אֵין־לוֹ סְנַפִּיר וְקַשְׂקֶשֶׂת לֹא תֹאכֵלוּ
you eat it   not   and scales   fin   to it - isn't   which   and all

טָמֵ֥א ה֖וּא לָכֶֽם׃
to you   he   unclean

10 And whatsoever hath not fins and scales ye may not eat; it is unclean unto you.

ס

כָּל־צִפּ֥וֹר טְהֹרָ֖ה תֹּאכֵֽלוּ׃
you may eat it   clean   bird - all

11 Of all clean birds ye shall eat.

וְזֶ֕ה אֲשֶׁ֥ר לֹֽא־תֹאכְל֖וּ מֵהֶ֑ם הַנֶּ֥שֶׁר וְהַפֶּ֖רֶס וְהָֽעָזְנִיָּֽה׃
and the black vulture and the vulture the eagle from them you may eat it - not which and this

12 But these are they of which ye shall not eat: the eagle, and the ossifrage, and the osprey,

וְהָרָאָה֙ וְאֶת־הָ֣אַיָּ֔ה וְהַדַּיָּ֖ה לְמִינָֽהּ׃
to it's kind   and the black kite   the falcon - and that   and the glede

13 And the glede, and the kite, and the vulture after his kind,

וְאֵ֥ת כָּל־עֹרֵ֖ב לְמִינֽוֹ׃
to it's kind   raven - all   and that

14 And every raven after his kind,

וְאֵת֙ בַּ֣ת הַֽיַּעֲנָ֔ה וְאֶת־הַתַּחְמָ֖ס וְאֶת־הַשָּֽׁחַף
the gull - and that   the screech owl - and that   the ostrich   daughter   and that

וְאֶת־הַנֵּ֖ץ לְמִינֵֽהוּ׃
to it's kind   the hawk - and that

15 And the owl, and the night hawk, and the cuckoo, and the hawk after his kind,

אֶת־הַכּ֥וֹס וְאֶת־הַיַּנְשׁ֖וּף וְהַתִּנְשָֽׁמֶת׃
and the ibis   the great owl - and that   and the little owl - that

16 The little owl, and the great owl, and the swan,

וְהַקָּאָ֥ת וְאֶת־הָרָחָ֖מָה וְאֶת־הַשָּׁלָֽךְ׃
the cormorant - and that   the Egyptian vulture - and that   and the pelican

17 And the pelican, and the gier eagle, and the cormorant,

וְהַ֣חֲסִידָ֔ה וְהָאֲנָפָ֖ה לְמִינָ֑הּ
to it's kind   and the heron   and the stork

וְהַדּוּכִיפַ֖ת וְהָעֲטַלֵּֽף׃
and the bat   and the hoopoe

18 And the stork, and the heron after her kind, and the lapwing, and the bat.

וְכֹל שֶׁרֶץ הָעוֹף טָמֵא הוּא לָכֶם
to you   he   unclean   the wing   swarmer   and all

לֹא יֵאָכֵלוּ׃
they may be eaten   not

19 And every creeping thing that flieth is unclean unto you: they shall not be eaten.

כָּל־עוֹף טָהוֹר תֹּאכֵלוּ׃
you may eat it   clean   fowls - all

20 But of all clean fowls ye may eat.

לֹא־תֹאכְלוּ כָל־נְבֵלָה
dead animal - all   you may eat it - not

לַגֵּר אֲשֶׁר־בִּשְׁעָרֶיךָ תִּתְּנֶנָּה וַאֲכָלָהּ אוֹ מָכֹר לְנָכְרִי
to foreigner   sell   or   and he may eat it   you may give it   in your gates - which   to alien

כִּי עַם קָדוֹשׁ אַתָּה לַיהוָה אֱלֹהֶיךָ
your elohim   to ihvh   you   holy   people   like

לֹא־תְבַשֵּׁל גְּדִי בַּחֲלֵב אִמּוֹ׃
his mother   in milk   young goat   you cook - not

21 Ye shall not eat of any thing that dieth of itself: thou shalt give it unto the stranger that is in thy gates, that he may eat it; or thou mayest sell it unto an alien: for thou art an holy people unto the LORD thy God. Thou shalt not seethe a kid in his mother's milk.

פ

[חמישי]

עַשֵּׂר תְּעַשֵּׂר אֵת כָּל־תְּבוּאַת זַרְעֶךָ
your seed   yield - all   that   you tenth   tenth

הַיֹּצֵא הַשָּׂדֶה שָׁנָה שָׁנָה׃
year   year   the field   the coming out one

22 Thou shalt truly tithe all the increase of thy seed, that the field bringeth forth year by year.

וְאָכַלְתָּ לִפְנֵי יְהוָה אֱלֹהֶיךָ
your Elohim   ihvh   before   and you eat

בַּמָּקוֹם אֲשֶׁר־יִבְחַר לְשַׁכֵּן שְׁמוֹ שָׁם
there   his name   to make dwell   he will choose - which   in place

מַעְשַׂר דְּגָנְךָ תִּירֹשְׁךָ וְיִצְהָרֶךָ
and your oil   your new wine   your grain   tithe

וּבְכֹרֹת בְּקָרְךָ וְצֹאנֶךָ
and your flock   your herd   and ones first born

לְמַ֣עַן תִּלְמַ֗ד לְיִרְאָ֛ה אֶת־יְהוָ֥ה אֱלֹהֶ֖יךָ כָּל־הַיָּמִֽים׃

   the days - all   your Elohim   ihvh - that   to fear   you learn   to end

23 And thou shalt eat before the LORD thy God, in the place which he shall choose to place his name there, the tithe of thy corn, of thy wine, and of thine oil, and the firstlings of thy herds and of thy flocks; that thou mayest learn to fear the LORD thy God always.

וְכִֽי־יִרְבֶּ֨ה מִמְּךָ֜ הַדֶּ֗רֶךְ

   the way   from you   he much - and like

כִּ֣י לֹ֣א תוּכַל֮ שְׂאֵתוֹ֒ כִּֽי־יִרְחַ֤ק מִמְּךָ֙ הַמָּק֔וֹם

   the place   from you   he is far - like   to carry him   you able   not   like

אֲשֶׁ֤ר יִבְחַר֙ יְהוָ֣ה אֱלֹהֶ֔יךָ לָשׂ֥וּם שְׁמ֖וֹ שָׁ֑ם

   there   his name   to put   your Elohim   ihvh   he will choose   which

כִּ֥י יְבָרֶכְךָ֖ יְהוָ֥ה אֱלֹהֶֽיךָ׃

   your Elohim   ihvh   he blessed you   like

24 And if the way be too long for thee, so that thou art not able to carry it; or if the place be too far from thee, which the LORD thy God shall choose to set his name there, when the LORD thy God hath blessed thee:

וְנָתַתָּ֖ה בַּכָּ֑סֶף וְצַרְתָּ֤ הַכֶּ֨סֶף֙ בְּיָ֣דְךָ֔

   in your hand   the silver   and you bundle   in silver   and you give

וְהָֽלַכְתָּ֙ אֶל־הַמָּק֔וֹם אֲשֶׁ֥ר יִבְחַ֛ר יְהוָ֥ה אֱלֹהֶ֖יךָ בּֽוֹ׃

   in it   your Elohim   ihvh   he will choose   which   the place - unto   and you walk

25 Then shalt thou turn it into money, and bind up the money in thine hand, and shalt go unto the place which the LORD thy God shall choose:

וְנָתַתָּ֣ה הַכֶּ֡סֶף בְּכֹל֩ אֲשֶׁר־תְּאַוֶּ֨ה נַפְשְׁךָ֜

   your soul   it wants - which   in all   the silver   and you give

בַּבָּקָ֣ר וּבַצֹּ֗אן וּבַיַּ֨יִן֙ וּבַשֵּׁכָ֔ר

   and in fermented drink   and in wine   and in flock   in cattle

וּבְכֹ֛ל אֲשֶׁ֥ר תִּֽשְׁאָלְךָ֖ נַפְשֶׁ֑ךָ

   your soul   it asks you   which   and in all

וְאָכַ֣לְתָּ שָּׁ֗ם לִפְנֵי֙ יְהוָ֣ה אֱלֹהֶ֔יךָ

   your Elohim   ihvh   before   there   and you eat

וְשָׂמַחְתָּ֖ אַתָּ֥ה וּבֵיתֶֽךָ׃

   and your household   you   and you rejoice

26 And thou shalt bestow that money for whatsoever thy soul lusteth after, for oxen, or for sheep, or for wine, or for strong drink, or for whatsoever thy soul desireth: and thou shalt eat there before the LORD thy God, and thou shalt rejoice, thou, and thine household,

וְהַלֵּוִי אֲשֶׁר־בִּשְׁעָרֶיךָ לֹא תַעַזְבֶנּוּ
and the Levite   in your gates - which   not   you forsake him

כִּי אֵין לוֹ חֵלֶק וְנַחֲלָה עִמָּךְ:
like   isn't   to him   allotment   and inheritance   with you

27 And the Levite that is within thy gates; thou shalt not forsake him; for he hath no part nor inheritance with thee.

ס

מִקְצֵה שָׁלֹשׁ שָׁנִים
from end   three   years

תּוֹצִיא אֶת־כָּל־מַעְשַׂר תְּבוּאָתְךָ בַּשָּׁנָה הַהִוא
you bring out   that - all - tithe   your produce   in year   the it

וְהִנַּחְתָּ בִּשְׁעָרֶיךָ:
and you store   in your gates

28 At the end of three years thou shalt bring forth all the tithe of thine increase the same year, and shalt lay it up within thy gates:

וּבָא הַלֵּוִי כִּי אֵין־לוֹ חֵלֶק
and he come   the Levite   like   isn't to him   allotment

וְנַחֲלָה עִמָּךְ וְהַגֵּר וְהַיָּתוֹם וְהָאַלְמָנָה אֲשֶׁר בִּשְׁעָרֶיךָ
and inheritance   with you   and the alien   and the orphan   and the widow   which   in your gates

וְאָכְלוּ וְשָׂבֵעוּ לְמַעַן יְבָרֶכְךָ יְהוָה אֱלֹהֶיךָ
and they eat   and they be satisfied   to end   he will bless you   ihvh   your Elohim

בְּכָל־מַעֲשֵׂה יָדְךָ אֲשֶׁר תַּעֲשֶׂה:
in all - work   your hand   which   you do

29 And the Levite, (because he hath no part nor inheritance with thee,) and the stranger, and the fatherless, and the widow, which are within thy gates, shall come, and shall eat and be satisfied; that the LORD thy God may bless thee in all the work of thine hand which thou doest.

ס

Chapter 15

ספר דברים פרק טו

[ששי]

מִקֵּץ שֶׁבַע־שָׁנִים תַּעֲשֶׂה שְׁמִטָּה:
from end   seven - years   you do   debt release

1 At the end of every seven years thou shalt make a release.

וְזֶה֙ דְּבַ֣ר הַשְּׁמִטָּ֔ה
and this   way   the release

שָׁמ֗וֹט כָּל־בַּ֙עַל֙ מַשֵּׁ֣ה יָד֔וֹ
creditor   master - all   loan   his hand

אֲשֶׁ֥ר יַשֶּׁ֖ה בְּרֵעֵ֑הוּ לֹֽא־יִגֹּ֤שׂ אֶת־רֵעֵ֙הוּ֙ וְאֶת־אָחִ֔יו
which   he loaned   his neighbor   not - he shall exact   that - his neighbor   and that - his brother

כִּֽי־קָרָ֥א שְׁמִטָּ֖ה לַיהֹוָֽה׃
like - he proclaimed   cancel debt   to ihvh

2 And this is the manner of the release: Every creditor that lendeth ought unto his neighbour shall release it; he shall not exact it of his neighbour, or of his brother; because it is called the LORD'S release.

אֶת־הַנָּכְרִ֖י תִּגֹּ֑שׂ
that - the foreigner   you require payment

וַאֲשֶׁ֨ר יִהְיֶ֥ה לְךָ֛ אֶת־אָחִ֖יךָ תַּשְׁמֵ֥ט יָדֶֽךָ׃
and which   it is   to you   that - your brother   you cancel debt   your hand

3 Of a foreigner thou mayest exact it again: but that which is thine with thy brother thine hand shall release;

אֶ֕פֶס כִּ֛י לֹ֥א יִֽהְיֶה־בְּךָ֖ אֶבְי֑וֹן
however   like   not   it be - in you   poor

כִּֽי־בָרֵ֤ךְ יְבָֽרֶכְךָ֙ יְהוָ֔ה בָּאָ֕רֶץ
like - to bless   he will bless you   ihvh   in the land

אֲשֶׁר֙ יְהוָ֣ה אֱלֹהֶ֔יךָ נֹתֵֽן־לְךָ֥ נַחֲלָ֖ה לְרִשְׁתָּֽהּ׃
which   ihvh   your Elohim   giving - to you   inheritance   to her possess

4 Save when there shall be no poor among you; for the LORD shall greatly bless thee in the land which the LORD thy God giveth thee for an inheritance to possess it:

רַ֚ק אִם־שָׁמ֣וֹעַ תִּשְׁמַ֔ע בְּק֖וֹל יְהוָ֣ה אֱלֹהֶ֑יךָ
only   if - listen   you listen   in voice   ihvh   your Elohim

לִשְׁמֹ֤ר לַעֲשׂוֹת֙ אֶת־כָּל־הַמִּצְוָ֣ה הַזֹּ֔את
to heed   to do   that - all - the commandments   the this

אֲשֶׁ֛ר אָנֹכִ֥י מְצַוְּךָ֖ הַיּֽוֹם׃
which   I am   commanding you   the day

5 Only if thou carefully hearken unto the voice of the LORD thy God, to observe to do all these commandments which I command thee this day.

כִּֽי־יְהוָ֤ה אֱלֹהֶ֙יךָ֙ בֵּֽרַכְךָ֔ כַּאֲשֶׁ֖ר דִּבֶּר־לָ֑ךְ
like - ihvh   your Elohim   will bless you   when   spoke - to you

Rehei - Chapter 15

וְהַעֲבַטְתָּ֙ גּוֹיִ֣ם רַבִּ֔ים וְאַתָּ֖ה לֹ֣א תַעֲבֹ֑ט
you will borrow not and you many nations and you will lend

וּמָ֣שַׁלְתָּ֔ בְּגוֹיִ֣ם רַבִּ֔ים וּבְךָ֖ לֹ֥א יִמְשֹֽׁלוּ׃
they will rule not and in you many ones in nations and you will rule

6 For the LORD thy God blesseth thee, as he promised thee: and thou shalt lend unto many nations, but thou shalt not borrow; and thou shalt reign over many nations, but they shall not reign over thee.

ס

כִּֽי־יִהְיֶה֩ בְךָ֨ אֶבְי֜וֹן מֵאַחַ֤ד אַחֶ֙יךָ֙
your brothers from one poor in you he is - like

בְּאַחַ֣ד שְׁעָרֶ֔יךָ בְּאַרְצְךָ֕
in your land your gates in one

אֲשֶׁר־יְהוָ֥ה אֱלֹהֶ֖יךָ נֹתֵ֣ן לָ֑ךְ
to you giving your Elohim ihvh - which

לֹ֧א תְאַמֵּ֛ץ אֶת־לְבָבְךָ֖
your heart - that you rigid not

וְלֹ֤א תִקְפֹּץ֙ אֶת־יָ֣דְךָ֔ מֵאָחִ֖יךָ הָאֶבְיֽוֹן׃
the poor from your brother your hand - that you tighten and not

7 If there be among you a poor man of one of thy brethren within any of thy gates in thy land which the LORD thy God giveth thee, thou shalt not harden thine heart, nor shut thine hand from thy poor brother:

כִּֽי־פָתֹ֧חַ תִּפְתַּ֛ח אֶת־יָדְךָ֖ ל֑וֹ
to him your hand - that you will open open - like

וְהַעֲבֵט֙ תַּעֲבִיטֶ֔נּוּ דֵּ֚י מַחְסֹר֔וֹ אֲשֶׁ֥ר יֶחְסַ֖ר לֽוֹ׃
to him he needs which his need enough you lend him and the lend

8 But thou shalt open thine hand wide unto him, and shalt surely lend him sufficient for his need, in that which he wanteth.

הִשָּׁ֣מֶר לְךָ֡ פֶּן־יִהְיֶ֣ה דָבָר֩ עִם־לְבָבְךָ֨ בְלִיַּ֜עַל לֵאמֹ֗ר
to say decadence your heart - if matter it be - lest to you heed

קָֽרְבָ֣ה שְׁנַֽת־הַשֶּׁ֗בַע שְׁנַ֣ת הַשְּׁמִטָּה֒
the release year the seventh - year she in near

וְרָעָ֣ה עֵֽינְךָ֗ בְּאָחִ֙יךָ֙ הָֽאֶבְי֔וֹן וְלֹ֥א תִתֵּ֖ן ל֑וֹ
to him you give and not the needy in your brother your eye and evil

וְקָרָ֤א עָלֶ֙יךָ֙ אֶל־יְהוָ֔ה וְהָיָ֥ה בְךָ֖ חֵֽטְא׃
guilt in you and he will be ihvh - unto upon you and he cries

9 Beware that there be not a thought in thy wicked heart, saying, The seventh year, the year of release, is at hand; and thine eye be evil against thy poor brother, and thou givest him nought; and he cry unto the LORD against thee, and it be sin unto thee.

נָת֤וֹן תִּתֵּן֙ ל֔וֹ וְלֹא־יֵרַ֥ע לְבָבְךָ֖ בְּתִתְּךָ֣ ל֑וֹ
give   you will give   to him   and not - he bad   your heart   in give you   to him

כִּ֞י בִּגְלַ֣ל ׀ הַדָּבָ֣ר הַזֶּ֗ה יְבָרֶכְךָ֙ יְהוָ֣ה אֱלֹהֶ֔יךָ
like   because   the thing   the this   he will bless you   ihvh   your Elohim

בְּכָֽל־מַעֲשֶׂ֔ךָ וּבְכֹ֖ל מִשְׁלַ֥ח יָדֶֽךָ׃
in all - your work   and in all   activity   your hand

10 Thou shalt surely give him, and thine heart shall not be grieved when thou givest unto him: because that for this thing the LORD thy God shall bless thee in all thy works, and in all that thou puttest thine hand unto.

כִּ֛י לֹא־יֶחְדַּ֥ל אֶבְי֖וֹן מִקֶּ֣רֶב הָאָ֑רֶץ
like   not - he will leave   poor   from close   the land

עַל־כֵּ֞ן אָנֹכִ֤י מְצַוְּךָ֙ לֵאמֹ֔ר
upon - this   I am   commanding you   to say

פָּ֠תֹחַ תִּפְתַּ֨ח אֶת־יָדְךָ֜
open   you open   that - your hand

לְאָחִ֧יךָ לַעֲנִיֶּ֛ךָ וּלְאֶבְיֹנְךָ֖ בְּאַרְצֶֽךָ׃
to your brother   to your poor   and to your needy   in your land

11 For the poor shall never cease out of the land: therefore I command thee, saying, Thou shalt open thine hand wide unto thy brother, to thy poor, and to thy needy, in thy land.

ס

כִּֽי־יִמָּכֵ֨ר לְךָ֜ אָחִ֣יךָ הָֽעִבְרִ֗י א֚וֹ הָֽעִבְרִיָּ֔ה
he sold - like   to you   your fellow   the Hebrew man   or   the Hebrew woman

וַעֲבָֽדְךָ֖ שֵׁ֣שׁ שָׁנִ֑ים וּבַשָּׁנָה֙ הַשְּׁבִיעִ֔ת
and he serves you   six   year   and in the year   the seventh

תְּשַׁלְּחֶ֥נּוּ חָפְשִׁ֖י מֵעִמָּֽךְ׃
you will send him   free   from with you

12 And if thy brother, an Hebrew man, or an Hebrew woman, be sold unto thee, and serve thee six years; then in the seventh year thou shalt let him go free from thee.

וְכִֽי־תְשַׁלְּחֶ֥נּוּ חָפְשִׁ֖י מֵֽעִמָּ֑ךְ לֹ֥א תְשַׁלְּחֶ֖נּוּ רֵיקָֽם׃
and like - you release him   free   from with you   not   you send him away   empty handed

13 And when thou sendest him out free from thee, thou shalt not let him go away empty:

הַעֲנֵיק תַּעֲנִיק לוֹ מִצֹּאנְךָ וּמִגָּרְנְךָ וּמִיִּקְבֶךָ
the necklace you necklace to him from your flock and from threshing your floor and from wine vat your

אֲשֶׁר בֵּרַכְךָ יְהוָה אֱלֹהֶיךָ תִּתֶּן־לוֹ:
which he blessed you ihvh your Elohim to him - you give

14 Thou shalt furnish him liberally out of thy flock, and out of thy floor, and out of thy winepress: of that wherewith the LORD thy God hath blessed thee thou shalt give unto him.

וְזָכַרְתָּ כִּי עֶבֶד הָיִיתָ בְּאֶרֶץ מִצְרַיִם
and you remember like slave you were in land Egypt

וַיִּפְדְּךָ יְהוָה אֱלֹהֶיךָ
and he reeemed you ihvh your elohim

עַל־כֵּן אָנֹכִי מְצַוְּךָ אֶת־הַדָּבָר הַזֶּה הַיּוֹם:
this - upon I am commanding you the matter - that the this the day

15 And thou shalt remember that thou wast a bondman in the land of Egypt, and the LORD thy God redeemed thee: therefore I command thee this thing to day.

וְהָיָה כִּי־יֹאמַר אֵלֶיךָ לֹא אֵצֵא מֵעִמָּךְ
and it will be he says - like unto you not I will go out from with you

כִּי אֲהֵבְךָ וְאֶת־בֵּיתֶךָ כִּי־טוֹב לוֹ עִמָּךְ:
like he loves you your house - and that good - like to him with you

16 And it shall be, if he say unto thee, I will not go away from thee; because he loveth thee and thine house, because he is well with thee;

וְלָקַחְתָּ אֶת־הַמַּרְצֵעַ וְנָתַתָּה בְאָזְנוֹ וּבַדֶּלֶת
and you take the awl - that and you give in his ear and in door

וְהָיָה לְךָ עֶבֶד עוֹלָם וְאַף לַאֲמָתְךָ תַּעֲשֶׂה־כֵּן:
and he will be to you servant for ever and also to your maidservant thus - you do

17 Then thou shalt take an awl, and thrust it through his ear unto the door, and he shall be thy servant for ever. And also unto thy maidservant thou shalt do likewise.

לֹא־יִקְשֶׁה בְעֵינֶךָ בְּשַׁלֵּחֲךָ אֹתוֹ חָפְשִׁי מֵעִמָּךְ
not - it will be hard in your eyes in send you to him free from with you

כִּי מִשְׁנֶה שְׂכַר שָׂכִיר עֲבָדְךָ שֵׁשׁ שָׁנִים
like twice worth hired hand he served you six years

וּבֵרַכְךָ יְהוָה אֱלֹהֶיךָ בְּכֹל אֲשֶׁר תַּעֲשֶׂה:
and he will bless you ihvh your Elohim in all which you do

18 It shall not seem hard unto thee, when thou sendest him away free from thee; for he hath been worth a double hired servant to thee, in serving thee six years: and the LORD thy God shall bless thee in all that thou doest.

פ

[שביעי]

כָּל־הַבְּכוֹר אֲשֶׁר יִוָּלֵד בִּבְקָרְךָ
in your herd　he born　which　the firstborn - all

וּבְצֹאנְךָ הַזָּכָר תַּקְדִּישׁ לַיהוָה אֱלֹהֶיךָ
Elohim your　to ihvh　you set apart　the male　and in your flock

לֹא תַעֲבֹד בִּבְכֹר שׁוֹרֶךָ
ox your　firstborn　you make work　not

וְלֹא תָגֹז בְּכוֹר צֹאנֶךָ׃
your flock　firstborn　you shear　and not

19 All the firstling males that come of thy herd and of thy flock thou shalt sanctify unto the LORD thy God: thou shalt do no work with the firstling of thy bullock, nor shear the firstling of thy sheep.

לִפְנֵי יְהוָה אֱלֹהֶיךָ תֹאכֲלֶנּוּ שָׁנָה בְשָׁנָה
in year　year　you eat him　your elohim　ihvh　before

בַּמָּקוֹם אֲשֶׁר־יִבְחַר יְהוָה אַתָּה וּבֵיתֶךָ׃
and your house　you　ihvh　he will coose - which　in place

20 Thou shalt eat it before the LORD thy God year by year in the place which the LORD shall choose, thou and thy household.

וְכִי־יִהְיֶה בוֹ מוּם פִּסֵּחַ אוֹ עִוֵּר
blind　or　lame　defect　in him　he is - and if

כֹּל מוּם רָע לֹא תִזְבָּחֶנּוּ לַיהוָה אֱלֹהֶיךָ׃
your elohim　to ihvh　you sacrifice him　not　serious　flaw　all

21 And if there be any blemish therein, as if it be lame, or blind, or have any ill blemish, thou shalt not sacrifice it unto the LORD thy God.

בִּשְׁעָרֶיךָ תֹּאכֲלֶנּוּ הַטָּמֵא
the unclean　you eat him　in gates your

וְהַטָּהוֹר יַחְדָּו כַּצְּבִי וְכָאַיָּל׃
and like deer　like gazelle　both　and the clean

22 Thou shalt eat it within thy gates: the unclean and the clean person shall eat it alike, as the roebuck, and as the hart.

רַק אֶת־דָּמוֹ לֹא תֹאכֵל עַל־הָאָרֶץ תִּשְׁפְּכֶנּוּ כַּמָּיִם׃
like waters　your pour out him　the ground - upon　you eat　not　his blood - that　only

23 Only thou shalt not eat the blood thereof; thou shalt pour it upon the ground as water.

Chapter 16

ס

ספר דברים פרק טז

שָׁמוֹר אֶת־חֹדֶשׁ הָאָבִיב
the Abib   month - that   to observe

וְעָשִׂיתָ פֶּסַח לַיהוָה אֱלֹהֶיךָ
elohim your to ihvh   passover and you celebrate

כִּי בְּחֹדֶשׁ הָאָבִיב הוֹצִיאֲךָ יְהוָה אֱלֹהֶיךָ מִמִּצְרַיִם לָיְלָה:
night from Egypt your Elohim ihvh he brought you the aviv in month like

1 Observe the month of Abib, and keep the passover unto the LORD thy God: for in the month of Abib the LORD thy God brought thee forth out of Egypt by night.

וְזָבַחְתָּ פֶּסַח לַיהוָה אֱלֹהֶיךָ צֹאן וּבָקָר
and heard flock your Elohim to ihvh passover and you sacrifice

בַּמָּקוֹם אֲשֶׁר־יִבְחַר יְהוָה לְשַׁכֵּן שְׁמוֹ שָׁם:
there his name to dwell ihvh he chooses which in place

2 Thou shalt therefore sacrifice the passover unto the LORD thy God, of the flock and the herd, in the place which the LORD shall choose to place his name there.

לֹא־תֹאכַל עָלָיו חָמֵץ
leavened upon it you eat - not

שִׁבְעַת יָמִים תֹּאכַל־עָלָיו מַצּוֹת לֶחֶם עֹנִי
affliction bread unleavened upon it - you eat days seven

כִּי בְחִפָּזוֹן יָצָאתָ מֵאֶרֶץ מִצְרַיִם
Egypt from land you came out in haste like

לְמַעַן תִּזְכֹּר אֶת־יוֹם צֵאתְךָ מֵאֶרֶץ מִצְרַיִם כֹּל יְמֵי חַיֶּיךָ:
your life days all Egypt from land you came out day - that you will remember to end

3 Thou shalt eat no leavened bread with it; seven days shalt thou eat unleavened bread therewith, even the bread of affliction; for thou camest forth out of the land of Egypt in haste: that thou mayest remember the day when thou camest forth out of the land of Egypt all the days of thy life.

וְלֹא־יֵרָאֶה לְךָ שְׂאֹר בְּכָל־גְּבֻלְךָ שִׁבְעַת יָמִים
days seven your borders - in all yeast to you he will see - and not

וְלֹא־יָלִין מִן־הַבָּשָׂר אֲשֶׁר תִּזְבַּח בָּעֶרֶב
in evening you sacrifice which the flesh - from he spend night - and not

בַּיּוֹם הָרִאשׁוֹן לַבֹּקֶר:
to morning the first in day

4 And there shall be no leavened bread seen with thee in all thy coast seven days; neither

shall there any thing of the flesh, which thou sacrificedst the first day at even, remain all night until the morning.

לֹא תוּכַל לִזְבֹּחַ אֶת־הַפֶּסַח בְּאַחַד שְׁעָרֶיךָ
your gates   in one   the passover - that   to sacrifice   you eat   not

אֲשֶׁר־יְהוָה אֱלֹהֶיךָ נֹתֵן לָךְ:
to you   given   your Elohim   ihvh - which

5 Thou mayest not sacrifice the passover within any of thy gates, which the LORD thy God giveth thee:

כִּי אִם־אֶל־הַמָּקוֹם אֲשֶׁר־יִבְחַר יְהוָה אֱלֹהֶיךָ
your Elohim   ihvh   he chooses - which   the place - unto - with   like

לְשַׁכֵּן שְׁמוֹ שָׁם תִּזְבַּח אֶת־הַפֶּסַח בָּעָרֶב
in evening   the passover - that   you will sacrifice   there   his name   to dwell

כְּבוֹא הַשֶּׁמֶשׁ מוֹעֵד צֵאתְךָ מִמִּצְרָיִם:
from Egypt   your coming out   appointed time   the sun   like comes

6 But at the place which the LORD thy God shall choose to place his name in, there thou shalt sacrifice the passover at even, at the going down of the sun, at the season that thou camest forth out of Egypt.

וּבִשַּׁלְתָּ וְאָכַלְתָּ בַּמָּקוֹם אֲשֶׁר יִבְחַר יְהוָה אֱלֹהֶיךָ בּוֹ
in it   your Elohim   ihvh   he will choose   which   in place   and you eat   and you roast

וּפָנִיתָ בַבֹּקֶר וְהָלַכְתָּ לְאֹהָלֶיךָ:
to your tents   and you will go   in morning   and you will face

7 And thou shalt roast and eat it in the place which the LORD thy God shall choose: and thou shalt turn in the morning, and go unto thy tents.

שֵׁשֶׁת יָמִים תֹּאכַל מַצּוֹת
unleaven   you eat   days   six

וּבַיּוֹם הַשְּׁבִיעִי עֲצֶרֶת לַיהוָה אֱלֹהֶיךָ
your Elohim   to ihvh   solemn assembly   the seventh   and in day

לֹא תַעֲשֶׂה מְלָאכָה:
work   you do   not

8 Six days thou shalt eat unleavened bread: and on the seventh day shall be a solemn assembly to the LORD thy God: thou shalt do no work therein.

ס

שִׁבְעָה שָׁבֻעֹת תִּסְפָּר־לָךְ
to you - you number   weeks   seven

מֵהָחֵל חֶרְמֵשׁ בַּקָּמָה
in raised grain   sickled   from the beginning

תָּחֵל לִסְפֹּר שִׁבְעָה שָׁבֻעוֹת:
weeks   seven   to number   begin

9 Seven weeks shalt thou number unto thee: begin to number the seven weeks from such time as thou beginnest to put the sickle to the corn.

וְעָשִׂיתָ חַג שָׁבֻעוֹת לַיהוָה אֱלֹהֶיךָ
your Elohim   to ihvh   weeks   feast   and you do

מִסַּת נִדְבַת יָדְךָ אֲשֶׁר תִּתֵּן
you will give   which   your hand   freewill offering   tribute

כַּאֲשֶׁר יְבָרֶכְךָ יְהוָה אֱלֹהֶיךָ:
your Elohim   ihvh   he blessed you   when

10 And thou shalt keep the feast of weeks unto the LORD thy God with a tribute of a freewill offering of thine hand, which thou shalt give unto the LORD thy God, according as the LORD thy God hath blessed thee:

וְשָׂמַחְתָּ לִפְנֵי יְהוָה אֱלֹהֶיךָ
your Elohim   ihvh   before   and you rejoice

אַתָּה וּבִנְךָ וּבִתֶּךָ וְעַבְדְּךָ וַאֲמָתֶךָ
and your maid   and your servant   and your daughter   and your son   you

וְהַלֵּוִי אֲשֶׁר בִּשְׁעָרֶיךָ וְהַגֵּר וְהַיָּתוֹם וְהָאַלְמָנָה
and the widow   and the fatherless   and the stranger   in your gates   which   and the Levite

אֲשֶׁר בְּקִרְבֶּךָ בַּמָּקוֹם אֲשֶׁר יִבְחַר יְהוָה אֱלֹהֶיךָ
your Elohim   ihvh   he chooses   which   in place   in among you   which

לְשַׁכֵּן שְׁמוֹ שָׁם:
there   his name   to dwell

11 And thou shalt rejoice before the LORD thy God, thou, and thy son, and thy daughter, and thy manservant, and thy maidservant, and the Levite that is within thy gates, and the stranger, and the fatherless, and the widow, that are among you, in the place which the LORD thy God hath chosen to place his name there.

וְזָכַרְתָּ כִּי־עֶבֶד הָיִיתָ בְּמִצְרָיִם
in Egypt   you were   slave - like   and you remember

וְשָׁמַרְתָּ וְעָשִׂיתָ אֶת־הַחֻקִּים הָאֵלֶּה:
the these   the statutes - that   and you do   and you heed

12 And thou shalt remember that thou wast a bondman in Egypt: and thou shalt observe and do these statutes.

פ

[מפטיר]

חַג הַסֻּכֹּת תַּעֲשֶׂה לְךָ שִׁבְעַת יָמִים
days   seven   to you   you do   the succot   festival

בְּאָסְפְּךָ מִגָּרְנְךָ וּמִיִּקְבֶךָ:
and from your wine vat   from threshing site   in your gathering

13 Thou shalt observe the feast of tabernacles seven days, after that thou hast gathered in thy corn and thy wine:

וְשָׂמַחְתָּ בְּחַגֶּךָ אַתָּה וּבִנְךָ וּבִתֶּךָ וְעַבְדְּךָ וַאֲמָתֶךָ
and your maid   and your servant   and your daughter   and your son   you   in your festival   and you rejoice

וְהַלֵּוִי וְהַגֵּר וְהַיָּתוֹם וְהָאַלְמָנָה אֲשֶׁר בִּשְׁעָרֶיךָ:
in your gates   which   and the widow   and the fatherless   and the stranger   and the Levite

14 And thou shalt rejoice in thy feast, thou, and thy son, and thy daughter, and thy manservant, and thy maidservant, and the Levite, the stranger, and the fatherless, and the widow, that are within thy gates.

שִׁבְעַת יָמִים תָּחֹג לַיהוָה אֱלֹהֶיךָ
your Elohim   to ihvh   you festival   days   seven

בַּמָּקוֹם אֲשֶׁר־יִבְחַר יְהוָה
ihvh   he chooses - which   in place

כִּי יְבָרֶכְךָ יְהוָה אֱלֹהֶיךָ בְּכֹל תְּבוּאָתְךָ
your production - in all   your Elohim   ihvh   he will bless you   like

וּבְכֹל מַעֲשֵׂה יָדֶיךָ וְהָיִיתָ אַךְ שָׂמֵחַ:
happy   surely   and you will be   your hands   works   and in all

15 Seven days shalt thou keep a solemn feast unto the LORD thy God in the place which the LORD shall choose: because the LORD thy God shall bless thee in all thine increase, and in all the works of thine hands, therefore thou shalt surely rejoice.

שָׁלוֹשׁ פְּעָמִים בַּשָּׁנָה יֵרָאֶה כָל־זְכוּרְךָ
all your males   he will appear   in year   times   three

אֶת־פְּנֵי יְהוָה אֱלֹהֶיךָ בַּמָּקוֹם אֲשֶׁר יִבְחָר
he chooses   which   in place   your Elohim   ihvh   face - that

בְּחַג הַמַּצּוֹת וּבְחַג הַשָּׁבֻעוֹת וּבְחַג הַסֻּכּוֹת
the succot   the festival   the weeks   and in festival   the unleavened   in festival

וְלֹא יֵרָאֶה אֶת־פְּנֵי יְהוָה רֵיקָם:
empty   ihvh   face - that   he appear   and not

16 Three times in a year shall all thy males appear before the LORD thy God in the place which he shall choose; in the feast of unleavened bread, and in the feast of weeks, and in the feast of tabernacles: and they shall not appear before the LORD empty:

אִ֕ישׁ כְּמַתְּנַ֣ת יָד֑וֹ
              his hand   like gift   man

כְּבִרְכַּ֛ת יְהוָ֥ה אֱלֹהֶ֖יךָ אֲשֶׁ֥ר נָֽתַן־לָֽךְ׃
to you - given which your Elohim ihvh like blessing

17 Every man shall give as he is able, according to the blessing of the LORD thy God which he hath given thee.

ס ס ס

Shofatim

Chapter 16 cont

[פרשת שופטים]

שֹׁפְטִ֣ים וְשֹֽׁטְרִ֗ים תִּֽתֶּן־לְךָ֙ בְּכָל־שְׁעָרֶ֔יךָ
judges · and officers · to you - you give · your gates - in all

אֲשֶׁ֨ר יְהֹוָ֧ה אֱלֹהֶ֛יךָ נֹתֵ֥ן לְךָ֖ לִשְׁבָטֶ֑יךָ
which · ihvh · your Elohim · gives · to you · to your tribes

וְשָׁפְט֥וּ אֶת־הָעָ֖ם מִשְׁפַּט־צֶֽדֶק׃
and they will judge · the people - that · righteous - judgement

18 Judges and officers shalt thou make thee in all thy gates, which the LORD thy God giveth thee, throughout thy tribes: and they shall judge the people with just judgment.

לֹא־תַטֶּ֣ה מִשְׁפָּ֔ט לֹ֥א תַכִּ֖יר פָּנִ֑ים
you turn aside - not · judgment · not · you respect · faces

וְלֹֽא־תִקַּ֣ח שֹׁ֔חַד כִּ֣י הַשֹּׁ֗חַד יְעַוֵּר֙ עֵינֵ֣י חֲכָמִ֔ים
you take - and not · bribe · like · the bribe · it blinds · eyes · wise ones

וִֽיסַלֵּ֖ף דִּבְרֵ֥י צַדִּיקִֽם׃
and it perverts · speakings · righteous ones

19 Thou shalt not wrest judgment; thou shalt not respect persons, neither take a gift: for a gift doth blind the eyes of the wise, and pervert the words of the righteous.

צֶ֥דֶק צֶ֖דֶק תִּרְדֹּ֑ף לְמַ֤עַן תִּֽחְיֶה֙
righteous · righteous · you will pursue · to end · you will live

וְיָרַשְׁתָּ֣ אֶת־הָאָ֔רֶץ אֲשֶׁר־יְהֹוָ֥ה אֱלֹהֶ֖יךָ נֹתֵ֥ן לָֽךְ׃
and you inherit · the land - that · ihvh - which · your Elohim · gives · to you

20 That which is altogether just shalt thou follow, that thou mayest live, and inherit the land which the LORD thy God giveth thee.

ס

לֹֽא־תִטַּ֥ע לְךָ֛ אֲשֵׁרָ֖ה כָּל־עֵ֑ץ
you plant - not · to you · grove · tree - all

אֵ֗צֶל מִזְבַּ֛ח יְהֹוָ֥ה אֱלֹהֶ֖יךָ אֲשֶׁ֥ר תַּעֲשֶׂה־לָּֽךְ׃
next to · altar · ihvh · your Elohim · which · to you - you will make

21 Thou shalt not plant thee a grove of any trees near unto the altar of the LORD thy God, which thou shalt make thee.

וְלֹֽא־תָקִ֥ים לְךָ֖ מַצֵּבָ֑ה אֲשֶׁ֥ר שָׂנֵ֖א יְהֹוָ֥ה אֱלֹהֶֽיךָ׃
and not - you place · to you · monument · which · hates · ihvh · your Elohim

22 Neither shalt thou set thee up any image; which the LORD thy God hateth.

ס

Chapter 17

ספר דברים פרק יז

לֹא־תִזְבַּח לַיהוָה אֱלֹהֶיךָ שׁוֹר וָשֶׂה
and sheep　ox　your Elohim　to ihvh　you sacrifice - not

אֲשֶׁר יִהְיֶה בוֹ מוּם כֹּל דָּבָר רָע
bad　matter　all　blemish　in it　it was　which

כִּי תוֹעֲבַת יְהוָה אֱלֹהֶיךָ הוּא׃
it　your Elohim　ihvh　abomination　like

1 Thou shalt not sacrifice unto the LORD thy God any bullock, or sheep, wherein is blemish, or any evil favouredness: for that is an abomination unto the LORD thy God.

ס

כִּי־יִמָּצֵא בְקִרְבְּךָ בְּאַחַד שְׁעָרֶיךָ
your gates　in one　in among you　he found - like

אֲשֶׁר־יְהוָה אֱלֹהֶיךָ נֹתֵן לָךְ
to you　gives　your Elohim　ihvh - which

אִישׁ אוֹ־אִשָּׁה אֲשֶׁר יַעֲשֶׂה אֶת־הָרַע בְּעֵינֵי יְהוָה־אֱלֹהֶיךָ
your Elohim - ihvh　in eyes　the bad - that　he does　which　woman - or　man

לַעֲבֹר בְּרִיתוֹ׃
his covenant　to pass

2 If there be found among you, within any of thy gates which the LORD thy God giveth thee, man or woman, that hath wrought wickedness in the sight of the LORD thy God, in transgressing his covenant,

וַיֵּלֶךְ וַיַּעֲבֹד אֱלֹהִים אֲחֵרִים
other ones　elohim　and he served　and he went

וַיִּשְׁתַּחוּ לָהֶם וְלַשֶּׁמֶשׁ אוֹ לַיָּרֵחַ
to moon　or　and to sun　to them　and he bowed down

אוֹ לְכָל־צְבָא הַשָּׁמַיִם אֲשֶׁר לֹא־צִוִּיתִי׃
I commanded - not　which　the heaven　host - to all　or

3 And hath gone and served other gods, and worshipped them, either the sun, or moon, or any of the host of heaven, which I have not commanded;

וְהֻגַּד־לְךָ וְשָׁמָעְתָּ וְדָרַשְׁתָּ הֵיטֵב
diligently　and you inquired　and you heard　to you - and told

Shofatim - Chapter 17

וְהִנֵּה אֱמֶת נָכוֹן הַדָּבָר נֶעֶשְׂתָה
and here   truth   correct   the matter   it was done

הַתּוֹעֵבָה הַזֹּאת בְּיִשְׂרָאֵל:
the abomination   the this   in Israel

4 And it be told thee, and thou hast heard of it, and inquired diligently, and, behold, it be true, and the thing certain, that such abomination is wrought in Israel:

וְהוֹצֵאתָ אֶת־הָאִישׁ הַהוּא אוֹ אֶת־הָאִשָּׁה הַהִוא
and you bring out   the man - that   or   the he   the woman - that   the she

אֲשֶׁר עָשׂוּ אֶת־הַדָּבָר הָרַע הַזֶּה אֶל־שְׁעָרֶיךָ
which   they did   the matter - that   the bad   the this   unto - your gates

אֶת־הָאִישׁ אוֹ אֶת־הָאִשָּׁה וּסְקַלְתָּם בָּאֲבָנִים וָמֵתוּ:
the man - that   or   the woman - that   and stone them   in stones   and they die

5 Then shalt thou bring forth that man or that woman, which have committed that wicked thing, unto thy gates, even that man or that woman, and shalt stone them with stones, till they die.

עַל־פִּי שְׁנַיִם עֵדִים אוֹ שְׁלֹשָׁה עֵדִים יוּמַת הַמֵּת
upon - and mouth   two ones   witnesses   or   three   witnesses   he dies   the death

לֹא יוּמַת עַל־פִּי עֵד אֶחָד:
not   he dies   upon - mouth   witness   one

6 At the mouth of two witnesses, or three witnesses, shall he that is worthy of death be put to death; but at the mouth of one witness he shall not be put to death.

יַד הָעֵדִים תִּהְיֶה־בּוֹ בָרִאשֹׁנָה לַהֲמִיתוֹ
the witnesses hand   in it - you will be   in first   to the his kill

וְיַד כָּל־הָעָם בָּאַחֲרֹנָה וּבִעַרְתָּ הָרַע מִקִּרְבֶּךָ:
and hand   all - the people   in afterwards   and you eradicate   the bad   from amongst you

7 The hands of the witnesses shall be first upon him to put him to death, and afterward the hands of all the people. So thou shalt put the evil away from among you.

פ

כִּי יִפָּלֵא מִמְּךָ דָבָר לַמִּשְׁפָּט
like   it difficult   from you   matter   to judgment

בֵּין־דָּם לְדָם בֵּין־דִּין לְדִין וּבֵין נֶגַע לָנֶגַע
between - blood   to blood   adjudication - between   to adjudication   and between   touch   to touch

דִּבְרֵי רִיבֹת בִּשְׁעָרֶיךָ וְקַמְתָּ וְעָלִיתָ אֶל־הַמָּקוֹם
matters   controversy   in your gates   and you will arise   and you ascend   unto - the place

אֲשֶׁר יִבְחַר יְהוָה אֱלֹהֶיךָ בּוֹ:
which   will choose   ihvh   your Elohim   in it

8 If there arise a matter too hard for thee in judgment, between blood and blood, between plea and plea, and between stroke and stroke, being matters of controversy within thy gates: then shalt thou arise, and get thee up into the place which the LORD thy God shall choose;

וּבָאתָ֗ אֶל־הַכֹּהֲנִים֙ הַלְוִיִּ֔ם וְאֶל־הַשֹּׁפֵ֔ט
and you will come unto - the priests the Levites and unto - the judge

אֲשֶׁ֥ר יִהְיֶ֖ה בַּיָּמִ֣ים הָהֵ֑ם וְדָרַשְׁתָּ֙
which it will be in days the them and you inquire

וְהִגִּ֣ידוּ לְךָ֔ אֵ֖ת דְּבַ֥ר הַמִּשְׁפָּֽט׃
and they cause to tell to you that matter the judgment

9 And thou shalt come unto the priests the Levites, and unto the judge that shall be in those days, and inquire; and they shall show thee the sentence of judgment:

וְעָשִׂ֗יתָ עַל־פִּ֤י הַדָּבָר֙
and you will do upon - mouth the matter

אֲשֶׁ֣ר יַגִּ֣ידֽוּ לְךָ֔ מִן־הַמָּק֣וֹם הַה֑וּא
which they tell to you from - the place the it

אֲשֶׁ֥ר יִבְחַ֖ר יְהוָ֑ה
which he choose ihvh

וְשָׁמַרְתָּ֣ לַעֲשׂ֔וֹת כְּכֹ֖ל אֲשֶׁ֥ר יוֹרֽוּךָ׃
and you will heed to do like all which they inform you

10 And thou shalt do according to the sentence, which they of that place which the LORD shall choose shall shew thee; and thou shalt observe to do according to all that they inform thee:

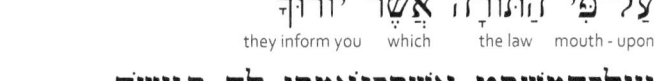
upon - mouth the law which they inform you

וְעַל־הַמִּשְׁפָּ֖ט אֲשֶׁר־יֹאמְר֣וּ לְךָ֑ תַּעֲשֶׂ֑ה
and upon - judgment which - they say to you you do

לֹ֣א תָס֗וּר מִן־הַדָּבָ֛ר אֲשֶׁר־יַגִּ֥ידֽוּ לְךָ֖ יָמִ֥ין וּשְׂמֹֽאל׃
not you withdraw from - the matter which - they tell to you right and left

11 According to the sentence of the law which they shall teach thee, and according to the judgment which they shall tell thee, thou shalt do: thou shalt not decline from the sentence which they shall shew thee, to the right hand, nor to the left.

וְהָאִ֞ישׁ אֲשֶׁר־יַעֲשֶׂ֣ה בְזָד֗וֹן לְבִלְתִּ֣י שְׁמֹ֣עַ
and the man which - he does in arrogance to without he hears

unto - the priest the one standing to minister there that - ihvh your Elohim

אוֹ אֶל־הַשֹּׁפֵט וּמֵת הָאִישׁ הַהוּא וּבִעַרְתָּ הָרָע מִיִּשְׂרָאֵל׃

| from Israel | the bad | and you eradicate | the he | the man | and will die | the judge - unto | or |

12 And the man that will do presumptuously, and will not hearken unto the priest that standeth to minister there before the LORD thy God, or unto the judge, even that man shall die: and thou shalt put away the evil from Israel.

וְכָל־הָעָם יִשְׁמְעוּ וְיִרָאוּ וְלֹא יְזִידוּן עוֹד׃

| again | he arrogant | and not | and they fear | they will hear | the people - and all |

13 And all the people shall hear, and fear, and do no more presumptuously.

ס

[שני]

כִּי־תָבֹא אֶל־הָאָרֶץ אֲשֶׁר יְהֹוָה אֱלֹהֶיךָ נֹתֵן לָךְ

| to you | gives | your Elohim | ihvh | which | the land - unto | your come - like |

וִירִשְׁתָּהּ וְיָשַׁבְתָּה בָּהּ

| in it | and you will dwell | and you possess it |

וְאָמַרְתָּ אָשִׂימָה עָלַי מֶלֶךְ כְּכָל־הַגּוֹיִם אֲשֶׁר סְבִיבֹתָי׃

| around me | which | the nations - like all | king | upon me | I will set | and you say |

14 When thou art come unto the land which the LORD thy God giveth thee, and shalt possess it, and shalt dwell therein, and shalt say, I will set a king over me, like as all the nations that are about me;

שׂוֹם תָּשִׂים עָלֶיךָ מֶלֶךְ אֲשֶׁר יִבְחַר יְהֹוָה אֱלֹהֶיךָ בּוֹ

| in him | your Elohim | ihvh | he chooses | which | king | upon you | you set | set |

מִקֶּרֶב אַחֶיךָ תָּשִׂים עָלֶיךָ מֶלֶךְ

| king | upon you | you will set | your brother | from among |

לֹא תוּכַל לָתֵת עָלֶיךָ אִישׁ נָכְרִי אֲשֶׁר לֹא־אָחִיךָ הוּא׃

| he | your brother - not | which | stranger | man | upon you | to give | you able | not |

15 Thou shalt in any wise set him king over thee, whom the LORD thy God shall choose: one from among thy brethren shalt thou set king over thee: thou mayest not set a stranger over thee, which is not thy brother.

רַק לֹא־יַרְבֶּה־לּוֹ סוּסִים

| horses | to him - he will multiply - not | only |

וְלֹא־יָשִׁיב אֶת־הָעָם מִצְרַיְמָה לְמַעַן הַרְבּוֹת סוּס

| horse | the multiplying | to end | towards Egypt | the people - that | he return - and not |

וַיהֹוָה אָמַר לָכֶם לֹא תֹסִפוּן לָשׁוּב בַּדֶּרֶךְ הַזֶּה עוֹד׃

| again | the this | in way | to return | you proceed | not | to you | said | and ihvh |

16 But he shall not multiply horses to himself, nor cause the people to return to Egypt, to the end that he should multiply horses: forasmuch as the LORD hath said unto you,

Ye shall henceforth return no more that way.

וְלֹא יַרְבֶּה־לּוֹ נָשִׁים וְלֹא יָסוּר לְבָבוֹ
and not   he multiply   to him - women   and not   turn   his heart

וְכֶסֶף וְזָהָב לֹא יַרְבֶּה־לּוֹ מְאֹד:
and silver   and gold   not   he multiply - to him   greatly

17 Neither shall he multiply wives to himself, that his heart turn not away: neither shall he greatly multiply to himself silver and gold.

וְהָיָה כְשִׁבְתּוֹ עַל כִּסֵּא מַמְלַכְתּוֹ
and it is   like his sitting   upon   throne   from his kingdom

וְכָתַב לוֹ אֶת־מִשְׁנֵה הַתּוֹרָה הַזֹּאת
and will write   to him   that - copy   the law   the this

עַל־סֵפֶר מִלִּפְנֵי הַכֹּהֲנִים הַלְוִיִּם:
book - upon   from before   the priests   the Levites

18 And it shall be, when he sitteth upon the throne of his kingdom, that he shall write him a copy of this law in a book out of that which is before the priests the Levites:

וְהָיְתָה עִמּוֹ וְקָרָא בוֹ כָּל־יְמֵי חַיָּיו
and it will be with him   and read   in it   all - days   his life

לְמַעַן יִלְמַד לְיִרְאָה אֶת־יְהוָה אֱלֹהָיו
to end   he learns   to fear   that - ihvh   his Elohim

לִשְׁמֹר אֶת־כָּל־דִּבְרֵי הַתּוֹרָה הַזֹּאת
to heed   that - all - speakings   the law   the this

וְאֶת־הַחֻקִּים הָאֵלֶּה לַעֲשֹׂתָם:
and that - the statutes   the these   to do them

19 And it shall be with him, and he shall read therein all the days of his life: that he may learn to fear the LORD his God, to keep all the words of this law and these statutes, to do them:

20 That his heart be not lifted up above his brethren, and that he turn not aside from the commandment, to the right hand, or to the left: to the end that he may prolong his

days in his kingdom, he, and his children, in the midst of Israel.

ס

Chapter 18

ספר דברים פרק יח

[שלישי]

לֹא־יִהְיֶה לַכֹּהֲנִים הַלְוִיִּם כָּל־שֵׁבֶט לֵוִי

Levy   tribe - all   the Levites   to priests   it will be - not

חֵלֶק וְנַחֲלָה עִם־יִשְׂרָאֵל

Israel - with   and inheritance   portion

אִשֵּׁי יְהוָה וְנַחֲלָתוֹ יֹאכֵלוּן׃

they will eat   and his inheritance   ihvh   fires

1 The priests the Levites, and all the tribe of Levi, shall have no part nor inheritance with Israel: they shall eat the offerings of the LORD made by fire, and his inheritance.

וְנַחֲלָה לֹא־יִהְיֶה־לּוֹ בְּקֶרֶב אֶחָיו

his brother   in among   to him - will be - not   and inheritance

יְהוָה הוּא נַחֲלָתוֹ כַּאֲשֶׁר דִּבֶּר־לוֹ׃

to him - spoke   when   his inheritance   he   ihvh

2 Therefore shall they have no inheritance among their brethren: the LORD is their inheritance, as he hath said unto them.

ס

וְזֶה יִהְיֶה מִשְׁפַּט הַכֹּהֲנִים מֵאֵת הָעָם

the people   from that   the priests   judgment   will be   and this

מֵאֵת זֹבְחֵי הַזֶּבַח אִם־שׁוֹר אִם־שֶׂה

sheep - with   ox - with   the sacrifice   sacrifice   from that

וְנָתַן לַכֹּהֵן הַזְּרֹעַ וְהַלְּחָיַיִם וְהַקֵּבָה׃

and the maw   and the cheeks   the shoulder   to priest   and will give

3 And this shall be the priest's due from the people, from them that offer a sacrifice, whether it be ox or sheep; and they shall give unto the priest the shoulder, and the two cheeks, and the maw.

רֵאשִׁית דְּגָנְךָ תִּירֹשְׁךָ וְיִצְהָרֶךָ

and your oil   your wine   grain   first

וְרֵאשִׁית גֵּז צֹאנְךָ תִּתֶּן־לוֹ׃

to him - you give   your sheep   fleece   and first

4 The firstfruit also of thy corn, of thy wine, and of thine oil, and the first of the fleece of thy sheep, shalt thou give him.

כִּי בוֹ בָּחַר יְהוָה אֱלֹהֶיךָ מִכָּל־שְׁבָטֶיךָ
לַעֲמֹד לְשָׁרֵת בְּשֵׁם־יְהוָה
הוּא וּבָנָיו כָּל־הַיָּמִים׃

5 For the LORD thy God hath chosen him out of all thy tribes, to stand to minister in the name of the LORD, him and his sons for ever.

ס

[רביעי]
וְכִי־יָבֹא הַלֵּוִי מֵאַחַד שְׁעָרֶיךָ מִכָּל־יִשְׂרָאֵל
אֲשֶׁר־הוּא גָּר שָׁם וּבָא בְּכָל־אַוַּת נַפְשׁוֹ
אֶל־הַמָּקוֹם אֲשֶׁר־יִבְחַר יְהוָה׃

6 And if a Levite come from any of thy gates out of all Israel, where he sojourned, and come with all the desire of his mind unto the place which the LORD shall choose;

וְשֵׁרֵת בְּשֵׁם יְהוָה אֱלֹהָיו
כְּכָל־אֶחָיו הַלְוִיִּם הָעֹמְדִים שָׁם לִפְנֵי יְהוָה׃

7 Then he shall minister in the name of the LORD his God, as all his brethren the Levites do, which stand there before the LORD.

חֵלֶק כְּחֵלֶק יֹאכֵלוּ לְבַד מִמְכָּרָיו עַל־הָאָבוֹת׃

8 They shall have like portions to eat, beside that which cometh of the sale of his patrimony.

ס

כִּי אַתָּה בָּא אֶל־הָאָרֶץ אֲשֶׁר־יְהוָה אֱלֹהֶיךָ נֹתֵן לָךְ
לֹא־תִלְמַד לַעֲשׂוֹת כְּתוֹעֲבֹת הַגּוֹיִם הָהֵם׃

9 When thou art come into the land which the LORD thy God giveth thee, thou shalt not learn to do after the abominations of those nations.

Shofatim - Chapter 18

לֹא־יִמָּצֵא בְךָ מַעֲבִיר בְּנוֹ־וּבִתּוֹ בָּאֵשׁ
in fire   and his daughter - his son   from passer   in you   he will be found - not

קֹסֵם קְסָמִים מְעוֹנֵן וּמְנַחֵשׁ וּמְכַשֵּׁף׃
and witch   and enchanter   observer of times   diviner ones   diviner

10 There shall not be found among you any one that maketh his son or his daughter to pass through the fire, or that useth divination, or an observer of times, or an enchanter, or a witch,

וְחֹבֵר חָבֶר וְשֹׁאֵל אוֹב וְיִדְּעֹנִי וְדֹרֵשׁ אֶל־הַמֵּתִים׃
the dead ones - unto   and inquirer   or wizard   contacter   and Shoel   friend   and charmer

11 Or a charmer, or a consulter with familiar spirits, or a wizard, or a necromancer.

כִּי־תוֹעֲבַת יְהוָה כָּל־עֹשֵׂה אֵלֶּה
these   does - all   ihvh   abomination - like

וּבִגְלַל הַתּוֹעֵבֹת הָאֵלֶּה יְהוָה אֱלֹהֶיךָ מוֹרִישׁ אוֹתָם מִפָּנֶיךָ׃
from before you   to them   drives out   your Elohim   ihvh   the these   the abomination   and because of

12 For all that do these things are an abomination unto the LORD: and because of these abominations the LORD thy God doth drive them out from before thee.

תָּמִים תִּהְיֶה עִם יְהוָה אֱלֹהֶיךָ׃
your Elohim   ihvh   with   you will be   perfect

13 Thou shalt be perfect with the LORD thy God.

[חמישי]

כִּי הַגּוֹיִם הָאֵלֶּה אֲשֶׁר אַתָּה יוֹרֵשׁ אוֹתָם
to them   possess   you   which   the these   the nations   like

אֶל־מְעֹנְנִים וְאֶל־קֹסְמִים יִשְׁמָעוּ
they listen   diviners - and unto   observers of times - unto

וְאַתָּה לֹא כֵן נָתַן לְךָ יְהוָה אֱלֹהֶיךָ׃
your Elohim   ihvh   to you   gives   thus   not   and you

14 For these nations, which thou shalt possess, hearkened unto observers of times, and unto diviners: but as for thee, the LORD thy God hath not suffered thee so to do.

נָבִיא מִקִּרְבְּךָ מֵאַחֶיךָ כָּמֹנִי יָקִים לְךָ
to you   he will rise   like me   from your brothers   from among you   prophet

יְהוָה אֱלֹהֶיךָ אֵלָיו תִּשְׁמָעוּן׃
you will listen   unto him   your Elohim   ihvh

15 The LORD thy God will raise up unto thee a Prophet from the midst of thee, of thy brethren, like unto me; unto him ye shall hearken;

כְּכֹל אֲשֶׁר־שָׁאַלְתָּ מֵעִם יְהוָה אֱלֹהֶיךָ
like all   which - you ask   from with   ihvh   your Elohim

בְּחֹרֵב בְּיוֹם הַקָּהָל לֵאמֹר
in Horeb   in day   the assembly   to say

לֹא אֹסֵף לִשְׁמֹעַ אֶת־קוֹל יְהוָה אֱלֹהָי
not   again   to listen   that - voice   ihvh   my Elohim

וְאֶת־הָאֵשׁ הַגְּדֹלָה הַזֹּאת לֹא־אֶרְאֶה עוֹד
and that - the fire   the great   the this   not - I will see   again

וְלֹא אָמוּת׃
and not   I die

16 According to all that thou desiredst of the LORD thy God in Horeb in the day of the assembly, saying, Let me not hear again the voice of the LORD my God, neither let me see this great fire any more, that I die not.

וַיֹּאמֶר יְהוָה אֵלָי הֵיטִיבוּ אֲשֶׁר דִּבֵּרוּ׃
and he said   ihvh   unto me   they did well   which   they spoke

17 And the LORD said unto me, They have well spoken that which they have spoken.

נָבִיא אָקִים לָהֶם מִקֶּרֶב אֲחֵיהֶם כָּמוֹךָ
prophet   I will raise   to them   from among   their brothers   like you

וְנָתַתִּי דְבָרַי בְּפִיו
and will I give   speakings   in his mouth

וְדִבֶּר אֲלֵיהֶם אֵת כָּל־אֲשֶׁר אֲצַוֶּנּוּ׃
and will speak   unto them   that   all - which   I will command him

18 I will raise them up a Prophet from among their brethren, like unto thee, and will put my words in his mouth; and he shall speak unto them all that I shall command him.

וְהָיָה הָאִישׁ אֲשֶׁר לֹא־יִשְׁמַע אֶל־דְּבָרַי
and it will be   the man   which   not - he will listen   unto - speakings

אֲשֶׁר יְדַבֵּר בִּשְׁמִי אָנֹכִי אֶדְרֹשׁ מֵעִמּוֹ׃
which   he speaks   in my name   I am   requiring   from with him

19 And it shall come to pass, that whosoever will not hearken unto my words which he shall speak in my name, I will require it of him.

אַךְ הַנָּבִיא אֲשֶׁר יָזִיד לְדַבֵּר דָּבָר בִּשְׁמִי
thus   the prophet   which   he will arrogantly   to speak   matter   in my name

אֵת אֲשֶׁר לֹא־צִוִּיתִיו לְדַבֵּר
that   which   not - I commanded him   to speak

וַאֲשֶׁר יְדַבֵּר בְּשֵׁם אֱלֹהִים אֲחֵרִים
and which   he will speak   in name   elohim   other ones

וּמֵת הַנָּבִיא הַהוּא:
the he   the prophet   and die

20 But the prophet, which shall presume to speak a word in my name, which I have not commanded him to speak, or that shall speak in the name of other gods, even that prophet shall die.

וְכִי תֹאמַר בִּלְבָבֶךָ
in your heart   you say   and like

אֵיכָה נֵדַע אֶת־הַדָּבָר אֲשֶׁר לֹא־דִבְּרוֹ יְהוָה:
ihvh   his speak - not   which   the speak - that   we know   where

21 And if thou say in thine heart, How shall we know the word which the LORD hath not spoken?

אֲשֶׁר יְדַבֵּר הַנָּבִיא בְּשֵׁם יְהוָה
ihvh   in name   the prophet   he speaks   which

וְלֹא־יִהְיֶה הַדָּבָר וְלֹא יָבוֹא הוּא הַדָּבָר
the matter   it   he comes   and not   the matter   it will be - and not

אֲשֶׁר לֹא־דִבְּרוֹ יְהוָה בְּזָדוֹן דִּבְּרוֹ הַנָּבִיא
the prophet   his speak   in arrogance   ihvh   his speak - not   which

לֹא תָגוּר מִמֶּנּוּ:
from him   you shrink   not

22 When a prophet speaketh in the name of the LORD, if the thing follow not, nor come to pass, that is the thing which the LORD hath not spoken, but the prophet hath spoken it presumptuously: thou shalt not be afraid of him.

ס

Chapter 19

ספר דברים פרק יט

כִּי־יַכְרִית יְהוָה אֱלֹהֶיךָ אֶת־הַגּוֹיִם
the nations - that   your Elohim   ihvh   he cuts off - like

אֲשֶׁר יְהוָה אֱלֹהֶיךָ נֹתֵן לְךָ אֶת־אַרְצָם
their land - that   to you   gives   your Elohim   ihvh   which

וִירִשְׁתָּם וְיָשַׁבְתָּ בְּעָרֵיהֶם וּבְבָתֵּיהֶם:
and in their houses   in their cities   and you dwell   and you possess

1 When the LORD thy God hath cut off the nations, whose land the LORD thy God giveth thee, and thou succeedest them, and dwellest in their cities, and in their houses;

שָׁלוֹשׁ עָרִים תַּבְדִּיל לָךְ בְּתוֹךְ אַרְצֶךָ
your land   in midst   to you   you separate   cities   three

DEVARIM/DEUTERONOMY

אֲשֶׁ֧ר יְהוָ֛ה אֱלֹהֶ֖יךָ נֹתֵ֥ן לְךָ֖ לְרִשְׁתָּֽהּ׃
to possess it — to you — gives — your Elohim — ihvh — which

2 Thou shalt separate three cities for thee in the midst of thy land, which the LORD thy God giveth thee to possess it.

תָּכִ֣ין לְךָ֒ הַדֶּ֔רֶךְ וְשִׁלַּשְׁתָּ֙ אֶת־גְּב֣וּל אַרְצְךָ֔
your land — border - that — and you trisect — the way — to you — prepare

אֲשֶׁ֥ר יַנְחִֽילְךָ֖ יְהוָ֣ה אֱלֹהֶ֑יךָ
your Elohim — ihvh — bequeaths you — which

וְהָיָ֕ה לָנ֥וּס שָׁ֖מָּה כָּל־רֹצֵֽחַ׃
slayer of men - all — there — to flee — and it will be

3 Thou shalt prepare thee a way, and divide the coasts of thy land, which the LORD thy God giveth thee to inherit, into three parts, that every slayer may flee thither.

וְזֶה֙ דְּבַ֣ר הָרֹצֵ֔חַ אֲשֶׁר־יָנ֥וּס שָׁ֖מָּה וָחָ֑י
and live — there — he flee - which — the slayer — matter — and this

אֲשֶׁ֨ר יַכֶּ֤ה אֶת־רֵעֵ֙הוּ֙ בִּבְלִי־דַ֔עַת
knowledge - in without — his neighbor - that — he kills — which

וְה֛וּא לֹא־שֹׂנֵ֥א ל֖וֹ מִתְּמֹ֥ל שִׁלְשֹֽׁם׃
past — yesterday — to him — hated - not — and he

4 And this is the case of the slayer, which shall flee thither, that he may live: Whoso killeth his neighbour ignorantly, whom he hated not in time past;

וַאֲשֶׁר֩ יָבֹ֨א אֶת־רֵעֵ֥הוּ בַיַּעַר֮ לַחְטֹ֣ב עֵצִים֒
wood — to chop — in city — his neighbor - that — he came — and which

וְנִדְּחָ֨ה יָד֤וֹ בַגַּרְזֶן֙ לִכְרֹ֣ת הָעֵ֔ץ
the tree — to cut — in ax — his hand — and strokes

וְנָשַׁ֤ל הַבַּרְזֶל֙ מִן־הָעֵ֔ץ וּמָצָ֥א אֶת־רֵעֵ֖הוּ וָמֵ֑ת ה֗וּא
he — and die — his neighbor - that — and finds — the tree - from — the iron — and slips

יָנ֛וּס אֶל־אַחַ֥ת הֶעָרִים־הָאֵ֖לֶּה וָחָֽי׃
and live — the these - the cities — one - unto — he will flee

5 As when a man goeth into the wood with his neighbour to hew wood, and his hand fetcheth a stroke with the axe to cut down the tree, and the head slippeth from the helve, and lighteth upon his neighbour, that he die; he shall flee unto one of those cities, and live:

פֶּן־יִרְדֹּף֩ גֹּאֵ֨ל הַדָּ֜ם אַחֲרֵ֣י הָרֹצֵ֗חַ
the slayer — after — the blood — redeeming — he pursue - lest

כִּי־יֵחַם֮ לְבָבוֹ֒ וְהִשִּׂיג֛וֹ כִּֽי־יִרְבֶּ֥ה הַדֶּ֖רֶךְ
the way — he multiply - like — and his overtake — his heart — he hot — like

וְהִכָּ֣הוּ נֶ֑פֶשׁ וְל֕וֹ אֵ֥ין מִשְׁפַּט־מָ֖וֶת
    death - judgment isn't and to him soul and cause slay him

כִּ֣י לֹ֥א שֹׂנֵ֛א ה֥וּא ל֖וֹ מִתְּמ֥וֹל שִׁלְשֹֽׁם׃
    past yesterday to him he hated - not like

6 Lest the avenger of the blood pursue the slayer, while his heart is hot, and overtake him, because the way is long, and slay him; whereas he was not worthy of death, inasmuch as he hated him not in time past.

עַל־כֵּ֛ן אָנֹכִ֥י מְצַוְּךָ֖ לֵאמֹ֑ר שָׁלֹ֥שׁ עָרִ֖ים תַּבְדִּ֥יל לָֽךְ׃
  to you you separate cities three to say commanding you I am thus - upon

7 Wherefore I command thee, saying, Thou shalt separate three cities for thee.

וְאִם־יַרְחִ֞יב יְהוָ֤ה אֱלֹהֶ֙יךָ֙ אֶת־גְּבֻ֣לְךָ֔
    your borders - that your Elohim ihvh he widens - and if

כַּאֲשֶׁ֥ר נִשְׁבַּ֖ע לַאֲבֹתֶ֑יךָ
    to your fathers he swore when

וְנָ֤תַן לְךָ֙ אֶת־כָּל־הָאָ֔רֶץ אֲשֶׁ֥ר דִּבֶּ֖ר לָתֵ֥ת לַאֲבֹתֶֽיךָ׃
  to your fathers to give he spoke which the land - all - that to you and gives

8 And if the LORD thy God enlarge thy coast, as he hath sworn unto thy fathers, and give thee all the land which he promised to give unto thy fathers;

כִּֽי־תִשְׁמֹר֩ אֶת־כָּל־הַמִּצְוָ֨ה הַזֹּ֜את לַעֲשֹׂתָ֗הּ
    to do it the this commandments - all - that you heed - like

אֲשֶׁ֨ר אָנֹכִ֣י מְצַוְּךָ֮ הַיּוֹם֒ לְאַהֲבָ֞ה אֶת־יְהוָ֤ה אֱלֹהֶ֙יךָ֙
    your Elohim ihvh - that to love the day commanding you I am which

וְלָלֶ֥כֶת בִּדְרָכָ֖יו כָּל־הַיָּמִ֑ים
    the days - all in his ways and to walk

וְיָסַפְתָּ֙ לְךָ֥ ע֛וֹד שָׁלֹ֥שׁ עָרִ֖ים עַ֥ל הַשָּׁלֹ֥שׁ הָאֵֽלֶּה׃
  the these the three upon cities three again to you and you will add

9 If thou shalt keep all these commandments to do them, which I command thee this day, to love the LORD thy God, and to walk ever in his ways; then shalt thou add three cities more for thee, beside these three:

וְלֹ֤א יִשָּׁפֵךְ֙ דָּ֣ם נָקִ֔י בְּקֶ֖רֶב אַרְצְךָ֑
    your land in among innocent blood he shed and not

אֲשֶׁר֙ יְהוָ֣ה אֱלֹהֶ֔יךָ נֹתֵ֥ן לְךָ֖ נַחֲלָ֑ה וְהָיָ֥ה עָלֶ֖יךָ דָּמִֽים׃
  bloods upon you and it will be inheritance to you gives your Elohim ihvh which

10 That innocent blood be not shed in thy land, which the LORD thy God giveth thee for an inheritance, and so blood be upon thee.

פ

וְכִי־יִהְיֶה אִישׁ שֹׂנֵא לְרֵעֵהוּ
to his neighbor   hate   man   it will be - and like

וְאָרַב לוֹ וְקָם עָלָיו וְהִכָּהוּ נֶפֶשׁ וָמֵת
and dies   soul   and smites his   upon him   and rises   to him   and ambushes

וְנָס אֶל־אַחַת הֶעָרִים הָאֵל׃
the these   the cities   one - unto   and flees

11 But if any man hate his neighbour, and lie in wait for him, and rise up against him, and smite him mortally that he die, and fleeth into one of these cities:

וְשָׁלְחוּ זִקְנֵי עִירוֹ וְלָקְחוּ אֹתוֹ מִשָּׁם
from there   to him   and they take   his city   elders   and they will send

וְנָתְנוּ אֹתוֹ בְּיַד גֹּאֵל הַדָּם וָמֵת׃
and dies   the blood   redeemer   in hand   to him   and they give

12 Then the elders of his city shall send and fetch him thence, and deliver him into the hand of the avenger of blood, that he may die.

לֹא־תָחוֹס עֵינְךָ עָלָיו
upon him   your eye   you pity - not

וּבִעַרְתָּ דַם־הַנָּקִי מִיִּשְׂרָאֵל וְטוֹב לָךְ׃
to you   and good   from Israel   the innocent - blood   and you eradicate

13 Thine eye shall not pity him, but thou shalt put away the guilt of innocent blood from Israel, that it may go well with thee.

ס

[שׁשׁי]

לֹא תַסִּיג גְּבוּל רֵעֲךָ אֲשֶׁר גָּבְלוּ רִאשֹׁנִים בְּנַחֲלָתְךָ
in your allotment   first ones   they bounded   which   your neighbor   landmark   remove   not

אֲשֶׁר תִּנְחַל בָּאָרֶץ
in land   you are allotted   which

אֲשֶׁר יְהוָה אֱלֹהֶיךָ נֹתֵן לְךָ לְרִשְׁתָּהּ׃
to possess   to you   gives   your Elohim   ihvh   which

14 Thou shalt not remove thy neighbour's landmark, which they of old time have set in thine inheritance, which thou shalt inherit in the land that the LORD thy God giveth thee to possess it.

ס

לֹא־יָקוּם עֵד אֶחָד בְּאִישׁ לְכָל־עָוֹן
inequity - to all   in man   one   witness   he will rise - not

Shofatim - Chapter 19

וּלְכָל־חַטָּאת בְּכָל־חֵטְא אֲשֶׁר יֶחֱטָא עַל־פִּי שְׁנֵי עֵדִים

witnesses two mouth - upon he sins which sin - in all sin - and to all

אוֹ עַל־פִּי שְׁלֹשָׁה־עֵדִים יָקוּם דָּבָר׃

matter it established witnesses - three mouth - upon or

15 One witness shall not rise up against a man for any iniquity, or for any sin, in any sin that he sinneth: at the mouth of two witnesses, or at the mouth of three witnesses, shall the matter be established.

כִּי־יָקוּם עֵד־חָמָס בְּאִישׁ לַעֲנוֹת בּוֹ סָרָה׃

stupid in it to answer in man violence - witness he rise - like

16 If a false witness rise up against any man to testify against him that which is wrong;

וְעָמְדוּ שְׁנֵי־הָאֲנָשִׁים אֲשֶׁר־לָהֶם הָרִיב

the controversy to them - which the men - two and they stood

לִפְנֵי יְהוָה לִפְנֵי הַכֹּהֲנִים וְהַשֹּׁפְטִים

and the judges the priests before ihvh before

אֲשֶׁר יִהְיוּ בַּיָּמִים הָהֵם׃

the them in days they were which

17 Then both the men, between whom the controversy is, shall stand before the LORD, before the priests and the judges, which shall be in those days;

וְדָרְשׁוּ הַשֹּׁפְטִים הֵיטֵב

cause good the judges and they inquire

וְהִנֵּה עֵד־שֶׁקֶר הָעֵד שֶׁקֶר עָנָה בְאָחִיו׃

in his brother answer lie the witness lie - witness and here

18 And the judges shall make diligent inquisition: and, behold, if the witness be a false witness, and hath testified falsely against his brother;

וַעֲשִׂיתֶם לוֹ כַּאֲשֶׁר זָמַם לַעֲשׂוֹת לְאָחִיו

to his brother to do planned when to him and you will do

וּבִעַרְתָּ הָרָע מִקִּרְבֶּךָ׃

from among you the evil and you eradicate

19 Then shall ye do unto him, as he had thought to have done unto his brother: so shalt thou put the evil away from among you.

וְהַנִּשְׁאָרִים יִשְׁמְעוּ וְיִרָאוּ

and they will fear they will hear and the remainder ones

וְלֹא־יֹסִפוּ לַעֲשׂוֹת עוֹד כַּדָּבָר הָרָע הַזֶּה בְּקִרְבֶּךָ׃

in among you the this the evil like matter again to do they proceed - and not

20 And those which remain shall hear, and fear, and shall henceforth commit no more any such evil among you.

וְלֹא תָחוֹס עֵינֶךָ

your eye — you pity — and not

נֶפֶשׁ בְּנֶפֶשׁ עַיִן בְּעַיִן שֵׁן בְּשֵׁן יָד בְּיָד רֶגֶל בְּרָגֶל׃

in foot — foot — in hand — hand — in tooth — tooth — in eye — eye — in soul — soul

21 And thine eye shall not pity; but life shall go for life, eye for eye, tooth for tooth, hand for hand, foot for foot.

ס

Chapter 20

ספר דברים פרק כ

כִּי־תֵצֵא לַמִּלְחָמָה עַל־אֹיְבֶךָ

your enemy - upon — to war — you go out - like

וְרָאִיתָ סוּס וָרֶכֶב עַם רַב מִמְּךָ לֹא תִירָא מֵהֶם

from them — you fear — not — from you — many — people — and rider — horse — and you see

כִּי־יְהוָה אֱלֹהֶיךָ עִמָּךְ הַמַּעַלְךָ מֵאֶרֶץ מִצְרָיִם׃

Egypt — from land — the ascended you — with you — your Elohim — ihvh - like

1 When thou goest out to battle against thine enemies, and seest horses, and chariots, and a people more than thou, be not afraid of them: for the LORD thy God is with thee, which brought thee up out of the land of Egypt.

וְהָיָה כְּקָרָבְכֶם אֶל־הַמִּלְחָמָה וְנִגַּשׁ הַכֹּהֵן וְדִבֶּר אֶל־הָעָם׃

the people - unto — and speaks — the priest — and touches — the war - unto — like you near — and it will be

2 And it shall be, when ye are come nigh unto the battle, that the priest shall approach and speak unto the people,

וְאָמַר אֲלֵהֶם שְׁמַע יִשְׂרָאֵל

Israel — hear — unto them — and says

אַתֶּם קְרֵבִים הַיּוֹם לַמִּלְחָמָה עַל־אֹיְבֵיכֶם

your enemies - upon — to war — the day — near ones — you

אַל־יֵרַךְ לְבַבְכֶם אַל־תִּירְאוּ

you fear it - don't — your hearts — you fear - don't

וְאַל־תַּחְפְּזוּ וְאַל־תַּעַרְצוּ מִפְּנֵיהֶם׃

from before them — you be terrified it - and don't — you tremble it - and don't

3 And shall say unto them, Hear, O Israel, ye approach this day unto battle against your enemies: let not your hearts faint, fear not, and do not tremble, neither be ye terrified because of them;

כִּי יְהוָה אֱלֹהֵיכֶם הַהֹלֵךְ עִמָּכֶם

with you — the walker — your Elohim — ihvh — like

Shofatim - Chapter 20

לְהִלָּחֵ֥ם לָכֶ֖ם עִם־אֹיְבֵיכֶ֑ם לְהוֹשִׁ֖יעַ אֶתְכֶֽם׃

| to fight | to you | your enemies - with | to save | that you |

4 For the LORD your God is he that goeth with you, to fight for you against your enemies, to save you.

וְדִבְּר֥וּ הַשֹּׁטְרִ֖ים אֶל־הָעָ֥ם לֵאמֹ֑ר

| and they will speak | the officers | the people - unto | to say |

מִֽי־הָאִ֞ישׁ אֲשֶׁ֨ר בָּנָ֤ה בַֽיִת־חָדָשׁ֙ וְלֹ֣א חֲנָכ֔וֹ

| the man - who | which | built | the new - house | and not | it dedicated |

יֵלֵ֖ךְ וְיָשֹׁ֣ב לְבֵית֑וֹ פֶּן־יָמוּת֙ בַּמִּלְחָמָ֔ה וְאִ֥ישׁ אַחֵ֖ר יַחְנְכֶֽנּוּ׃

| he goes | and he returns | to his house | lest - he die | in war | and man | another | he dedicates it |

5 And the officers shall speak unto the people, saying, What man is there that hath built a new house, and hath not dedicated it? let him go and return to his house, lest he die in the battle, and another man dedicate it.

וּמִֽי־הָאִ֞ישׁ אֲשֶׁר־נָטַ֥ע כֶּ֛רֶם וְלֹ֥א חִלְּל֖וֹ

| the man - and who | which | planted | vineyard | and not | his started |

יֵלֵ֖ךְ וְיָשֹׁ֣ב לְבֵית֑וֹ פֶּן־יָמוּת֙ בַּמִּלְחָמָ֔ה וְאִ֥ישׁ אַחֵ֖ר יְחַלְּלֶֽנּוּ׃

| he goes | and he returns | to his house | lest - he die | in war | and man | another | he started it |

6 And what man is he that hath planted a vineyard, and hath not yet eaten of it? let him also go and return unto his house, lest he die in the battle, and another man eat of it.

וּמִֽי־הָאִ֞ישׁ אֲשֶׁר־אֵרַ֤שׂ אִשָּׁה֙ וְלֹ֣א לְקָחָ֔הּ

| the man - and who | which | betrothed | wife | and not | to take her |

יֵלֵ֖ךְ וְיָשֹׁ֣ב לְבֵית֑וֹ פֶּן־יָמוּת֙ בַּמִּלְחָמָ֔ה

| he goes | and he returns | to his house | lest - he dies | in war |

וְאִ֥ישׁ אַחֵ֖ר יִקָּחֶֽנָּה׃

| and man | another | he takes her |

7 And what man is there that hath betrothed a wife, and hath not taken her? let him go and return unto his house, lest he die in the battle, and another man take her.

וְיָסְפ֣וּ הַשֹּׁטְרִים֮ לְדַבֵּ֣ר אֶל־הָעָם֒

| and he will story | the officers | to speak | the people - unto |

וְאָמְר֗וּ מִֽי־הָאִ֤ישׁ הַיָּרֵא֙ וְרַ֣ךְ הַלֵּבָ֔ב

| and they say | the man - who | the fearful | and soft | the heart |

יֵלֵ֖ךְ וְיָשֹׁ֣ב לְבֵית֑וֹ וְלֹ֥א יִמַּ֛ס אֶת־לְבַ֥ב אֶחָ֖יו כִּלְבָבֽוֹ׃

| he goes | and he returns | to his house | and not | he melt | heart - that | his brother | like his heart |

8 And the officers shall speak further unto the people, and they shall say, What man is there that is fearful and fainthearted? let him go and return unto his house, lest his brethren's heart faint as well as his heart.

וְהָיָה כְּכַלֹּת הַשֹּׁטְרִים לְדַבֵּר אֶל־הָעָם
וּפָקְדוּ שָׂרֵי צְבָאוֹת בְּרֹאשׁ הָעָם:

9 And it shall be, when the officers have made an end of speaking unto the people, that they shall make captains of the armies to lead the people.

ס

[שביעי]

כִּי־תִקְרַב אֶל־עִיר לְהִלָּחֵם עָלֶיהָ
וְקָרָאתָ אֵלֶיהָ לְשָׁלוֹם:

10 When thou comest nigh unto a city to fight against it, then proclaim peace unto it.

וְהָיָה אִם־שָׁלוֹם תַּעַנְךָ וּפָתְחָה לָךְ
וְהָיָה כָּל־הָעָם הַנִּמְצָא־בָהּ יִהְיוּ לְךָ לָמַס וַעֲבָדוּךָ:

11 And it shall be, if it make thee answer of peace, and open unto thee, then it shall be, that all the people that is found therein shall be tributaries unto thee, and they shall serve thee.

וְאִם־לֹא תַשְׁלִים עִמָּךְ
וְעָשְׂתָה עִמְּךָ מִלְחָמָה וְצַרְתָּ עָלֶיהָ:

12 And if it will make no peace with thee, but will make war against thee, then thou shalt besiege it:

וּנְתָנָהּ יְהוָה אֱלֹהֶיךָ בְּיָדֶךָ
וְהִכִּיתָ אֶת־כָּל־זְכוּרָהּ לְפִי־חָרֶב:

13 And when the LORD thy God hath delivered it into thine hands, thou shalt smite every male thereof with the edge of the sword:

רַק הַנָּשִׁים וְהַטַּף וְהַבְּהֵמָה

וְכֹל אֲשֶׁר יִהְיֶה בָעִיר כָּל־שְׁלָלָהּ תָּבֹז לָךְ
to you you plunder loot - all in city will be which and all

וְאָכַלְתָּ אֶת־שְׁלַל אֹיְבֶיךָ
your enemies loot - that and you eat

אֲשֶׁר נָתַן יְהוָה אֱלֹהֶיךָ לָךְ׃
to you your Elohim ihvh gives which

14 But the women, and the little ones, and the cattle, and all that is in the city, even all the spoil thereof, shalt thou take unto thyself; and thou shalt eat the spoil of thine enemies, which the LORD thy God hath given thee.

כֵּן תַּעֲשֶׂה לְכָל־הֶעָרִים הָרְחֹקֹת מִמְּךָ מְאֹד
very from you the far off ones the cities - to all you do thus

אֲשֶׁר לֹא־מֵעָרֵי הַגּוֹיִם־הָאֵלֶּה הֵנָּה׃
here the these - the nations from cities - not which

15 Thus shalt thou do unto all the cities which are very far off from thee, which are not of the cities of these nations.

רַק מֵעָרֵי הָעַמִּים הָאֵלֶּה
the these the people cities only

אֲשֶׁר יְהוָה אֱלֹהֶיךָ נֹתֵן לְךָ נַחֲלָה
inheritance to you gives your Elohim ihvh which

לֹא תְחַיֶּה כָּל־נְשָׁמָה׃
breath - all you let live not

16 But of the cities of these people, which the LORD thy God doth give thee for an inheritance, thou shalt save alive nothing that breatheth:

כִּי־הַחֲרֵם תַּחֲרִימֵם
you utterly destroy them the utterly destroy them - like

הַחִתִּי וְהָאֱמֹרִי הַכְּנַעֲנִי וְהַפְּרִזִּי הַחִוִּי וְהַיְבוּסִי
the Jebusites the Hivites and the Perizzites the Canaanites and the Amorites the Hittites

כַּאֲשֶׁר צִוְּךָ יְהוָה אֱלֹהֶיךָ׃
your Elohim ihvh commanded you when

17 But thou shalt utterly destroy them; namely, the Hittites, and the Amorites, the Canaanites, and the Perizzites, the Hivites, and the Jebusites; as the LORD thy God hath commanded thee:

לְמַעַן אֲשֶׁר לֹא־יְלַמְּדוּ אֶתְכֶם לַעֲשׂוֹת כְּכֹל תּוֹעֲבֹתָם
their abominations like all to do that you they teach - not which to end

אֲשֶׁר עָשׂוּ לֵאלֹהֵיהֶם וַחֲטָאתֶם לַיהוָה אֱלֹהֵיכֶם׃
your Elohim to ihvh and you sin to their elohim they did which

18 That they teach you not to do after all their abominations, which they have done unto their gods; so should ye sin against the LORD your God.

ס

כִּי־תָצוּר אֶל־עִיר יָמִים רַבִּים לְהִלָּחֵם עָלֶיהָ לְתָפְשָׂהּ
you will besiege - like   city - unto   days   many   to fight   upon them   to grab it

לֹא־תַשְׁחִית אֶת־עֵצָהּ לִנְדֹּחַ עָלָיו גַּרְזֶן
you will destroy - not   trees - that   to forcing   upon it   axe

כִּי מִמֶּנּוּ תֹאכֵל וְאֹתוֹ לֹא תִכְרֹת
like   from it   you eat   and to it   not   you cut

כִּי הָאָדָם עֵץ הַשָּׂדֶה לָבֹא מִפָּנֶיךָ בַּמָּצוֹר׃
like   the Adam   tree   the field   to come   from before you   in siege

19 When thou shalt besiege a city a long time, in making war against it to take it, thou shalt not destroy the trees thereof by forcing an axe against them: for thou mayest eat of them, and thou shalt not cut them down (for the tree of the field is man's life) to employ them in the siege:

רַק עֵץ אֲשֶׁר־תֵּדַע כִּי לֹא־עֵץ מַאֲכָל הוּא
only   trees   which - you know   like   not - trees   food   it

אֹתוֹ תַשְׁחִית וְכָרָתָּ וּבָנִיתָ מָצוֹר עַל־הָעִיר
to it   you will destroy   and you cut down   and you will build   bulwarks   the city - upon

אֲשֶׁר־הִוא עֹשָׂה עִמְּךָ מִלְחָמָה עַד רִדְתָּהּ׃
it - which   did   with you   war   till   subdued

20 Only the trees which thou knowest that they be not trees for meat, thou shalt destroy and cut them down; and thou shalt build bulwarks against the city that maketh war with thee, until it be subdued.

פ

Chapter 21

ספר דברים פרק כא

כִּי־יִמָּצֵא חָלָל בָּאֲדָמָה
like - he finds   slain   in ground

אֲשֶׁר יְהוָה אֱלֹהֶיךָ נֹתֵן לְךָ לְרִשְׁתָּהּ
which   ihvh   your Elohim   gives   to you   to possess

נֹפֵל בַּשָּׂדֶה לֹא נוֹדַע מִי הִכָּהוּ׃
fallen   in field   not   known   who   slain him

1 If one be found slain in the land which the LORD thy God giveth thee to possess it, lying in the field, and it be not known who hath slain him:

Shofatim - Chapter 21

וְיָצְאוּ   זְקֵנֶיךָ וְשֹׁפְטֶיךָ
and they will come out   your elders   and your judges

וּמָדְדוּ   אֶל־הֶעָרִים אֲשֶׁר סְבִיבֹת הֶחָלָל׃
and they will measure   the cities - unto   which   surround   the slain

2 Then thy elders and thy judges shall come forth, and they shall measure unto the cities which are round about him that is slain:

וְהָיָה הָעִיר הַקְּרֹבָה אֶל־הֶחָלָל
and it will be   the city   the near   the slain - unto

וְלָקְחוּ זִקְנֵי הָעִיר הַהִוא עֶגְלַת בָּקָר
and they to take   elders   the city   the it   heifer   cattle

אֲשֶׁר לֹא־עֻבַּד בָּהּ אֲשֶׁר לֹא־מָשְׁכָה בְּעֹל׃
which   served - not   in it   which   not - drawn   in yoke

3 And it shall be, that the city which is next unto the slain man, even the elders of that city shall take an heifer, which hath not been wrought with, and which hath not drawn in the yoke;

וְהוֹרִדוּ זִקְנֵי הָעִיר הַהִוא אֶת־הָעֶגְלָה
and they bring down   elders   the city   the it   the heifer - that

אֶל־נַחַל אֵיתָן אֲשֶׁר לֹא־יֵעָבֵד בּוֹ
river - unto   perineal   which   not served   in it

וְלֹא יִזָּרֵעַ וְעָרְפוּ־שָׁם אֶת־הָעֶגְלָה בַּנָּחַל׃
and not   it sown   there - and they break neck   the heifer - that   in valley

4 And the elders of that city shall bring down the heifer unto a rough valley, which is neither eared nor sown, and shall strike off the heifer's neck there in the valley:

וְנִגְּשׁוּ הַכֹּהֲנִים בְּנֵי לֵוִי
and they touch   the priests   sons   Levites

כִּי בָם בָּחַר יְהוָה אֱלֹהֶיךָ לְשָׁרְתוֹ וּלְבָרֵךְ בְּשֵׁם יְהוָה
like   chosen in them   ihvh   your Elohim   to minister him   and to bless   in name   ihvh

וְעַל־פִּיהֶם יִהְיֶה כָּל־רִיב וְכָל־נָגַע׃
and upon - their mouth   it will be   all - contention   and all - stroke

5 And the priests the sons of Levi shall come near; for them the LORD thy God hath chosen to minister unto him, and to bless in the name of the LORD; and by their word shall every controversy and every stroke be tried:

וְכֹל זִקְנֵי הָעִיר הַהִוא הַקְּרֹבִים אֶל־הֶחָלָל
and all   elders   the city   the it   the near ones   slain - unto

יִרְחֲצוּ אֶת־יְדֵיהֶם עַל־הָעֶגְלָה הָעֲרוּפָה בַנָּחַל׃
they will wash   that - their hands   upon - the heifer   the broken neck   in river

6 And all the elders of that city, that are next unto the slain man, shall wash their hands over the heifer that is beheaded in the valley:

[מפטיר]

וְעָנוּ וְאָמְרוּ יָדֵינוּ לֹא שָׁפְכָה [שָׁפְכוּ] אֶת־הַדָּם הַזֶּה
and they will answer · and they will say · our hands · not · shed it · the blood - that · the this

וְעֵינֵינוּ לֹא רָאוּ׃
and our eyes · not · saw it

7 And they shall answer and say, Our hands have not shed this blood, neither have our eyes seen it.

כַּפֵּר לְעַמְּךָ יִשְׂרָאֵל אֲשֶׁר־פָּדִיתָ יְהוָה
shelter · to your people · Israel · which - you redeemed · ihvh

וְאַל־תִּתֵּן דָּם נָקִי בְּקֶרֶב עַמְּךָ יִשְׂרָאֵל
and don't - you give · blood · innocent · in near · your people · Israel

וְנִכַּפֵּר לָהֶם הַדָּם׃
and we shelter · to them · the blood

8 Be merciful, O LORD, unto thy people Israel, whom thou hast redeemed, and lay not innocent blood unto thy people of Israel's charge. And the blood shall be forgiven them.

וְאַתָּה תְּבַעֵר הַדָּם הַנָּקִי מִקִּרְבֶּךָ
and you · you eradicate · the blood · the innocent · from among you

כִּי־תַעֲשֶׂה הַיָּשָׁר בְּעֵינֵי יְהוָה׃
like - you do · the upright · in eyes · ihvh

9 So shalt thou put away the guilt of innocent blood from among you, when thou shalt do that which is right in the sight of the LORD.

ס ס ס

Ki Tetzeh

Chapter 21 cont

[פרשת כי תצא]

כִּי־תֵצֵא לַמִּלְחָמָה עַל־אֹיְבֶיךָ
_{enemies - upon   to war   you go out - like}

וּנְתָנוֹ יְהוָה אֱלֹהֶיךָ בְּיָדֶךָ וְשָׁבִיתָ שִׁבְיוֹ׃
_{his captive   and you captured   in your hand   your Elohim   ihvh   and his gift}

10 When thou goest forth to war against thine enemies, and the LORD thy God hath delivered them into thine hands, and thou hast taken them captive,

וְרָאִיתָ בַּשִּׁבְיָה אֵשֶׁת יְפַת־תֹּאַר
_{appearance - beautiful   woman   in captive   and you sees}

וְחָשַׁקְתָּ בָהּ וְלָקַחְתָּ לְךָ לְאִשָּׁה׃
_{to wife   to her   and you take   in her   and you attach}

11 And seest among the captives a beautiful woman, and hast a desire unto her, that thou wouldest have her to thy wife;

וַהֲבֵאתָהּ אֶל־תּוֹךְ בֵּיתֶךָ
_{your house   inside - unto   and the bring}

וְגִלְּחָה אֶת־רֹאשָׁהּ וְעָשְׂתָה אֶת־צִפָּרְנֶיהָ׃
_{her nails - that   and do her   her head - that   and shave her}

12 Then thou shalt bring her home to thine house; and she shall shave her head, and pare her nails;

וְהֵסִירָה אֶת־שִׂמְלַת שִׁבְיָהּ מֵעָלֶיהָ וְיָשְׁבָה בְּבֵיתֶךָ
_{in your house   and she sits   from upon her   captivity   dress - that   and she takes off}

וּבָכְתָה אֶת־אָבִיהָ וְאֶת־אִמָּהּ יֶרַח יָמִים
_{days   full month   and her mother - that   her father - that   and she cries}

וְאַחַר כֵּן תָּבוֹא אֵלֶיהָ וּבְעַלְתָּהּ וְהָיְתָה לְךָ לְאִשָּׁה׃
_{to wife   to her   and will be   and master her   unto her   you come   thus   and after}

13 And she shall put the raiment of her captivity from off her, and shall remain in thine house, and bewail her father and her mother a full month: and after that thou shalt go in unto her, and be her husband, and she shall be thy wife.

וְהָיָה אִם־לֹא חָפַצְתָּ בָּהּ וְשִׁלַּחְתָּהּ לְנַפְשָׁהּ
_{to her soul   and cast her   in her   you delight   not - if   and it will be}

וּמָכֹר לֹא־תִמְכְּרֶנָּה בַּכָּסֶף
_{in money   you sell her - not   and sell}

Ki Tetzeh - Chapter 21 cont

לֹא־תִתְעַמֵּר בָּהּ תַּחַת אֲשֶׁר עִנִּיתָהּ׃
humbled her   which   instead   in her   you merchandise - not

14 And it shall be, if thou have no delight in her, then thou shalt let her go whither she will; but thou shalt not sell her at all for money, thou shalt not make merchandise of her, because thou hast humbled her.

ס

כִּי־תִהְיֶיןָ לְאִישׁ שְׁתֵּי נָשִׁים
women   two   to wife   you have - like

הָאַחַת אֲהוּבָה וְהָאַחַת שְׂנוּאָה
hated   and one   beloved   the one

וְיָלְדוּ־לוֹ בָנִים הָאֲהוּבָה וְהַשְּׂנוּאָה
and the hated   the beloved   sons   to him - and they bore

וְהָיָה הַבֵּן הַבְּכוֹר לַשְּׂנִיאָה׃
to hated one   the first born   the son   and it be

15 If a man have two wives, one beloved, and another hated, and they have born him children, both the beloved and the hated; and if the firstborn son be hers that was hated:

וְהָיָה בְּיוֹם הַנְחִילוֹ אֶת־בָּנָיו אֵת אֲשֶׁר־יִהְיֶה לוֹ
to him   will be - which   that   his sons - that   the his inheritance   in day   and it will be

לֹא יוּכַל לְבַכֵּר אֶת־בֶּן־הָאֲהוּבָה
the beloved - son - that   to make firstborn   he able   not

עַל־פְּנֵי בֶן־הַשְּׂנוּאָה הַבְּכֹר׃
the first born   the hated - son   face - upon

16 Then it shall be, when he maketh his sons to inherit that which he hath, that he may not make the son of the beloved firstborn before the son of the hated, which is indeed the firstborn:

כִּי אֶת־הַבְּכֹר בֶּן־הַשְּׂנוּאָה יַכִּיר
he will recognize   the hated - son   the first born - that   like

לָתֶת לוֹ פִּי שְׁנַיִם בְּכֹל אֲשֶׁר־יִמָּצֵא לוֹ
to him   he finds - which   in all   twice   face   to him   to give

כִּי־הוּא רֵאשִׁית אֹנוֹ לוֹ מִשְׁפַּט הַבְּכֹרָה׃
the first born   judgment   to him   his being   first   he - like

17 But he shall acknowledge the son of the hated for the firstborn, by giving him a double portion of all that he hath: for he is the beginning of his strength; the right of the firstborn is his.

ס

כִּי־יִהְיֶה לְאִישׁ בֵּן סוֹרֵר וּמוֹרֶה אֵינֶנּוּ שֹׁמֵעַ בְּקוֹל אָבִיו וּבְקוֹל אִמּוֹ וְיִסְּרוּ אֹתוֹ וְלֹא יִשְׁמַע אֲלֵיהֶם:

18 If a man have a stubborn and rebellious son, which will not obey the voice of his father, or the voice of his mother, and that, when they have chastened him, will not hearken unto them:

וְתָפְשׂוּ בוֹ אָבִיו וְאִמּוֹ וְהוֹצִיאוּ אֹתוֹ אֶל־זִקְנֵי עִירוֹ וְאֶל־שַׁעַר מְקֹמוֹ:

19 Then shall his father and his mother lay hold on him, and bring him out unto the elders of his city, and unto the gate of his place;

וְאָמְרוּ אֶל־זִקְנֵי עִירוֹ בְּנֵנוּ זֶה סוֹרֵר וּמֹרֶה אֵינֶנּוּ שֹׁמֵעַ בְּקֹלֵנוּ זוֹלֵל וְסֹבֵא:

20 And they shall say unto the elders of his city, This our son is stubborn and rebellious, he will not obey our voice; he is a glutton, and a drunkard.

וּרְגָמֻהוּ כָּל־אַנְשֵׁי עִירוֹ בָאֲבָנִים וָמֵת וּבִעַרְתָּ הָרָע מִקִּרְבֶּךָ וְכָל־יִשְׂרָאֵל יִשְׁמְעוּ וְיִרָאוּ:

21 And all the men of his city shall stone him with stones, that he die: so shalt thou put evil away from among you; and all Israel shall hear, and fear.

ס

[שני]

וְכִי־יִהְיֶה בְאִישׁ חֵטְא מִשְׁפַּט־מָוֶת וְהוּמָת וְתָלִיתָ אֹתוֹ עַל־עֵץ:

22 And if a man have committed a sin worthy of death, and he be to be put to death, and thou hang him on a tree:

Ki Tetzeh - Chapter 22

לֹא־תָלִין נִבְלָתוֹ עַל־הָעֵץ
the tree - upon   his carcass   you lodge - not

כִּי־קָבוֹר תִּקְבְּרֶנּוּ בַּיּוֹם הַהוּא
the it   in day   you bury it   bury - like

כִּי־קִלְלַת אֱלֹהִים תָּלוּי
hanged one   Elohim   cursed - like

וְלֹא תְטַמֵּא אֶת־אַדְמָתְךָ
your ground - that   you defiled   and not

אֲשֶׁר יְהוָה אֱלֹהֶיךָ נֹתֵן לְךָ נַחֲלָה׃
inheritance   to you   gives   your Elohim   ihvh   which

23 His body shall not remain all night upon the tree, but thou shalt in any wise bury him that day; (for he that is hanged is accursed of God;) that thy land be not defiled, which the LORD thy God giveth thee for an inheritance.

ס

Chapter 22

ספר דברים פרק כב

לֹא־תִרְאֶה אֶת־שׁוֹר אָחִיךָ אוֹ אֶת־שֵׂיוֹ נִדָּחִים
go astray   his sheep - that   or   your brother   ox - that   you see - not

וְהִתְעַלַּמְתָּ מֵהֶם
from them   and you hide yourself

הָשֵׁב תְּשִׁיבֵם לְאָחִיךָ׃
to your brother   you return them   the return

1 Thou shalt not see thy brother's ox or his sheep go astray, and hide thyself from them: thou shalt in any case bring them again unto thy brother.

וְאִם־לֹא קָרוֹב אָחִיךָ אֵלֶיךָ
unto you   your brother   bring near   not - and if

וְלֹא יְדַעְתּוֹ וַאֲסַפְתּוֹ אֶל־תּוֹךְ בֵּיתֶךָ
your house   inside - unto   and his gathering   his knowing   and not

וְהָיָה עִמְּךָ עַד דְּרֹשׁ אָחִיךָ אֹתוֹ וַהֲשֵׁבֹתוֹ לוֹ׃
to him   and the his restore   to it   your brother   seek   till   with you   and it will be

2 And if thy brother be not nigh unto thee, or if thou know him not, then thou shalt bring it unto thine own house, and it shall be with thee until thy brother seek after it, and thou shalt restore it to him again.

וְכֵן תַּעֲשֶׂה לַחֲמֹרוֹ וְכֵן תַּעֲשֶׂה לְשִׂמְלָתוֹ
to his raiment   you will do   and thus   to his ass   you will do   and thus

וְכֵ֣ן תַּעֲשֶׂ֔ה לְכָל־אֲבֵדַ֖ת אָחִ֑יךָ
     your brother   lost - to all   you will do   and thus

אֲשֶׁר־תֹּאבַ֥ד מִמֶּ֖נּוּ וּמְצָאתָ֑הּ לֹ֥א תוּכַ֖ל לְהִתְעַלֵּֽם׃
to cause to hide you you able not and you found from it   lost - which

3 In like manner shalt thou do with his ass; and so shalt thou do with his raiment; and with all lost thing of thy brother's, which he hath lost, and thou hast found, shalt thou do likewise: thou mayest not hide thyself.

ס

לֹא־תִרְאֶה֩ אֶת־חֲמ֨וֹר אָחִ֜יךָ א֤וֹ שׁוֹרוֹ֙ נֹפְלִ֣ים בַּדֶּ֔רֶךְ
 in way falling ones his ox or your brother ass - that you see - not

וְהִתְעַלַּמְתָּ֖ מֵהֶ֑ם הָקֵ֥ם תָּקִ֖ים עִמּֽוֹ׃
with him you raise the raise from them and you hide yourself

4 Thou shalt not see thy brother's ass or his ox fall down by the way, and hide thyself from them: thou shalt surely help him to lift them up again.

ס

לֹא־יִהְיֶ֤ה כְלִי־גֶ֙בֶר֙ עַל־אִשָּׁ֔ה
woman - upon gentleman - instrument   it will be - not

וְלֹא־יִלְבַּ֥שׁ גֶּ֖בֶר שִׂמְלַ֣ת אִשָּׁ֑ה
woman dress man dress - and not

כִּ֧י תוֹעֲבַ֛ת יְהוָ֥ה אֱלֹהֶ֖יךָ כָּל־עֹ֥שֵׂה אֵֽלֶּה׃
these doing - all your Elohim ihvh abomination like

5 The woman shall not wear that which pertaineth unto a man, neither shall a man put on a woman's garment: for all that do so are abomination unto the LORD thy God.

פ

כִּ֣י יִקָּרֵ֣א קַן־צִפּ֣וֹר ׀ לְפָנֶ֡יךָ בַּדֶּ֜רֶךְ בְּכָל־עֵ֣ץ
tree - in all in way before you bird - nest it comes near like

א֣וֹ עַל־הָאָ֗רֶץ אֶפְרֹחִים֙ א֣וֹ בֵיצִ֔ים
eggs or young bird ones the ground - upon or

וְהָאֵ֤ם רֹבֶ֙צֶת֙ עַל־הָֽאֶפְרֹחִ֔ים א֖וֹ עַל־הַבֵּיצִ֑ים
the eggs - upon or young bird ones - upon reclining and the mother

לֹא־תִקַּ֥ח הָאֵ֖ם עַל־הַבָּנִֽים׃
the sons - upon the mother you take - not

6 If a bird's nest chance to be before thee in the way in any tree, or on the ground, whether they be young ones, or eggs, and the dam sitting upon the young, or upon the eggs, thou shalt not take the dam with the young:

Ki Tetzeh - Chapter 22

שַׁלֵּחַ תְּשַׁלַּח אֶת־הָאֵם
cast off   you cast   the mother - that

וְאֶת־הַבָּנִים תִּקַּח־לָךְ
and the sons - and that   to you - you take

לְמַעַן יִיטַב לָךְ וְהַאֲרַכְתָּ יָמִים:
to reason   it will be good   to you   and the you prolong   days

7 But thou shalt in any wise let the dam go, and take the young to thee; that it may be well with thee, and that thou mayest prolong thy days.

ס

[שלישי]

כִּי תִבְנֶה בַּיִת חָדָשׁ וְעָשִׂיתָ מַעֲקֶה לְגַגֶּךָ
like   you build   house   new   and you will do   parapet   to your roof

וְלֹא־תָשִׂים דָּמִים בְּבֵיתֶךָ כִּי־יִפֹּל הַנֹּפֵל מִמֶּנּוּ:
from it   the faller   he fall - like   in your house   bloods   you put - and not

8 When thou buildest a new house, then thou shalt make a battlement for thy roof, that thou bring not blood upon thine house, if any man fall from thence.

לֹא־תִזְרַע כַּרְמְךָ כִּלְאָיִם
you sow - not   your vineyard   two types

פֶּן־תִּקְדַּשׁ הַמְלֵאָה הַזֶּרַע אֲשֶׁר תִּזְרָע
it be holy - lest   the fullness   the seed   which   you sow

וּתְבוּאַת הַכָּרֶם:
and defiled   the vineyard

9 Thou shalt not sow thy vineyard with divers seeds: lest the fruit of thy seed which thou hast sown, and the fruit of thy vineyard, be defiled.

ס

לֹא־תַחֲרֹשׁ בְּשׁוֹר־וּבַחֲמֹר יַחְדָּו:
you plow - not   and in ass - in ox   together

10 Thou shalt not plow with an ox and an ass together.

לֹא תִלְבַּשׁ שַׁעַטְנֵז צֶמֶר וּפִשְׁתִּים יַחְדָּו:
not   you wear   mixed garment   woollen   and linen   together

11 Thou shalt not wear a garment of divers sorts, as of woollen and linen together.

ס

גְּדִלִ֖ים תַּעֲשֶׂה־לָּ֑ךְ עַל־אַרְבַּ֛ע כַּנְפ֥וֹת כְּסוּתְךָ֖
<small>vesture   quarters   four - upon   to you - you make   fringes</small>

אֲשֶׁ֥ר תְּכַסֶּה־בָּֽהּ׃
<small>in it - you cover   which</small>

12 Thou shalt make thee fringes upon the four quarters of thy vesture, wherewith thou coverest thyself.

ס

כִּֽי־יִקַּ֥ח אִ֛ישׁ אִשָּׁ֖ה וּבָ֣א אֵלֶ֑יהָ וּשְׂנֵאָֽהּ׃
<small>and hate her   unto her   and comes   wife   man   he take - like</small>

13 If any man take a wife, and go in unto her, and hate her,

וְשָׂ֥ם לָהּ֙ עֲלִילֹ֣ת דְּבָרִ֔ים וְהוֹצִ֥א עָלֶ֖יהָ שֵׁ֣ם רָ֑ע
<small>bad   name   upon her   and came out   speakings   cursing   to her   and put</small>

וְאָמַ֗ר אֶת־הָאִשָּׁ֤ה הַזֹּאת֙ לָקַ֔חְתִּי וָאֶקְרַ֖ב אֵלֶ֑יהָ
<small>unto her   and I came near   I took   the this   the wife - that   and say</small>

וְלֹא־מָצָ֥אתִי לָ֖הּ בְּתוּלִֽים׃
<small>virgin ones   to her   and I found - and not</small>

14 And give occasions of speech against her, and bring up an evil name upon her, and say, I took this woman, and when I came to her, I found her not a maid:

וְלָקַ֛ח אֲבִ֥י הַֽנַּעֲרָ֖ה וְאִמָּ֑הּ
<small>and mother   the child   father   and will take</small>

וְהוֹצִ֜יאוּ אֶת־בְּתוּלֵ֧י הַֽנַּעֲרָ֛ה אֶל־זִקְנֵ֥י הָעִ֖יר הַשָּֽׁעְרָה׃
<small>the gate   the city   elders - unto   the child   virginities - that   and they bring out</small>

15 Then shall the father of the damsel, and her mother, take and bring forth the tokens of the damsel's virginity unto the elders of the city in the gate:

וְאָמַ֛ר אֲבִ֥י הַֽנַּעֲרָ֖ה אֶל־הַזְּקֵנִ֑ים
<small>the elders - unto   the child   father   and say</small>

אֶת־בִּתִּ֗י נָתַ֜תִּי לָאִ֥ישׁ הַזֶּ֛ה לְאִשָּׁ֖ה וַיִּשְׂנָאֶֽהָ׃
<small>and he hates her   to wife   the this   to wife   I gave   my daughter - that</small>

16 And the damsel's father shall say unto the elders, I gave my daughter unto this man to wife, and he hateth her;

וְהִנֵּה־ה֗וּא שָׂ֚ם עֲלִילֹ֣ת דְּבָרִ֔ים לֵאמֹ֔ר
<small>to say   speakings   curses   puts on   he - and here</small>

לֹא־מָצָ֤אתִי לְבִתְּךָ֙ בְּתוּלִ֔ים וְאֵ֖לֶּה בְּתוּלֵ֣י בִתִּ֑י
<small>my daughter   virginities   and these   virginities ones   to your daughter   I found - not</small>

Ki Tetzeh - Chapter 22

וּפָרְשׂוּ֙ הַשִּׂמְלָ֔ה לִפְנֵ֖י זִקְנֵ֥י הָעִֽיר׃
the city   elders   before   the dress   and it token

17 And, lo, he hath given occasions of speech against her, saying, I found not thy daughter a maid; and yet these are the tokens of my daughter's virginity. And they shall spread the cloth before the elders of the city.

וְלָֽקְח֛וּ זִקְנֵ֥י הָעִיר־הַהִ֖וא אֶת־הָאִ֑ישׁ וְיִסְּר֖וּ אֹתֽוֹ׃
to him   and they chastise   the man - that   the it - the city   elders   and take him

18 And the elders of that city shall take that man and chastise him;

וְעָנְשׁ֨וּ אֹת֜וֹ מֵ֣אָה כֶ֗סֶף וְנָֽתְנוּ֙ לַאֲבִ֣י הַֽנַּעֲרָ֔ה
the child   to father   and give it   silver   hundred   to him   and they fine

כִּ֤י הוֹצִיא֙ שֵׁ֣ם רָ֔ע עַ֖ל בְּתוּלַ֣ת יִשְׂרָאֵ֑ל
Israel   virgin   upon   bad   name   brought out   like

וְלֽוֹ־תִהְיֶ֣ה לְאִשָּׁ֔ה לֹא־יוּכַ֥ל לְשַׁלְּחָ֖הּ כָּל־יָמָֽיו׃
his days - all   to cast her   he able - not   to wife   she will be - and to him

19 And they shall amerce him in an hundred shekels of silver, and give them unto the father of the damsel, because he hath brought up an evil name upon a virgin of Israel: and she shall be his wife; he may not put her away all his days.

ס

וְאִם־אֱמֶ֣ת הָיָ֔ה הַדָּבָ֖ר הַזֶּ֑ה
the this   the matter   it be   true - and if

לֹא־נִמְצְא֥וּ בְתוּלִ֖ים לַֽנַּעֲרָֽה׃
to child   virginity ones   it found - not

20 But if this thing be true, and the tokens of virginity be not found for the damsel:

וְהוֹצִ֨יאוּ אֶת־הַֽנַּעֲרָ֜ה אֶל־פֶּ֣תַח בֵּית־אָבִ֗יהָ
her father - house   opening - unto   the child - that   and they bring out

וּסְקָל֩וּהָ֩ אַנְשֵׁ֨י עִירָ֤הּ בָּֽאֲבָנִים֙ וָמֵ֔תָה
and she die   in stones   her city   men   and stone her

כִּֽי־עָשְׂתָ֤ה נְבָלָה֙ בְּיִשְׂרָאֵ֔ל לִזְנ֖וֹת בֵּ֣ית אָבִ֑יהָ
her father   house   to whoredom   in Israel   decadence   she did - like

וּבִֽעַרְתָּ֥ הָרָ֖ע מִקִּרְבֶּֽךָ׃
from among you   the bad   and you eradicate

21 Then they shall bring out the damsel to the door of her father's house, and the men of her city shall stone her with stones that she die: because she hath wrought folly in Israel, to play the whore in her father's house: so shalt thou put evil away from among you.

ס

כִּי־יִמָּצֵא אִישׁ שֹׁכֵב עִם־אִשָּׁה בְעֻלַת־בַּעַל
husband - married   wife - with   lying   man   he finds - like

וּמֵתוּ גַּם־שְׁנֵיהֶם הָאִישׁ הַשֹּׁכֵב עִם־הָאִשָּׁה וְהָאִשָּׁה
and the wife   the wife - with   the lying one   the man   both them - also   and they die

וּבִעַרְתָּ הָרָע מִיִּשְׂרָאֵל׃
from Israel   the bad   and you eradicate

22 If a man be found lying with a woman married to an husband, then they shall both of them die, both the man that lay with the woman, and the woman: so shalt thou put away evil from Israel

ס

כִּי יִהְיֶה נַעֲרָ בְתוּלָה מְאֹרָשָׂה לְאִישׁ
to man   betrothed   virgin   young girl   it be   like

וּמְצָאָהּ אִישׁ בָּעִיר וְשָׁכַב עִמָּהּ׃
with her   and lie   in city   man   and finds her

23 If a damsel that is a virgin be betrothed unto an husband, and a man find her in the city, and lie with her;

וְהוֹצֵאתֶם אֶת־שְׁנֵיהֶם
two of them - that   and you bring out

אֶל־שַׁעַר הָעִיר הַהִוא וּסְקַלְתֶּם אֹתָם בָּאֲבָנִים
in stones   to them   and you stone   the it   the city   gate - unto

וָמֵתוּ אֶת־הַנַּעֲרָ עַל־דְּבַר אֲשֶׁר לֹא־צָעֲקָה בָעִיר
in city   she cried - not   which   matter - upon   young girl - that   and they die

וְאֶת־הָאִישׁ עַל־דְּבַר אֲשֶׁר־עִנָּה אֶת־אֵשֶׁת רֵעֵהוּ
his neighbor   wife - that   humbled - which   the matter - upon   the man - and that

וּבִעַרְתָּ הָרָע מִקִּרְבֶּךָ׃
from among you   the bad   and you eradicate

24 Then ye shall bring them both out unto the gate of that city, and ye shall stone them with stones that they die; the damsel, because she cried not, being in the city; and the man, because he hath humbled his neighbour's wife: so thou shalt put away evil from among you.

ס

וְאִם־בַּשָּׂדֶה יִמְצָא הָאִישׁ אֶת־הַנַּעֲרָ הַמְאֹרָשָׂה
the betrothed   young woman - that   the man   he finds   in field - and if

וְהֶחֱזִיק־בָּהּ הָאִישׁ וְשָׁכַב עִמָּהּ
with her   and lie   the man   in her - and the force

Ki Tetzeh - Chapter 22

וּמֵת הָאִישׁ אֲשֶׁר־שָׁכַב עִמָּהּ לְבַדּוֹ:
alone with her lay - which the man and die

25 But if a man find a betrothed damsel in the field, and the man force her, and lie with her: then the man only that lay with her shall die:

וְלַנַּעֲרָ לֹא־תַעֲשֶׂה דָבָר
matter she does - not and the young woman

אֵין לַנַּעֲרָ חֵטְא מָוֶת
death sin to young woman isn't

כִּי כַּאֲשֶׁר יָקוּם אִישׁ עַל־רֵעֵהוּ וּרְצָחוֹ נֶפֶשׁ
soul and slays him his neighbor - upon man he rises when like

כֵּן הַדָּבָר הַזֶּה:
the this the matter thus

26 But unto the damsel thou shalt do nothing; there is in the damsel no sin worthy of death: for as when a man riseth against his neighbour, and slayeth him, even so is this matter:

כִּי בַשָּׂדֶה מְצָאָהּ צָעֲקָה הַנַּעֲרָ הַמְאֹרָשָׂה
the betrothed the young woman cried found her in field like

וְאֵין מוֹשִׁיעַ לָהּ:
to her saviour and isn't

27 For he found her in the field, and the betrothed damsel cried, and there was none to save her.

ס

כִּי־יִמְצָא אִישׁ נַעֲרָ בְתוּלָה אֲשֶׁר לֹא־אֹרָשָׂה
betrothed - not which virgin young woman man he finds - like

וּתְפָשָׂהּ וְשָׁכַב עִמָּהּ וְנִמְצָאוּ:
and they be found with her and lie and grabs her

28 If a man find a damsel that is a virgin, which is not betrothed, and lay hold on her, and lie with her, and they be found;

וְנָתַן הָאִישׁ הַשֹּׁכֵב עִמָּהּ לַאֲבִי הַנַּעֲרָ חֲמִשִּׁים כָּסֶף
silver fifty the young woman to father with her the laying the man and will give

וְלוֹ־תִהְיֶה לְאִשָּׁה תַּחַת אֲשֶׁר עִנָּהּ
humbled her which under to wife she will be - and to him

לֹא־יוּכַל שַׁלְּחָהּ כָּל־יָמָיו:
his days - all send her he able - not

29 Then the man that lay with her shall give unto the damsel's father fifty shekels of silver, and she shall be his wife; because he hath humbled her, he may not put her away

all his days.

לֹא־יִקַּח אִישׁ אֶת־אֵשֶׁת אָבִיו וְלֹא יְגַלֶּה כְּנַף אָבִיו׃
_{he take - not   man   wife - that   his father   and not   he expose   skirt   his father}

30 A man shall not take his father's wife, nor discover his father's skirt.

Chapter 23

ספר דברים פרק כג

לֹא־יָבֹא פְצוּעַ־דַּכָּה
_{he comes - and not   crushed - wounded}

וּכְרוּת שָׁפְכָה בִּקְהַל יְהוָה׃
_{and cut off   genitals   in congregation   ihvh}

1 He that is wounded in the stones, or hath his privy member cut off, shall not enter into the congregation of the LORD.

לֹא־יָבֹא מַמְזֵר בִּקְהַל יְהוָה
_{he will come - not   bastard   in congregation   ihvh}

גַּם דּוֹר עֲשִׂירִי לֹא־יָבֹא לוֹ בִּקְהַל יְהוָה׃
_{also generation   tenth   he will come - not   to him   in congregation   ihvh}

2 A bastard shall not enter into the congregation of the LORD; even to his tenth generation shall he not enter into the congregation of the LORD.

לֹא־יָבֹא עַמּוֹנִי וּמוֹאָבִי בִּקְהַל יְהוָה
_{he will come - not   Ammonite   and Moabite   in congregation   ihvh}

גַּם דּוֹר עֲשִׂירִי לֹא־יָבֹא לָהֶם בִּקְהַל יְהוָה עַד־עוֹלָם׃
_{also generation   tenth   he will come - not   to them   in congregation   ihvh   forever - till}

3 An Ammonite or Moabite shall not enter into the congregation of the LORD; even to their tenth generation shall they not enter into the congregation of the LORD for ever:

עַל־דְּבַר אֲשֶׁר לֹא־קִדְּמוּ אֶתְכֶם בַּלֶּחֶם
_{upon - matter   which   not - they give assistance   you   in bread}

וּבַמַּיִם בַּדֶּרֶךְ בְּצֵאתְכֶם מִמִּצְרָיִם
_{and in water   in way   in you coming out   from Egypt}

וַאֲשֶׁר שָׂכַר עָלֶיךָ אֶת־בִּלְעָם בֶּן־בְּעוֹר
_{and which   hired   upon you   Balaam - that   Beor - son}

Ki Tetzeh - Chapter 23

מִפְּתוֹר אֲרַם נַהֲרַיִם לְקַלְלֶךָּ׃
from Pethor - Mesopotamia - to curse you

4 Because they met you not with bread and with water in the way, when ye came forth out of Egypt; and because they hired against thee Balaam the son of Beor of Pethor of Mesopotamia, to curse thee.

וְלֹא־אָבָה יְהוָה אֱלֹהֶיךָ לִשְׁמֹעַ אֶל־בִּלְעָם
and not - would ihvh your Elohim to hear unto - Balaam

וַיַּהֲפֹךְ יְהוָה אֱלֹהֶיךָ לְּךָ אֶת־הַקְּלָלָה לִבְרָכָה
and he turned ihvh your Elohim to you that - the curse to blessing

כִּי אֲהֵבְךָ יְהוָה אֱלֹהֶיךָ׃
like loved you ihvh your Elohim

5 Nevertheless the LORD thy God would not hearken unto Balaam; but the LORD thy God turned the curse into a blessing unto thee, because the LORD thy God loved thee.

לֹא־תִדְרֹשׁ שְׁלֹמָם וְטֹבָתָם כָּל־יָמֶיךָ לְעוֹלָם׃
not - you seek their peace and their good all - days you to forever

6 Thou shalt not seek their peace nor their prosperity all thy days for ever.

ס

[רביעי]

לֹא־תְתַעֵב אֲדֹמִי כִּי אָחִיךָ הוּא
not - you will abhor Edomite like your brother he

לֹא־תְתַעֵב מִצְרִי כִּי־גֵר הָיִיתָ בְאַרְצוֹ׃
not - you will abhor Egyptian like - stranger you were in his land

7 Thou shalt not abhor an Edomite; for he is thy brother: thou shalt not abhor an Egyptian; because thou wast a stranger in his land.

בָּנִים אֲשֶׁר־יִוָּלְדוּ לָהֶם
sons which - they begotten to them

דּוֹר שְׁלִישִׁי יָבֹא לָהֶם בִּקְהַל יְהוָה׃
generation third he will come to them in congregation ihvh

8 The children that are begotten of them shall enter into the congregation of the LORD in their third generation.

ס

כִּי־תֵצֵא מַחֲנֶה עַל־אֹיְבֶיךָ וְנִשְׁמַרְתָּ מִכֹּל דָּבָר רָע׃
like - you go out camp upon - your enemies and you heed from all matter bad

9 When the host goeth forth against thine enemies, then keep thee from every wicked thing.

כִּי־יִהְיֶה בְךָ אִישׁ אֲשֶׁר לֹא־יִהְיֶה טָהוֹר מִקְּרֵה־לָיְלָה
night - from happening pure will be - not which man in you it will be - like

וְיָצָא אֶל־מִחוּץ לַמַּחֲנֶה
to camp outside - unto and he goes out

לֹא יָבֹא אֶל־תּוֹךְ הַמַּחֲנֶה׃
the camp among - unto he will come not

10 If there be among you any man, that is not clean by reason of uncleanness that chanceth him by night, then shall he go abroad out of the camp, he shall not come within the camp:

וְהָיָה לִפְנוֹת־עֶרֶב יִרְחַץ בַּמָּיִם
in water he will wash evening - to faces and it will be

וּכְבֹא הַשֶּׁמֶשׁ יָבֹא אֶל־תּוֹךְ הַמַּחֲנֶה׃
the camp among - unto he will come the sun and like comes

11 But it shall be, when evening cometh on, he shall wash himself with water: and when the sun is down, he shall come into the camp again.

וְיָד תִּהְיֶה לְךָ מִחוּץ לַמַּחֲנֶה וְיָצָאתָ שָּׁמָּה חוּץ׃
outside there and you will go out to camp outside to you it will be and hand

12 Thou shalt have a place also without the camp, whither thou shalt go forth abroad:

וְיָתֵד תִּהְיֶה לְךָ עַל־אֲזֵנֶךָ
your weapon - upon to you it will have and paddle

וְהָיָה בְּשִׁבְתְּךָ חוּץ וְחָפַרְתָּה בָהּ
in it and you will dig outside in your returning and it will be

וְשַׁבְתָּ וְכִסִּיתָ אֶת־צֵאָתֶךָ׃
your goings out - that and you cover and you will return

13 And thou shalt have a paddle upon thy weapon; and it shall be, when thou wilt ease thyself abroad, thou shalt dig therewith, and shalt turn back and cover that which cometh from thee:

כִּי יְהוָה אֱלֹהֶיךָ מִתְהַלֵּךְ בְּקֶרֶב מַחֲנֶךָ לְהַצִּילְךָ
to your delivery your camp in near walks your Elohim ihvh like

וְלָתֵת אֹיְבֶיךָ לְפָנֶיךָ וְהָיָה מַחֲנֶיךָ קָדוֹשׁ
holy your camp and it will be to before you your enemy and to give

וְלֹא־יִרְאֶה בְךָ עֶרְוַת דָּבָר וְשָׁב מֵאַחֲרֶיךָ׃
from after you and return matter nakedness in you he see - and not

14 For the LORD thy God walketh in the midst of thy camp, to deliver thee, and to give up thine enemies before thee; therefore shall thy camp be holy: that he see no unclean thing in thee, and turn away from thee.

Ki Tetzeh - Chapter 23

לֹא־תַסְגִּיר עֶבֶד אֶל־אֲדֹנָיו
his master - unto   servant   you will surrender - not

אֲשֶׁר־יִנָּצֵל אֵלֶיךָ מֵעִם אֲדֹנָיו׃
his master   from with   unto you   he rescued - which

15 Thou shalt not deliver unto his master the servant which is escaped from his master unto thee:

עִמְּךָ יֵשֵׁב בְּקִרְבְּךָ בַּמָּקוֹם
in place   in your near   he will dwell   with you

אֲשֶׁר־יִבְחַר בְּאַחַד שְׁעָרֶיךָ בַּטּוֹב לוֹ
to him   in good   your gates   in one   he will choose - which

לֹא תּוֹנֶנּוּ׃
you oppress him   not

16 He shall dwell with thee, even among you, in that place which he shall choose in one of thy gates, where it liketh him best: thou shalt not oppress him.

לֹא־תִהְיֶה קְדֵשָׁה מִבְּנוֹת יִשְׂרָאֵל
Israel   from daughters   "holy"whore   you will be - not

וְלֹא־יִהְיֶה קָדֵשׁ מִבְּנֵי יִשְׂרָאֵל׃
Israel   from sons   "holy" man whore   he will be   and not

17 There shall be no whore of the daughters of Israel, nor a sodomite of the sons of Israel.

לֹא־תָבִיא אֶתְנַן זוֹנָה
prostitute   fee   you will bring - not

וּמְחִיר כֶּלֶב בֵּית יְהוָה אֱלֹהֶיךָ לְכָל־נֶדֶר
vow - to all   your Elohim   ihvh   house   dog   and hire

כִּי תוֹעֲבַת יְהוָה אֱלֹהֶיךָ גַּם־שְׁנֵיהֶם׃
both them - also   your Elohim   ihvh   abomination   like

18 Thou shalt not bring the hire of a whore, or the price of a dog, into the house of the LORD thy God for any vow: for even both these are abomination unto the LORD thy God.

לֹא־תַשִּׁיךְ לְאָחִיךָ נֶשֶׁךְ כֶּסֶף נֶשֶׁךְ אֹכֶל
food   interest   money   interest   to your brother   you charge interest - not

נֶ֕שֶׁךְ כָּל־דָּבָ֖ר אֲשֶׁ֥ר יִשָּֽׁךְ׃
he interest   which   matter - all   interest

19 Thou shalt not lend upon usury to thy brother; usury of money, usury of victuals, usury of any thing that is lent upon usury:

לַנָּכְרִ֣י תַשִּׁ֔יךְ וּלְאָחִ֖יךָ לֹ֣א תַשִּׁ֑יךְ
you charge interest   not   and to your brother   you charge interest   to stranger

לְמַ֨עַן יְבָרֶכְךָ֜ יְהוָ֣ה אֱלֹהֶ֗יךָ בְּכֹל֙ מִשְׁלַ֣ח יָדֶ֔ךָ עַל־הָאָ֕רֶץ
the land - upon   your hand   undertaking   in all   your Elohim   ihvh   he bless you   to end

אֲשֶׁר־אַתָּ֥ה בָא־שָׁ֖מָּה לְרִשְׁתָּֽהּ׃
to possess it   there - come   you - which

20 Unto a stranger thou mayest lend upon usury; but unto thy brother thou shalt not lend upon usury: that the LORD thy God may bless thee in all that thou settest thine hand to in the land whither thou goest to possess it.

ס

כִּֽי־תִדֹּ֥ר נֶ֨דֶר֙ לַיהוָ֣ה אֱלֹהֶ֔יךָ לֹ֥א תְאַחֵ֖ר לְשַׁלְּמ֑וֹ
to his pay   you delay   not   your Elohim   to ihvh   vow   you vow- like

כִּֽי־דָרֹ֨שׁ יִדְרְשֶׁ֜נּוּ יְהוָ֤ה אֱלֹהֶ֨יךָ֙ מֵֽעִמָּ֔ךְ
from with you   your Elohim   ihvh   he will require it   require - like

וְהָיָ֥ה בְךָ֖ חֵֽטְא׃
sin   in you   and it will be

21 When thou shalt vow a vow unto the LORD thy God, thou shalt not slack to pay it: for the LORD thy God will surely require it of thee; and it would be sin in thee.

וְכִ֥י תֶחְדַּ֖ל לִנְדֹּ֑ר לֹֽא־יִהְיֶ֥ה בְךָ֖ חֵֽטְא׃
sin   in you   it will be - not   to vow   you will forbear   and like

22 But if thou shalt forbear to vow, it shall be no sin in thee.

מוֹצָ֥א שְׂפָתֶ֖יךָ תִּשְׁמֹ֣ר
you heed   your lips   go out

וְעָשִׂ֑יתָ כַּאֲשֶׁ֨ר נָדַ֜רְתָּ לַיהוָ֤ה אֱלֹהֶ֨יךָ֙
your Elohim   to ihvh   you vowed   when   and you will do

נְדָבָ֔ה אֲשֶׁ֥ר דִּבַּ֖רְתָּ בְּפִֽיךָ׃
in your mouth   you spoke   which   voluntary

23 That which is gone out of thy lips thou shalt keep and perform; even a freewill offering, according as thou hast vowed unto the LORD thy God, which thou hast promised with thy mouth.

ס

Ki Tetzeh - Chapter 24

[חמישי]

כִּי תָבֹא בְּכֶרֶם רֵעֶךָ וְאָכַלְתָּ עֲנָבִים כְּנַפְשְׁךָ שָׂבְעֶךָ
like   you come   in vineyard   your neighbor   and you eat   grapes   like your soul   your fullness

וְאֶל־כֶּלְיְךָ לֹא תִתֵּן:
your vessel - and unto   not   you will give

24 When thou comest into thy neighbour's vineyard, then thou mayest eat grapes thy fill at thine own pleasure; but thou shalt not put any in thy vessel.

ס

כִּי תָבֹא בְּקָמַת רֵעֶךָ וְקָטַפְתָּ מְלִילֹת בְּיָדֶךָ
like   you come   in raised grain   your neighbor   and you pluck   snippets   in your hand

וְחֶרְמֵשׁ לֹא תָנִיף עַל קָמַת רֵעֶךָ:
and sickle   not   you swing   upon   raised grain   your neighbor

25 When thou comest into the standing corn of thy neighbour, then thou mayest pluck the ears with thine hand; but thou shalt not move a sickle unto thy neighbour's standing corn.

ס

Chapter 24

ספר דברים פרק כד

כִּי־יִקַּח אִישׁ אִשָּׁה וּבְעָלָהּ
he takes - like   man   wife   and marries her

וְהָיָה אִם־לֹא תִמְצָא־חֵן בְּעֵינָיו כִּי־מָצָא בָהּ עֶרְוַת דָּבָר
and it be   not - with   grace - she finds   in his eyes   finds - like   in her   nakedness   matter

וְכָתַב לָהּ סֵפֶר כְּרִיתֻת וְנָתַן בְּיָדָהּ וְשִׁלְּחָהּ מִבֵּיתוֹ:
and write   to her   book   divorcement   and give   in her hand   and sends her   from his house

1 When a man hath taken a wife, and married her, and it come to pass that she find no favour in his eyes, because he hath found some uncleanness in her: then let him write her a bill of divorcement, and give it in her hand, and send her out of his house.

וְיָצְאָה מִבֵּיתוֹ וְהָלְכָה וְהָיְתָה לְאִישׁ־אַחֵר:
and she goes out   from his house   and she goes   and she will be   another - to man

2 And when she is departed out of his house, she may go and be another man's wife.

וּשְׂנֵאָהּ הָאִישׁ הָאַחֲרוֹן וְכָתַב לָהּ סֵפֶר כְּרִיתֻת
and hate her   the man   the after one   and write   to her   book   divorcement

וְנָתַן בְּיָדָהּ וְשִׁלְּחָהּ מִבֵּיתוֹ
and give   in her hand   and send her   from his house

DEVARIM/DEUTERONOMY

אוֹ כִי־יָמוּת הָאִישׁ הָאַחֲרוֹן אֲשֶׁר־לְקָחָהּ לוֹ לְאִשָּׁה׃
or like he die the man the after one which - took her to him to wife

3 And if the latter husband hate her, and write her a bill of divorcement, and giveth it in her hand, and sendeth her out of his house; or if the latter husband die, which took her to be his wife;

לֹא־יוּכַל בַּעְלָהּ הָרִאשׁוֹן אֲשֶׁר־שִׁלְּחָהּ
not - he able husband the first one which - sent her

לָשׁוּב לְקַחְתָּהּ לִהְיוֹת לוֹ לְאִשָּׁה אַחֲרֵי אֲשֶׁר הֻטַּמָּאָה
to return to take her to be to him to wife after which she defiled

כִּי־תוֹעֵבָה הִוא לִפְנֵי יְהוָה
like - abomination she before ihvh

וְלֹא תַחֲטִיא אֶת־הָאָרֶץ אֲשֶׁר יְהוָה אֱלֹהֶיךָ נֹתֵן לְךָ נַחֲלָה׃
and not you will sin the - land that ihvh your Elohim gives to you inheritance

4 Her former husband, which sent her away, may not take her again to be his wife, after that she is defiled; for that is abomination before the LORD: and thou shalt not cause the land to sin, which the LORD thy God giveth thee for an inheritance.

ס

[ששי]

כִּי־יִקַּח אִישׁ אִשָּׁה חֲדָשָׁה לֹא יֵצֵא בַּצָּבָא
like - he takes man wife new not he go out to battle

וְלֹא־יַעֲבֹר עָלָיו לְכָל־דָּבָר נָקִי
and not - he pass upon him to all - matter innocent

יִהְיֶה לְבֵיתוֹ שָׁנָה אֶחָת וְשִׂמַּח אֶת־אִשְׁתּוֹ אֲשֶׁר־לָקָח׃
he be to his house year one and make happy that - his wife which - taken

5 When a man hath taken a new wife, he shall not go out to war, neither shall he be charged with any business: but he shall be free at home one year, and shall cheer up his wife which he hath taken.

לֹא־יַחֲבֹל רֵחַיִם וָרָכֶב כִּי־נֶפֶשׁ הוּא חֹבֵל׃
not - he take pledge millstones and rider like - soul it pledge

6 No man shall take the nether or the upper millstone to pledge: for he taketh a man's life to pledge.

ס

כִּי־יִמָּצֵא אִישׁ גֹּנֵב נֶפֶשׁ מֵאֶחָיו מִבְּנֵי יִשְׂרָאֵל
like - he found man stealer soul from his brother from sons Israel

Ki Tetzeh - Chapter 24

וְהִתְעַמֶּר־בּוֹ   וּמְכָרוֹ   וּמֵת הַגַּנָּב הַהוּא
the he the thief and dies and it sells in it - causes to be merchandise

וּבִעַרְתָּ   הָרָע   מִקִּרְבֶּךָ׃
from near you the bad and you eradicate

7 If a man be found stealing any of his brethren of the children of Israel, and maketh merchandise of him, or selleth him; then that thief shall die; and thou shalt put evil away from among you.

ס

הִשָּׁמֶר   בְּנֶגַע־הַצָּרַעַת   לִשְׁמֹר   מְאֹד
greatly to heed the leprosy - in plague cause to heed

וְלַעֲשׂוֹת   כְּכֹל   אֲשֶׁר־יוֹרוּ   אֶתְכֶם הַכֹּהֲנִים הַלְוִיִּם
the Levites the priests that you they direct - which like all and to do

כַּאֲשֶׁר   צִוִּיתִם   תִּשְׁמְרוּ   לַעֲשׂוֹת׃
to do you will heed it I commanded them when

8 Take heed in the plague of leprosy, that thou observe diligently, and do according to all that the priests the Levites shall teach you: as I commanded them, so ye shall observe to do.

זָכוֹר   אֵת אֲשֶׁר־עָשָׂה יְהוָה אֱלֹהֶיךָ לְמִרְיָם בַּדָּרֶךְ
in way to Miriam your Elohim ihvh did - which that remember

בְּצֵאתְכֶם מִמִּצְרָיִם׃
from Egypt in your going out

9 Remember what the LORD thy God did unto Miriam by the way, after that ye were come forth out of Egypt.

ס

כִּי־תַשֶּׁה בְרֵעֲךָ   מַשַּׁאת   מְאוּמָה
from speck lending in your neighbor you do - like

לֹא־תָבֹא אֶל־בֵּיתוֹ לַעֲבֹט עֲבֹטוֹ׃
his security to repossess his house - unto you come - not

10 When thou dost lend thy brother any thing, thou shalt not go into his house to fetch his pledge.

בַּחוּץ   תַּעֲמֹד   וְהָאִישׁ אֲשֶׁר אַתָּה נֹשֶׁה בּוֹ
in it lending you which and the man you will stand in outside

יוֹצִיא   אֵלֶיךָ   אֶת־הָעֲבוֹט   הַחוּצָה׃
the outside the security - that unto you he will come out

11 Thou shalt stand abroad, and the man to whom thou dost lend shall bring out the pledge abroad unto thee.

וְאִם־אִישׁ עָנִי הוּא לֹא תִשְׁכַּב בַּעֲבֹטוֹ:
in his security   you lie down   not   he   poor   man - and if

12 And if the man be poor, thou shalt not sleep with his pledge:

הָשֵׁב תָּשִׁיב לוֹ אֶת־הַעֲבוֹט כְּבוֹא הַשֶּׁמֶשׁ
the sun   like comes   the security - that   to him   you will return   the return

וְשָׁכַב בְּשַׂלְמָתוֹ וּבֵרֲכֶךָּ
and will bless you   in his garment covering   and lies down

וּלְךָ תִּהְיֶה צְדָקָה לִפְנֵי יְהוָה אֱלֹהֶיךָ:
your Elohim   ihvh   before   righteous giving   it will be   and to you

13 In any case thou shalt deliver him the pledge again when the sun goeth down, that he may sleep in his own raiment, and bless thee: and it shall be righteousness unto thee before the LORD thy God.

ס

[שביעי]

לֹא־תַעֲשֹׁק שָׂכִיר עָנִי וְאֶבְיוֹן מֵאַחֶיךָ
from your brother   and needy   poor   hired   you extort - not

אוֹ מִגֵּרְךָ אֲשֶׁר בְּאַרְצְךָ בִּשְׁעָרֶיךָ:
in your gates   in your land   which   from your stranger   or

14 Thou shalt not oppress an hired servant that is poor and needy, whether he be of thy brethren, or of thy strangers that are in thy land within thy gates:

בְּיוֹמוֹ תִתֵּן שְׂכָרוֹ וְלֹא־תָבוֹא עָלָיו הַשֶּׁמֶשׁ
the sun   upon him   it will come - and not   his hire   you will give   in his day

כִּי עָנִי הוּא וְאֵלָיו הוּא נֹשֵׂא אֶת־נַפְשׁוֹ
his soul - that   lifting   he   and unto his   he   poor   like

וְלֹא־יִקְרָא עָלֶיךָ אֶל־יְהוָה וְהָיָה בְךָ חֵטְא:
sin   in you   and it will be   ihvh - unto   upon you   he call - and not

15 At his day thou shalt give him his hire, neither shall the sun go down upon it; for he is poor, and setteth his heart upon it: lest he cry against thee unto the LORD, and it be sin unto thee.

ס

לֹא־יוּמְתוּ אָבוֹת עַל־בָּנִים
sons - upon   fathers   they will be put to death - not

וּבָנִים לֹא־יוּמְתוּ עַל־אָבוֹת
fathers - upon   they will be put to death - not   and sons

Ki Tetzeh - Chapter 24

אִישׁ בְּחֶטְאוֹ יוּמָתוּ׃
man / in his sin / they will be put to death

16 The fathers shall not be put to death for the children, neither shall the children be put to death for the fathers: every man shall be put to death for his own sin.

ס

לֹא תַטֶּה מִשְׁפַּט גֵּר יָתוֹם וְלֹא תַחֲבֹל בֶּגֶד אַלְמָנָה׃
not / you will pervert / judgment / stranger / fatherless / and not / you take pledge / garment / widow

17 Thou shalt not pervert the judgment of the stranger, nor of the fatherless; nor take a widow's raiment to pledge:

וְזָכַרְתָּ כִּי עֶבֶד הָיִיתָ בְּמִצְרַיִם
and you remember / like / slave / you were / in Egypt

וַיִּפְדְּךָ יְהוָה אֱלֹהֶיךָ מִשָּׁם
and he redeemed you / ihvh / your Elohim / from there

עַל־כֵּן אָנֹכִי מְצַוְּךָ לַעֲשׂוֹת אֶת־הַדָּבָר הַזֶּה׃
upon - thus / I am / commanding you / to do / that - the matter / the this

18 But thou shalt remember that thou wast a bondman in Egypt, and the LORD thy God redeemed thee thence: therefore I command thee to do this thing.

ס

כִּי תִקְצֹר קְצִירְךָ בְשָׂדֶךָ וְשָׁכַחְתָּ עֹמֶר בַּשָּׂדֶה
like / you cut down / your harvest / in your field / and you forgot / sheaf / in field

לֹא תָשׁוּב לְקַחְתּוֹ
not / you return / to it's taking

לַגֵּר לַיָּתוֹם וְלָאַלְמָנָה יִהְיֶה
to stranger / to fatherless / and to widow / it will be

לְמַעַן יְבָרֶכְךָ יְהוָה אֱלֹהֶיךָ בְּכֹל מַעֲשֵׂה יָדֶיךָ׃
to end / he will bless you / ihvh / your Elohim / in all / work / your hand

19 When thou cuttest down thine harvest in thy field, and hast forgot a sheaf in the field, thou shalt not go again to fetch it: it shall be for the stranger, for the fatherless, and for the widow: that the LORD thy God may bless thee in all the work of thine hands.

ס

כִּי תַחְבֹּט זֵיתְךָ לֹא תְפָאֵר אַחֲרֶיךָ
like / you beatest / your olive tree / not / you will go over / your afterwards

לַגֵּר לַיָּתוֹם וְלָאַלְמָנָה יִהְיֶה׃
to stranger / to fatherless / and to widow / it will be

20 When thou beatest thine olive tree, thou shalt not go over the boughs again: it shall be for the stranger, for the fatherless, and for the widow.

כִּי תַבְצֹר כַּרְמְךָ לֹא תְעוֹלֵל אַחֲרֶיךָ
your afterwards   you glean   not   your vineyard   you pick   like

לַגֵּר לַיָּתוֹם וְלָאַלְמָנָה יִהְיֶה:
it will be   and to widow   to fatherless   to stranger

21 When thou gatherest the grapes of thy vineyard, thou shalt not glean it afterward: it shall be for the stranger, for the fatherless, and for the widow.

וְזָכַרְתָּ כִּי־עֶבֶד הָיִיתָ בְּאֶרֶץ מִצְרָיִם
Egypt   in land   you were   slave - like   you remember

עַל־כֵּן אָנֹכִי מְצַוְּךָ לַעֲשׂוֹת אֶת־הַדָּבָר הַזֶּה:
the this   the matter - that   to do   commanding you   I am   thus - upon

22 And thou shalt remember that thou wast a bondman in the land of Egypt: therefore I command thee to do this thing.

ס

Chapter 24

ספר דברים פרק כה

כִּי־יִהְיֶה רִיב בֵּין אֲנָשִׁים
men   between   strife   it be - like

וְנִגְּשׁוּ אֶל־הַמִּשְׁפָּט וּשְׁפָטוּם
and judges   judgment - unto   and they touch

וְהִצְדִּיקוּ אֶת־הַצַּדִּיק וְהִרְשִׁיעוּ אֶת־הָרָשָׁע:
the wicked - that   and they condemn   the righteous - that   and they will justify

1 If there be a controversy between men, and they come unto judgment, that the judges may judge them; then they shall justify the righteous, and condemn the wicked.

וְהָיָה אִם־בִּן הַכּוֹת הָרָשָׁע וְהִפִּילוֹ הַשֹּׁפֵט
the judge   and cause his fall   the wicked   strike   between - if   and it will be

וְהִכָּהוּ לְפָנָיו כְּדֵי רִשְׁעָתוֹ בְּמִסְפָּר:
in number   his wickedness   sufficient   before him   and he struck

2 And it shall be, if the wicked man be worthy to be beaten, that the judge shall cause him to lie down, and to be beaten before his face, according to his fault, by a certain number.

אַרְבָּעִים יַכֶּנּוּ לֹא יֹסִיף
it add   not   he strikes him   forty

Ki Tetzeh - Chapter 24

פֶּן־יֹסִיף לְהַכֹּתוֹ עַל־אֵלֶּה מַכָּה רַבָּה
_{much   beat   these - upon   to his strike   it add - lest}

וְנִקְלָה אָחִיךָ לְעֵינֶיךָ:
_{to your eyes   your brother   and slighted}

3 Forty stripes he may give him, and not exceed: lest, if he should exceed, and beat him above these with many stripes, then thy brother should seem vile unto thee.

לֹא־תַחְסֹם שׁוֹר בְּדִישׁוֹ:
_{in his treading   ox   muzzle - not}

4 Thou shalt not muzzle the ox when he treadeth out the corn.

ס

כִּי־יֵשְׁבוּ אַחִים יַחְדָּו וּמֵת אַחַד מֵהֶם
_{from them   one   and die   together   brothers   they dwell - like}

וּבֵן אֵין־לוֹ לֹא־תִהְיֶה אֵשֶׁת־הַמֵּת הַחוּצָה לְאִישׁ זָר
_{stranger   to man   the outside   the dead - wife   she will be - not   to him - isn't   and son}

יְבָמָהּ יָבֹא עָלֶיהָ וּלְקָחָהּ לוֹ לְאִשָּׁה וְיִבְּמָהּ:
_{and he be husbands brother   to wife   to him   and take her   upon her   he will come   husband's brother}

5 If brethren dwell together, and one of them die, and have no child, the wife of the dead shall not marry without unto a stranger: her husband's brother shall go in unto her, and take her to him to wife, and perform the duty of an husband's brother unto her.

וְהָיָה הַבְּכוֹר אֲשֶׁר תֵּלֵד יָקוּם עַל־שֵׁם אָחִיו הַמֵּת
_{the dead   his brother   name - upon   he gets up   you go   which   the first born   and it will be}

וְלֹא־יִמָּחֶה שְׁמוֹ מִיִּשְׂרָאֵל:
_{from Israel   his name   he wiped out - and not}

6 And it shall be, that the firstborn which she beareth shall succeed in the name of his brother which is dead, that his name be not put out of Israel.

וְאִם־לֹא יַחְפֹּץ הָאִישׁ לָקַחַת אֶת־יְבִמְתּוֹ
_{his brothers wife - that   to take   the man   he pleases   not - and if}

וְעָלְתָה יְבִמְתּוֹ הַשַּׁעְרָה אֶל־הַזְּקֵנִים וְאָמְרָה
_{and she says   the elders - unto   the gate   his brothers wife   and she goes up}

מֵאֵן יְבָמִי לְהָקִים לְאָחִיו שֵׁם בְּיִשְׂרָאֵל
_{in Israel   name   to his brother   to takings   my husbands brother   refuses}

לֹא אָבָה יַבְּמִי:
_{my brothers wife   I come   not}

7 And if the man like not to take his brother's wife, then let his brother's wife go up to the gate unto the elders, and say, My husband's brother refuseth to raise up unto his brother a name in Israel, he will not perform the duty of my husband's brother.

וְקָרְאוּ־לוֹ זִקְנֵי־עִירוֹ וְדִבְּרוּ אֵלָיו
וְעָמַד וְאָמַר לֹא חָפַצְתִּי לְקַחְתָּהּ:

8 Then the elders of his city shall call him, and speak unto him: and if he stand to it, and say, I like not to take her;

וְנִגְּשָׁה יְבִמְתּוֹ אֵלָיו לְעֵינֵי הַזְּקֵנִים
וְחָלְצָה נַעֲלוֹ מֵעַל רַגְלוֹ
וְיָרְקָה בְּפָנָיו וְעָנְתָה וְאָמְרָה כָּכָה יֵעָשֶׂה לָאִישׁ
אֲשֶׁר לֹא־יִבְנֶה אֶת־בֵּית אָחִיו:

9 Then shall his brother's wife come unto him in the presence of the elders, and loose his shoe from off his foot, and spit in his face, and shall answer and say, So shall it be done unto that man that will not build up his brother's house.

וְנִקְרָא שְׁמוֹ בְּיִשְׂרָאֵל בֵּית חֲלוּץ הַנָּעַל:

10 And his name shall be called in Israel, The house of him that hath his shoe loosed.

ס

כִּי־יִנָּצוּ אֲנָשִׁים יַחְדָּו אִישׁ וְאָחִיו
וְקָרְבָה אֵשֶׁת הָאֶחָד לְהַצִּיל אֶת־אִישָׁהּ מִיַּד מַכֵּהוּ
וְשָׁלְחָה יָדָהּ וְהֶחֱזִיקָה בִּמְבֻשָׁיו:

11 When men strive together one with another, and the wife of the one draweth near for to deliver her husband out of the hand of him that smiteth him, and putteth forth her hand, and taketh him by the secrets:

וְקַצֹּתָה אֶת־כַּפָּהּ לֹא תָחוֹס עֵינֶךָ:

12 Then thou shalt cut off her hand, thine eye shall not pity her.

ס

Ki Tetzeh - Chapter 24

לֹא־יִהְיֶ֥ה לְךָ֛ בְּכִֽיסְךָ֖ אֶ֣בֶן וָאָ֑בֶן גְּדוֹלָ֖ה וּקְטַנָּֽה׃
and small   big   and stone   stone   in your purse   to you   it will be - not

13 Thou shalt not have in thy bag divers weights, a great and a small.

לֹא־יִהְיֶ֥ה לְךָ֛ בְּבֵיתְךָ֖
in your house   to you   there will be - not

אֵיפָ֥ה וְאֵיפָ֑ה גְּדוֹלָ֖ה וּקְטַנָּֽה׃
and small   big   and measure   measure

14 Thou shalt not have in thine house divers measures, a great and a small.

אֶ֣בֶן שְׁלֵמָ֤ה וָצֶ֙דֶק֙ יִֽהְיֶה־לָּ֔ךְ
to you - it will be   and just   equitable   stone

אֵיפָ֥ה שְׁלֵמָ֛ה וָצֶ֖דֶק יִֽהְיֶה־לָּ֑ךְ
to you - it will be   and just   equitable   measure

לְמַ֙עַן֙ יַאֲרִ֣יכוּ יָמֶ֔יךָ עַ֚ל הָֽאֲדָמָ֔ה
the ground   upon   your days   it will prolong   to end

אֲשֶׁר־יְהוָ֥ה אֱלֹהֶ֖יךָ נֹתֵ֥ן לָֽךְ׃
to you   gives   your Elohim   ihvh - which

15 But thou shalt have a perfect and just weight, a perfect and just measure shalt thou have: that thy days may be lengthened in the land which the LORD thy God giveth thee.

כִּ֧י תוֹעֲבַ֛ת יְהוָ֥ה אֱלֹהֶ֖יךָ
your Elohim   ihvh   abomination   like

כָל־עֹ֣שֵׂה אֵ֑לֶּה כֹּ֖ל עֹ֥שֵׂה עָֽוֶל׃
inequity   doing   all   these   doing - all

16 For all that do such things, and all that do unrighteously, are an abomination unto the LORD thy God.

פ

[מפטיר]

זָכ֕וֹר אֵ֛ת אֲשֶׁר־עָשָׂ֥ה לְךָ֖ עֲמָלֵ֑ק
Amalek   to you   done - which   that   remember

בַּדֶּ֖רֶךְ בְּצֵאתְכֶ֥ם מִמִּצְרָֽיִם׃
from Egypt   in your going out   in way

17 Remember what Amalek did unto thee by the way, when ye were come forth out of Egypt;

אֲשֶׁ֨ר קָֽרְךָ֜ בַּדֶּ֗רֶךְ וַיְזַנֵּ֤ב בְּךָ֙ כָּל־הַנֶּחֱשָׁלִ֣ים אַחֲרֶ֔יךָ
after you   the overcome ones - all   in you   and he curtailing   in way   you met   which

וְאַתָּה עָיֵף וְיָגֵעַ וְלֹא יָרֵא אֱלֹהִים׃
   Elohim he feared and not and weary tired and you

18 How he met thee by the way, and smote the hindmost of thee, even all that were feeble behind thee, when thou wast faint and weary; and he feared not God.

וְהָיָה בְּהָנִיחַ יְהוָה אֱלֹהֶיךָ לְךָ מִכָּל־אֹיְבֶיךָ מִסָּבִיב בָּאָרֶץ
in land from around your enemies - from all to you your Elohim ihvh in the rest and it was

אֲשֶׁר יְהוָה־אֱלֹהֶיךָ נֹתֵן לְךָ נַחֲלָה לְרִשְׁתָּהּ
to possess inheritance to you gives your Elohim - ihvh which

תִּמְחֶה אֶת־זֵכֶר עֲמָלֵק מִתַּחַת הַשָּׁמָיִם לֹא תִּשְׁכָּח׃
you will forget not the heavens from under Amalek remembrance - that you blot out

19 Therefore it shall be, when the LORD thy God hath given thee rest from all thine enemies round about, in the land which the LORD thy God giveth thee for an inheritance to possess it, that thou shalt blot out the remembrance of Amalek from under heaven; thou shalt not forget it.

פ פ פ

Ki Tavo
Chapter 26

ספר דברים פרק כו

[פרשת כי תבוא]

וְהָיָה֙ כִּֽי־תָב֣וֹא אֶל־הָאָ֔רֶץ
and it will be   you come - like   the land - unto

אֲשֶׁר֙ יְהוָ֣ה אֱלֹהֶ֔יךָ נֹתֵ֥ן לְךָ֖ נַחֲלָ֑ה
which   ihvh   your Elohim   gives   to you   inheritance

וִֽירִשְׁתָּ֖הּ וְיָשַׁ֥בְתָּ בָּֽהּ׃
and you possess it   and you dwell   in it

1 And it shall be, when thou art come in unto the land which the LORD thy God giveth thee for an inheritance, and possessest it, and dwellest therein;

וְלָקַחְתָּ֞ מֵרֵאשִׁ֣ית ׀ כָּל־פְּרִ֣י הָאֲדָמָ֗ה
and you will take   from first   fruit - all   the ground

אֲשֶׁ֨ר תָּבִ֧יא מֵֽאַרְצְךָ֛ אֲשֶׁ֨ר יְהוָ֧ה אֱלֹהֶ֛יךָ נֹתֵ֥ן לָ֖ךְ
which   you bring   from your land   which   ihvh   your Elohim   gives   to you

וְשַׂמְתָּ֣ בַטֶּ֑נֶא וְהָֽלַכְתָּ֙ אֶל־הַמָּק֔וֹם
and you put   in basket   and you go   the place - unto

אֲשֶׁ֤ר יִבְחַר֙ יְהוָ֣ה אֱלֹהֶ֔יךָ לְשַׁכֵּ֥ן שְׁמ֖וֹ שָֽׁם׃
which   he chooses   ihvh   your Elohim   to tabernacle   his name   there

2 That thou shalt take of the first of all the fruit of the earth, which thou shalt bring of thy land that the LORD thy God giveth thee, and shalt put it in a basket, and shalt go unto the place which the LORD thy God shall choose to place his name there.

וּבָאתָ֙ אֶל־הַכֹּהֵ֔ן אֲשֶׁ֥ר יִהְיֶ֖ה בַּיָּמִ֣ים הָהֵ֑ם
and you come   the priest - unto   which   ihvh   in days   the them

וְאָמַרְתָּ֣ אֵלָ֗יו הִגַּ֤דְתִּי הַיּוֹם֙ לַיהוָ֣ה אֱלֹהֶ֔יךָ
and you say   unto him   I tell   the day   to ihvh   your Elohim

כִּי־בָ֙אתִי֙ אֶל־הָאָ֔רֶץ
I come - like   the land - unto

אֲשֶׁ֨ר נִשְׁבַּ֧ע יְהוָ֛ה לַאֲבֹתֵ֖ינוּ לָ֥תֶת לָֽנוּ׃
which   swore   ihvh   to our fathers   to give   to us

3 And thou shalt go unto the priest that shall be in those days, and say unto him, I profess this day unto the LORD thy God, that I am come unto the country which the LORD sware unto our fathers for to give us.

וְלָקַח הַכֹּהֵן הַטֶּנֶא מִיָּדֶךָ
from your hand the basket the priest and will take

וְהִנִּיחוֹ לִפְנֵי מִזְבַּח יְהוָה אֱלֹהֶיךָ:
your Elohim ihvh altar before and leaves it

4 And the priest shall take the basket out of thine hand, and set it down before the altar of the LORD thy God.

וְעָנִיתָ וְאָמַרְתָּ לִפְנֵי יְהוָה אֱלֹהֶיךָ
your Elohim ihvh before and you will say and you answer

אֲרַמִּי אֹבֵד אָבִי וַיֵּרֶד מִצְרַיְמָה
towards Egypt and he descended my father lost Syrian

וַיָּגָר שָׁם בִּמְתֵי מְעָט וַיְהִי־שָׁם לְגוֹי גָּדוֹל עָצוּם וָרָב:
and many mighty great to nation there - and it was few in deaths there and he lived

5 And thou shalt speak and say before the LORD thy God, A Syrian ready to perish was my father, and he went down into Egypt, and sojourned there with a few, and became there a nation, great, mighty, and populous:

וַיָּרֵעוּ אֹתָנוּ הַמִּצְרִים וַיְעַנּוּנוּ
and they afflicted us the Egyptians to us and they did evil

וַיִּתְּנוּ עָלֵינוּ עֲבֹדָה קָשָׁה:
hard work upon us and they gave

6 And the Egyptians evil entreated us, and afflicted us, and laid upon us hard bondage:

וַנִּצְעַק אֶל־יְהוָה אֱלֹהֵי אֲבֹתֵינוּ
our fathers Elohim ihvh - unto and we cried

וַיִּשְׁמַע יְהוָה אֶת־קֹלֵנוּ
our voice - that ihvh and he heard

וַיַּרְא אֶת־עָנְיֵנוּ וְאֶת־עֲמָלֵנוּ וְאֶת־לַחֲצֵנוּ:
to our oppression - and that our labor - and that our affliction - that and he saw

7 And when we cried unto the LORD God of our fathers, the LORD heard our voice, and looked on our affliction, and our labour, and our oppression:

וַיּוֹצִאֵנוּ יְהוָה מִמִּצְרַיִם בְּיָד חֲזָקָה וּבִזְרֹעַ נְטוּיָה
arm and in outstretched strong in hand from Egypt ihvh and he brought us out

וּבְמֹרָא גָּדֹל וּבְאֹתוֹת וּבְמֹפְתִים:
and in miracles and it signs great and in trembling fear

8 And the LORD brought us forth out of Egypt with a mighty hand, and with an outstretched arm, and with great terribleness, and with signs, and with wonders:

וַיְבִאֵנוּ אֶל־הַמָּקוֹם הַזֶּה וַיִּתֶּן־לָנוּ אֶת־הָאָרֶץ הַזֹּאת
the this the land - that to us - and he gave the this the place - unto and he brought us

Ki Tavo - Chapter 26

אֶרֶץ זָבַת חָלָב וּדְבָשׁ׃
land flowing milk and honey

9 And he hath brought us into this place, and hath given us this land, even a land that floweth with milk and honey.

וְעַתָּה הִנֵּה הֵבֵאתִי אֶת־רֵאשִׁית פְּרִי הָאֲדָמָה
and now here I brought that - first fruits the ground

אֲשֶׁר־נָתַתָּה לִּי יְהֹוָה וְהִנַּחְתּוֹ לִפְנֵי יְהֹוָה אֱלֹהֶיךָ
which - gave it to me ihvh and leave him before ihvh our Elohim

וְהִשְׁתַּחֲוִיתָ לִפְנֵי יְהֹוָה אֱלֹהֶיךָ׃
and you worship before ihvh your Elohim

10 And now, behold, I have brought the firstfruits of the land, which thou, O LORD, hast given me. And thou shalt set it before the LORD thy God, and worship before the LORD thy God:

וְשָׂמַחְתָּ בְכָל־הַטּוֹב אֲשֶׁר נָתַן־לְךָ יְהֹוָה אֱלֹהֶיךָ
and you rejoice in all - the good which gave - to you ihvh your Elohim

וּלְבֵיתֶךָ אַתָּה וְהַלֵּוִי וְהַגֵּר אֲשֶׁר בְּקִרְבֶּךָ׃
and to your house you and the Levite and the stranger which in amongst you

11 And thou shalt rejoice in every good thing which the LORD thy God hath given unto thee, and unto thine house, thou, and the Levite, and the stranger that is among you.

ס

[שני]

כִּי תְכַלֶּה לַעְשֵׂר אֶת־כָּל־מַעְשַׂר תְּבוּאָתְךָ
like you finish to tithe that - all - tithing your produce

בַּשָּׁנָה הַשְּׁלִישִׁת שְׁנַת הַמַּעֲשֵׂר
in year the third year the tithing

וְנָתַתָּה לַלֵּוִי לַגֵּר לַיָּתוֹם וְלָאַלְמָנָה
and you gave to Levite to stranger to fatherless and to widow

וְאָכְלוּ בִשְׁעָרֶיךָ וְשָׂבֵעוּ׃
and they ate in your gate and they full

12 When thou hast made an end of tithing all the tithes of thine increase the third year, which is the year of tithing, and hast given it unto the Levite, the stranger, the fatherless, and the widow, that they may eat within thy gates, and be filled;

וְאָמַרְתָּ לִפְנֵי יְהֹוָה אֱלֹהֶיךָ בִּעַרְתִּי הַקֹּדֶשׁ מִן־הַבַּיִת
and you said before ihvh your Elohim I brought away the holy from - the house

וְגַם נְתַתִּיו לַלֵּוִי וְלַגֵּר לַיָּתוֹם וְלָאַלְמָנָה
and to widow   to fatherless and to stranger   to Levite   I gave him   and also

כְּכָל־מִצְוָתְךָ אֲשֶׁר צִוִּיתָנִי
you commanded me   which   your commandments - like all

לֹא־עָבַרְתִּי מִמִּצְוֹתֶיךָ וְלֹא שָׁכָחְתִּי׃
I forgot   and not   from your commandments   I passed - not

13 Then thou shalt say before the LORD thy God, I have brought away the hallowed things out of mine house, and also have given them unto the Levite, and unto the stranger, to the fatherless, and to the widow, according to all thy commandments which thou hast commanded me: I have not transgressed thy commandments, neither have I forgotten them:

לֹא־אָכַלְתִּי בְאֹנִי מִמֶּנּוּ וְלֹא־בִעַרְתִּי מִמֶּנּוּ בְּטָמֵא
in unclean use   from it   I taken away - and not   from it   in mourning   I ate - not

וְלֹא־נָתַתִּי מִמֶּנּוּ לְמֵת
to dead   from it   I gave - and not

שָׁמַעְתִּי בְּקוֹל יְהֹוָה אֱלֹהָי עָשִׂיתִי כְּכֹל אֲשֶׁר צִוִּיתָנִי׃
you commanded me   which   like all   I did   Elohim   ihvh   in voice   I heard

14 I have not eaten thereof in my mourning, neither have I taken away ought thereof for any unclean use, nor given ought thereof for the dead: but I have hearkened to the voice of the LORD my God, and have done according to all that thou hast commanded me.

הַשְׁקִיפָה מִמְּעוֹן קָדְשְׁךָ מִן־הַשָּׁמַיִם
the heaven - from   holy   from habitation   you gaze

וּבָרֵךְ אֶת־עַמְּךָ אֶת־יִשְׂרָאֵל וְאֵת הָאֲדָמָה
the ground   and that   Israel - that   your people - that   and bless

אֲשֶׁר נָתַתָּה לָנוּ כַּאֲשֶׁר נִשְׁבַּעְתָּ לַאֲבֹתֵינוּ
to our fathers   you swore   when   to us   you gave   which

אֶרֶץ זָבַת חָלָב וּדְבָשׁ׃
and honey   milk   flowing   land

15 Look down from thy holy habitation, from heaven, and bless thy people Israel, and the land which thou hast given us, as thou swarest unto our fathers, a land that floweth with milk and honey.

ס

[שְׁלִישִׁי]

הַיּוֹם הַזֶּה יְהֹוָה אֱלֹהֶיךָ מְצַוְּךָ
commanded you   your Elohim   ihvh   the this   the day

לַעֲשׂוֹת אֶת־הַחֻקִּים הָאֵלֶּה וְאֶת־הַמִּשְׁפָּטִים
to do   that - the statutes   the these   and that - the judgments

וְשָׁמַרְתָּ וְעָשִׂיתָ אוֹתָם בְּכָל־לְבָבְךָ וּבְכָל־נַפְשֶׁךָ׃
and you heed   and you do   to them   in all - your heart   and in all - your soul

16 This day the LORD thy God hath commanded thee to do these statutes and judgments: thou shalt therefore keep and do them with all thine heart, and with all thy soul.

אֶת־יְהֹוָה הֶאֱמַרְתָּ הַיּוֹם לִהְיוֹת לְךָ לֵאלֹהִים
ihvh - that   you vouched   the day   to be   to you   to Elohim

וְלָלֶכֶת בִּדְרָכָיו וְלִשְׁמֹר חֻקָּיו וּמִצְוֺתָיו וּמִשְׁפָּטָיו
and to walk   in his way   and to heed   his statutes   and his commandments   and his judgments

וְלִשְׁמֹעַ בְּקֹלוֹ׃
and to hear   in his voice

17 Thou hast avouched the LORD this day to be thy God, and to walk in his ways, and to keep his statutes, and his commandments, and his judgments, and to hearken unto his voice:

וַיהֹוָה הֶאֱמִירְךָ הַיּוֹם לִהְיוֹת לוֹ לְעַם סְגֻלָּה
and ihvh   the affirms you   the day   to be   to him   to people   special

כַּאֲשֶׁר דִּבֶּר־לָךְ וְלִשְׁמֹר כָּל־מִצְוֺתָיו׃
when   spoke - to you   and to heed   all - his commandments

18 And the LORD hath avouched thee this day to be his peculiar people, as he hath promised thee, and that thou shouldest keep all his commandments;

וּלְתִתְּךָ עֶלְיוֹן עַל כָּל־הַגּוֹיִם
and to give you   supreme   upon   all - the nations

אֲשֶׁר עָשָׂה לִתְהִלָּה וּלְשֵׁם וּלְתִפְאָרֶת
which   did   to praise   and to name   and to beauty

וְלִהְיֹתְךָ עַם־קָדֹשׁ לַיהֹוָה אֱלֹהֶיךָ כַּאֲשֶׁר דִּבֵּר׃
and to be you   people - holy   to ihvh   your Elohim   when   he spoke

19 And to make thee high above all nations which he hath made, in praise, and in name, and in honour; and that thou mayest be an holy people unto the LORD thy God, as he hath spoken.

פ

Chapter 27

ספר דברים פרק כז

[רביעי]

וַיְצַ֤ו מֹשֶׁה֙ וְזִקְנֵ֣י יִשְׂרָאֵ֔ל אֶת־הָעָ֖ם לֵאמֹ֑ר
    and he commanded Moses and elders Israel that - the people to say

שָׁמֹר֙ אֶת־כָּל־הַמִּצְוָ֔ה אֲשֶׁ֧ר אָנֹכִ֛י מְצַוֶּ֥ה אֶתְכֶ֖ם הַיּֽוֹם׃
heed that - all - the commandment which I am commanding that you the day

1 And Moses with the elders of Israel commanded the people, saying, Keep all the commandments which I command you this day.

וְהָיָ֗ה בַּיּוֹם֙ אֲשֶׁ֨ר תַּעַבְר֤וּ אֶת־הַיַּרְדֵּן֙ אֶל־הָאָ֔רֶץ
and it will be in day which you will pass that - the Jordan unto - the land

אֲשֶׁר־יְהוָ֥ה אֱלֹהֶ֖יךָ נֹתֵ֣ן לָ֑ךְ
which - ihvh your Elohim gives to you

וַהֲקֵמֹתָ֤ לְךָ֙ אֲבָנִ֣ים גְּדֹל֔וֹת וְשַׂדְתָּ֥ אֹתָ֖ם בַּשִּֽׂיד׃
and you will set up to you stones great ones and you plaster to them in plaster

2 And it shall be on the day when ye shall pass over Jordan unto the land which the LORD thy God giveth thee, that thou shalt set thee up great stones, and plaster them with plaster:

וְכָתַבְתָּ֣ עֲלֵיהֶ֗ן אֶת־כָּל־דִּבְרֵ֛י הַתּוֹרָ֥ה הַזֹּ֖את בְּעָבְרֶ֑ךָ
and you will write upon them that - all - speakings the law the this in your passing

לְמַ֙עַן֙ אֲשֶׁ֣ר תָּבֹ֔א אֶל־הָאָ֜רֶץ
to end which you come unto - the land

אֲשֶׁר־יְהוָ֨ה אֱלֹהֶ֤יךָ ׀ נֹתֵ֨ן לְךָ֜ אֶ֣רֶץ זָבַ֤ת חָלָב֙ וּדְבַ֔שׁ
ihvh - which your Elohim gave to you land flowing milk and honey

כַּאֲשֶׁ֥ר דִּבֶּ֛ר יְהוָ֥ה אֱלֹהֵֽי־אֲבֹתֶ֖יךָ לָֽךְ׃
when spoke ihvh Elohim - your fathers to you

3 And thou shalt write upon them all the words of this law, when thou art passed over, that thou mayest go in unto the land which the LORD thy God giveth thee, a land that floweth with milk and honey; as the LORD God of thy fathers hath promised thee.

וְהָיָה֙ בְּעָבְרְכֶ֣ם אֶת־הַיַּרְדֵּ֔ן תָּקִ֛ימוּ אֶת־הָאֲבָנִ֥ים הָאֵ֖לֶּה
and it will be in you passing that - the Jordan you will set up that - the stones the these

אֲשֶׁ֨ר אָנֹכִ֜י מְצַוֶּ֥ה אֶתְכֶ֖ם הַיּ֑וֹם
which I am commanding that you the day

בְּהַ֖ר עֵיבָ֑ל וְשַׂדְתָּ֥ אוֹתָ֖ם בַּשִּֽׂיד׃
in mountain Ebal and you will plaster to them in plaster

Ki Tavo - Chapter 27

4 Therefore it shall be when ye be gone over Jordan, that ye shall set up these stones, which I command you this day, in mount Ebal, and thou shalt plaster them with plaster.

וּבָנִ֤יתָ שָּׁם֙ מִזְבֵּ֔חַ לַיהוָ֖ה אֱלֹהֶ֑יךָ
your Elohim   to ihvh   altar   there   you will build

מִזְבַּ֣ח אֲבָנִ֔ים לֹא־תָנִ֥יף עֲלֵיהֶ֖ם בַּרְזֶֽל׃
iron   upon them   you swing - not   stones   altar

5 And there shalt thou build an altar unto the LORD thy God, an altar of stones: thou shalt not lift up any iron tool upon them.

אֲבָנִ֤ים שְׁלֵמוֹת֙ תִּבְנֶ֔ה אֶת־מִזְבַּ֖ח יְהוָ֣ה אֱלֹהֶ֑יךָ
your Elohim   ihvh   altar - that   you will build   whole   stones

וְהַעֲלִ֤יתָ עָלָיו֙ עוֹלֹ֔ת לַיהוָ֖ה אֱלֹהֶֽיךָ׃
your Elohim   to ihvh   burnt offerings   upon it   and you will offer

6 Thou shalt build the altar of the LORD thy God of whole stones: and thou shalt offer burnt offerings thereon unto the LORD thy God:

וְזָבַחְתָּ֥ שְׁלָמִ֖ים וְאָכַ֣לְתָּ שָּׁ֑ם
there   and you will eat   peace offerings   and you will offer offerings

וְשָׂ֣מַחְתָּ֔ לִפְנֵ֖י יְהוָ֥ה אֱלֹהֶֽיךָ׃
your Elohim   ihvh   before   and you rejoice

7 And thou shalt offer peace offerings, and shalt eat there, and rejoice before the LORD thy God.

וְכָתַבְתָּ֣ עַל־הָאֲבָנִ֔ים
the stones - upon   and you will write

אֶת־כָּל־דִּבְרֵ֛י הַתּוֹרָ֥ה הַזֹּ֖את בַּאֵ֥ר הֵיטֵֽב׃
good   plainly   the this   the law   speakings - all - that

8 And thou shalt write upon the stones all the words of this law very plainly.

ס

וַיְדַבֵּ֤ר מֹשֶׁה֙ וְהַכֹּהֲנִ֣ים הַלְוִיִּ֔ם אֶל־כָּל־יִשְׂרָאֵ֖ל לֵאמֹ֑ר
to say   Israel - all - unto   the Levites   and the priests   Moses   and he spoke

הַסְכֵּ֤ת ׀ וּשְׁמַע֙ יִשְׂרָאֵ֔ל
Israel   and hear   the quiet

הַיּ֤וֹם הַזֶּה֙ נִהְיֵ֣יתָ לְעָ֔ם לַיהוָ֖ה אֱלֹהֶֽיךָ׃
your Elohim   to ihvh   to people   you are   the this   the day

9 And Moses and the priests the Levites spake unto all Israel, saying, Take heed, and hearken, O Israel; this day thou art become the people of the LORD thy God.

וְשָׁמַעְתָּ֙ בְּקוֹל֙ יְהֹוָ֣ה אֱלֹהֶ֔יךָ
              your Elohim   ihvh   in voice and you will hear

וְעָשִׂ֣יתָ אֶת־מִצְוֺתָ֗יו וְאֶת־חֻקָּ֔יו אֲשֶׁ֛ר אָנֹכִ֥י מְצַוְּךָ֖ הַיּֽוֹם׃
the day commanding I am which his statutes - and that his commandments - that and you do

10 Thou shalt therefore obey the voice of the LORD thy God, and do his commandments and his statutes, which I command thee this day.

ס

[חמישי]

וַיְצַ֤ו מֹשֶׁה֙ אֶת־הָעָ֔ם בַּיּ֥וֹם הַה֖וּא לֵאמֹֽר׃
            to say the it in day the people - that Moses and he commanded

11 And Moses charged the people the same day, saying,

אֵ֠לֶּה יַֽעַמְד֞וּ לְבָרֵ֤ךְ אֶת־הָעָם֙
        the people - that to bless they will stand these

עַל־הַ֣ר גְּרִזִ֔ים בְּעָבְרְכֶ֖ם אֶת־הַיַּרְדֵּ֑ן
       the Jordan - that in you passing Gerizim mountain - upon

שִׁמְעוֹן֙ וְלֵוִ֣י וִֽיהוּדָ֔ה וְיִשָּׂשכָ֥ר וְיוֹסֵ֖ף וּבִנְיָמִֽן׃
and Benjamin and Joseph and Issachar and Judah and Levi Simeon

12 These shall stand upon mount Gerizim to bless the people, when ye are come over Jordan; Simeon, and Levi, and Judah, and Issachar, and Joseph, and Benjamin:

וְאֵ֛לֶּה יַֽעַמְד֥וּ עַל־הַקְּלָלָ֖ה בְּהַ֣ר עֵיבָ֑ל
Ebal in mountain the curse - upon they will stand and these

רְאוּבֵן֙ גָּ֣ד וְאָשֵׁ֔ר וּזְבוּלֻ֖ן דָּ֥ן וְנַפְתָּלִֽי׃
and Naphtali Dan and Zebulun and Asher Gad Reuben

13 And these shall stand upon mount Ebal to curse; Reuben, Gad, and Asher, and Zebulun, Dan, and Naphtali.

וְעָנ֣וּ הַלְוִיִּ֗ם וְאָֽמְר֛וּ אֶל־כׇּל־אִ֥ישׁ יִשְׂרָאֵ֖ל ק֥וֹל רָֽם׃
loud voice Israel man - all - unto and they will say the Levites and they answer

14 And the Levites shall speak, and say unto all the men of Israel with a loud voice,

ס

אָר֣וּר הָאִ֗ישׁ אֲשֶׁ֨ר יַעֲשֶׂ֥ה פֶ֨סֶל֙
        graven idol he makes which the man cursed

וּמַסֵּכָ֜ה תּוֹעֲבַ֣ת יְהֹוָ֗ה מַעֲשֵׂ֛ה יְדֵ֥י חָרָ֖שׁ
craftsman hand work ihvh abomination and molten idol

Ki Tavo - Chapter 27

וְשָׂ֣ם בַּסָּ֑תֶר
   in hiding and puts

וְעָנ֧וּ כָל־הָעָ֛ם וְאָמְר֖וּ אָמֵֽן׃
and they will answer the people - all and they say Amen

15 Cursed be the man that maketh any graven or molten image, an abomination unto the LORD, the work of the hands of the craftsman, and putteth it in a secret place. And all the people shall answer and say, Amen.

ס

אָר֕וּר מַקְלֶ֥ה אָבִ֖יו וְאִמּ֑וֹ וְאָמַ֥ר כָּל־הָעָ֖ם אָמֵֽן׃
cursed slighting his father and his mother and will say the people - all Amen

16 Cursed be he that setteth light by his father or his mother. And all the people shall say, Amen.

ס

אָר֕וּר מַסִּ֖יג גְּב֣וּל רֵעֵ֑הוּ וְאָמַ֥ר כָּל־הָעָ֖ם אָמֵֽן׃
cursed remover landmark his neighbor and will say the people - all Amen

17 Cursed be he that removeth his neighbour's landmark. And all the people shall say, Amen.

ס

אָר֕וּר מַשְׁגֶּ֥ה עִוֵּ֖ר בַּדָּ֑רֶךְ וְאָמַ֥ר כָּל־הָעָ֖ם אָמֵֽן׃
cursed making err blind in way and will say the people - all Amen

18 Cursed be he that maketh the blind to wander out of the way. And all the people shall say, Amen.

ס

אָר֗וּר מַטֶּ֛ה מִשְׁפַּ֥ט גֵּר־יָת֖וֹם וְאַלְמָנָ֑ה
cursed perverts judgment stranger - fatherless and widow

וְאָמַ֥ר כָּל־הָעָ֖ם אָמֵֽן׃
and will say the people - all Amen

19 Cursed be he that perverteth the judgment of the stranger, fatherless, and widow. And all the people shall say, Amen.

אָר֗וּר שֹׁכֵב֙ עִם־אֵ֣שֶׁת אָבִ֔יו כִּ֥י גִלָּ֖ה כְּנַ֥ף אָבִ֑יו
cursed lying one wife - with his father like exposes hem his father

וְאָמַ֥ר כָּל־הָעָ֖ם אָמֵֽן׃
and will say the people - all Amen

ס

20 Cursed be he that lieth with his father's wife; because he uncovereth his father's skirt. And all the people shall say, Amen.

אָרוּר שֹׁכֵב עִם־כָּל־בְּהֵמָה
cursed　lying one　with - all - beast

וְאָמַר כָּל־הָעָם אָמֵן׃
and will say　the people - all　Amen

ס

21 Cursed be he that lieth with any manner of beast. And all the people shall say, Amen.

אָרוּר שֹׁכֵב עִם־אֲחֹתוֹ בַּת־אָבִיו אוֹ בַת־אִמּוֹ
cursed　lying one　with - his sister　his father - daughter　or　his mother - daughter

וְאָמַר כָּל־הָעָם אָמֵן׃
and will say　the people - all　Amen

22 Cursed be he that lieth with his sister, the daughter of his father, or the daughter of his mother. And all the people shall say, Amen.

ס

אָרוּר שֹׁכֵב עִם־חֹתַנְתּוֹ וְאָמַר כָּל־הָעָם אָמֵן׃
cursed　lying one　with - mother in law　and will say　the people - all　Amen

23 Cursed be he that lieth with his mother in law. And all the people shall say, Amen.

ס

אָרוּר מַכֵּה רֵעֵהוּ בַּסָּתֶר וְאָמַר כָּל־הָעָם אָמֵן׃
cursed　smiter　his neighbor　in secret　and will say　the people - all　Amen

24 Cursed be he that smiteth his neighbour secretly. And all the people shall say, Amen.

ס

אָרוּר לֹקֵחַ שֹׁחַד לְהַכּוֹת נֶפֶשׁ דָּם נָקִי
cursed　taker　bribe　to slay　soul　blood　innocent

וְאָמַר כָּל־הָעָם אָמֵן׃
and will say　the people - all　Amen

25 Cursed be he that taketh reward to slay an innocent person. And all the people shall say, Amen.

ס

אָרוּר אֲשֶׁר לֹא־יָקִים אֶת־דִּבְרֵי הַתּוֹרָה־הַזֹּאת לַעֲשׂוֹת אוֹתָם
cursed　which　not - he establishes　that - speakings　the law - the this　to do　to them

וְאָמַר כָּל־הָעָם אָמֵן׃
and will say　the people - all　Amen

Ki Tavo - Chapter 28

26 Cursed be he that confirmeth not all the words of this law to do them. And all the people shall say, Amen.

פ

Chapter 28

ספר דברים פרק כח

וְהָיָ֞ה אִם־שָׁמ֤וֹעַ תִּשְׁמַע֙ בְּקוֹל֙ יְהֹוָ֣ה אֱלֹהֶ֔יךָ
and it will be — listen - if — you listen — in voice — ihvh — your Elohim

לִשְׁמֹ֤ר לַעֲשׂוֹת֙ אֶת־כָּל־מִצְוֺתָ֔יו
to heed — to do — that - all - his commandments

אֲשֶׁ֛ר אָנֹכִ֥י מְצַוְּךָ֖ הַיּ֑וֹם
which — I am — commanding you — the day

וּנְתָ֨נְךָ֜ יְהֹוָ֤ה אֱלֹהֶ֙יךָ֙ עֶלְי֔וֹן עַ֖ל כָּל־גּוֹיֵ֥י הָאָֽרֶץ׃
and give you — ihvh — your Elohim — supreme — upon — all - nations — the land

1 And it shall come to pass, if thou shalt hearken diligently unto the voice of the LORD thy God, to observe and to do all his commandments which I command thee this day, that the LORD thy God will set thee on high above all nations of the earth:

וּבָ֧אוּ עָלֶ֛יךָ כָּל־הַבְּרָכ֥וֹת הָאֵ֖לֶּה וְהִשִּׂיגֻ֑ךָ
and it will come — upon you — the blessings - all — the these — and cause overtake you

כִּ֣י תִשְׁמַ֔ע בְּק֖וֹל יְהֹוָ֥ה אֱלֹהֶֽיךָ׃
like — you will hear — in voice — ihvh — your Elohim

2 And all these blessings shall come on thee, and overtake thee, if thou shalt hearken unto the voice of the LORD thy God.

בָּר֥וּךְ אַתָּ֖ה בָּעִ֑יר וּבָר֥וּךְ אַתָּ֖ה בַּשָּׂדֶֽה׃
will be blessed — you — in city — and will be blessed — you — in field

3 Blessed shalt thou be in the city, and blessed shalt thou be in the field.

בָּר֧וּךְ פְּרִֽי־בִטְנְךָ֛ וּפְרִ֥י אַדְמָתְךָ֖
will be blessed — fruit - your stomach — and fruit — your ground

וּפְרִ֣י בְהֶמְתֶּ֑ךָ שְׁגַ֥ר אֲלָפֶ֖יךָ
and fruit — your cattle — drop — your kine

וְעַשְׁתְּר֥וֹת צֹאנֶֽךָ׃
and doing ones — your sheep

4 Blessed shall be the fruit of thy body, and the fruit of thy ground, and the fruit of thy cattle, the increase of thy kine, and the flocks of thy sheep.

בָּר֥וּךְ טַנְאֲךָ֖ וּמִשְׁאַרְתֶּֽךָ׃
will be blesssed — your basket — and your store

5 Blessed shall be thy basket and thy store.

בָּרוּךְ אַתָּה בְּבֹאֶךָ וּבָרוּךְ אַתָּה בְּצֵאתֶךָ:
will be blessed　you　in your coming　and will be blessed　your　your going out

6 Blessed shalt thou be when thou comest in, and blessed shalt thou be when thou goest out.

[ששי]

יִתֵּן יְהוָה אֶת־אֹיְבֶיךָ הַקָּמִים עָלֶיךָ
he gives　ihvh　your enemies - that　the rising up ones　upon you

נִגָּפִים לְפָנֶיךָ בְּדֶרֶךְ אֶחָד יֵצְאוּ אֵלֶיךָ
slain ones　before you　in way　one　they will come out　unto you

וּבְשִׁבְעָה דְרָכִים יָנוּסוּ לְפָנֶיךָ:
and in seven　ways　they flee　before you

7 The LORD shall cause thine enemies that rise up against thee to be smitten before thy face: they shall come out against thee one way, and flee before thee seven ways.

יְצַו יְהוָה אִתְּךָ אֶת־הַבְּרָכָה בַּאֲסָמֶיךָ
will command　ihvh　to you　the blessing - that　in your storehouses

וּבְכֹל מִשְׁלַח יָדֶךָ
and in all　delivered　your hand

וּבֵרַכְךָ בָּאָרֶץ אֲשֶׁר־יְהוָה אֱלֹהֶיךָ נֹתֵן לָךְ:
and will bless you　in land　ihvh - which　your Elohim　gives　to you

8 The LORD shall command the blessing upon thee in thy storehouses, and in all that thou settest thine hand unto; and he shall bless thee in the land which the LORD thy God giveth thee.

יְקִימְךָ יְהוָה לוֹ לְעַם קָדוֹשׁ כַּאֲשֶׁר נִשְׁבַּע־לָךְ
will establish　ihvh　to him　to people　holy　when　to you - swore

כִּי תִשְׁמֹר אֶת־מִצְוֹת יְהוָה אֱלֹהֶיךָ וְהָלַכְתָּ בִּדְרָכָיו:
like　you heed　commandment - that　ihvh　your Elohim　and you walk　in his ways

9 The LORD shall establish thee an holy people unto himself, as he hath sworn unto thee, if thou shalt keep the commandments of the LORD thy God, and walk in his ways.

וְרָאוּ כָּל־עַמֵּי הָאָרֶץ כִּי שֵׁם יְהוָה נִקְרָא עָלֶיךָ
and they will see　my people - all　the land　like　name　ihvh　called　upon you

וְיָרְאוּ מִמֶּךָּ:
and they will be afraid　from you

10 And all people of the earth shall see that thou art called by the name of the LORD; and they shall be afraid of thee.

Ki Tavo - Chapter 28

וְהוֹתִרְךָ֤ יְהוָ֨ה לְטוֹבָ֔ה בִּפְרִ֥י בִטְנְךָ֖
    your belly   in fruit   to good   ihvh   and will make you plenteous

וּבִפְרִ֧י בְהֶמְתְּךָ֛ וּבִפְרִ֥י אַדְמָתֶ֖ךָ עַ֚ל הָאֲדָמָ֔ה
    the ground   upon   your ground   and in fruit   your cattle   and in fruit

אֲשֶׁ֨ר נִשְׁבַּ֧ע יְהוָ֛ה לַאֲבֹתֶ֖יךָ לָ֥תֶת לָֽךְ׃
    to you   to give   to your fathers   ihvh   swore   which

11 And the LORD shall make thee plenteous in goods, in the fruit of thy body, and in the fruit of thy cattle, and in the fruit of thy ground, in the land which the LORD sware unto thy fathers to give thee.

יִפְתַּ֣ח יְהוָ֣ה ׀ לְךָ֡ אֶת־אוֹצָר֨וֹ הַטּ֜וֹב
    the good   his treasure - that   to you   ihvh   he will open

אֶת־הַשָּׁמַ֜יִם לָתֵ֥ת מְטַֽר־אַרְצְךָ֛ בְּעִתּ֔וֹ
    in it's season   your land - rain   to give   the heaven - that

וּלְבָרֵ֕ךְ אֵ֖ת כָּל־מַעֲשֵׂ֣ה יָדֶ֑ךָ
    your hand   work - all   that   and to bless

וְהִלְוִ֨יתָ גּוֹיִ֣ם רַבִּ֔ים וְאַתָּ֖ה לֹ֥א תִלְוֶֽה׃
    you will borrow   not   and you   many   nations   and you will lend

12 The LORD shall open unto thee his good treasure, the heaven to give the rain unto thy land in his season, and to bless all the work of thine hand: and thou shalt lend unto many nations, and thou shalt not borrow.

וּנְתָֽנְךָ֨ יְהוָ֤ה לְרֹאשׁ֙ וְלֹ֣א לְזָנָ֔ב
    to tail   and not   to head   ihvh   and will give you

וְהָיִ֨יתָ רַ֣ק לְמַ֔עְלָה וְלֹ֥א תִהְיֶ֖ה לְמָ֑טָּה
    to beneath   you will be   and not   to above   only   and you will be

כִּֽי־תִשְׁמַ֞ע אֶל־מִצְוֹ֣ת ׀ יְהוָ֣ה אֱלֹהֶ֗יךָ
    your Elohim   ihvh   commandment - unto   you will hear - like

אֲשֶׁ֨ר אָנֹכִ֧י מְצַוְּךָ֛ הַיּ֖וֹם לִשְׁמֹ֥ר וְלַעֲשֽׂוֹת׃
    and to do   to heed   the day   commanding you   I am   which

13 And the LORD shall make thee the head, and not the tail; and thou shalt be above only, and thou shalt not be beneath; if that thou hearken unto the commandments of the LORD thy God, which I command thee this day, to observe and to do them:

וְלֹ֣א תָס֗וּר מִכָּל־הַדְּבָרִ֔ים
    the speakings - from all   you remove   and not

אֲשֶׁ֨ר אָנֹכִ֜י מְצַוֶּ֥ה אֶתְכֶ֛ם הַיּ֖וֹם יָמִ֣ין וּשְׂמֹ֑אול
    and left   right   the day   that you   commanding   I am   which

לָלֶכֶת אַחֲרֵי אֱלֹהִים אֲחֵרִים לְעָבְדָם׃
to serve them   other ones   elohim   after   to go

14 And thou shalt not go aside from any of the words which I command thee this day, to the right hand, or to the left, to go after other gods to serve them.

פ

וְהָיָה אִם־לֹא תִשְׁמַע בְּקוֹל יְהוָה אֱלֹהֶיךָ לִשְׁמֹר
and it will be   not - if   you hear   in voice   ihvh   your Elohim   to heed

לַעֲשׂוֹת אֶת־כָּל־מִצְוֺתָיו וְחֻקֹּתָיו אֲשֶׁר אָנֹכִי מְצַוְּךָ הַיּוֹם
to do   that - all - his commandments   and his statutes   which   I am   commanding you   the day

וּבָאוּ עָלֶיךָ כָּל־הַקְּלָלוֹת הָאֵלֶּה וְהִשִּׂיגוּךָ׃
and it come   upon you   all - the curses   the these   and they overtake you

15 But it shall come to pass, if thou wilt not hearken unto the voice of the LORD thy God, to observe to do all his commandments and his statutes which I command thee this day; that all these curses shall come upon thee, and overtake thee:

אָרוּר אַתָּה בָּעִיר וְאָרוּר אַתָּה בַּשָּׂדֶה׃
in field   you   and cursed   in city   you   cursed

16 Cursed shalt thou be in the city, and cursed shalt thou be in the field.

אָרוּר טַנְאֲךָ וּמִשְׁאַרְתֶּךָ׃
and your store   your basket   cursed

17 Cursed shall be thy basket and thy store.

אָרוּר פְּרִי־בִטְנְךָ וּפְרִי אַדְמָתֶךָ
cursed   fruit - your stomach   and fruit   your land

שְׁגַר אֲלָפֶיךָ וְעַשְׁתְּרֹת צֹאנֶךָ׃
drop   your kine   and doings   your sheep

18 Cursed shall be the fruit of thy body, and the fruit of thy land, the increase of thy kine, and the flocks of thy sheep.

אָרוּר אַתָּה בְּבֹאֶךָ
cursed   you   in your coming

וְאָרוּר אַתָּה בְּצֵאתֶךָ׃
cursed   you   your going out

19 Cursed shalt thou be when thou comest in, and cursed shalt thou be when thou goest out.

יְשַׁלַּח יְהוָה בְּךָ
he will send   ihvh   in you

Ki Tavo - Chapter 28

אֶת־הַמְּאֵרָה אֶת־הַמְּהוּמָה וְאֶת־הַמִּגְעֶרֶת
the cursing - that   the vexation - that   the rebuke - and that

בְּכָל־מִשְׁלַח יָדְךָ אֲשֶׁר תַּעֲשֶׂה עַד הִשָּׁמֶדְךָ
exterminated you   till   you do   which   your hand   undertaking - in all

וְעַד־אֲבָדְךָ מַהֵר מִפְּנֵי רֹעַ מַעֲלָלֶיךָ אֲשֶׁר עֲזַבְתָּנִי׃
you forsaken me   which   from your actions   evil   from presence   quickly   you perish - and till

20 The LORD shall send upon thee cursing, vexation, and rebuke, in all that thou settest thine hand unto for to do, until thou be destroyed, and until thou perish quickly; because of the wickedness of thy doings, whereby thou hast forsaken me.

יַדְבֵּק יְהֹוָה בְּךָ אֶת־הַדָּבֶר
he clings   ihvh   in you   the pestilence - that

עַד כַּלֹּתוֹ אֹתְךָ מֵעַל הָאֲדָמָה
till   his consumed   to you   from upon   the ground

אֲשֶׁר־אַתָּה בָא־שָׁמָּה לְרִשְׁתָּהּ׃
you - which   there - come   to possess

21 The LORD shall make the pestilence cleave unto thee, until he have consumed thee from off the land, whither thou goest to possess it.

יַכְּכָה יְהֹוָה בַּשַּׁחֶפֶת
and he will smite   ihvh   in consumption

וּבַקַּדַּחַת וּבַדַּלֶּקֶת וּבַחַרְחֻר וּבַחֶרֶב וּבַשִּׁדָּפוֹן וּבַיֵּרָקוֹן
and in fever   and in inflammation   and in extreme burning   and in sword   and in blasting   and in mildew

וּרְדָפוּךָ עַד אָבְדֶךָ׃
and they will pursue you   till   you perish

22 The LORD shall smite thee with a consumption, and with a fever, and with an inflammation, and with an extreme burning, and with the sword, and with blasting, and with mildew; and they shall pursue thee until thou perish.

וְהָיוּ שָׁמֶיךָ אֲשֶׁר עַל־רֹאשְׁךָ נְחֹשֶׁת
and it will be   your heaven   which   your head - upon   brass

וְהָאָרֶץ אֲשֶׁר־תַּחְתֶּיךָ בַּרְזֶל׃
and the land   under you - which   iron

23 And thy heaven that is over thy head shall be brass, and the earth that is under thee shall be iron.

יִתֵּן יְהֹוָה אֶת־מְטַר אַרְצְךָ אָבָק וְעָפָר
he will give   ihvh   rain - that   your ground   powder   and dust

מִן־הַשָּׁמַיִם יֵרֵד עָלֶיךָ עַד הִשָּׁמְדָךְ׃
the heaven - from   descends   upon you   till   exterminated you

24 The LORD shall make the rain of thy land powder and dust: from heaven shall it come down upon thee, until thou be destroyed.

25 The LORD shall cause thee to be smitten before thine enemies: thou shalt go out one way against them, and flee seven ways before them: and shalt be removed into all the kingdoms of the earth.

וְהָיְתָה נִבְלָתְךָ לְמַאֲכָל לְכָל־עוֹף הַשָּׁמַיִם
  and it will be   your carcass   to food   bird - to all   the heaven

וּלְבֶהֱמַת הָאָרֶץ וְאֵין מַחֲרִיד׃
  and to beast   the earth   and isn't   trembeling

26 And thy carcase shall be meat unto all fowls of the air, and unto the beasts of the earth, and no man shall fray them away.

יַכְּכָה יְהוָה בִּשְׁחִין מִצְרַיִם
  he will smite   ihvh   in boil   Egypt

וּבַעְפֹלִים [וּבַטְּחֹרִים] וּבַגָּרָב וּבֶחָרֶס
  and in humps   and in scab   and in itch

אֲשֶׁר לֹא־תוּכַל לְהֵרָפֵא׃
  which   able - not   to be healed

27 The LORD will smite thee with the botch of Egypt, and with the emerods, and with the scab, and with the itch, whereof thou canst not be healed.

יַכְּכָה יְהוָה בְּשִׁגָּעוֹן וּבְעִוָּרוֹן וּבְתִמְהוֹן לֵבָב׃
  he will smite   ihvh   in madness   and blindness   and in astonishment   heart

28 The LORD shall smite thee with madness, and blindness, and astonishment of heart:

Ki Tavo - Chapter 28

29 And thou shalt grope at noonday, as the blind gropeth in darkness, and thou shalt not prosper in thy ways: and thou shalt be only oppressed and spoiled evermore, and no man shall save thee.

אִשָּׁה תְאָרֵשׂ וְאִישׁ אַחֵר יִשְׁגָּלֶנָּה [יִשְׁכָּבֶנָּה]
wife   you will betroth   and man   one   he lavish with her

בַּיִת תִּבְנֶה
house   you will build

וְלֹא־תֵשֵׁב בּוֹ כֶּרֶם תִּטַּע וְלֹא תְחַלְּלֶנּוּ׃
and not - you will dwell   in it   vineyard   you plant   and not   you will start it

30 Thou shalt betroth a wife, and another man shall lie with her: thou shalt build an house, and thou shalt not dwell therein: thou shalt plant a vineyard, and shalt not gather the grapes thereof.

שׁוֹרְךָ טָבוּחַ לְעֵינֶיךָ וְלֹא תֹאכַל מִמֶּנּוּ
your ox   will be slaughtered   to your eyes   and not   you will eat   from it

חֲמֹרְךָ גָּזוּל מִלְּפָנֶיךָ וְלֹא יָשׁוּב לָךְ
your ass   violently stolen   from before you   and not   he returned   to you

צֹאנְךָ נְתֻנוֹת לְאֹיְבֶיךָ
your sheep   given ones   to your enemies

וְאֵין לְךָ מוֹשִׁיעַ׃
and isn't   to you   savior

31 Thine ox shall be slain before thine eyes, and thou shalt not eat thereof: thine ass shall be violently taken away from before thy face, and shall not be restored to thee: thy sheep shall be given unto thine enemies, and thou shalt have none to rescue them.

בָּנֶיךָ וּבְנֹתֶיךָ נְתֻנִים לְעַם אַחֵר
your sons   and your daughters   given ones   to people   another

וְעֵינֶיךָ רֹאוֹת וְכָלוֹת אֲלֵיהֶם כָּל־הַיּוֹם
and your eyes   will see   and fail   unto them   all - the day

וְאֵין לְאֵל יָדֶךָ׃
and isn't   to El   your hand

32 Thy sons and thy daughters shall be given unto another people, and thine eyes shall look, and fail with longing for them all the day long: and there shall be no might in thine hand.

פְּרִי אַדְמָתְךָ וְכָל־יְגִיעֲךָ יֹאכַל עַם
fruit   your ground   and all - your effort   he eats   people

אֲשֶׁר לֹא־יָדָעְתָּ וְהָיִיתָ רַק עָשׁוּק וְרָצוּץ כָּל־הַיָּמִים׃
which   not - you know   and it will be   only   oppressed   and bruised   all - the days

33 The fruit of thy land, and all thy labours, shall a nation which thou knowest not eat up; and thou shalt be only oppressed and crushed alway:

וְהָיִ֖יתָ מְשֻׁגָּ֑ע מִמַּרְאֵ֥ה עֵינֶ֖יךָ אֲשֶׁ֥ר תִּרְאֶֽה׃
you will see   which   your eyes   from sight   made mad   and you will be

34 So that thou shalt be mad for the sight of thine eyes which thou shalt see.

יַכְּכָ֨ה יְהוָ֜ה בִּשְׁחִ֣ין רָ֗ע עַל־הַבִּרְכַּ֙יִם֙ וְעַל־הַשֹּׁקַ֔יִם
the legs - and upon   the knees - upon   bad   in boil   ihvh   he will smite

אֲשֶׁ֥ר לֹא־תוּכַ֖ל לְהֵרָפֵ֑א מִכַּ֥ף רַגְלְךָ֖ וְעַ֥ד קָדְקֳדֶֽךָ׃
your scalp   and till   your foot   from sole   to the heal   you able - not   which

35 The LORD shall smite thee in the knees, and in the legs, with a sore botch that cannot be healed, from the sole of thy foot unto the top of thy head.

יוֹלֵ֨ךְ יְהוָ֜ה אֹתְךָ֗ וְאֶֽת־מַלְכְּךָ֙
your king - and that   to you   ihvh   and he goes

אֲשֶׁ֣ר תָּקִ֣ים עָלֶ֔יךָ אֶל־גּ֕וֹי
nations - unto   upon you   you set   which

אֲשֶׁ֥ר לֹא־יָדַ֖עְתָּ אַתָּ֣ה וַאֲבֹתֶ֑יךָ
and your fathers   you   you knew - not   which

וְעָבַ֤דְתָּ שָּׁם֙ אֱלֹהִ֣ים אֲחֵרִ֔ים עֵ֖ץ וָאָֽבֶן׃
and stone   wood   other ones   elohim   there   and you will serve

36 The LORD shall bring thee, and thy king which thou shalt set over thee, unto a nation which neither thou nor thy fathers have known; and there shalt thou serve other gods, wood and stone.

וְהָיִ֣יתָ לְשַׁמָּ֔ה לְמָשָׁ֖ל וְלִשְׁנִינָ֑ה
and to byword   to proverb   to hear   and you will be

בְּכֹל֙ הָֽעַמִּ֔ים אֲשֶׁר־יְנַהֶגְךָ֥ יְהוָ֖ה שָֽׁמָּה׃
there   ihvh   he leads you - which   the people   in all

37 And thou shalt become an astonishment, a proverb, and a byword, among all nations whither the LORD shall lead thee.

זֶ֥רַע רַ֛ב תּוֹצִ֥יא הַשָּׂדֶ֖ה
the field   it comes out   much   seed

וּמְעַ֣ט תֶּאֱסֹ֑ף כִּ֥י יַחְסְלֶ֖נּוּ הָאַרְבֶּֽה׃
the locust   they will eat up it   like   you gather   and little

38 Thou shalt carry much seed out into the field, and shalt gather but little in; for the locust shall consume it.

כְּרָמִ֥ים תִּטַּ֖ע וְעָבָ֑דְתָּ
and you serve   you plant   vineyards

Ki Tavo - Chapter 28

וְיַיִן לֹא־תִשְׁתֶּה וְלֹא תֶאֱגֹר
and wine   not - you will drink   and not   you hoard

כִּי תֹאכְלֶנּוּ הַתֹּלָעַת׃
like   they devour   the worms

39 Thou shalt plant vineyards, and dress them, but shalt neither drink of the wine, nor gather the grapes; for the worms shall eat them.

זֵיתִים יִהְיוּ לְךָ בְּכָל־גְּבוּלֶךָ
olives   they will be   to you   in all - your borders

וְשֶׁמֶן לֹא תָסוּךְ כִּי יִשַּׁל זֵיתֶךָ׃
and oil   not   you anoint   like   it ease off   your olive

40 Thou shalt have olive trees throughout all thy coasts, but thou shalt not anoint thyself with the oil; for thine olive shall cast his fruit.

בָּנִים וּבָנוֹת תּוֹלִיד
sons   and daughters   you beget

וְלֹא־יִהְיוּ לָךְ כִּי יֵלְכוּ בַּשֶּׁבִי׃
they will be - and not   to you   like   they will go   into captivity

41 Thou shalt beget sons and daughters, but thou shalt not enjoy them; for they shall go into captivity.

כָּל־עֵצְךָ וּפְרִי אַדְמָתֶךָ יְיָרֵשׁ הַצְּלָצַל׃
all - your trees   and fruit   your ground   desolate   the ciada

42 All thy trees and fruit of thy land shall the locust consume.

הַגֵּר אֲשֶׁר בְּקִרְבְּךָ יַעֲלֶה עָלֶיךָ מַעְלָה מָּעְלָה
the stranger   which   in among your   he will ascend   upon you   upward   upward

וְאַתָּה תֵרֵד מַטָּה מָּטָּה׃
and you   you will descend   downward   downward

43 The stranger that is within thee shall get up above thee very high; and thou shalt come down very low.

הוּא יַלְוְךָ וְאַתָּה לֹא תַלְוֶנּוּ
he   he will lend you   and you   not   you lend him

הוּא יִהְיֶה לְרֹאשׁ וְאַתָּה תִּהְיֶה לְזָנָב׃
he   will be   to head   and you   you will be   to tail

44 He shall lend to thee, and thou shalt not lend to him: he shall be the head, and thou shalt be the tail.

וּבָאוּ עָלֶיךָ כָּל־הַקְּלָלוֹת הָאֵלֶּה
and it comes   upon you   all - the curses   the these

וּרְדָפ֖וּךְ וְהִשִּׂיג֑וּךָ עַ֣ד הִשָּׁמְדָ֑ךְ
and pursues you   and it overtakes you   till   exterminate you

כִּי־לֹ֣א שָׁמַ֔עְתָּ בְּק֖וֹל יְהֹוָ֣ה אֱלֹהֶ֑יךָ
not - like   you listened   in voice   ihvh   your Elohim

לִשְׁמֹ֧ר מִצְוֺתָ֛יו וְחֻקֹּתָ֖יו אֲשֶׁ֥ר צִוָּֽךְ׃
to heed   his commandments   and his statutes   which   commanded you

45 Moreover all these curses shall come upon thee, and shall pursue thee, and overtake thee, till thou be destroyed; because thou hearkenedst not unto the voice of the LORD thy God, to keep his commandments and his statutes which he commanded thee:

וְהָי֣וּ בְךָ֔ לְא֖וֹת וּלְמוֹפֵ֑ת וּבְזַרְעֲךָ֖ עַד־עוֹלָֽם׃
and they will be   in you   to sign   and to miracle   and in your seed   till - forever

46 And they shall be upon thee for a sign and for a wonder, and upon thy seed for ever.

תַּ֗חַת אֲשֶׁ֤ר לֹא־עָבַ֙דְתָּ֙ אֶת־יְהֹוָ֣ה אֱלֹהֶ֔יךָ בְּשִׂמְחָ֖ה
instead   which   not - you serve   that - ihvh   your Elohim   in happiness

וּבְט֣וּב לֵבָ֑ב מֵרֹ֖ב כֹּֽל׃
and in goodness   heart   from much   all

47 Because thou servedst not the LORD thy God with joyfulness, and with gladness of heart, for the abundance of all things;

וְעָבַדְתָּ֣ אֶת־אֹיְבֶ֗יךָ אֲשֶׁ֨ר יְשַׁלְּחֶ֤נּוּ יְהֹוָה֙ בָּ֔ךְ
and you will serve   that - your enemies   which   he will send you   ihvh   in it

בְּרָעָ֧ב וּבְצָמָ֛א וּבְעֵירֹ֖ם וּבְחֹ֣סֶר כֹּ֑ל
in hunger   and in thirst   and in nakedness   and in lack   all

וְנָתַ֞ן עֹ֤ל בַּרְזֶל֙ עַל־צַוָּארֶ֔ךָ עַ֥ד הִשְׁמִיד֖וֹ אֹתָֽךְ׃
and gives   upon   iron   upon - your neck   till   his destroying   to you

48 Therefore shalt thou serve thine enemies which the LORD shall send against thee, in hunger, and in thirst, and in nakedness, and in want of all things: and he shall put a yoke of iron upon thy neck, until he have destroyed thee.

יִשָּׂ֣א יְהֹוָה֩ עָלֶ֨יךָ גּ֤וֹי מֵרָחֹק֙ מִקְצֵ֣ה הָאָ֔רֶץ
he will lift   ihvh   upon you   nations   from far   from end   the earth

כַּאֲשֶׁ֥ר יִדְאֶ֖ה הַנָּ֑שֶׁר גּ֕וֹי אֲשֶׁ֥ר לֹא־תִשְׁמַ֖ע לְשֹׁנֽוֹ׃
when   swoops   the eagle   nations   which   not - you will hear   to his tongue

49 The LORD shall bring a nation against thee from far, from the end of the earth, as swift as the eagle flieth; a nation whose tongue thou shalt not understand;

גּ֖וֹי עַ֣ז פָּנִ֑ים
nation   strong   faces

Ki Tavo - Chapter 28

אֲשֶׁר לֹא־יִשָּׂא פָנִים לְזָקֵן וְנַעַר לֹא יָחֹן:
which he lifts - not faces to old and young not he gracious

50 A nation of fierce countenance, which shall not regard the person of the old, nor shew favour to the young:

וְאָכַל פְּרִי בְהֶמְתְּךָ וּפְרִי־אַדְמָתְךָ עַד הִשָּׁמְדָךְ
and will eat fruit your cattle fruit - and your ground till your extermination

אֲשֶׁר לֹא־יַשְׁאִיר לְךָ דָּגָן תִּירוֹשׁ וְיִצְהָר
which not - he remain to you corn grape juice and oil

שְׁגַר אֲלָפֶיךָ וְעַשְׁתְּרֹת צֹאנֶךָ עַד הַאֲבִידוֹ אֹתָךְ:
drop your kine and doings your sheep till the his destroyed to you

51 And he shall eat the fruit of thy cattle, and the fruit of thy land, until thou be destroyed: which also shall not leave thee either corn, wine, or oil, or the increase of thy kine, or flocks of thy sheep, until he have destroyed thee.

וְהֵצַר לְךָ בְּכָל־שְׁעָרֶיךָ עַד רֶדֶת חֹמֹתֶיךָ הַגְּבֹהֹת
and lay siege to you your gates - in all till tear down your walls the high ones

וְהַבְּצֻרוֹת אֲשֶׁר אַתָּה בֹּטֵחַ בָּהֵן בְּכָל־אַרְצֶךָ
and the defended ones which you trust in grace your land - in all

וְהֵצַר לְךָ בְּכָל־שְׁעָרֶיךָ בְּכָל־אַרְצְךָ
and will lay siege to you your gates - in all your land - in all

אֲשֶׁר נָתַן יְהוָה אֱלֹהֶיךָ לָךְ:
which gave ihvh your Elohim to you

52 And he shall besiege thee in all thy gates, until thy high and fenced walls come down, wherein thou trustedst, throughout all thy land: and he shall besiege thee in all thy gates throughout all thy land, which the LORD thy God hath given thee.

וְאָכַלְתָּ פְרִי־בִטְנְךָ בְּשַׂר בָּנֶיךָ וּבְנֹתֶיךָ
and you will eat fruit - your stomach flesh your sons and your daughters

אֲשֶׁר נָתַן־לְךָ יְהוָה אֱלֹהֶיךָ בְּמָצוֹר
which given - to you ihvh your Elohim in siege

וּבְמָצוֹק אֲשֶׁר־יָצִיק לְךָ אֹיְבֶךָ:
in constraint which - will distress to you your enemies

53 And thou shalt eat the fruit of thine own body, the flesh of thy sons and of thy daughters, which the LORD thy God hath given thee, in the siege, and in the straitness, wherewith thine enemies shall distress thee:

הָאִישׁ הָרַךְ בְּךָ וְהֶעָנֹג מְאֹד תֵּרַע עֵינוֹ בְאָחִיו
the man the tender in you and the delicate very it bad his eye in his brother

וּבְאֵ֣שֶׁת חֵיק֔וֹ וּבְיֶ֥תֶר בָּנָ֖יו אֲשֶׁ֥ר יוֹתִֽיר׃
he will leave which his sons and in remnant his bosom and in woman

54 So that the man that is tender among you, and very delicate, his eye shall be evil toward his brother, and toward the wife of his bosom, and toward the remnant of his children which he shall leave:

מִתֵּ֣ת ׀ לְאַחַ֣ד מֵהֶ֗ם מִבְּשַׂ֣ר בָּנָיו֙
his sons from flesh from them to one from giving

אֲשֶׁ֣ר יֹאכֵ֔ל מִבְּלִ֥י הִשְׁאִֽיר־ל֖וֹ כֹּ֑ל בְּמָצוֹר֙
in siege all to him - remained from nothing he will eat which

וּבְמָצ֔וֹק אֲשֶׁ֨ר יָצִ֥יק לְךָ֛ אֹיִבְךָ֖ בְּכָל־שְׁעָרֶֽיךָ׃
your gates - in all your enemies to you he distress which and in constraint

55 So that he will not give to any of them of the flesh of his children whom he shall eat: because he hath nothing left him in the siege, and in the straitness, wherewith thine enemies shall distress thee in all thy gates.

הָרַכָּ֥ה בְךָ֖ וְהָעֲנֻגָּ֑ה
and the delicate one in you the tender

אֲשֶׁ֨ר לֹא־נִסְּתָ֤ה כַף־רַגְלָהּ֙ הַצֵּ֣ג עַל־הָאָ֔רֶץ מֵהִתְעַנֵּ֖ג
from delicate the earth - upon the put her foot - sole she tries - not which

וּמֵרֹ֑ךְ תֵּרַ֤ע עֵינָהּ֙ בְּאִ֣ישׁ חֵיקָ֔הּ וּבִבְנָ֖הּ וּבְבִתָּֽהּ׃
and in her daughter and in her son her bosom in man her eye it bad and from tender

56 The tender and delicate woman among you, which would not adventure to set the sole of her foot upon the ground for delicateness and tenderness, her eye shall be evil toward the husband of her bosom, and toward her son, and toward her daughter,

וּֽבְשִׁלְיָתָ֞הּ הַיּוֹצֵ֣ת ׀ מִבֵּ֣ין רַגְלֶ֗יהָ וּבְבָנֶ֙יהָ֙ אֲשֶׁ֣ר תֵּלֵ֔ד
she will birth which and in her sons her feet from between the coming out and in her afterbirth

כִּֽי־תֹאכְלֵ֥ם בְּחֹֽסֶר־כֹּ֖ל בַּסָּ֑תֶר בְּמָצוֹר֙
in siege in secret all - in lack she will eat them - like

וּבְמָצ֔וֹק אֲשֶׁ֨ר יָצִ֥יק לְךָ֛ אֹיִבְךָ֖ בִּשְׁעָרֶֽיךָ׃
in your gates your enemies to her it distress which and in constraint

57 And toward her young one that cometh out from between her feet, and toward her children which she shall bear: for she shall eat them for want of all things secretly in the siege and straitness, wherewith thine enemy shall distress thee in thy gates.

אִם־לֹ֣א תִשְׁמֹ֗ר לַעֲשׂוֹת֙ אֶת־כָּל־דִּבְרֵי֙ הַתּוֹרָ֣ה הַזֹּ֔את
the this the law speakings - all - that to do you heed not - if

הַכְּתוּבִ֖ים בַּסֵּ֣פֶר הַזֶּ֑ה
the this in book the written ones

Ki Tavo - Chapter 28

לְיִרְאָה אֶת־הַשֵּׁם הַנִּכְבָּד וְהַנּוֹרָא הַזֶּה
the this   and the awesome   the glorious   the name - that   to fear

אֵת יְהוָה אֱלֹהֶיךָ
your Elohim   ihvh   that

58 If thou wilt not observe to do all the words of this law that are written in this book, that thou mayest fear this glorious and fearful name, THE LORD THY GOD;

וְהִפְלָא יְהוָה אֶת־מַכֹּתְךָ
your plague - that   ihvh   and cause to be miraculous

וְאֵת מַכּוֹת זַרְעֶךָ מַכּוֹת גְּדֹלֹת וְנֶאֱמָנוֹת
and constant ones   great   smitings   your seed   smitings   and that

וָחֳלָיִם רָעִים וְנֶאֱמָנִים:
and constant ones   bad ones   and sicknesses

59 Then the LORD will make thy plagues wonderful, and the plagues of thy seed, even great plagues, and of long continuance, and sore sicknesses, and of long continuance.

ס

וְהֵשִׁיב בְּךָ אֵת כָּל־מַדְוֵה מִצְרַיִם
Egypt   disease - all   that   in you   and the return

אֲשֶׁר יָגֹרְתָּ מִפְּנֵיהֶם וְדָבְקוּ בָּךְ:
in you   and they will cleave   before them   you shrank away   which

60 Moreover he will bring upon thee all the diseases of Egypt, which thou wast afraid of; and they shall cleave unto thee.

גַּם כָּל־חֳלִי וְכָל־מַכָּה
plague - and all   sickness - all   also

אֲשֶׁר לֹא כָתוּב בְּסֵפֶר הַתּוֹרָה הַזֹּאת
the this   the law   in book   written   not   which

יַעְלֵם יְהוָה עָלֶיךָ עַד הִשָּׁמְדָךְ:
exterminate you   till   upon you   ihvh   he will ascend them

61 Also every sickness, and every plague, which is not written in the book of this law, them will the LORD bring upon thee, until thou be destroyed.

וְנִשְׁאַרְתֶּם בִּמְתֵי מְעָט תַּחַת
instead   little   in deaths   and you remained

אֲשֶׁר הֱיִיתֶם כְּכוֹכְבֵי הַשָּׁמַיִם לָרֹב
to much   the heavens   like stars   they were   which

כִּי־לֹא שָׁמַעְתָּ בְּקוֹל יְהוָה אֱלֹהֶיךָ:
your Elohim   ihvh   in voice   you heard   not - like

62 And ye shall be left few in number, whereas ye were as the stars of heaven for multitude; because thou wouldest not obey the voice of the LORD thy God.

63 And it shall come to pass, that as the LORD rejoiced over you to do you good, and to multiply you; so the LORD will rejoice over you to destroy you, and to bring you to nought; and ye shall be plucked from off the land whither thou goest to possess it.

64 And the LORD shall scatter thee among all people, from the one end of the earth even unto the other; and there thou shalt serve other gods, which neither thou nor thy fathers have known, even wood and stone.

65 And among these nations shalt thou find no ease, neither shall the sole of thy foot have rest: but the LORD shall give thee there a trembling heart, and failing of eyes, and

Ki Tavo - Chapter 29

sorrow of mind:

וְהָיוּ חַיֶּיךָ תְּלֻאִים לְךָ מִנֶּגֶד
and it will be　your life　hung ones　to you　from in front

וּפָחַדְתָּ לַיְלָה וְיוֹמָם
and you afraid　night　and by day

וְלֹא תַאֲמִין בְּחַיֶּיךָ׃
and not　you assured　in your life

66 And thy life shall hang in doubt before thee; and thou shalt fear day and night, and shalt have none assurance of thy life:

בַּבֹּקֶר תֹּאמַר מִי־יִתֵּן עֶרֶב
in morning　you will say　he gives - who　evening

וּבָעֶרֶב תֹּאמַר מִי־יִתֵּן בֹּקֶר מִפַּחַד לְבָבְךָ
and in evening　you will say　gives - who　morning　from afraid　your heart

אֲשֶׁר תִּפְחָד וּמִמַּרְאֵה עֵינֶיךָ אֲשֶׁר תִּרְאֶה׃
which　you afraid　and from sight　your eyes　which　your will see

67 In the morning thou shalt say, Would God it were even! and at even thou shalt say, Would God it were morning! for the fear of thine heart wherewith thou shalt fear, and for the sight of thine eyes which thou shalt see.

וֶהֱשִׁיבְךָ יְהוָה מִצְרַיִם בָּאֳנִיּוֹת בַּדֶּרֶךְ
and your returning　ihvh　Egypt　in ships　in way

אֲשֶׁר אָמַרְתִּי לְךָ לֹא־תֹסִיף עוֹד לִרְאֹתָהּ
which　I said　to you　you continue - not　still　to see it

וְהִתְמַכַּרְתֶּם שָׁם לְאֹיְבֶיךָ לַעֲבָדִים וְלִשְׁפָחוֹת וְאֵין קֹנֶה׃
and will sell yourselves　there　to your enemies　to serving men　and to maids　and isn't　buyer

68 And the LORD shall bring thee into Egypt again with ships, by the way whereof I spake unto thee, Thou shalt see it no more again: and there ye shall be sold unto your enemies for bondmen and bondwomen, and no man shall buy you.

ס

Chapter 29

ספר דברים פרק כט
[שביעי]

אֵלֶּה דִבְרֵי הַבְּרִית אֲשֶׁר־צִוָּה יְהוָה אֶת־מֹשֶׁה
these　words　the covenant　commanded - which　ihvh　Moses - that

לִכְרֹת אֶת־בְּנֵי יִשְׂרָאֵל בְּאֶרֶץ מוֹאָב מִלְּבַד הַבְּרִית
to cut　sons - that　Israel　in land　Moab　besides　the covenant

אֲשֶׁר־כָּרַת אִתָּם בְּחֹרֵב׃
in Horeb　　with them　　cut - which

1 These are the words of the covenant, which the LORD commanded Moses to make with the children of Israel in the land of Moab, beside the covenant which he made with them in Horeb.

פ

וַיִּקְרָא מֹשֶׁה אֶל־כָּל־יִשְׂרָאֵל וַיֹּאמֶר אֲלֵהֶם
unto them　　and he said　　Israel - all - unto　　Moses and he called

אַתֶּם רְאִיתֶם אֵת כָּל־אֲשֶׁר עָשָׂה יְהוָה לְעֵינֵיכֶם
to your eyes　　ihvh　　did　　which - all　　that　　you saw　　you

בְּאֶרֶץ מִצְרַיִם לְפַרְעֹה
to Pharaoh　　Egypt　　in land

וּלְכָל־עֲבָדָיו וּלְכָל־אַרְצוֹ׃
his land - and to all　　his servants - and to all

2 And Moses called unto all Israel, and said unto them, Ye have seen all that the LORD did before your eyes in the land of Egypt unto Pharaoh, and unto all his servants, and unto all his land;

הַמַּסּוֹת הַגְּדֹלֹת אֲשֶׁר רָאוּ עֵינֶיךָ הָאֹתֹת
the signs　　your eyes　　you saw　　which　　the great ones　　the temptations

וְהַמֹּפְתִים הַגְּדֹלִים הָהֵם׃
the them　　the great ones　　and the miracles

3 The great temptations which thine eyes have seen, the signs, and those great miracles:

וְלֹא־נָתַן יְהוָה לָכֶם לֵב לָדַעַת
to know　　heart　　to you　　ihvh　　given - and not

וְעֵינַיִם לִרְאוֹת וְאָזְנַיִם לִשְׁמֹעַ עַד הַיּוֹם הַזֶּה׃
the this　　the day　　till　　to hear　　and ears　　to see　　and eyes

4 Yet the LORD hath not given you an heart to perceive, and eyes to see, and ears to hear, unto this day.

וָאוֹלֵךְ אֶתְכֶם אַרְבָּעִים שָׁנָה בַּמִּדְבָּר
in wilderness　　year　　forty　　that you　　and I caused go

לֹא־בָלוּ שַׂלְמֹתֵיכֶם מֵעֲלֵיכֶם
from upon you　　your clothes　　they decayed - not

וְנַעַלְךָ לֹא־בָלְתָה מֵעַל רַגְלֶךָ׃
your foot　　from upon　　it decayed - not　　and your shoe

5 And I have led you forty years in the wilderness: your clothes are not waxen old upon you, and thy shoe is not waxen old upon thy foot.

Ki Tavo - Chapter 29

לֶ֤חֶם לֹ֣א אֲכַלְתֶּ֔ם וְיַ֥יִן וְשֵׁכָ֖ר לֹ֣א שְׁתִיתֶ֑ם
bread   not   you ate   and wine   and liquor   not   you drank

לְמַ֙עַן֙ תֵּֽדְע֔וּ כִּ֛י אֲנִ֥י יְהֹוָ֖ה אֱלֹהֵיכֶֽם׃
to end   you know   I   like   ihvh   your Elohim

6 Ye have not eaten bread, neither have ye drunk wine or strong drink: that ye might know that I am the LORD your God.

[מפטיר]

וַתָּבֹ֖אוּ אֶל־הַמָּק֣וֹם הַזֶּ֑ה
and you came   unto - the place   the this

וַיֵּצֵ֣א סִיחֹ֣ן מֶֽלֶךְ־חֶשְׁבּ֗וֹן וְע֛וֹג מֶֽלֶךְ־הַבָּשָׁ֥ן
and he came out   Sihon   king - Heshbon   and Og   king - the Bashan

לִקְרָאתֵ֛נוּ לַמִּלְחָמָ֖ה וַנַּכֵּֽם׃
to meet us   to war   and we smote them

7 And when ye came unto this place, Sihon the king of Heshbon, and Og the king of Bashan, came out against us unto battle, and we smote them:

וַנִּקַּח֙ אֶת־אַרְצָ֔ם וַנִּתְּנָ֣הּ לְנַחֲלָ֔ה לָרֽאוּבֵנִ֖י
and we took   that - their land   and we gave it   to inheritance   to Reubenites

וְלַגָּדִ֑י וְלַחֲצִ֖י שֵׁ֥בֶט הַֽמְנַשִּֽׁי׃
and to Gadites   and to half   tribe   the Manasseh

8 And we took their land, and gave it for an inheritance unto the Reubenites, and to the Gadites, and to the half tribe of Manasseh.

וּשְׁמַרְתֶּ֗ם אֶת־דִּבְרֵי֙ הַבְּרִ֣ית הַזֹּ֔את
and you heed   that - speakings   the covenant   the this

וַעֲשִׂיתֶ֖ם אֹתָ֑ם
and you do   to them

לְמַ֣עַן תַּשְׂכִּ֔ילוּ אֵ֖ת כׇּל־אֲשֶׁ֥ר תַּעֲשֽׂוּן׃
to end   you will be intelligent   that   all - which   you do

9 Keep therefore the words of this covenant, and do them, that ye may prosper in all that ye do.

פ פ פ

Nitzavim

Chapter 29 cont

ספר דברים פרק כט
[פרשת נצבים]

10 Ye stand this day all of you before the LORD your God; your captains of your tribes, your elders, and your officers, with all the men of Israel,

11 Your little ones, your wives, and thy stranger that is in thy camp, from the hewer of thy wood unto the drawer of thy water:

לְעָבְרְךָ בִּבְרִית יְהוָה אֱלֹהֶיךָ
to your passing   in covenant   ihvh   your Elohim

וּבְאָלָתוֹ אֲשֶׁר יְהוָה אֱלֹהֶיךָ כֹּרֵת עִמְּךָ הַיּוֹם:
and his oath   which   ihvh   your Elohim   cut   with you   the day

12 That thou shouldest enter into covenant with the LORD thy God, and into his oath, which the LORD thy God maketh with thee this day:

[שני]

13 That he may establish thee to day for a people unto himself, and that he may be unto thee a God, as he hath said unto thee, and as he hath sworn unto thy fathers, to Abraham, to Isaac, and to Jacob.

Nitzavim - Chapter 29 cont

וְלֹא אִתְּכֶם לְבַדְּכֶם אָנֹכִי כֹּרֵת אֶת־הַבְּרִית הַזֹּאת
the this   the covenant - that   cutting   I am   you alone   with you   and not

וְאֶת־הָאָלָה הַזֹּאת:
the this   the oath - and that

14 Neither with you only do I make this covenant and this oath;

כִּי אֶת־אֲשֶׁר יֶשְׁנוֹ פֹּה עִמָּנוּ עֹמֵד הַיּוֹם לִפְנֵי יְהוָה אֱלֹהֵינוּ
our Elohim   ihvh   before   the day   stands   with us   here   his "is"ness   which - that   like

וְאֵת אֲשֶׁר אֵינֶנּוּ פֹּה עִמָּנוּ הַיּוֹם:
the day   with us   here   aren't   which   and that

15 But with him that standeth here with us this day before the LORD our God, and also with him that is not here with us this day:

[שלישי]

כִּי־אַתֶּם יְדַעְתֶּם אֵת אֲשֶׁר־יָשַׁבְנוּ בְּאֶרֶץ מִצְרָיִם
Egypt   in land   we dwelt - which   that   you know   you - like

וְאֵת אֲשֶׁר־עָבַרְנוּ בְּקֶרֶב הַגּוֹיִם אֲשֶׁר עֲבַרְתֶּם:
you passed   which   the nations   in near   we passed - which   and that

16 (For ye know how we have dwelt in the land of Egypt; and how we came through the nations which ye passed by;

וַתִּרְאוּ אֶת־שִׁקּוּצֵיהֶם וְאֵת גִּלֻּלֵיהֶם
their vile idols   and that   abominations - that   and you saw it

עֵץ וָאֶבֶן כֶּסֶף וְזָהָב אֲשֶׁר עִמָּהֶם:
with them   which   and gold   silver   and stone   wood

17 And ye have seen their abominations, and their idols, wood and stone, silver and gold, which were among them:)

פֶּן־יֵשׁ בָּכֶם אִישׁ אוֹ־אִשָּׁה אוֹ מִשְׁפָּחָה אוֹ־שֵׁבֶט
tribe - or   family   or   woman - or   man   in you   there is - lest

אֲשֶׁר לְבָבוֹ פֹנֶה הַיּוֹם מֵעִם יְהוָה אֱלֹהֵינוּ
our Elohim   ihvh   from with   the day   faces away   his heart   which

לָלֶכֶת לַעֲבֹד אֶת־אֱלֹהֵי הַגּוֹיִם הָהֵם
the them   the nations   elohim - that   to serve   to go

פֶּן־יֵשׁ בָּכֶם שֹׁרֶשׁ פֹּרֶה רֹאשׁ וְלַעֲנָה:
and wormwood   gall   bearing   root   in them   there is - lest

18 Lest there should be among you man, or woman, or family, or tribe, whose heart turneth away this day from the LORD our God, to go and serve the gods of these nations; lest there should be among you a root that beareth gall and wormwood;

וְהָיָ֡ה בְּשָׁמְעוֹ֩ אֶת־דִּבְרֵ֨י הָאָלָ֜ה הַזֹּ֗את
            the this   the these   speakings - that in his hearing and it will be

וְהִתְבָּרֵ֨ךְ בִּלְבָב֤וֹ לֵאמֹר֙ שָׁל֣וֹם יִֽהְיֶה־לִּ֔י
to me - it will be   peace   to say   in his heart and caused to bless

כִּ֛י בִּשְׁרִר֥וּת לִבִּ֖י אֵלֵ֑ךְ
        unto me my heart in imaginations like

לְמַ֛עַן סְפ֥וֹת הָרָוָ֖ה אֶת־הַצְּמֵאָֽה׃
        the thirst - that drunkenness sweep up to end

19 And it come to pass, when he heareth the words of this curse, that he bless himself in his heart, saying, I shall have peace, though I walk in the imagination of mine heart, to add drunkenness to thirst:

לֹא־יֹאבֶ֣ה יְהוָה֮ סְלֹ֣חַֽ ל֒וֹ
        to him pardon ihvh   he willing - not

כִּ֣י אָ֠ז יֶעְשַׁ֨ן אַף־יְהוָ֤ה וְקִנְאָתוֹ֙ בָּאִ֣ישׁ הַה֔וּא
the it in man and his jealousy ihvh - anger he will smoke then like

וְרָ֤בְצָה בּוֹ֙ כָּל־הָ֣אָלָ֔ה הַכְּתוּבָ֖ה בַּסֵּ֣פֶר הַזֶּ֑ה
       the this in book the written the curses - all in it and reclining

וּמָחָ֤ה יְהוָה֙ אֶת־שְׁמ֔וֹ מִתַּ֖חַת הַשָּׁמָֽיִם׃
      the heavens from under his name - that ihvh and will blot out

20 The LORD will not spare him, but then the anger of the LORD and his jealousy shall smoke against that man, and all the curses that are written in this book shall lie upon him, and the LORD shall blot out his name from under heaven.

וְהִבְדִּיל֤וֹ יְהוָה֙ לְרָעָ֔ה מִכֹּ֖ל שִׁבְטֵ֣י יִשְׂרָאֵ֑ל
        Israel tribes from all to evil ihvh and cause to separate him

כְּכֹל֙ אָל֣וֹת הַבְּרִ֔ית הַכְּתוּבָ֕ה בְּסֵ֥פֶר הַתּוֹרָ֖ה הַזֶּֽה׃
    the this the law in book the written the covenant curses like all

21 And the LORD shall separate him unto evil out of all the tribes of Israel, according to all the curses of the covenant that are written in this book of the law:

וְאָמַ֞ר הַדּ֣וֹר הָֽאַחֲר֗וֹן בְּנֵיכֶם֙ אֲשֶׁ֤ר יָק֙וּמוּ֙ מֵאַ֣חֲרֵיכֶ֔ם
from after you they rise up which your sons the after the generation and said

וְהַ֨נָּכְרִ֔י אֲשֶׁ֥ר יָבֹ֖א מֵאֶ֣רֶץ רְחוֹקָ֑ה
         far away from land he will come which and the stranger

וְרָא֗וּ אֶת־מַכּ֛וֹת הָאָ֥רֶץ הַהִ֖וא
        the it the land smitings - that and they see

וְאֶת־תַּ֣חֲלֻאֶ֔יהָ אֲשֶׁר־חִלָּ֥ה יְהוָ֖ה בָּֽהּ׃
      in it ihvh made ill - which her ailments - and that

Nitzavim - Chapter 29 cont

22 So that the generation to come of your children that shall rise up after you, and the stranger that shall come from a far land, shall say, when they see the plagues of that land, and the sicknesses which the LORD hath laid upon it;

גׇּפְרִית וָמֶלַח שְׂרֵפָה כׇל־אַרְצָהּ
brimstone and salt burnt waste land - all

לֹא תִזָּרַע וְלֹא תַצְמִחַ וְלֹא־יַעֲלֶה בָהּ כׇּל־עֵשֶׂב
not it sow and not it grow and not it ascend - in it all - grass

כְּמַהְפֵּכַת סְדֹם וַעֲמֹרָה אַדְמָה וּצְבֹיִים [וּצְבוֹיִם]
like overthrow Sodom and Gomorrah Admah Zeboim

אֲשֶׁר הָפַךְ יְהֹוָה בְּאַפּוֹ וּבַחֲמָתוֹ׃
which overthrew ihvh in his anger and in his wrath

23 And that the whole land thereof is brimstone, and salt, and burning, that it is not sown, nor beareth, nor any grass groweth therein, like the overthrow of Sodom, and Gomorrah, Admah, and Zeboim, which the LORD overthrew in his anger, and in his wrath:

וְאָמְרוּ כׇּל־הַגּוֹיִם עַל־מֶה עָשָׂה יְהֹוָה כָּכָה לָאָרֶץ הַזֹּאת
and they will say all - the nations upon - what did ihvh like thus to land the this

מֶה חֳרִי הָאַף הַגָּדוֹל הַזֶּה׃
what heat the anger the great the this

24 Even all nations shall say, Wherefore hath the LORD done thus unto this land? what meaneth the heat of this great anger?

וְאָמְרוּ עַל אֲשֶׁר עָזְבוּ אֶת־בְּרִית יְהֹוָה אֱלֹהֵי אֲבֹתָם
and they said upon which they forsaken that - covenant ihvh Elohim their fathers

אֲשֶׁר כָּרַת עִמָּם בְּהוֹצִיאוֹ אֹתָם מֵאֶרֶץ מִצְרָיִם׃
which cut with them in his bringing out to them from land Egypt

25 Then men shall say, Because they have forsaken the covenant of the LORD God of their fathers, which he made with them when he brought them forth out of the land of Egypt:

וַיֵּלְכוּ וַיַּעַבְדוּ אֱלֹהִים אֲחֵרִים
and they went and they served elohim other ones

וַיִּשְׁתַּחֲווּ לָהֶם אֱלֹהִים אֲשֶׁר לֹא־יְדָעוּם
and they bowed the them elohim which not - they knew

וְלֹא חָלַק לָהֶם׃
and not portion to them

26 For they went and served other gods, and worshipped them, gods whom they knew not, and whom he had not given unto them:

וַיִּחַר־אַף יְהֹוָה בָּאָרֶץ הַהִוא
the it   in land   ihvh   anger - and it kindled

לְהָבִיא עָלֶיהָ אֶת־כָּל־הַקְּלָלָה הַכְּתוּבָה בַּסֵּפֶר הַזֶּה׃
the this   in book   the written   the curses - all - that   upon it   to bring

27 And the anger of the LORD was kindled against this land, to bring upon it all the curses that are written in this book:

וַיִּתְּשֵׁם יְהֹוָה מֵעַל אַדְמָתָם בְּאַף
in anger   their ground   from upon   ihvh   and he plucked

וּבְחֵמָה וּבְקֶצֶף גָּדוֹל
great   and in fury   and in wrath

וַיַּשְׁלִכֵם אֶל־אֶרֶץ אַחֶרֶת כַּיּוֹם הַזֶּה׃
the this   like day   another   land - unto   and he cast them

28 And the LORD rooted them out of their land in anger, and in wrath, and in great indignation, and cast them into another land, as it is this day.

הַנִּסְתָּרֹת לַיהֹוָה אֱלֹהֵינוּ וְהַנִּגְלֹת לָנוּ וּלְבָנֵינוּ עַד־עוֹלָם
forever - till   and to our sons   to us   and the revealed   our Elohim   the ihvh   the hidden ones

לַעֲשׂוֹת אֶת־כָּל־דִּבְרֵי הַתּוֹרָה הַזֹּאת׃
the this   the law   speakings - all - that   to do

29 The secret things belong unto the LORD our God: but those things which are revealed belong unto us and to our children for ever, that we may do all the words of this law.

ס

CHAPTER 30

ספר דברים פרק ל

[רביעי] [שני כשהן מחוברין]

וְהָיָה כִי־יָבֹאוּ עָלֶיךָ כָּל־הַדְּבָרִים הָאֵלֶּה הַבְּרָכָה וְהַקְּלָלָה
and the curse   the blessing   the these   the speakings - all   upon you   they will come - like   and it will be

אֲשֶׁר נָתַתִּי לְפָנֶיךָ וַהֲשֵׁבֹתָ אֶל־לְבָבֶךָ בְּכָל־הַגּוֹיִם
the nations - in all   your heart - unto   and the you recall   to before you   I give   which

אֲשֶׁר הִדִּיחֲךָ יְהֹוָה אֱלֹהֶיךָ שָׁמָּה׃
there   your Elohim   ihvh   caused you expelled   which

1 And it shall come to pass, when all these things are come upon thee, the blessing and the curse, which I have set before thee, and thou shalt call them to mind among all the nations, whither the LORD thy God hath driven thee,

Nitzavim - Chapter 30

וְשַׁבְתָּ֞ עַד־יְהוָ֤ה אֱלֹהֶ֙יךָ֙
and you will return   ihvh - till   your Elohim

וְשָׁמַעְתָּ֣ בְקֹל֗וֹ כְּכֹ֤ל אֲשֶׁר־אָנֹכִ֛י מְצַוְּךָ֖ הַיּ֑וֹם
and you will hear   in his voice   like all   I am - which   commanding you   the day

אַתָּ֣ה וּבָנֶ֔יךָ בְּכָל־לְבָבְךָ֖ וּבְכָל־נַפְשֶֽׁךָ׃
you   and your sons   in all - your heart   and in all - your soul

2 And shalt return unto the LORD thy God, and shalt obey his voice according to all that I command thee this day, thou and thy children, with all thine heart, and with all thy soul;

וְשָׁ֨ב יְהוָ֧ה אֱלֹהֶ֛יךָ אֶת־שְׁבוּתְךָ֖
and return   ihvh   your Elohim   that - your captivity

וְרִֽחֲמֶ֑ךָ וְשָׁ֗ב וְקִבֶּצְךָ֙ מִכָּל־הָ֣עַמִּ֔ים
and your compassion   and will return   and you convene   from all - the people

אֲשֶׁ֧ר הֱפִֽיצְךָ֛ יְהוָ֥ה אֱלֹהֶ֖יךָ שָֽׁמָּה׃
which   scattered you   ihvh   your Elohim   there

3 That then the LORD thy God will turn thy captivity, and have compassion upon thee, and will return and gather thee from all the nations, whither the LORD thy God hath scattered thee.

אִם־יִהְיֶ֥ה נִֽדַּחֲךָ֖ בִּקְצֵ֣ה הַשָּׁמָ֑יִם
if - it be   you expelled   in outmost parts   the heaven

מִשָּׁ֗ם יְקַבֶּצְךָ֙ יְהוָ֣ה אֱלֹהֶ֔יךָ וּמִשָּׁ֖ם יִקָּחֶֽךָ׃
from there   he will convene   ihvh   your Elohim   and from there   he will take you

4 If any of thine be driven out unto the outmost parts of heaven, from thence will the LORD thy God gather thee, and from thence will he fetch thee:

וֶהֱבִֽיאֲךָ֞ יְהוָ֣ה אֱלֹהֶ֗יךָ אֶל־הָאָ֛רֶץ
and cause to bring you   ihvh   your Elohim   unto - the land

אֲשֶׁר־יָרְשׁ֥וּ אֲבֹתֶ֖יךָ וִֽירִשְׁתָּ֑הּ
which - they possessed   your fathers   and you will possess it

וְהֵיטִֽבְךָ֥ וְהִרְבְּךָ֖ מֵאֲבֹתֶֽיךָ׃
and causes benefit you   and will multiply you   from your fathers

5 And the LORD thy God will bring thee into the land which thy fathers possessed, and thou shalt possess it; and he will do thee good, and multiply thee above thy fathers.

וּמָ֨ל יְהוָ֧ה אֱלֹהֶ֛יךָ אֶת־לְבָבְךָ֖
and circumcises   ihvh   your Elohim   that - your heart

וְאֶת־לְבַ֣ב זַרְעֶ֑ךָ לְאַהֲבָ֞ה אֶת־יְהוָ֤ה אֱלֹהֶ֙יךָ֙
and that - heart   your seed   to love   that - ihvh   your Elohim

בְּכָל־לְבָבְךָ וּבְכָל־נַפְשְׁךָ לְמַעַן חַיֶּיךָ:
    you will live to end   your soul - and in all   your heart - in all

6 And the LORD thy God will circumcise thine heart, and the heart of thy seed, to love the LORD thy God with all thine heart, and with all thy soul, that thou mayest live.

[חמישי]

[שלישי כשהן מחוברין]

וְנָתַן יְהוָה אֱלֹהֶיךָ אֵת כָּל־הָאָלוֹת הָאֵלֶּה
   the these   the curses - all that your Elohim   ihvh and gave

עַל־אֹיְבֶיךָ וְעַל־שֹׂנְאֶיךָ אֲשֶׁר רְדָפוּךָ:
    they persecuted you which your haters - and upon your enemies - upon

7 And the LORD thy God will put all these curses upon thine enemies, and on them that hate thee, which persecuted thee.

וְאַתָּה תָשׁוּב וְשָׁמַעְתָּ בְּקוֹל יְהוָה
    ihvh in voice and you hear your will return and you

וְעָשִׂיתָ אֶת־כָּל־מִצְוֹתָיו אֲשֶׁר אָנֹכִי מְצַוְּךָ הַיּוֹם:
  the day commanding you I am which his commandments - all - that and you do

8 And thou shalt return and obey the voice of the LORD, and do all his commandments which I command thee this day.

וְהוֹתִירְךָ יְהוָה אֱלֹהֶיךָ בְּכֹל מַעֲשֵׂה יָדֶךָ
   your hand works in all your Elohim ihvh and will prosper you

בִּפְרִי בִטְנְךָ וּבִפְרִי בְהֶמְתְּךָ
    your beasts and in fruit your stomach in fruit

וּבִפְרִי אַדְמָתְךָ לְטֹבָה
    to good your ground and in fruit

כִּי יָשׁוּב יְהוָה לָשׂוּשׂ עָלֶיךָ לְטוֹב
    to good upon you to elated ihvh he will return like

כַּאֲשֶׁר־שָׂשׂ עַל־אֲבֹתֶיךָ:
    your fathers - upon elated - when

9 And the LORD thy God will make thee plenteous in every work of thine hand, in the fruit of thy body, and in the fruit of thy cattle, and in the fruit of thy land, for good: for the LORD will again rejoice over thee for good, as he rejoiced over thy fathers:

כִּי תִשְׁמַע בְּקוֹל יְהוָה אֱלֹהֶיךָ
    your Elohim ihvh in voice you will hear like

לִשְׁמֹר מִצְוֹתָיו וְחֻקֹּתָיו הַכְּתוּבָה בְּסֵפֶר הַתּוֹרָה הַזֶּה
  the this the law in book the written and his statutes his commandments to heed

Nitzavim - Chapter 30

כִּי תָשׁוּב אֶל־יְהוָה אֱלֹהֶיךָ בְּכָל־לְבָבְךָ וּבְכָל־נַפְשֶׁךָ:

like   you return   ihvh - unto   your Elohim   your heart - in all   your soul - and in all

10 If thou shalt hearken unto the voice of the LORD thy God, to keep his commandments and his statutes which are written in this book of the law, and if thou turn unto the LORD thy God with all thine heart, and with all thy soul.

ס

[ששי]

כִּי הַמִּצְוָה הַזֹּאת אֲשֶׁר אָנֹכִי מְצַוְּךָ הַיּוֹם

like   the commandment   the this   which   I am   commanding you   the day

לֹא־נִפְלֵאת הִוא מִמְּךָ וְלֹא־רְחֹקָה הִוא:

not - miraculous   it   from you   and not - far   it

11 For this commandment which I command thee this day, it is not hidden from thee, neither is it far off.

לֹא בַשָּׁמַיִם הִוא לֵאמֹר מִי יַעֲלֶה־לָּנוּ הַשָּׁמַיְמָה

not   in heaven   it   to say   who   he will ascend - to us   the towards heaven

וְיִקָּחֶהָ לָּנוּ וְיַשְׁמִעֵנוּ אֹתָהּ וְנַעֲשֶׂנָּה:

and he take it   to us   and we will hear   to it   to we will do

12 It is not in heaven, that thou shouldest say, Who shall go up for us to heaven, and bring it unto us, that we may hear it, and do it?

וְלֹא־מֵעֵבֶר לַיָּם הִוא לֵאמֹר

and not - from across   to sea   it   to say

מִי יַעֲבָר־לָנוּ אֶל־עֵבֶר הַיָּם

who   he pass - to us   and unto - pass   the sea

וְיִקָּחֶהָ לָּנוּ וְיַשְׁמִעֵנוּ אֹתָהּ וְנַעֲשֶׂנָּה:

and he take it   to us   and we hear it   to it   and we will do it

13 Neither is it beyond the sea, that thou shouldest say, Who shall go over the sea for us, and bring it unto us, that we may hear it, and do it?

כִּי־קָרוֹב אֵלֶיךָ הַדָּבָר מְאֹד בְּפִיךָ

like - near   unto you   the matter   very   in your mouth

וּבִלְבָבְךָ לַעֲשֹׂתוֹ:

and in your heart   to its doing

14 But the word is very nigh unto thee, in thy mouth, and in thy heart, that thou mayest do it.

ס

[שביעי ומפטיר]

[רביעי כשהן מחוברין]

רְאֵ֨ה נָתַ֤תִּי לְפָנֶ֙יךָ֙ הַיּ֔וֹם אֶת־הַֽחַיִּ֖ים
the life - that   the day   before you   I give   see

וְאֶת־הַטּ֑וֹב וְאֶת־הַמָּ֖וֶת וְאֶת־הָרָֽע׃
the evil - and that   the death - and that   the good - and that

15 See, I have set before thee this day life and good, and death and evil;

אֲשֶׁ֨ר אָנֹכִ֣י מְצַוְּךָ֮ הַיּוֹם֒ לְאַהֲבָ֞ה אֶת־יְהוָ֤ה אֱלֹהֶ֙יךָ֙
your Elohim   ihvh - that   to love   the day   commanding you   I am   which

לָלֶ֣כֶת בִּדְרָכָ֔יו וְלִשְׁמֹ֛ר מִצְוֺתָ֥יו וְחֻקֹּתָ֖יו וּמִשְׁפָּטָ֑יו
and his judgments   and his statutes   his commandments   and to heed   in his way   to go

וְחָיִ֣יתָ וְרָבִ֔יתָ וּבֵֽרַכְךָ֙ יְהוָ֣ה אֱלֹהֶ֔יךָ
your Elohim   ihvh   and will bless you   and you will multiply   and you will live

בָּאָ֕רֶץ אֲשֶׁר־אַתָּ֥ה בָא־שָׁ֖מָּה לְרִשְׁתָּֽהּ׃
to possess it   there - come   you - which   in land

16 In that I command thee this day to love the LORD thy God, to walk in his ways, and to keep his commandments and his statutes and his judgments, that thou mayest live and multiply: and the LORD thy God shall bless thee in the land whither thou goest to possess it.

וְאִם־יִפְנֶ֥ה לְבָבְךָ֖ וְלֹ֣א תִשְׁמָ֑ע וְנִדַּחְתָּ֗
and you impelled   you hear   and not   your heart   he face - and if

וְהִֽשְׁתַּחֲוִ֛יתָ לֵאלֹהִ֥ים אֲחֵרִ֖ים וַעֲבַדְתָּֽם׃
and serve them   other ones   to elohim   and you bow down

17 But if thine heart turn away, so that thou wilt not hear, but shalt be drawn away, and worship other gods, and serve them;

הִגַּ֤דְתִּי לָכֶם֙ הַיּ֔וֹם כִּ֥י אָבֹ֖ד תֹּאבֵד֑וּן
you will perish   perish   like   the day   to you   I cause to tell

לֹא־תַאֲרִיכֻ֣ן יָמִ֔ים עַל־הָ֣אֲדָמָ֔ה
the ground - upon   days   you will prolong - not

אֲשֶׁ֨ר אַתָּ֤ה עֹבֵר֙ אֶת־הַיַּרְדֵּ֔ן לָב֥וֹא שָׁ֖מָּה לְרִשְׁתָּֽהּ׃
to possess it   there   to come   the Jordan - that   pass   you   which

18 I denounce unto you this day, that ye shall surely perish, and that ye shall not prolong your days upon the land, whither thou passest over Jordan to go to possess it.

הַעִידֹ֨תִי בָכֶ֤ם הַיּוֹם֙ אֶת־הַשָּׁמַ֣יִם וְאֶת־הָאָ֔רֶץ
the earth - and that   the heaven - that   the day   in you   the I testify

Nitzavim - Chapter 30

הַחַיִּים וְהַמָּוֶת נָתַתִּי לְפָנֶיךָ
the life / and the death / I give / to before you

הַבְּרָכָה וְהַקְּלָלָה וּבָחַרְתָּ בַּחַיִּים
the blessing / and the cursing / and you choosing / in life

לְמַעַן תִּחְיֶה אַתָּה וְזַרְעֶךָ:
to end / you will live / you / and your seed

19 I call heaven and earth to record this day against you, that I have set before you life and death, blessing and cursing: therefore choose life, that both thou and thy seed may live:

לְאַהֲבָה אֶת־יְהוָה אֱלֹהֶיךָ לִשְׁמֹעַ בְּקֹלוֹ
to love / ihvh - that / your Elohim / to hear / in his voice

וּלְדָבְקָה־בוֹ כִּי הוּא חַיֶּיךָ
to cling - and in it / like / it / your life

וְאֹרֶךְ יָמֶיךָ לָשֶׁבֶת עַל־הָאֲדָמָה
and length / your days / to dwell / upon - the ground

אֲשֶׁר נִשְׁבַּע יְהוָה לַאֲבֹתֶיךָ
which / swore / ihvh / to your fathers

לְאַבְרָהָם לְיִצְחָק וּלְיַעֲקֹב לָתֵת לָהֶם:
to Abraham / to Isaac / and to Jacob / to give / to them

20 That thou mayest love the LORD thy God, and that thou mayest obey his voice, and that thou mayest cleave unto him: for he is thy life, and the length of thy days: that thou mayest dwell in the land which the LORD sware unto thy fathers, to Abraham, to Isaac, and to Jacob, to give them.

פ פ פ

Vayeilech

Chapter 31

ספר דברים פרק לא

[פרשת וילך]

וַיֵּלֶךְ מֹשֶׁה וַיְדַבֵּר אֶת־הַדְּבָרִים הָאֵלֶּה אֶל־כָּל־יִשְׂרָאֵל׃
_{Israel - all - unto   the these   the speakings - that   and he spoke   Moses   and he went}

1 And Moses went and spake these words unto all Israel.

וַיֹּאמֶר אֲלֵהֶם בֶּן־מֵאָה וְעֶשְׂרִים שָׁנָה אָנֹכִי הַיּוֹם
_{the day   I am   year   and twenty   hundred - age   unto them   and he said}

לֹא־אוּכַל עוֹד לָצֵאת וְלָבוֹא
_{and to come   to go out   again   able - not}

וַיהוָה אָמַר אֵלַי לֹא תַעֲבֹר אֶת־הַיַּרְדֵּן הַזֶּה׃
_{the this   the Jordan - that   you pass   not   unto me   said   and ihvh}

2 And he said unto them, I am an hundred and twenty years old this day; I can no more go out and come in: also the LORD hath said unto me, Thou shalt not go over this Jordan.

יְהוָה אֱלֹהֶיךָ הוּא עֹבֵר לְפָנֶיךָ
_{before you   will pass   he   your Elohim   ihvh}

הוּא־יַשְׁמִיד אֶת־הַגּוֹיִם הָאֵלֶּה מִלְּפָנֶיךָ וִירִשְׁתָּם
_{and you will possess them   from before you   the these   the nations - that   he will exterminate - he}

יְהוֹשֻׁעַ הוּא עֹבֵר לְפָנֶיךָ כַּאֲשֶׁר דִּבֶּר יְהוָה׃
_{ihvh   spoke   when   before you   will pass   he   Joshua}

3 The LORD thy God, he will go over before thee, and he will destroy these nations from before thee, and thou shalt possess them: and Joshua, he shall go over before thee, as the LORD hath said.

[שני]

וְעָשָׂה יְהוָה לָהֶם כַּאֲשֶׁר עָשָׂה לְסִיחוֹן וּלְעוֹג מַלְכֵי הָאֱמֹרִי
_{the Amorites   kings   and to Og   to Sihon   did   when   to them   ihvh   and will do}

וּלְאַרְצָם אֲשֶׁר הִשְׁמִיד אֹתָם׃
_{to them   caused to exterminate   which   and to their land}

4 And the LORD shall do unto them as he did to Sihon and to Og, kings of the Amorites, and unto the land of them, whom he destroyed.

וּנְתָנָם יְהוָה לִפְנֵיכֶם
_{before you   ihvh   and will give them}

VAYEILECH - CHAPTER 31

וַעֲשִׂיתֶם לָהֶם כְּכָל־הַמִּצְוָה אֲשֶׁר צִוִּיתִי אֶתְכֶם:
_{that you   I commanded   which   the commandment - like all   to them   and you will do}

5 And the LORD shall give them up before your face, that ye may do unto them according unto all the commandments which I have commanded you.

חִזְקוּ וְאִמְצוּ אַל־תִּירְאוּ וְאַל־תַּעַרְצוּ מִפְּנֵיהֶם
_{from presence them   you terrified it - and don't   you fear it - don't   and you be courageous   you be strong}

כִּי יְהוָה אֱלֹהֶיךָ הוּא הַהֹלֵךְ עִמָּךְ
_{with you   the walker   he   your Elohim   ihvh   like}

לֹא יַרְפְּךָ וְלֹא יַעַזְבֶךָּ:
_{he forsake you   and not   he will fail you   not}

6 Be strong and of a good courage, fear not, nor be afraid of them: for the LORD thy God, he it is that doth go with thee; he will not fail thee, nor forsake thee.

ס

[שלישי]

[חמישי כשהן מחוברין]

וַיִּקְרָא מֹשֶׁה לִיהוֹשֻׁעַ
_{to Joshua   Moses   and he called}

וַיֹּאמֶר אֵלָיו לְעֵינֵי כָל־יִשְׂרָאֵל
_{Israel - all   to eyes   unto him   and he said}

חֲזַק וֶאֱמָץ כִּי אַתָּה תָּבוֹא אֶת־הָעָם הַזֶּה
_{the this   the people - that   you come   you   like   and courage   strong}

אֶל־הָאָרֶץ אֲשֶׁר נִשְׁבַּע יְהוָה לַאֲבֹתָם לָתֵת לָהֶם
_{to them   to give   to their fathers   ihvh   swore   which   the land - unto}

וְאַתָּה תַּנְחִילֶנָּה אוֹתָם:
_{to them   you cause to inherit   and you}

7 And Moses called unto Joshua, and said unto him in the sight of all Israel, Be strong and of a good courage: for thou must go with this people unto the land which the LORD hath sworn unto their fathers to give them; and thou shalt cause them to inherit it.

וַיהוָה הוּא הַהֹלֵךְ לְפָנֶיךָ
_{before you   the goer   he   and ihvh}

הוּא יִהְיֶה עִמָּךְ לֹא יַרְפְּךָ
_{he fail you   not   with you   will be   he}

וְלֹא יַעַזְבֶךָּ לֹא תִירָא וְלֹא תֵחָת׃
and not he will forsake you not you fear and not you dismayed

8 And the LORD, he it is that doth go before thee; he will be with thee, he will not fail thee, neither forsake thee: fear not, neither be dismayed.

וַיִּכְתֹּב מֹשֶׁה אֶת־הַתּוֹרָה הַזֹּאת
and he wrote Moses that - the law the this

וַיִּתְּנָהּ אֶל־הַכֹּהֲנִים בְּנֵי לֵוִי
and he gave it unto - the priests sons Levi

הַנֹּשְׂאִים אֶת־אֲרוֹן בְּרִית יְהוָה
the bearing ones that - ark covenant ihvh

וְאֶל־כָּל־זִקְנֵי יִשְׂרָאֵל׃
and unto - all - elders Israel

9 And Moses wrote this law, and delivered it unto the priests the sons of Levi, which bare the ark of the covenant of the LORD, and unto all the elders of Israel.

וַיְצַו מֹשֶׁה אוֹתָם לֵאמֹר
and he commanded Moses to them to say

מִקֵּץ שֶׁבַע שָׁנִים בְּמֹעֵד שְׁנַת הַשְּׁמִטָּה בְּחַג הַסֻּכּוֹת׃
from end seven years in appointed time of year the release in feast the booths

10 And Moses commanded them, saying, At the end of every seven years, in the solemnity of the year of release, in the feast of tabernacles,

[רביעי]

בְּבוֹא כָל־יִשְׂרָאֵל לֵרָאוֹת אֶת־פְּנֵי יְהוָה אֱלֹהֶיךָ
in come all - Israel to see that - face ihvh your Elohim

בַּמָּקוֹם אֲשֶׁר יִבְחָר תִּקְרָא אֶת־הַתּוֹרָה הַזֹּאת
in place which he will choose you will read that - the law the this

נֶגֶד כָּל־יִשְׂרָאֵל בְּאָזְנֵיהֶם׃
in front all - Israel in their ears

11 When all Israel is come to appear before the LORD thy God in the place which he shall choose, thou shalt read this law before all Israel in their hearing.

הַקְהֵל אֶת־הָעָם הָאֲנָשִׁים וְהַנָּשִׁים וְהַטַּף וְגֵרְךָ
the gathering that - the people the men and the women and the children and your stranger

אֲשֶׁר בִּשְׁעָרֶיךָ לְמַעַן יִשְׁמְעוּ
which in your gate to end they will hear

וּלְמַעַן יִלְמְדוּ וְיָרְאוּ אֶת־יְהוָה אֱלֹהֵיכֶם
and to end they will learn and they will fear that - ihvh your Elohim

VAYEILECH - CHAPTER 31

וְשָׁמְרוּ לַעֲשׂוֹת אֶת־כָּל־דִּבְרֵי הַתּוֹרָה הַזֹּאת׃
    the this   the law   speakings - all - that   to do   and they heed

12 Gather the people together, men, and women, and children, and thy stranger that is within thy gates, that they may hear, and that they may learn, and fear the LORD your God, and observe to do all the words of this law:

וּבְנֵיהֶם אֲשֶׁר לֹא־יָדְעוּ
    they know - not   which   and their sons

יִשְׁמְעוּ וְלָמְדוּ לְיִרְאָה אֶת־יְהוָה אֱלֹהֵיכֶם כָּל־הַיָּמִים
the days - all your Elohim ihvh - that to fear and they will learn they will hear

אֲשֶׁר אַתֶּם חַיִּים עַל־הָאֲדָמָה
    the ground - upon live you which

אֲשֶׁר אַתֶּם עֹבְרִים אֶת־הַיַּרְדֵּן שָׁמָּה לְרִשְׁתָּהּ׃
  to possess it there the Jordan - that passings you which

13 And that their children, which have not known any thing, may hear, and learn to fear the LORD your God, as long as ye live in the land whither ye go over Jordan to possess it.

פ

[חמישי] [ששי כשהן מחוברין]

וַיֹּאמֶר יְהוָה אֶל־מֹשֶׁה הֵן קָרְבוּ יָמֶיךָ לָמוּת
  to die your days you come near grace Moses - unto ihvh and he said

קְרָא אֶת־יְהוֹשֻׁעַ וְהִתְיַצְּבוּ בְּאֹהֶל מוֹעֵד וַאֲצַוֶּנּוּ
and I charge you appointment in tent and cause to present you Joshua - that meet

וַיֵּלֶךְ מֹשֶׁה וִיהוֹשֻׁעַ וַיִּתְיַצְּבוּ בְּאֹהֶל מוֹעֵד׃
appointment in tent and they presented and Joshua Moses and he went

14 And the LORD said unto Moses, Behold, thy days approach that thou must die: call Joshua, and present yourselves in the tabernacle of the congregation, that I may give him a charge. And Moses and Joshua went, and presented themselves in the tabernacle of the congregation.

וַיֵּרָא יְהוָה בָּאֹהֶל בְּעַמּוּד עָנָן
  cloud in pillar in tent ihvh and he appeared

וַיַּעֲמֹד עַמּוּד הֶעָנָן עַל־פֶּתַח הָאֹהֶל׃
  the tent opening - upon the cloud pillar and it stood

15 And the LORD appeared in the tabernacle in a pillar of a cloud: and the pillar of the cloud stood over the door of the tabernacle.

וַיֹּאמֶר יְהוָה אֶל־מֹשֶׁה הִנְּךָ שֹׁכֵב עִם־אֲבֹתֶיךָ
your fathers - with   laying   here you   Moses - unto   ihvh   and he said

וְקָם הָעָם הַזֶּה וְזָנָה אַחֲרֵי אֱלֹהֵי נֵכַר־הָאָרֶץ
the earth - strange   elohim   after   and whore   the this   the people   and will rise up

אֲשֶׁר הוּא בָא־שָׁמָּה בְּקִרְבּוֹ וַעֲזָבַנִי
and forsake me   in his near   there - come   he   which

וְהֵפֵר אֶת־בְּרִיתִי אֲשֶׁר כָּרַתִּי אִתּוֹ׃
with them   I cut   which   my covenant - that   and annuls

16 And the LORD said unto Moses, Behold, thou shalt sleep with thy fathers; and this people will rise up, and go a whoring after the gods of the strangers of the land, whither they go to be among them, and will forsake me, and break my covenant which I have made with them.

וְחָרָה אַפִּי בוֹ בַיּוֹם־הַהוּא וַעֲזַבְתִּים
and I will forsake them   the it - in day   in it   my anger   and kindles

וְהִסְתַּרְתִּי פָנַי מֵהֶם וְהָיָה לֶאֱכֹל
to consumed   and it will be   from them   my face   and I will cause hide

וּמְצָאֻהוּ רָעוֹת רַבּוֹת וְצָרוֹת וְאָמַר בַּיּוֹם הַהוּא
the it   in day   and say   and troubles   many   evils   and they will find it

הֲלֹא עַל כִּי־אֵין אֱלֹהַי בְּקִרְבִּי מְצָאוּנִי הָרָעוֹת הָאֵלֶּה׃
the these   the evils   they found me   in among us   Elohim   isn't - like   upon   the not

17 Then my anger shall be kindled against them in that day, and I will forsake them, and I will hide my face from them, and they shall be devoured, and many evils and troubles shall befall them; so that they will say in that day, Are not these evils come upon us, because our God is not among us?

וְאָנֹכִי הַסְתֵּר אַסְתִּיר פָּנַי בַּיּוֹם הַהוּא עַל כָּל־הָרָעָה
the evils - all   upon   the it   in day   my face   I will hide   the hide   and I am

אֲשֶׁר עָשָׂה כִּי פָנָה אֶל־אֱלֹהִים אֲחֵרִים׃
other ones   elohim - unto   faced   like   did   which

18 And I will surely hide my face in that day for all the evils which they shall have wrought, in that they are turned unto other gods.

וְעַתָּה כִּתְבוּ לָכֶם אֶת־הַשִּׁירָה הַזֹּאת
the this   the song - that   to them   you write   and now

וְלַמְּדָהּ אֶת־בְּנֵי־יִשְׂרָאֵל שִׂימָהּ בְּפִיהֶם
in their mouth   place it   Israel - sons - that   and teach it

לְמַעַן תִּהְיֶה־לִּי הַשִּׁירָה הַזֹּאת לְעֵד בִּבְנֵי יִשְׂרָאֵל׃
Israel   in sons   to witness   the this   the song   to me - it will be   to end

Vayeilech - Chapter 31

19 Now therefore write ye this song for you, and teach it the children of Israel: put it in their mouths, that this song may be a witness for me against the children of Israel.

[שׁשׁי] [שביעי כשהן מחוברין]

כִּי־אֲבִיאֶנּוּ אֶל־הָאֲדָמָה אֲשֶׁר־נִשְׁבַּעְתִּי לַאֲבֹתָיו
to his father   I swore - which   the ground - unto   I will bring them - like

זָבַת חָלָב וּדְבַשׁ וְאָכַל וְשָׂבַע וְדָשֵׁן
and be fat and be full and will eat and honey milk flowing

וּפָנָה אֶל־אֱלֹהִים אֲחֵרִים וַעֲבָדוּם
and serve them   other ones   elohim - unto   and face

וְנִאֲצוּנִי וְהֵפֵר אֶת־בְּרִיתִי׃
my covenant - that   and annul   and provoke me

20 For when I shall have brought them into the land which I sware unto their fathers, that floweth with milk and honey; and they shall have eaten and filled themselves, and waxen fat; then will they turn unto other gods, and serve them, and provoke me, and break my covenant.

וְהָיָה כִּי־תִמְצֶאןָ אֹתוֹ רָעוֹת רַבּוֹת וְצָרוֹת
and troubles   many   evils   to it   they will find - like   and will be

וְעָנְתָה הַשִּׁירָה הַזֹּאת לְפָנָיו לְעֵד
to witness before him the this the song and it answers

כִּי לֹא תִשָּׁכַח מִפִּי זַרְעוֹ
his seed from mouth you forget not like

כִּי יָדַעְתִּי אֶת־יִצְרוֹ אֲשֶׁר הוּא עֹשֶׂה הַיּוֹם
the day does he which his form - that I know like

בְּטֶרֶם אֲבִיאֶנּוּ אֶל־הָאָרֶץ אֲשֶׁר נִשְׁבָּעְתִּי׃
I swore which the land - unto I brought them in before

21 And it shall come to pass, when many evils and troubles are befallen them, that this song shall testify against them as a witness; for it shall not be forgotten out of the mouths of their seed: for I know their imagination which they go about, even now, before I have brought them into the land which I sware.

22 Moses therefore wrote this song the same day, and taught it the children of Israel.

וְאֱמָץ	חֲזַק	וַיֹּאמֶר	בִּן־נוּן	אֶת־יְהוֹשֻׁעַ		וַיְצַו
and be courageous	be strong	and he said	Nun - son	Joshua - that		and he commanded

אֶל־הָאָרֶץ	אֶת־בְּנֵי יִשְׂרָאֵל		תָּבִיא	אַתָּה	כִּי
the land - unto	Israel sons - that		will bring	you	like

עִמָּךְ:	אֶהְיֶה	וְאָנֹכִי	לָהֶם	אֲשֶׁר־נִשְׁבַּעְתִּי
with them	"Ehieh"	and I am	to them	I swore - which

23 And he gave Joshua the son of Nun a charge, and said, Be strong and of a good courage: for thou shalt bring the children of Israel into the land which I sware unto them: and I will be with thee.

הַתּוֹרָה־הַזֹּאת	אֶת־דִּבְרֵי	לִכְתֹּב	מֹשֶׁה	כְּכַלּוֹת	וַיְהִי
the this - the law	speakings - that	to write	Moses	like finished	and it was

תֻּמָּם:	עַד	עַל־סֵפֶר
it's end	till	book - upon

24 And it came to pass, when Moses had made an end of writing the words of this law in a book, until they were finished,

[שביעי]

לֵאמֹר:	בְּרִית־יְהֹוָה	אֲרוֹן	נֹשְׂאֵי	אֶת־הַלְוִיִּם	מֹשֶׁה	וַיְצַו
to say	ihvh - covenant	ark	carry	the Levites - that	Moses	and he commanded

25 That Moses commanded the Levites, which bare the ark of the covenant of the LORD, saying,

הַזֶּה	הַתּוֹרָה	סֵפֶר	אֵת לָקֹחַ
the this	the law	book	that take

אֱלֹהֵיכֶם	בְּרִית־יְהֹוָה	אֲרוֹן	מִצַּד	וְשַׂמְתֶּם אֹתוֹ
your Elohim	ihvh - covenant	ark	from side	to it and you put

לְעֵד:	בְּךָ	וְהָיָה־שָׁם
to witness	in you	there - and it will be

26 Take this book of the law, and put it in the side of the ark of the covenant of the LORD your God, that it may be there for a witness against thee.

הַקָּשֶׁה	וְאֶת־עָרְפְּךָ	אֶת־מֶרְיְךָ	יָדַעְתִּי	אָנֹכִי	כִּי
the hard	your neck - and that	your rebellion - that	I know	I am	like

עִם־יְהֹוָה	הֱיִתֶם	מַמְרִים	הַיּוֹם	עִמָּכֶם	חַי	הֵן בְּעוֹדֶנִּי
ihvh - with	you have been	from rebellions	the day	with you	live	thus in we still

מוֹתִי:	וְאַף כִּי־אַחֲרֵי
I die	after - like and indeed

27 For I know thy rebellion, and thy stiff neck: behold, while I am yet alive with you this

day, ye have been rebellious against the LORD; and how much more after my death?

[מפטיר]

הַקְהִילוּ אֵלַי אֶת־כָּל־זִקְנֵי שִׁבְטֵיכֶם
the you assemble unto me that - all - elders your tribes

וְשֹׁטְרֵיכֶם וַאֲדַבְּרָה בְאָזְנֵיהֶם אֵת הַדְּבָרִים הָאֵלֶּה
and your officers and I will speak in their ears that the speakings the these

וְאָעִידָה בָּם אֶת־הַשָּׁמַיִם וְאֶת־הָאָרֶץ:
and I will witness in them that - the heavens and that - the earth

28 Gather unto me all the elders of your tribes, and your officers, that I may speak these words in their ears, and call heaven and earth to record against them.

כִּי יָדַעְתִּי אַחֲרֵי מוֹתִי כִּי־הַשְׁחֵת תַּשְׁחִתוּן
like I know after my death like - the destroy you will destroy

וְסַרְתֶּם מִן־הַדֶּרֶךְ אֲשֶׁר צִוִּיתִי אֶתְכֶם
and you depart from - the way which I commanded you that

וְקָרָאת אֶתְכֶם הָרָעָה בְּאַחֲרִית הַיָּמִים
and meet you that the evil in afterwards the days

כִּי־תַעֲשׂוּ אֶת־הָרַע בְּעֵינֵי יְהוָֹה
like - you will do that - the bad in eye ihvh

לְהַכְעִיסוֹ בְּמַעֲשֵׂה יְדֵיכֶם:
to the his anger in work your hands

29 For I know that after my death ye will utterly corrupt yourselves, and turn aside from the way which I have commanded you; and evil will befall you in the latter days; because ye will do evil in the sight of the LORD, to provoke him to anger through the work of your hands.

וַיְדַבֵּר מֹשֶׁה בְּאָזְנֵי כָּל־קְהַל יִשְׂרָאֵל
and he spoke Moses in ears all - assembly Israel

אֶת־דִּבְרֵי הַשִּׁירָה הַזֹּאת עַד תֻּמָּם:
that - speakings the song the this till they ended

30 And Moses spake in the ears of all the congregation of Israel the words of this song, until they were ended.

פ פ פ

HA'AZINU

CHAPTER 32

ספר דברים פרק לב
[פרשת האזינו]

הַאֲזִינוּ הַשָּׁמַיִם וַאֲדַבֵּרָה וְתִשְׁמַע הָאָרֶץ אִמְרֵי־פִי:
my mouth - my words   the earth   and you hear   and I will speak   the heavens   the you ear

1 Give ear, O ye heavens, and I will speak; and hear, O earth, the words of my mouth.

יַעֲרֹף כַּמָּטָר לִקְחִי תִּזַּל כַּטַּל אִמְרָתִי
my words   like dew   it will distill   to my take   like rain   it will drop

כִּשְׂעִירִם עֲלֵי־דֶשֶׁא וְכִרְבִיבִים עֲלֵי־עֵשֶׂב:
grass - upon   and like showers   vegetation – upon   like drizzle

2 My doctrine shall drop as the rain, my speech shall distil as the dew, as the small rain upon the tender herb, and as the showers upon the grass:

כִּי שֵׁם יְהוָה אֶקְרָא הָבוּ גֹדֶל לֵאלֹהֵינוּ:
to our Elohim   greatness   ascribe   I will call   ihvh   name   like

3 Because I will publish the name of the LORD: ascribe ye greatness unto our God.

הַצּוּר תָּמִים פָּעֳלוֹ כִּי כָל־דְּרָכָיו מִשְׁפָּט
judgment   his ways - all   like   his work   perfect   the rock

אֵל אֱמוּנָה וְאֵין עָוֶל צַדִּיק וְיָשָׁר הוּא:
he   and upright   righteous   iniquity   and isn't   truthful   El

4 He is the Rock, his work is perfect: for all his ways are judgment: a God of truth and without iniquity, just and right is he.

שִׁחֵת לוֹ לֹא בָּנָיו מוּמָם דּוֹר עִקֵּשׁ וּפְתַלְתֹּל:
and crooked   perverse   generation   blemish   his sons   not   to him   corrupted

5 They have corrupted themselves, their spot is not the spot of his children: they are a perverse and crooked generation.

הַלְיהוָה תִּגְמְלוּ־זֹאת עַם נָבָל וְלֹא חָכָם
wise   and not   decadent   people   this - you be requite   the to ihvh

הֲלוֹא־הוּא אָבִיךָ קָּנֶךָ הוּא עָשְׂךָ וַיְכֹנְנֶךָ:
and established you   your doing   he   bought you   your father   he - the to him

6 Do ye thus requite the LORD, O foolish people and unwise? is not he thy father that hath bought thee? hath he not made thee, and established thee?

HA'AZINU - CHAPTER 32

[שֵׁנִי]

וָדֹר	דֹּר	שְׁנוֹת	בִּינוּ	עוֹלָם	יְמוֹת	זְכֹר
and generation	generation	years	you understand	ever	days	remember

לָךְ׃	וְיֹאמְרוּ	זְקֵנֶיךָ	וְיַגֵּדְךָ	אָבִיךָ	שְׁאַל
to you	and they will say	your elder	and he will tell you	your father	ask

7 Remember the days of old, consider the years of many generations: ask thy father, and he will shew thee; thy elders, and they will tell thee.

אָדָם	בְּנֵי	בְּהַפְרִידוֹ	גּוֹיִם	עֶלְיוֹן	בְּהַנְחֵל
Adam	sons	in his dividing	nations	most high	the inheritance

יִשְׂרָאֵל׃	בְּנֵי	לְמִסְפַּר	עַמִּים	גְּבֻלֹת	יַצֵּב
Israel	sons	to number	peoples	borders	he set

8 When the Most High divided to the nations their inheritance, when he separated the sons of Adam, he set the bounds of the people according to the number of the children of Israel.

נַחֲלָתוֹ׃	חֶבֶל	יַעֲקֹב	עַמּוֹ	יְהוָה	חֵלֶק	כִּי
his inheritance	portion	Jacob	his people	ihvh	portion	like

9 For the LORD'S portion is his people; Jacob is the lot of his inheritance.

יְשִׁמֹן	יְלֵל	וּבְתֹהוּ	מִדְבָּר	בְּאֶרֶץ	יִמְצָאֵהוּ
he desolation	howling	and in void	wilderness	in land	he found him

עֵינוֹ׃	כְּאִישׁוֹן	יִצְּרֶנְהוּ	יְבוֹנְנֵהוּ	יְסֹבְבֶנְהוּ
his eye	like pupil	he kept him	he made understand him	he led him around

10 He found him in a desert land, and in the waste howling wilderness; he led him about, he instructed him, he kept him as the apple of his eye.

כְּנָפָיו	יִפְרֹשׂ	יְרַחֵף	עַל־גּוֹזָלָיו	קִנּוֹ	יָעִיר	כְּנֶשֶׁר
his wings	he spreads	he vibrating	his young birds - upon	his nest	he stirs up	like eagle

עַל־אֶבְרָתוֹ׃	יִשָּׂאֵהוּ	יִקָּחֵהוּ
his passing - upon	he carries it	he takes them

11 As an eagle stirreth up her nest, fluttereth over her young, spreadeth abroad her wings, taketh them, beareth them on her wings:

נֵכָר׃	אֵל	עִמּוֹ	וְאֵין	יַנְחֶנּוּ	בָּדָד	יְהוָה
strange	el	with him	and isn't	leads him	alone	ihvh

12 So the LORD alone did lead him, and there was no strange god with him.

[שְׁלִישִׁי]

שָׂדַי	תְּנוּבֹת	וַיֹּאכַל	אֶרֶץ	עַל־בָּמֳתֵי	יַרְכִּבֵהוּ
field	produces	and he ate	earth	high places - upon	and he rode him

וַיֵּנִקֵהוּ דְבַשׁ מִסֶּלַע וְשֶׁמֶן מֵחַלְמִישׁ צוּר׃
rock from flint and oil from rock crag honey and he sucked

13 He made him ride on the high places of the earth, that he might eat the increase of the fields; and he made him to suck honey out of the rock, and oil out of the flinty rock;

חֶמְאַת בָּקָר וַחֲלֵב צֹאן עִם־חֵלֶב כָּרִים וְאֵילִים בְּנֵי־בָשָׁן
Bashan - sons and butting rams lambs milk - with sheep and milk herd butter

וְעַתּוּדִים עִם־חֵלֶב כִּלְיוֹת חִטָּה וְדַם־עֵנָב תִּשְׁתֶּה־חָמֶר׃
thick wine - you drank grape - and blood wheat kidneys fat - with and he goats

14 Butter of kine, and milk of sheep, with fat of lambs, and rams of the breed of Bashan, and goats, with the fat of kidneys of wheat; and thou didst drink the pure blood of the grape.

וַיִּשְׁמַן יְשֻׁרוּן
Jeshurun and grew fat

וַיִּבְעָט שָׁמַנְתָּ עָבִיתָ כָּשִׂיתָ
you burly you thick stout and he kicking

וַיִּטֹּשׁ אֱלוֹהַּ עָשָׂהוּ וַיְנַבֵּל צוּר יְשֻׁעָתוֹ׃
his salvation rock and he is disgracing made him Elohim and he abandoning

15 But Jeshurun waxed fat, and kicked: thou art waxen fat, thou art grown thick, thou art covered with fatness; then he forsook God which made him, and lightly esteemed the Rock of his salvation.

יַקְנִאֻהוּ בְּזָרִים בְּתוֹעֵבֹת יַכְעִיסֻהוּ׃
they made angry him in abominations in strange ones and he became jealous

16 They provoked him to jealousy with strange gods, with abominations provoked they him to anger.

יִזְבְּחוּ לַשֵּׁדִים לֹא אֱלֹהַּ
Elohim not to devils he sacrificed him

אֱלֹהִים לֹא יְדָעוּם
they knew them not elohim

חֲדָשִׁים מִקָּרֹב בָּאוּ לֹא שְׂעָרוּם אֲבֹתֵיכֶם׃
your fathers horrified by them not they came from close new ones

17 They sacrificed unto devils, not to God; to gods whom they knew not, to new gods that came newly up, whom your fathers feared not.

צוּר יְלָדְךָ תֶּשִׁי וַתִּשְׁכַּח אֵל מְחֹלְלֶךָ׃
travailing of you El and you forgot oblivious he begat you rock

18 Of the Rock that begat thee thou art unmindful, and hast forgotten God that formed thee.

HA'AZINU - CHAPTER 32

[רביעי]

וַיַּרְא יְהֹוָה וַיִּנְאָץ מִכַּעַס בָּנָיו וּבְנֹתָיו:
and his daughters his sons from anger and he spurning ihvh and he saw

19 And when the LORD saw it, he abhorred them, because of the provoking of his sons, and of his daughters.

וַיֹּאמֶר אַסְתִּירָה פָנַי מֵהֶם
from them my face I will hide and he said

אֶרְאֶה מָה אַחֲרִיתָם
after them what I will see

כִּי דוֹר תַּהְפֻּכֹת הֵמָּה בָּנִים לֹא־אֵמֻן בָּם:
in them faithfulness - not sons they are it froward generation like

20 And he said, I will hide my face from them, I will see what their end shall be: for they are a very froward generation, children in whom is no faith.

הֵם קִנְאוּנִי בְלֹא־אֵל כִּעֲסוּנִי בְּהַבְלֵיהֶם
in vanities of them like they provoked me El - without make jealous me them

וַאֲנִי אַקְנִיאֵם בְּלֹא־עָם בְּגוֹי נָבָל אַכְעִיסֵם:
I will anger them decadent in nation people - nothing I will make jealous to them and I

21 They have moved me to jealousy with that which is not God; they have provoked me to anger with their vanities: and I will move them to jealousy with those which are not a people; I will provoke them to anger with a foolish nation.

כִּי־אֵשׁ קָדְחָה בְאַפִּי וַתִּיקַד עַד־שְׁאוֹל תַּחְתִּית
lowest Shoel - till and it will glow in my anger kindled fire - like

וַתֹּאכַל אֶרֶץ וִיבֻלָהּ וַתְּלַהֵט מוֹסְדֵי הָרִים:
mountains foundations and it set afire and its produce land and it will consume

22 For a fire is kindled in mine anger, and shall burn unto the lowest hell, and shall consume the earth with her increase, and set on fire the foundations of the mountains.

אַסְפֶּה עָלֵימוֹ רָעוֹת חִצַּי אֲכַלֶּה־בָּם:
in them - I will spend arrows evils upon them I will heap

23 I will heap mischiefs upon them; I will spend mine arrows upon them.

מְזֵי רָעָב וּלְחֻמֵי רֶשֶׁף וְקֶטֶב מְרִירִי
bitter and sting burning heat and devoured hunger skinny

וְשֶׁן־בְּהֵמֹת אֲשַׁלַּח־בָּם עִם־חֲמַת זֹחֲלֵי עָפָר:
dust sulking ones venom - with in them - I will send beasts - and teeth

24 They shall be burnt with hunger, and devoured with burning heat, and with bitter destruction: I will also send the teeth of beasts upon them, with the poison of serpents of the dust.

מִחוּץ תְּשַׁכֶּל־חֶרֶב וּמֵחֲדָרִים אֵימָה
גַּם־בָּחוּר גַּם־בְּתוּלָה יוֹנֵק עִם־אִישׁ שֵׂיבָה׃

25 The sword without, and terror within, shall destroy both the young man and the virgin, the suckling also with the man of gray hairs.

אָמַרְתִּי אַפְאֵיהֶם אַשְׁבִּיתָה מֵאֱנוֹשׁ זִכְרָם׃

26 I said, I would scatter them into corners, I would make the remembrance of them to cease from among men:

לוּלֵי כַּעַס אוֹיֵב אָגוּר פֶּן־יְנַכְּרוּ צָרֵימוֹ
פֶּן־יֹאמְרוּ יָדֵנוּ רָמָה וְלֹא יְהוָה פָּעַל כָּל־זֹאת׃

27 Were it not that I feared the wrath of the enemy, lest their adversaries should behave themselves strangely, and lest they should say, Our hand is high, and the LORD hath not done all this.

כִּי־גוֹי אֹבַד עֵצוֹת הֵמָּה וְאֵין בָּהֶם תְּבוּנָה׃

28 For they are a nation void of counsel, neither is there any understanding in them.

[חמישי]

לוּ חָכְמוּ יַשְׂכִּילוּ זֹאת יָבִינוּ לְאַחֲרִיתָם׃

29 O that they were wise, that they understood this, that they would consider their latter end!

אֵיכָה יִרְדֹּף אֶחָד אֶלֶף וּשְׁנַיִם יָנִיסוּ רְבָבָה
אִם־לֹא כִּי־צוּרָם מְכָרָם וַיהוָה הִסְגִּירָם׃

30 How should one chase a thousand, and two put ten thousand to flight, except their Rock had sold them, and the LORD had shut them up?

כִּי לֹא כְצוּרֵנוּ צוּרָם וְאֹיְבֵינוּ פְּלִילִים׃

31 For their rock is not as our Rock, even our enemies themselves being judges.

כִּי־מִגֶּפֶן סְדֹם גַּפְנָם וּמִשַּׁדְמֹת עֲמֹרָה

HA'AZINU - CHAPTER 32

עֲנָבֵמוֹ עִנְּבֵי־רוֹשׁ אַשְׁכְּלֹת מְרֹרֹת לָמוֹ׃
to it   bitter   grape clusters   gall - grapes   his grapes

32 For their vine is of the vine of Sodom, and of the fields of Gomorrah: their grapes are grapes of gall, their clusters are bitter:

חֲמַת תַּנִּינִם יֵינָם וְרֹאשׁ פְּתָנִים אַכְזָר׃
cruel   cobras   and head   their wine   snakes   venom

33 Their wine is the poison of dragons, and the cruel venom of asps.

הֲלֹא־הוּא כָּמֻס עִמָּדִי חָתוּם בְּאוֹצְרֹתָי׃
in my treasures   sealed   with me   amassed   it - the not

34 Is not this laid up in store with me, and sealed up among my treasures?

לִי נָקָם וְשִׁלֵּם לְעֵת תָּמוּט רַגְלָם
their foot   will slip   to time   and repayment   vengeance   to me

כִּי קָרוֹב יוֹם אֵידָם וְחָשׁ עֲתִדֹת לָמוֹ׃
to them   impending   and haste   their calamity   day   near   like

35 To me belongeth vengeance, and recompence; their foot shall slide in due time: for the day of their calamity is at hand, and the things that shall come upon them make haste.

כִּי־יָדִין יְהוָה עַמּוֹ וְעַל־עֲבָדָיו יִתְנֶחָם
he comforts them   his servants - and upon   his people   ihvh   he will judge - like

כִּי יִרְאֶה כִּי־אָזְלַת יָד וְאֶפֶס עָצוּר וְעָזוּב׃
and forsaken   restraint   and limit   hand   power - like   he sees   like

36 For the LORD shall judge his people, and repent himself for his servants, when he seeth that their power is gone, and there is none shut up, or left.

וְאָמַר אֵי אֱלֹהֵימוֹ צוּר חָסָיוּ בוֹ׃
in him   they took refuge   rock   their Elohim   where   and will say

37 And he shall say, Where are their gods, their rock in whom they trusted,

אֲשֶׁר חֵלֶב זְבָחֵימוֹ יֹאכֵלוּ יִשְׁתּוּ יֵין נְסִיכָם
their drink offerings   wine   they drank   they ate   his sacrifices   fat   which

יָקוּמוּ וְיַעְזְרֻכֶם יְהִי עֲלֵיכֶם סִתְרָה׃
concealment   upon you   it be   and they help you   they rise up

38 Which did eat the fat of their sacrifices, and drank the wine of their drink offerings? let them rise up and help you, and be your protection.

רְאוּ עַתָּה כִּי אֲנִי אֲנִי הוּא
he   I   I   like   now   you see

וְאֵין אֱלֹהִים עִמָּדִי אֲנִי אָמִית וַאֲחַיֶּה
and I make live   I kill   I   with you   Elohim   and isn't

מָחַצְתִּי וַאֲנִי אֶרְפָּא וְאֵין מִיָּדִי מַצִּיל:
rescuer from my hand and isn't I heal and I I wound

39 See now that I, even I, am he, and there is no god with me: I kill, and I make alive; I wound, and I heal: neither is there any that can deliver out of my hand.

[ששי]

כִּי־אֶשָּׂא אֶל־שָׁמַיִם יָדִי וְאָמַרְתִּי חַי אָנֹכִי לְעֹלָם:
to forever I am live and I say my hand heaven - unto I lift - like

40 For I lift up my hand to heaven, and say, I live for ever.

אִם־שַׁנּוֹתִי בְּרַק חַרְבִּי
my sword glittering I whet - if

וְתֹאחֵז בְּמִשְׁפָּט יָדִי אָשִׁיב נָקָם לְצָרַי
to my adversaries vengeance I will return my hand in judgment and it takes hold

וְלִמְשַׂנְאַי אֲשַׁלֵּם:
I will repay and to from my haters

41 If I whet my glittering sword, and mine hand take hold on judgment; I will render vengeance to mine enemies, and will reward them that hate me.

אַשְׁכִּיר חִצַּי מִדָּם וְחַרְבִּי תֹּאכַל בָּשָׂר מִדַּם חָלָל וְשִׁבְיָה
and captives slain from blood flesh it will eat and my sword from blood my arrows I will make drunk

מֵרֹאשׁ פַּרְעוֹת אוֹיֵב:
enemy captains from head

42 I will make mine arrows drunk with blood, and my sword shall devour flesh; and that with the blood of the slain and of the captives, from the beginning of revengers upon the enemy.

הַרְנִינוּ גוֹיִם עַמּוֹ כִּי דַם־עֲבָדָיו יִקּוֹם
he will avenge his servants - blood like his people nations the rejoice

וְנָקָם יָשִׁיב לְצָרָיו וְכִפֶּר אַדְמָתוֹ עַמּוֹ:
his people his ground and shelters to his adversaries he will return and vengeance

43 Rejoice, O ye nations, with his people: for he will avenge the blood of his servants, and will render vengeance to his adversaries, and will be merciful unto his land, and to his people.

[שביעי]

וַיָּבֹא מֹשֶׁה וַיְדַבֵּר אֶת־כָּל־דִּבְרֵי הַשִּׁירָה־הַזֹּאת
the this - the song speakings - all - that and he spoke Moses and he came

בְּאָזְנֵי הָעָם הוּא וְהוֹשֵׁעַ בִּן־נוּן:
Nun - son and Hoshea he the people in ears

Ha'azinu - Chapter 32

44 And Moses came and spake all the words of this song in the ears of the people, he, and Hoshea the son of Nun.

וַיָּבֹא מֹשֶׁה לְדַבֵּר אֶת־כָּל־הַדְּבָרִים הָאֵלֶּה אֶל־כָּל־יִשְׂרָאֵל:
and he finished   Moses   to speak   that - all - the speakings   the these   unto - all - Israel

45 And Moses made an end of speaking all these words to all Israel:

וַיֹּאמֶר אֲלֵהֶם שִׂימוּ לְבַבְכֶם לְכָל־הַדְּבָרִים
and he said   unto them   you place   your hearts   to all - the speakings

אֲשֶׁר אָנֹכִי מֵעִיד בָּכֶם הַיּוֹם
which   I am   testifying   in you   the day

אֲשֶׁר תְּצַוֻּם אֶת־בְּנֵיכֶם לִשְׁמֹר לַעֲשׂוֹת
which   you will command them   that - your sons   to heed   to do

אֶת־כָּל־דִּבְרֵי הַתּוֹרָה הַזֹּאת:
that - all - speakings   the law   the this

46 And he said unto them, Set your hearts unto all the words which I testify among you this day, which ye shall command your children to observe to do, all the words of this law.

כִּי לֹא־דָבָר רֵק הוּא מִכֶּם כִּי־הוּא חַיֵּיכֶם
like   not - speak   empty   it   from you   like - it   your life

וּבַדָּבָר הַזֶּה תַּאֲרִיכוּ יָמִים עַל־הָאֲדָמָה
and in matter   the this   you will prolong   days   upon - the ground

אֲשֶׁר אַתֶּם עֹבְרִים אֶת־הַיַּרְדֵּן שָׁמָּה לְרִשְׁתָּהּ:
which   you   pass over   that - the Jordan   there   to possess it

47 For it is not a vain thing for you; because it is your life: and through this thing ye shall prolong your days in the land, whither ye go over Jordan to possess it.

פ

[מפטיר]

וַיְדַבֵּר יְהוָה אֶל־מֹשֶׁה בְּעֶצֶם הַיּוֹם הַזֶּה לֵאמֹר:
and he spoke   ihvh   unto - Moses   in exact same   the day   the this   to say

48 And the LORD spake unto Moses that selfsame day, saying,

עֲלֵה אֶל־הַר הָעֲבָרִים הַזֶּה
ascend   unto - mountain   the Abarim   the this

הַר־נְבוֹ אֲשֶׁר בְּאֶרֶץ מוֹאָב
mountain - Nebo   which   in land   Moab

אֲשֶׁר עַל־פְּנֵי יְרֵחוֹ וּרְאֵה אֶת־הָאָרֶץ כְּנָעַן
which   upon - face   Jericho   and see   that - land   Canaan

אֲשֶׁר אֲנִי נֹתֵן לִבְנֵי יִשְׂרָאֵל לַאֲחֻזָּה׃

49 Get thee up into this mountain Abarim, unto mount Nebo, which is in the land of Moab, that is over against Jericho; and behold the land of Canaan, which I give unto the children of Israel for a possession:

וּמֻת בָּהָר אֲשֶׁר אַתָּה עֹלֶה שָׁמָּה

וְהֵאָסֵף אֶל־עַמֶּיךָ כַּאֲשֶׁר־מֵת אַהֲרֹן אָחִיךָ בְּהֹר הָהָר

וַיֵּאָסֶף אֶל־עַמָּיו׃

50 And die in the mount whither thou goest up, and be gathered unto thy people; as Aaron thy brother died in mount Hor, and was gathered unto his people:

עַל אֲשֶׁר מְעַלְתֶּם בִּי בְּתוֹךְ בְּנֵי יִשְׂרָאֵל

בְּמֵי־מְרִיבַת קָדֵשׁ מִדְבַּר־צִן

עַל אֲשֶׁר לֹא־קִדַּשְׁתֶּם אוֹתִי בְּתוֹךְ בְּנֵי יִשְׂרָאֵל׃

51 Because ye trespassed against me among the children of Israel at the waters of Meribah-Kadesh, in the wilderness of Zin; because ye sanctified me not in the midst of the children of Israel.

כִּי מִנֶּגֶד תִּרְאֶה אֶת־הָאָרֶץ

וְשָׁמָּה לֹא תָבוֹא אֶל־הָאָרֶץ

אֲשֶׁר־אֲנִי נֹתֵן לִבְנֵי יִשְׂרָאֵל׃

52 Yet thou shalt see the land before thee; but thou shalt not go thither unto the land which I give the children of Israel.

פ פ פ

Ha Barakah

Chapter 33

ספר דברים פרק לג

[פרשת וזאת הברכה]

וְזֹאת הַבְּרָכָה אֲשֶׁר בֵּרַךְ מֹשֶׁה
     Moses   blessed   which   the blessing   and this

אִישׁ הָאֱלֹהִים אֶת־בְּנֵי יִשְׂרָאֵל לִפְנֵי מוֹתוֹ:
his death   before   Israel   sons - that   the Elohim   man

1. And this is the blessing, with which Moses the man of God blessed the people of Israel before his death.

וַיֹּאמַר יְהֹוָה מִסִּינַי בָּא
   came   from Sinai   ihvh   and he said

וְזָרַח מִשֵּׂעִיר לָמוֹ הוֹפִיעַ מֵהַר פָּארָן
Paran   from mountain   shining   to them   from Seir   and rose up

וְאָתָה מֵרִבְבֹת קֹדֶשׁ מִימִינוֹ אֵשְׁדָּת לָמוֹ:
to them   fire edict   from his right hand   holy   from ten thousands   and you

2. (K) And he said, The Lord came from Sinai, and rose up from Seir to them; he shone forth from Mount Paran, and he came with holy tens of thousands; from his right hand went a fiery law for them.

אַף חֹבֵב עַמִּים כָּל־קְדֹשָׁיו בְּיָדֶךָ
in your hand   his holy ones - all   people   fondling   thus

וְהֵם תֻּכּוּ לְרַגְלֶךָ יִשָּׂא מִדַּבְּרֹתֶיךָ:
from your speakings   he lifts   to your feet   midst   and them

3. He truly loves the people; all his holy ones are in your hand; and they sat down at your feet; every one shall receive of your words.

תּוֹרָה צִוָּה־לָנוּ מֹשֶׁה
Moses   to us - commanded   law

מוֹרָשָׁה קְהִלַּת יַעֲקֹב:
Jacob   congregation   teaching tool

4. Moses commanded us a Torah, the inheritance of the congregation of Jacob.

וַיְהִי בִישֻׁרוּן מֶלֶךְ
king   in Jeshurun   and it was

בְּהִתְאַסֵּף רָאשֵׁי עָם יַחַד שִׁבְטֵי יִשְׂרָאֵל:
Israel   tribes   together   people   heads   in causing gather

5. And he was king in Jeshurun, when the heads of the people and the tribes of Israel

were gathered together.

יְחִי רְאוּבֵן וְאַל־יָמֹת וִיהִי מְתָיו מִסְפָּר׃

6. Let Reuben live, and not die; and let not his men be few.

ס

וְזֹאת לִיהוּדָה וַיֹּאמַר שְׁמַע יְהוָה קוֹל יְהוּדָה
וְאֶל־עַמּוֹ תְּבִיאֶנּוּ יָדָיו רָב לוֹ
וְעֵזֶר מִצָּרָיו תִּהְיֶה׃

7. And this is the blessing of Judah; and he said, Hear, Lord, the voice of Judah, and bring him to his people; let his hands be sufficient for him; and be you a help to him from his enemies.

פ

[שני]

וּלְלֵוִי אָמַר תֻּמֶּיךָ וְאוּרֶיךָ לְאִישׁ חֲסִידֶךָ
אֲשֶׁר נִסִּיתוֹ בְּמַסָּה תְּרִיבֵהוּ עַל־מֵי מְרִיבָה׃

8. And of Levi he said, Let your Thummim and your Urim be with your pious one, whom you did test at Massah, and with whom you fought at the waters of Meribah;

הָאֹמֵר לְאָבִיו וּלְאִמּוֹ לֹא רְאִיתִיו
וְאֶת־אֶחָיו לֹא הִכִּיר וְאֶת־בָּנָו לֹא יָדָע
כִּי שָׁמְרוּ אִמְרָתֶךָ וּבְרִיתְךָ יִנְצֹרוּ׃

9. Who said to his father and to his mother, I have not seen him; nor did he acknowledge his brothers, nor knew his own children; for they have observed your word, and kept your covenant.

יוֹרוּ מִשְׁפָּטֶיךָ לְיַעֲקֹב וְתוֹרָתְךָ לְיִשְׂרָאֵל
יָשִׂימוּ קְטוֹרָה בְּאַפֶּךָ וְכָלִיל עַל־מִזְבְּחֶךָ׃

10. They shall teach Jacob your judgments, and Israel your Torah; they shall put incense before you, and whole burnt sacrifice upon your altar.

בָּרֵךְ יְהוָה חֵילוֹ וּפֹעַל יָדָיו
bless　ihvh　his estate　and work　his hand

תִּרְצֶה מְחַץ מָתְנַיִם קָמָיו וּמְשַׂנְאָיו מִן־יְקוּמוּן׃
you want　impale　loins　his arising ones　and from his haters　they will arise - from

11. Bless, Lord, his substance, and accept the work of his hands; strike through the loins of those who rise against him, and of those who hate him, that they rise not again.

ס

לְבִנְיָמִן אָמַר יְדִיד יְהוָה יִשְׁכֹּן לָבֶטַח עָלָיו
to Benjamin　said　beloved　ihvh　he will dwell　to safety　upon him

חֹפֵף עָלָיו כָּל־הַיּוֹם וּבֵין כְּתֵפָיו שָׁכֵן׃
spreading over　upon him　the day - all　and between　his shoulders　he tabernacles

12. And of Benjamin he said, The beloved of the Lord shall live in safety by him; and the Lord shall cover him all the day long, and he shall live between his shoulders.

ס

[שלישי]

וּלְיוֹסֵף אָמַר מְבֹרֶכֶת יְהוָה אַרְצוֹ
and to Joseph　said　blessed　ihvh　his land

מִמֶּגֶד שָׁמַיִם מִטָּל וּמִתְּהוֹם רֹבֶצֶת תָּחַת׃
from precious　heaven　from dew　and from deep　reclining　underneath

13. And of Joseph he said, Blessed of the Lord be his land, for the precious things of heaven, for the dew, and for the deep that couches beneath,

וּמִמֶּגֶד תְּבוּאֹת שָׁמֶשׁ וּמִמֶּגֶד גֶּרֶשׁ יְרָחִים׃
and from precious　produces　sun　and from precious　driven out　moons

14. And for the precious fruits brought forth by the sun, and for the precious things put forth by the moon,

וּמֵרֹאשׁ הַרְרֵי־קֶדֶם וּמִמֶּגֶד גִּבְעוֹת עוֹלָם׃
and from head　ancient - the mountains　and from precious　hills　forever

15. And for the chief things of the ancient mountains, and for the precious things of the lasting hills,

וּמִמֶּגֶד אֶרֶץ וּמְלֹאָהּ וּרְצוֹן שֹׁכְנִי סְנֶה
and from precious　land　and fullness　and desire　dwelling　bush

תָּבוֹאתָה לְרֹאשׁ יוֹסֵף וּלְקָדְקֹד נְזִיר אֶחָיו׃
you bring　to head　Joseph　and to scalp　separated　his brother

16. And for the precious things of the earth and its fullness, and for the good will of him who lived in the bush; let the blessing come upon the head of Joseph, and upon the top of the head of him who was separated from his brothers.

בְּכוֹר שׁוֹרוֹ הָדָר לוֹ וְקַרְנֵי רְאֵם קַרְנָיו
first born his ox honor to him and horns wild ox his horns

בָּהֶם עַמִּים יְנַגַּח יַחְדָּו אַפְסֵי־אָרֶץ
in them people he will gore together earth - ends

וְהֵם רִבְבוֹת אֶפְרַיִם וְהֵם אַלְפֵי מְנַשֶּׁה׃
and them ten thousands Ephraim and them thousands Manasseh

17. The firstling of his herd, grandeur is his, and his horns are like the horns of a wild ox; with them he shall push the people together to the ends of the earth; and they are the ten thousands of Ephraim, and they are the thousands of Manasseh.

ס

[רביעי]

וְלִזְבוּלֻן אָמַר שְׂמַח זְבוּלֻן בְּצֵאתֶךָ
and to Zebulun said be happy Zebulun in your going out

וְיִשָּׂשכָר בְּאֹהָלֶיךָ׃
and Issachar in your tents

18. And of Zebulun he said, Rejoice, Zebulun, in your going out; and, Issachar, in your tents.

עַמִּים הַר־יִקְרָאוּ שָׁם יִזְבְּחוּ זִבְחֵי־צֶדֶק
people they call - mountain there they will sacrifice righteous - sacrifices

כִּי שֶׁפַע יַמִּים יִינָקוּ וּשְׂפֻנֵי טְמוּנֵי חוֹל׃
like abundance seas they will suck and treasures buried sand

19. They shall call the people to the mountain; there they shall offer sacrifices of righteousness; for they shall suck of the abundance of the seas, and of treasures hidden in the sand.

ס

וּלְגָד אָמַר בָּרוּךְ מַרְחִיב גָּד
and to Gad said blessed widening Gad

כְּלָבִיא שָׁכֵן וְטָרַף זְרוֹעַ אַף־קָדְקֹד׃
like grown lion tabernacles and tears arm crown - surely

20. And of Gad he said, Blessed be he who enlarges Gad; he lives as a lion, and tears the arm with the crown of the head.

וַיַּרְא רֵאשִׁית לוֹ כִּי־שָׁם חֶלְקַת מְחֹקֵק סָפוּן
and he saw first to him there - like portion sculpture installed

Ha Barakah - Chapter 33

וַיֵּ֣תֵא רָאשֵׁ֣י עָ֔ם צִדְקַ֤ת יְהוָה֙ עָשָׂ֔ה
_{did ihvh righteousness people heads and he arrived}

וּמִשְׁפָּטָ֖יו עִם־יִשְׂרָאֵֽל׃
_{Israel - with and his judgments}

21. And he provided the first part for himself, because there, in a portion of the lawgiver, was he seated; and he came with the heads of the people, he executed the justice of the Lord, and his judgments with Israel.

ס

[חמישי]

וּלְדָ֣ן אָמַ֔ר דָּ֖ן גּ֣וּר אַרְיֵ֑ה יְזַנֵּ֖ק מִן־הַבָּשָֽׁן׃
_{the Bashan - from he will leap lion cub stranger Dan said and to Dan}

22. And of Dan he said, Dan is a lion's cub; he shall leap from Bashan.

וּלְנַפְתָּלִ֣י אָמַ֔ר נַפְתָּלִי֙ שְׂבַ֣ע רָצ֔וֹן
_{favor full Naphtali said and to Naphtali}

וּמָלֵ֖א בִּרְכַּ֣ת יְהוָ֑ה יָ֥ם וְדָר֖וֹם יְרָֽשָׁה׃
_{he possess and south sea ihvh blessing and full}

23. And of Naphtali he said, O Naphtali, satisfied with favor, and full with the blessing of the Lord; possess you the west and the south.

ס

וּלְאָשֵׁ֣ר אָמַ֔ר בָּר֥וּךְ מִבָּנִ֖ים אָשֵׁ֑ר יְהִ֤י רְצוּי֙ אֶחָ֔יו
_{his brother acceptable he will be Asher from the sons blessed said and to Asher}

וְטֹבֵ֥ל בַּשֶּׁ֖מֶן רַגְלֽוֹ׃
_{his foot in oil and dip}

24. And of Asher he said, Let Asher be blessed with children; let him be acceptable to his brothers, and let him dip his foot in oil.

בַּרְזֶ֥ל וּנְחֹ֖שֶׁת מִנְעָלֶ֑ךָ וּכְיָמֶ֖יךָ דָּבְאֶֽךָ׃
_{will cling you and like your days from your sandals and brass iron}

25. Your shoes shall be iron and bronze; and as your days, so shall your strength be.

אֵ֣ין כָּאֵ֖ל יְשֻׁר֑וּן רֹכֵ֤ב שָׁמַ֙יִם֙ בְעֶזְרֶ֔ךָ
_{in your help heaven riding Jeshurun like El isn't}

וּבְגַאֲוָת֖וֹ שְׁחָקִֽים׃
_{sky and in his greatness}

26. There is none like the God of Jeshurun, who rides upon the heaven in your help, and in his excellency on the sky.

[ששי]

מְעֹנָה אֱלֹהֵי קֶדֶם וּמִתַּחַת זְרֹעֹת עוֹלָם
forever   arms   and from beneath   eternal   Elohim   habitation

וַיְגָרֶשׁ מִפָּנֶיךָ אוֹיֵב וַיֹּאמֶר הַשְׁמֵד:
destroy   and he will say   enemy   from your presence   and he will drive out

27. The eternal God is your dwelling place, and underneath are the everlasting arms; and he shall thrust out the enemy from before you; and shall say, Destroy them.

וַיִּשְׁכֹּן יִשְׂרָאֵל בֶּטַח בָּדָד
alone   safely   Israel   and it will tabernacle

עֵין יַעֲקֹב אֶל־אֶרֶץ דָּגָן וְתִירוֹשׁ
and grape juice   grain   land - unto   Jacob   fountain

אַף־שָׁמָיו יַעַרְפוּ־טָל:
dew - they will drop   his heaven - thus

28. Israel then shall live in safety alone; the fountain of Jacob shall be upon a land of grain and wine; also his heavens shall drop down dew.

אַשְׁרֶיךָ יִשְׂרָאֵל מִי כָמוֹךָ
like you   who   Israel   your happiness

עַם נוֹשַׁע בַּיהוָה מָגֵן עֶזְרֶךָ
your help   shield   in ihvh   saved   people

וַאֲשֶׁר־חֶרֶב גַּאֲוָתֶךָ
your greatness   sword - and which

וְיִכָּחֲשׁוּ אֹיְבֶיךָ לָךְ וְאַתָּה עַל־בָּמוֹתֵימוֹ תִדְרֹךְ:
you will tread   in their high places - upon   and you   to you   your enemies   and they will submit

29. Happy are you, O Israel; who is like you, O people saved by the Lord, the shield of your help, and who is the sword of your excellency! and your enemies shall submit themselves to you; and you shall tread upon their high places.

ס

Chapter 34

ספר דברים פרק לד

[שביעי]

וַיַּעַל מֹשֶׁה מֵעַרְבֹת מוֹאָב אֶל־הַר נְבוֹ
Nebo   mountain - unto   Moab   from plains   Moses   and he ascended

רֹאשׁ הַפִּסְגָּה אֲשֶׁר עַל־פְּנֵי יְרֵחוֹ
Jericho   face - upon   which   the Pisgah   top

Ha Barakah - Chapter 34

וַיַּרְאֵהוּ יְהוָה אֶת־כָּל־הָאָרֶץ אֶת־הַגִּלְעָד עַד־דָּן׃
<small>Dan - till   the Gilead - that   the land - all - that   ihvh   and he showed it</small>

1 And Moses went up from the plains of Moab unto the mountain of Nebo, to the top of Pisgah, that is over against Jericho. And the LORD shewed him all the land of Gilead, unto Dan,

וְאֵת כָּל־נַפְתָּלִי וְאֶת־אֶרֶץ אֶפְרַיִם
<small>Ephraim   land - and that   Naphtali - all   and that</small>

וּמְנַשֶּׁה וְאֵת כָּל־אֶרֶץ יְהוּדָה עַד הַיָּם הָאַחֲרוֹן׃
<small>the behind   the sea   till   Judah   land - all   and that   and Manasseh</small>

2 And all Naphtali, and the land of Ephraim, and Manasseh, and all the land of Judah, unto the utmost sea,

וְאֶת־הַנֶּגֶב וְאֶת־הַכִּכָּר בִּקְעַת יְרֵחוֹ
<small>Jericho   in valley   the basin - and that   the south - and that</small>

עִיר הַתְּמָרִים עַד־צֹעַר׃
<small>Zoar - till   the palm trees   city</small>

3 And the south, and the plain of the valley of Jericho, the city of palm trees, unto Zoar.

וַיֹּאמֶר יְהוָה אֵלָיו זֹאת הָאָרֶץ אֲשֶׁר נִשְׁבַּעְתִּי
<small>I swore   which   the land   this   unto him   ihvh   and he said</small>

לְאַבְרָהָם לְיִצְחָק וּלְיַעֲקֹב לֵאמֹר לְזַרְעֲךָ אֶתְּנֶנָּה
<small>I will give it   to your seed   to say   and to Jacob   to Isaac   to Abraham</small>

הֶרְאִיתִיךָ בְעֵינֶיךָ וְשָׁמָּה לֹא תַעֲבֹר׃
<small>you pass over   not   and there   in your eyes   I caused you to see</small>

4 And the LORD said unto him, This is the land which I sware unto Abraham, unto Isaac, and unto Jacob, saying, I will give it unto thy seed: I have caused thee to see it with thine eyes, but thou shalt not go over thither.

וַיָּמָת שָׁם מֹשֶׁה עֶבֶד־יְהוָה בְּאֶרֶץ מוֹאָב עַל־פִּי יְהוָה׃
<small>ihvh   mouth - upon   Moab   in land   ihvh - servant   Moses   there   and he died</small>

5 So Moses the servant of the LORD died there in the land of Moab, according to the word of the LORD.

וַיִּקְבֹּר אֹתוֹ בַגַּי בְּאֶרֶץ מוֹאָב מוּל בֵּית פְּעוֹר
<small>Peor   Beth   at side   Moab   in land   in ravine   to him   and he buried</small>

וְלֹא־יָדַע אִישׁ אֶת־קְבֻרָתוֹ עַד הַיּוֹם הַזֶּה׃
<small>the this   the day   till   his sepulchre - that   man   he knows - and not</small>

6 And he buried him in a valley in the land of Moab, over against Beth-peor: but no man knoweth of his sepulchre unto this day.

וּמֹשֶׁה בֶּן־מֵאָה וְעֶשְׂרִים שָׁנָה
בְּמֹתוֹ לֹא־כָהֲתָה עֵינוֹ וְלֹא־נָס לֵחֹה׃

7 And Moses was an hundred and twenty years old when he died: his eye was not dim, nor his natural force abated.

וַיִּבְכּוּ בְנֵי יִשְׂרָאֵל אֶת־מֹשֶׁה בְּעַרְבֹת מוֹאָב
שְׁלֹשִׁים יוֹם וַיִּתְּמוּ יְמֵי בְכִי אֵבֶל מֹשֶׁה׃

8 And the children of Israel wept for Moses in the plains of Moab thirty days: so the days of weeping and mourning for Moses were ended.

וִיהוֹשֻׁעַ בִּן־נוּן מָלֵא רוּחַ חָכְמָה
כִּי־סָמַךְ מֹשֶׁה אֶת־יָדָיו עָלָיו
וַיִּשְׁמְעוּ אֵלָיו בְּנֵי־יִשְׂרָאֵל
וַיַּעֲשׂוּ כַּאֲשֶׁר צִוָּה יְהוָה אֶת־מֹשֶׁה׃

9 And Joshua the son of Nun was full of the spirit of wisdom; for Moses had laid his hands upon him: and the children of Israel hearkened unto him, and did as the LORD commanded Moses.

וְלֹא־קָם נָבִיא עוֹד בְּיִשְׂרָאֵל כְּמֹשֶׁה
אֲשֶׁר יְדָעוֹ יְהוָה פָּנִים אֶל־פָּנִים׃

10 And there arose not a prophet since in Israel like unto Moses, whom the LORD knew face to face,

לְכָל־הָאֹתֹת וְהַמּוֹפְתִים
אֲשֶׁר שְׁלָחוֹ יְהוָה לַעֲשׂוֹת בְּאֶרֶץ מִצְרָיִם
לְפַרְעֹה וּלְכָל־עֲבָדָיו וּלְכָל־אַרְצוֹ׃

11 In all the signs and the wonders, which the LORD sent him to do in the land of

Egypt to Pharaoh, and to all his servants, and to all his land,

וּלְכֹל הַיָּד הַחֲזָקָה וּלְכֹל הַמּוֹרָא הַגָּדוֹל
and to all the hand the mighty and to all the terror the great

אֲשֶׁר עָשָׂה מֹשֶׁה לְעֵינֵי כָּל־יִשְׂרָאֵל׃
which did Moses to eyes Israel - all

12 And in all that mighty hand, and in all the great terror which Moses shewed in the sight of all Israel.

פ פ פ

www.ingramcontent.com/pod-product-compliance
Lightning Source LLC
Chambersburg PA
CBHW071452040426
42444CB00008B/1309